pp 302-303 advice on writing

p 348
353

Turgenev's Letters

A SELECTION

Dec 3, 1984

To Alan Brown
She loved you
Dearly

from
Evelyn Bransford
Hyde

TURGENEV
(Painting, 1884; *The Bettmann Archive*)

TURGENEV'S
LETTERS

A SELECTION

EDITED AND TRANSLATED

FROM THE RUSSIAN, FRENCH, AND GERMAN

ORIGINALS BY

EDGAR · H · LEHRMAN

ALFRED · A · KNOPF : NEW YORK
(1 9 6 1)

L. C. catalog card number: 60-10817

THIS IS A BORZOI BOOK,
PUBLISHED BY ALFRED A. KNOPF, INC.

FIRST EDITION

THIS VOLUME IS DEDICATED

TO

Ernest J. Simmons

AND

Philip E. Mosely

Preface

SOMETIMES, in the history of nations, the same family name recurs with new distinction. Such a name was Turgenev in eighteenth- and nineteenth-century Russia. One Turgenev, Ivan Petrovich, introduced the future historian Nikolai Mikhailovich Karamzin to the Moscow Freemasons in 1784; a second, Nikolai Ivanovich, author of *Russia and the Russians*, was involved in the Decembrist plot in 1825 and, shortly after its collapse, fled Russia to take refuge in Paris; a third, Aleksandr Ivanovich, was a noted historian and author of *Historica Russiae Monumenta*.

Ivan Sergeevich Turgenev was born at Orel on October 28 [O. S., 1818]; his father, then a man of twenty-five, was married to an heiress six years his senior, the mistress of a huge property who owned thousands of "souls," a disappointed and cruel woman who was a brutal tyrant to her children, as well as to her serfs. In 1822 Ivan's parents took the child on a trip to Germany, France, and Switzerland, and when they returned to the Russian provinces, Ivan began his schooling with private tutors, French and German. In 1830 the family moved to Moscow.

Ivan attended the universities of Moscow and St.

Petersburg, and in 1837 passed his examinations for a degree from St. Petersburg. He then did graduate work in philosophy at the University of Berlin, where he became quite friendly with Granovski, Stankevich, and Bakunin. Upon returning to Russia, Turgenev took his master's degree in philosophy in 1842, after which he entered the civil service and served under the lexicographer Dal'.

It was but two years later that he resigned from this post to devote himself to writing. At first he concentrated on verse, and in 1843 his narrative poem *Parasha* was enthusiastically received by Belinski, the leading critic of the day. His poetic activity lasted from 1838 to 1845, at which time he abandoned verse for prose. Two years later Nekrasov's *Sovremennik* started the publication of the "word pictures" and short stories that were to appear in book form in 1852 under the title *A Sportsman's Sketches*. The book was a great success—apparently too great: generally viewed as a protest against serfdom, it alarmed the authorities, and the censor who had passed it was immediately fired. Shortly after that, Ivan wrote a laudatory obituary of Gogol, an act that was in part responsible for the author's banishment to his estate at Spasskoe, where he remained until the end of the following year.

Late in 1843 Turgenev met one of the most famous opera singers of the day—Mme Viardot (nee Pauline Garcia), whose husband was a theater manager and literary critic. The nature of the sexual relations between Turgenev and Mme Viardot has been the matter of endless speculation; whatever it may have been, she soon gained an emotional domination over Turgenev strong enough to cause him to rearrange his entire life to be with and serve her.

His mother's death, in 1850, made him a very well-to-do man. Turgenev never married. One of his mother's laundresses bore him an illegitimate daughter.

After A *Sportsman's Sketches*, his fame continued to grow. He finished his pre-Chekhovian play, *A Month in the Country*, in 1850 and five years later completed *Rudin*, his first novel. *A House of Gentlefolk*, his next novel, was published in 1859, the same year he did most of the work for *On the Eve*. Two years later his favorite and most famous book appeared: *Fathers and Children*.

The critical reception of *Fathers and Children* was predominantly hostile; profoundly disturbed, Turgenev decided to forsake Russia and Russian literature, and so went abroad, returning to Russia only for short periods. Five years passed before his next novel—*Smoke*—came out. During this period more than one person told Turgenev that his prolonged residence in Germany and France, destroying his empathy with Russia, was harming his work. Although Turgenev agreed, he felt unable to make a change. His last long work, *Virgin Soil*, appeared in 1877 and brought him some of his harshest notices.

In the few remaining years of his life, he published *Poems in Prose* and other short pieces. Soon after his last visit to Russia, Turgenev fell ill. He died in Bougival, near Paris, on September 27 [O.S., 1883], and his remains were sent to Russia, where they were buried, as he had wished, near Belinski's tomb.

Throughout his adult life Turgenev was passionately interested in the work of other writers and in the writers themselves. In France, where he resided for the greater part of the final dozen years of his life, he knew,

among others, Mérimée, Mme Sand, Edmond de
Goncourt, Zola, Maupassant, Daudet, and Flaubert.
In the English-speaking world his acquaintances in-
cluded Robert Browning, Harriet Beecher Stowe, and
Henry James. Of the Russians, he has left us (in his
Reminiscences) brief descriptions of Pushkin, Lermon-
tov, and Gogol; he corresponded with Lev Tolstoy,
Herzen, Dostoevski, Fet, Ostrovski, Saltykov-Shchedrin,
Garshin, Uspenski, and others. If, as Pushkin once re-
marked, Lomonosov was "Russia's first university,"
then Turgenev may be called Russia's first full professor of comparative literature.

Turgenev was also interested in the other arts. When
Glinka died in 1857, Turgenev declared that the future
of Russian music, "if there should be any," would be
traced back to the composer of *Ruslan and Liudmila*.
At Georges Bizet's death in 1875, Turgenev wrote to
a friend that *Carmen* had been the most original
piece of French music to appear since Gounod's *Faust*.
He also left tantalizingly brief comments on Tchaikovsky, Gounod, and Balakirev.

Turgenev's letters touch upon painting, too. Briulov—the man whose famous canvas inspired Bulwer-
Lytton's *Last Days of Pompeii*—was a *bête noire* to
him.

Perhaps more interesting than his attitude toward
any single artist are his remarks on ax-grinding in the
arts; these can be applied, almost as they were written,
to much of what has been written in the Soviet Union.

Turgenev the man emerges from his letters in a
rather surprising way. Who, judging from his novels
and stories, would have thought that he found himself
drawn reluctantly toward, atheism? In one of his letters
to Mme Viardot he wonders whether, in view of the

"bad and useless" things in the world, God might not be "a misanthrope." Writing to Countess Lambert, he admits to not being a Christian, but adds that he would prefer to drop the subject lest it lead to misunderstandings. In fact, he kept such ideas largely to himself, perhaps because he may have known about Pushkin's troubles after the secret police had intercepted one of the poet's letters in which atheism was discussed as a plausible concept. Sometimes Turgenev's attitude toward literature makes us wonder whether, for him, literature was not a surrogate for religion—something in which he could believe unhesitatingly, unreservedly, and enthusiastically, something that somehow would make man in general and Turgenev in particular a little bit happier.

Politically, Turgenev was a frustrated man. Russia was scarcely a congenial country for an English-style liberal, as he called himself. In 1850 he compared his native land to a sphinx that would devour him at its leisure if he did not solve its riddle. Nor were French politics to his taste. In fact, the fripperies of the Second Empire disgusted him; and he had nothing but scorn for Gambetta. At any rate, Turgenev did not believe in "absolutes or systems."

He had learned French and German in early childhood, and had begun to study English, as a twelve-year-old boy, after the family moved to Moscow. Alphonse Daudet testifies to the "very pure" French Turgenev spoke; according to Ely Halperine-Kaminsky, Turgenev's French reminded Hippolyte Taine of the language spoken in the salons of the *ancien régime*. According to Georg Brandes, Turgenev's German was as good as a native's. And Henry Holt, the American publisher, stated that Turgenev's English was very good. He also knew enough Spanish to read Calderón in the original, enough Latin to help the famous Russian poet Fet translate Horace, and enough Polish to dislike a Russian version of Mickiewicz's *Konrad Wallenrode*. He also dabbled in Greek and Italian.

Before Turgenev was twenty, he tried to render parts of *King Lear, Othello,* and Byron's *Manfred* into Russian. He expressed a desire to translate Montaigne, Rabelais, Cervantes, and Whitman. He did translate Charles Perrault and two of Flaubert's *Légendes*; indeed, one of the Flaubert translations seems to have seen print in Russian before the work appeared in the original. Turgenev corrected Emile Durand's French translations of Ostrovski's plays, and also checked a Russian translation of Heinrich Heine's *Deutschland* before recommending it to a Russian publisher. At one point he helped Louis Viardot (whose Russian was, at best, not good) to translate Pushkin's *Evgeni Onegin* into French prose.

It is not too much to call Turgenev a literary missionary for both contemporary French writers in Russia and nineteenth-century Russian writers in France. He suggested to the editor of the *Otechestvennye zapiski* that Edmond de Goncourt be signed up forthwith; he bargained on Maupassant's behalf with the editor of the *Vestnik Evropy;* and he offered to forego payment for his translation of Flaubert's *Légendes* if the Russian publisher would increase Flaubert's fee.

Turgenev was the first Russian writer to win widespread acclaim in the West. He used his fame, with altruism, humility, and generosity, to further the cause of Russian literature. He planned a veritable campaign to popularize *War and Peace* in Paris; he sent to Russia for some copies of the novel in Princess Paskevich's

French translation to distribute them among such literary figures as Taine, Edmond About (then editor of
Le XIXème Siècle), and Flaubert.

This was a period when even as outstanding a
writer as Daudet admitted that the French just did not
read the literature of other nations, and when the lack
of any communication was such that Flaubert, tremendously impressed by *War and Peace*, asked Turgenev whether that novel was Tolstoy's maiden effort;
Tolstoy then was almost fifty years old. Matthew Arnold
received his impressions of *Anna Karenina* (about which
he wrote an essay) from a French translation. That
language was serving both Englishmen and Americans
as a prism through which to view the new and brilliant
light of Russian literature. Turgenev himself comments
that an English translation of a work of his (by Eugene
Schuyler) shows that the latter had translated from a
French edition. Indeed, the ignorance of cultured men
in the West about Russian literature was so widespread
that Matthew Arnold could write, decades after Pushkin
and Lermontov had been buried: "The crown of literature is poetry, and the Russians have not yet had a great
poet." That such remarks soon became all but unthink-
able is in large part the result of Turgenev's educational
campaign.

Turgenev's interest in Tolstoy long antedated the
publication of *War and Peace*. As early as 1852, when
Tolstoy's first published work *Childhood* appeared in
the *Sovremennik*, his talent caught Turgenev's attention. Two years later he wrote about young Tolstoy as
one of the best writers who "now has to write some
other work in order to take the first place which is his
by right . . ." Let us recall that at this time *War and
Peace* was still a decade and more in the future. In

1858—over twenty years before Tolstoy's widely publicized "conversion"—Turgenev, who then was horrified by Tolstoy's headstrong and quasi-nihilistic squandering of his talents, asked Tolstoy whether he wished to become the founder of a new religion. No doubt Turgenev recognized genius when he saw it. Once, by implication, he compared Tolstoy to a tree, remarking that other writers will "sit in [his] shade"; on another occasion he called Tolstoy "new wine"—"when it ripens, it will be a drink fit for the gods." Yet the fatalism of *War and Peace* incensed Turgenev. As early as January 1857 he had warned Tolstoy against all philosophical systems: "[Philosophical] systems are valued only by those who do not have their hands on the entire truth and wish to grab it by the tail; a system is just like the tail of the truth—but the truth is like a lizard; it leaves its tail in your hand and runs away; it knows that it will shortly grow another one." In 1861 he was challenged to a duel by Tolstoy; scarcely had the quarrel been patched up when Turgenev sent Tolstoy a challenge of his own. Fortunately for Russian literature, the second disagreement was also resolved without recourse to swords or pistols. However, it led to a social break between the two men which lasted for seventeen years.

Politics seems to have contributed to the misunderstandings between Turgenev and Dostoevski—Turgenev was a liberal; Dostoevski, more Orthodox than the Tsar. Also Turgenev earned more per signature, at least at first, and Dostoevski may well have resented this. Moreover, Turgenev had once lent Dostoevski fifty thalers and, to complicate matters (in what was an honest mistake), thought the amount to be one hundred. The hostility between the two men was not eased by Dostoevski's vicious satire of Turgenev in *The Devils* (which

Constance Garnett has called *The Possessed*). It is interesting to see in Turgenev's letters how vigorously he denied being conquered by Dostoevski's famous speech at the dedication of the Pushkin statue in Moscow, and how—decades before Sigmund Freud would imply the same comparison—Turgenev compared Dostoevski to the "notorious Marquis de Sade."

To many Russian writers Turgenev showed encouragement and consideration. He urged Sergei Aksakov to write a story about a child for children; he encouraged Aleksandr Herzen to continue and finish his memoirs; he told Saltykov-Shchedrin that his creation, Iudushka, was so impressive he ought to try writing a novel with Iudushka in it. Today, almost any introductory course in nineteenth-century Russian literature at least mentions, besides Aksakov's *Years of Childhood* and Herzen's *My Past and Thoughts*, Saltykov-Shchedrin's *Golovlyov Family* as being among the masterpieces of Russian literature. When Garshin—one of Russian literature's many morning glories—suffered what today we might call a nervous breakdown, Turgenev not only wrote the younger man a letter filled with sympathy, but even suggested that Garshin's mother and brother take the sick man to recuperate on Turgenev's estate at Spasskoe.

Turgenev's accomplishments as a newspaper and magazine correspondent have been all but forgotten. His letter to the *Sovremennik* from Berlin in the 1840's gives an excellent picture of the Prussian capital before Bismarck's ascendancy. His fascinating letters to a St. Petersburg newspaper on the Franco-Prussian War of 1870 contain many brilliant passages: the Second Empire compared to an old oak tree rotten to the core; the woman who laughs at the column of French prisoners wending their way to Rastatt; the anecdotes from and about the bloodthirsty compatriots of General Chauvin; the way in which Turgenev's sympathies—like Karl Marx's at the same time—began to shift from Prussia to France once the outcome of the War becomes apparent. One regrets only that he did not continue writing these letters until the end of the war.

Turgenev's letters illuminate his own writings—and in an important way. When he tells Sluchevski about *Fathers and Children:* "where I wrote 'nihilist' read 'revolutionary'"; when he mentions to another friend that he once wanted to write a story for *A Sportsman's Sketches* about a land-grasping landholder whose peasants finally killed him by stuffing eight pounds of the very best black earth down his throat; when he tells a woman correspondent that he has based Rudin on the character of Mikhail Bakunin; or when he tells us that the "metal plow" (*plug*) mentioned in the epigraph of *Virgin Soil* refers not to revolution but to education, he is aiding the reader enormously to evaluate his own achievement. William Wordsworth suggested that criticism concern itself with three questions: what was the author trying to do; to what extent did he succeed in doing it; and was it worth it. Turgenev's self-criticism in his letters helps us to answer directly the first question as applied to himself, and to answer the other two indirectly.

In the selected letters of a professional author we expect to find a number of passages that reveal either the writer's soul or the world around him. Both are to be found in Turgenev's correspondence. His letters to Maria Savin contain, at least in the Russian, a bouquet of magnificently expressed frustration. We can feel the

sadness of his lost opportunity when he writes her: "I
am profoundly sorry that this enchanting instant [of
being *à deux*] is thus lost forever without having
touched me with its wings." We can see the Russian
countryside when Turgenev writes Princess Khilkovoi
how he misses "St. Egor's Day, the nightingales, the
smell of the straw and of the birch-buds, the sun, and
the puddles on the road." We can feel famine—the
curse of old Russia—haunting the country when Turgenev writes to his brother in 1866: "A terrible year is
on the way: the spring crops have perished; the rye is
enormous in the stalk, but the ears contain not a
kernel. And what an appearance Russia presents now—
this land which everyone maintains is so rich! The roofs
are *all* uncovered, the fences are down. Not a single new
building is to be seen except for taverns. The horses
and the cows are dead. The people are thin—three
coachmen could hardly lift my trunk! Dust is everywhere, like a cloud; around St. Petersburg, everything is
burning up—the forests, the houses, the very *land!*
[. . .] All you see is people, stretched out prone and at
full length, sleeping on their bellies. Feebleness, inertia,
deep filth, and poverty are everywhere."

Turgenev's letters, then, are part of his legacy.
Those readers who wish to find out more about the man
and his life may consult the biographies by Avrahm
Yarmolinsky (*Turgenev: The Man—His Art—And His
Age* [London: Hodder and Stoughton; 1926. Revised
edition, New York: Orion; 1959]) and David Magarshack (*Turgenev: A Life* [London: Faber and Faber;
1954]). A good book for the history of the period is
Michael T. Florinsky's *Russia: A History and an Interpretation* (New York: The Macmillan Co.; 1955).

A Note to Scholars

TURGENEV's popularity in the West is almost a century old. Yet the one volume of his letters published in English, *Tourguéneff and His French Circle* (ed. by Ely Halpérine-Kaminsky, tr. by Ethel M. Arnold, London, Fisher Unwin, 1898), contains only letters originally written in French. Turgenev wrote several hundred letters in that language, over a hundred in German, and a few in English. The overwhelming bulk of his correspondence was, of course, in Russian. Until now this material has been all but neglected by Englishmen and Americans.

The Russians themselves have not yet finished collecting Turgenev's letters—as they have Pushkin's and Chekhov's—into a single, reasonably complete, and scholarly edition. However, Mme Bagrov, of the Lenin Library in Moscow, has informed me that a twelve-volume edition of Turgenev's letters will be published, between 1960 and 1964, by the Academy of Sciences of the U.S.S.R.

As there was no single and reasonably complete collection available in 1959, I have had to work exclusively from other sources. As an aid to scholars, the source of each letter is given in an appendix to this volume. A letter may be assumed to have been written in the language in which the appendix note is given, unless I have specifically indicated otherwise.

A dozen or so of these letters have been translated from translations. This could not be avoided—the letters in their original languages were not available—but this too has been indicated in the appendix.

Any book dealing with nineteenth-century Russia is almost forced to mention that Russia was then on the Julian calendar, which, at the time, was twelve days behind the Gregorian calendar in use in the West. In this book all dates are assumed to be New Style unless either both dates are given or "O.S." is written in brackets after a date. However, when a Russian traveled and lived in the West as much as Turgenev did, pinpoint accuracy about the complicated and frustrating matter of calendars cannot be guaranteed.

A word ought also to be said about the transliteration system used here. Basically, it is the system used by the Library of Congress in Washington, but without ligatures or diacritical marks. However, Tolstoy, Tchaikovsky, and Herzen have been spelled the way they are in this sentence. Also, Gogol's name has been left without the apostrophe to indicate a *soft sign* at the end, lest the apostrophe interfere with the possessive-case form in English. Family names have invariably been given in the masculine, nominative form, so that Polonski's wife is called Polonski rather than Polonskaia.

This name brings up my final departure from the Library of Congress transliteration system: after a *yerry* (ы) or an *ee* (и), I have not rendered the *short ee* (й) at all. The reason is that anyone familiar with Russian will know the Russian spelling of *Polonski* or *novy,* whereas a reader who is limited to English may find such forms as *Polonskii* and *novyi* eyesores. To be consistent, I have transliterated Russian names which Turgenev gives in a different language (such as French) as if they had come directly from the Russian.

In regard to the names of Turgenev's creative works, I have given the titles used by Constance Garnett. This is not done to give that worthy pioneer additional authority, but merely because so many adults who have read Turgenev in English have done so through Garnett-colored glasses. Names of other authors' works and of periodicals are given in their original languages, except if they are as widely known as *War and Peace* or *Dead Souls*.

A distinction has been made between a plain ellipsis and an ellipsis enclosed in brackets. The bracketed ellipsis indicates that material has been omitted from the source; the plain ellipsis shows that the dots appear in the source used. Brackets have also been generally used to translate various words and phrases given by Turgenev in languages other than the main language of a given letter; this was one of his favorite devices. Where such translations are given in parentheses rather than in brackets, they have been done by Turgenev himself. (The only exceptions to this are the rare cases, already mentioned, in which the source was a translation; in those cases, parentheses may be used to indicate a word given in the language the letter was originally written in.) In general, salutations and formal closings have been omitted.

Turgenev frequently wrote letters in phrases whose main punctuation was the dash. Because English and Russian syntax differ so greatly, this device has been altered considerably.

A brief statement of the principles used in adjusting what material to include and what material to reject in the preparation of this volume is in order. One of my aims has been to shed light on works Turgenev himself wrote; thus, his letter to Annenkov of October 25/November 6, 1872 gives the plot for a story which Turgenev never completed—and tells why he never finished it. A second goal has been to give Turgenev's comments about his own state of mind; hence, for instance, the repeated variations on the theme of his being a bachelor. A third objective has been to indicate his reactions to the works of others—particularly Tolstoy—and to the men who wrote them; this is why I have included his letters to Tolstoy about their duel *manqué* and his comments on Tolstoy's writings, particularly *War and Peace*. A fourth purpose has been to mention Turgenev's ideas about the political events and figures of his time; hence, his letters on the Franco-Prussian War, his comments on such phenomena as the physical appearance of Napoleon III, and the story of his own interviews with French political figures in his attempt to help Flaubert, are found in this volume. On the other hand, I did not deem it necessary to include all the letters of Toporov in which Turgenev asks Toporov to run a specific but minor errand. Also, I have tried to avoid repetition; if Turgenev says to Aksakov many of the same things about Charrière's version of the *Sportman's Sketches* that he says in his letter to the *Journal de St. Petersbourg*, there is no need to give the same material twice. I cannot deny that a subjective factor has entered my choice, but I have tried to keep my subjectivity under control.

One last observation: perhaps after the Soviet government brings out its quasi-complete version of Turgenev's letters, someone else will wish to supplement—or even to finish—what has been started here. Such a task would be a worthy one, and whoever does undertake it will deserve the best of luck.

Acknowledgments

TURGENEV himself remarks that in a translation from the Russian, mistakes cannot be avoided. But many of them can be caught before a book sees print. To aid me in catching them, I have elicited the unstinting assistance of a platoon of generous persons whom I would like to thank here. First and foremost has been my sister-in-law Emily (Mrs. Nathaniel S.) Lehrman; she has sat with me for hours by the clock, helping me to overcome difficult passages of syntax which had eluded me. Professor Leon Stilman of Columbia University has also been of tremendous help to me.

I would also like to thank the following professors, currently on the staff of The Pennsylvania State University, for their assistance: Dr. Simon Belasco (in French); Dr. Dagobert de Levie (in German); Dr. Alfred A. Triolo (in Italian); Dr. Samuel F. Will, Jr. (in Latin); and Dr. Edward C. Thaden (in Russian history). Dr. Deming Brown and Dr. Thomas G. Winner, both of the University of Michigan, have been kind enough to comment on my Preface. This work could not have been undertaken at all had it not been for the brilliant use made of the limited library funds at The Pennsylvania State University by Dr. William B. Edgerton, now of Indiana University, and Dr. Peter Rudy, now of Northwestern University. It goes without saying, however, that whatever errors have crept into this volume are exclusively my responsibility.

The Pennsylvania State University made a grant of money available to me to aid in the typing of this manuscript. The men responsible for this generosity are Professor Nicholas M. Brentin (formerly Acting Chairman, Department of Romance Languages), Professor Frederick R. Matson (Assistant Dean for Research, College of the Liberal Arts), and Dr. Michael A. Farrell (Vice-President for Research at The Pennsylvania State University). They too deserve my thanks.

The personnel in the Slavonic Division of the New York Public Library have been wonderful to me—even to the point of letting me look through books on exhibition. The Lenin Library in Moscow too has, through the mails, been responsive to my request for information.

Mr. Herbert Weinstock and Mr. Robert Pick of Alfred A. Knopf, Inc., have been most generous to me.

Last but not least I thank Mrs. Hilda Hessel Stark, who shamed me into submitting the idea for this volume to a publisher.

State College, Pennsylvania

March 24, 1959

CONTENTS

ILLUSTRATIONS

Turgenev's Letters

A SELECTION

THE LETTERS

{ 1 }

[*Moscow*], *March 31—April 2* [O.S.], *1831* [*aet. 13*]
TO NIKOLAI NIKOLAEVICH TURGENEV

Dear Uncle,

My diary:

Tuesday, March 31. Mr. Doublet visited us in the morning; my composition was "*L'Homme vain*" ["The Vain Man"] and the conclusion of Mirabeau's speech; it was even better than the beginning. I cannot express how enraptured I was by reading that speech. Later, Platon Nikolaevich [Dubenski, the mathematics teacher] arrived. We did very interesting problems in algebra. Mr. Shchurovski came after dinner. We talked after class, as you have assumed, about philosophy . . . ; even more . . . , we delved deep into the most profound sagacity, etc., etc. For some days, now, it has been warm outside and it is now 12.5° [55° F.].

Wednesday, April 1. I played a trick, I was tricked, and I laughed at tricked persons on this day. In the

morning, as I was getting ready [my older brother],
Nicky brought me a folded piece of paper and said:
"Here is a letter." I unfolded it and it was not anything.
I went to Mr. Meyer and said that Mr. Vladimirov's
servant had come to see him; he jumped up, but there
was no one. But my younger brother [Serezha] was
tricked best of all. Nikanor and I made an agreement
and wrote in an old-fashioned handwriting:

"Dear Sir:

Allow me to inform you about the death of your
beloved Mother Vasil'evna.[1] As Nikolai Nikolaevich
has no time, he has instructed me to write. Yours, etc.,
Paul Moskalev."

We smeared on the seal from the house-man-
ager's office at Spasskoe, and sent [the letter] to Serezha.
Then the sighs, the tears, and God knows what else
began; he was finally undeceived. Of the teachers,
the one for drawing and Mr. Dubenski were here
today.

First, *Verses:*

Or along the swamp banks/ in the high grass, in
the forest thicket,/ . . . they await their prey/ The
free cliffs are their exile/ But life raves in their hearts/
On the crutches of sullen laziness.[2]

Second, *Geography:* Turkey. Do you know how
they obtain meerschaum in Turkey? The foam is
found in the earth; it is white and as soft as wax, but
after a week's exposure to the sun, it hardens, turns
yellow, and the result is meerschaum pipes.

Third, *History:* About the Franks.

Thursday, April 2. Valentin was here today. They

---

[1] One of the sources prints this as *Vasil'eva.*
[2] These verses are evidently in iambic tetrameter. No effort
has been made to reproduce the rhymes or rhythms in English.

had wanted to turn him away, but he was here and gave his lesson. Then Mr. Platon Nikolaevich [Dubenski] was here; he took good care of me.

Here is our lesson:

From the line AB and the angle k, form a triangle and analyse all cases (of which there are 3 for acute angles, 1 for an obtuse angle, and 1 for a right angle). It seems easy, but it is very hard. After dinner, Mr. Hardorf was here with the heir to the throne of the German language, Mr. Grigorius. Our translations impressed him as being very difficult; he liked my composition very much, gave us lessons, and left.

And now amen to my diary.

I have much to write you in my letter now, Uncle. The first and main thing is that we have not received any letters from Father so far—not because he has not written, but because the mail has not arrived yet on account of the nasty roads. In Moscow, dust rises up even now from the greater part of the streets when you drive along. The [Moscow] River has broken up and a huge crowd is gathering on the Kamenny Most to watch the enormous ice floes, almost in the middle of the river, suddenly fly—bang!—against the arcade and get smashed with a roar into small pieces of ice; a second one after it, a third, a fourth. . . . One can say of them:

They swallow each other in the wrestling of the waters/The ice floes are born of other ice floes,/A sea is born of another sea.[3]

And there is another verse: other ice floes will be born of the ice floes.

Answer me by return mail, please, even if only this once. I kiss you with all my heart, and I remain

[3] These verses are written in amphibrachic tetrameter.

your nephew who loves you just as much as you love
me.

Ivan Turgenev

P.S. Serezha does not wish to write you, saying that he
does not know what to write. Nicky writes you only the
nouns: "Fel'kertsam, brace, box." Answer the letter.
Especially, I beg of you, do not forget this last.

[2]

St. Petersburg, March 26/April 7, 1837

TO ALEKSANDR VASIL'EVICH NIKITENKO

In sending you my first, weak efforts in Russian
poetry, I ask you not to think that I have the slightest
wish to publish them. If I am asking for your advice, it
is solely to learn your opinion of my works, an opinion
I value highly. I have been vacillating over whether I
ought to send you the drama I wrote at 16 (my first
work);[4] I see so many shortcomings in it, and I now
so dislike its entire plan that if I did not hope for your
indulgence—and, most of all, did not think that the
first step might at least foreshadow the future—I
would never have decided to send it to you. About a
year ago I gave it to [Professor] P. A. Pletnev; he told
me what I had long been thinking myself: that it was
all exaggerated, inaccurate, and immature . . . , and
if it had anything that was fairly good, it was some details (very few). I consider it my duty to observe (you,
of course, will observe this right away) that the meter

---

[4] According to a note to the Russian source, Turgenev
began to write *Steno*, a drama in verse, in 1834. All the other
manuscripts mentioned here, including the translations, have
been lost. A few of Turgenev's early poems were published in
the *Sovremennik* in 1838 and in the *Otechestvennye zapiski*
during 1841–4, and are available in Russian editions of Turgenev's complete works.

of the verses is very faulty. To rework them now would not be worth the trouble. I was ready to consign them to total oblivion, when my very close acquaintanceship with you prompted me to show them to you. The *"Povest' starika"* ["Old Man's Tale"]—a poem that is unfinished and scarcely finishable—was written in 1835. And, finally, *"Nash vek"* ["Our Age"] is a work that was begun in mid-February of the current year in a fit of malicious annoyance at the despotism and monopoly of certain persons in our literature. Last year was devoted to translating: Shakespeare's *Othello* (which I did only up to the middle of Act II), *King Lear* (heavily abridged), and [Byron's] *Manfred.* I destroyed the first two translations; they struck me as being too poor after the translations of Vronchenko and Panaev. . . . Furthermore, it was the wrong road; I am completely unsuited for translating. I have no copy of my *Manfred,* and hence am not sending it to you.

If what I sent you does not strike you as being completely bad, and if you would care to tell me to do so, I shall give you three additional short—but finished —poems: *"Shtil' na more"* ["A Calm at Sea"], *"Fantasmagoriia v letniuiu noch'"* ["Phantasmagoria on a Summer Night"], and *"Son"* ["A Dream"]. I have about 100 minor poems beyond those, but not all of them have been copied, and they are scattered about. . . . "Our Age" is not finished; I am working on it now. Moreover, whether I ought to continue will depend on your decision. One more request: do not talk about this to Petr Aleksandrovich [Pletnev]; before I met you, I had promised to give my works to *him* (and I have not kept my promise yet). His opinions, which, of course, I respect very much, do not jibe with mine.

Furthermore, I tell you frankly that when I first met
you I felt unlimited confidence in you. . . . I have
also forgotten to tell you that I began a drama last
year; the first act and entire plan have been completely
finished; I hope to bring it in finished form when I
come back from the village in September. With this, I
ask your indulgence for the boldness with which I have
undertaken to disturb you, and I beg you to believe the
feelings of esteem and complete respect with which I
remain,

Your very humble servant.

〔 3 〕

[place not given], June 12 [O.S.], 1837

TO SERGEI MIKHAILOVICH FIGLEV

[. . .] I would have been sad at heart if I had
thought that you were ascribing my prolonged silence
(which I am not justifying) [to] anything else than my
innate laziness—and also my lack of the letter-writing
habit. [. . .]

〔 4 〕

Frankfurt [am Main], May 17, 1840

TO ALEKSANDR PAVLOVICH EFREMOV

Upon approaching Wiesbaden
I glanced at my trousers
And thought of your curls
And that you were there.

N.B.: My trousers are a golden yellow. Seriously,
it would have been sinful for me to pass so close to
Wiesbaden without leaving you a note. What have I
experienced in these thirteen days? Where have I not

been? In Leghorn, in Pisa, in Genoa; I have traveled through the entire Kingdom of Sardinia, seen the statue of St. Carlo Borromeo,[5] sailed on Lago Maggiore, sleighed at St. Gotthard—the devil take it—been, it seems, in Lucerne, in Basel, in Kehl, in Mannheim, in Mainz—and lost bit by bit my umbrella, cloak, cash box, stick, lorgnette, hat, cushion, pocket knife, wallet, three towels, two silk handkerchiefs, and two shirts, and I am now galloping to Leipzig with my trunk, my *sacco di nòtte* [overnight bag], my passport in my pocket, my p——s in my trousers, and that is all; And laughter and sorrow! By God, I am not exaggerating. I hasten to inform you of some very pleasant news: it seems that my money will take me to Berlin—and I was really afraid that they would throw me in jail somewhere and I would have no way to buy myself out, everything being lost. But:

Ugh! Prosaic nonsense.

Where is she? What is she? By God, I would have told another girl: "I am in love, ma'am—and his mother!" And I would have said it in vain. It is not love, but frivolousness, melancholy, craving—the same thing, for example, this letter smacks of; but what does it smack of? I am beginning to suspect that I drank too much Rhine wine yesterday, when I was in Mainz, for I am sentimental and giggly, and ready to use foul language. And today I let myself order a bottle of Altmannshausen,[6] and quickly and quietly I drooled over it and lapped it up in a corner of the rassterant [*sic*]. As a result of all this, I caught myself at a strange occupation. I looked at a German girl sitting opposite

---

[5] Presumably the statue at Stresa.
[6] Perhaps Turgenev is thinking of Assmannshauser, a famous Rhine wine.

me (I am writing this illustrious letter in one of the local *caffés* [*sic*], to the thunder of billiard balls) and thought: why does she have a pimple at the end of her nose, and where does it come from?

What a ridiculous word *pryshch* [pimple] is!

Try to say it several times in a row, with a great rolling of the "r"—after revealing the corners of the mouth—and look in the mirror without smiling. It will be very odd.

You think I am lying? A drunk friend sends greetings to you.

I shall write you from Berlin. I shall always be drunk.

[5]

Berlin, July 4 [*O.S.*], *1840*

TO TIMOFEI NIKOLAEVICH GRANOVSKI

A terrible misfortune has overtaken us, Granovski. I can scarcely gather the strength to write. We have lost a man whom we loved, whom we believed in, and who was our pride and hope. . . . Stankevich passed away, in Novi [in northern Italy], on June 24. What is there left for me to say; why do you need my words now? I am continuing this letter not for you, but rather for myself. I became friendly with him in Rome; I saw him every day and began to value his lucid mind, his warm heart, and all the charm of his soul. . . . Even then the cloud of early death was hovering over him.

We often spoke about death; he admitted it was the boundary of thought, and it seems to me he secretly shuddered. Death has a profound significance if it ap-

pears as the last event of a full heart and a prolonged
life; it is a reconciliation for an old man; but for us—
for him—it is the command of fate. He—die? He so
profoundly and sincerely acknowledged and loved the
sacredness of life. Despite his illness, he rejoiced in the
bliss of thinking, acting, and loving; he was preparing
to dedicate himself to the work Russia needs. . . . The
cold hand of death has fallen upon his head, and an
entire world has perished. Here it is, *die kalte Teufels-
faust . . . die sich—nicht vergebens tückisch ballt* [the
cold hand of the Devil which is not without reason
maliciously clenched in a fist]. [. . .]

Oh, my God! how this blow will stagger Neverov,
the Frolovs, you, . . . and all his other friends and
acquaintances! I could not bring myself to tell Werder
about it; I wrote him a letter. How profoundly he was
staggered! I told him when I saw him: *"In ihm ist
auch ein Theil von Ihnen gestorben."* ["In him, a part
of you also has died."] He almost began to sob. He
told me: *"Ich fühle es. Ich bin auf dem halben Wege
meines Lebens: meine besten Schüler, meine Jünger
sterben, ob ich überlebe sie! [sic]"* ["I feel it. I am at
the halfway point of my life. My best students, my
disciples, are dying, and I am outliving them."] He read
me a magnificent poem—*"Der Tod"* ["Death"] he had
written upon receiving the news. If he is willing, I shall
copy it and send it to you.

I look around, I seek—in vain. Who of our generation can replace our loss? Who will be worthy of
inheriting the dead man's legacy of great thoughts?
Who will prevent his influence from perishing? Who
will walk along his path, in his spirit, and with his
strength? . . .

Oh, if anything could make me doubt the future, I would now, having outlived Stankevich, part with my last hope. Why did not someone else die—a thousand others—such as myself, for example? When, oh when, will the time come when a more developed spirit will be an unalterable condition for the highest development of the body, and our very life will be a condition and the fruit of the Creator's delight? Why can the beautiful perish or suffer on earth? Until now it has seemed that thought is sacrilege, and punishment awaits everyone who exceeds blessed mediocrity. Or is God's envy aroused, as the envy of the Greek gods used to be? Or are we to believe that everything beautiful and holy—love and thought—is Jehovah's cold irony? What, oh what, is our life then?

But no, we must not despair or submit.

Let us meet; we shall shake hands and grow closer; one of us has fallen—perhaps the best. But others are appearing and will appear. The hand of God never ceases to sow embryos of great aspirations in the soul. Sooner or later, light will conquer darkness.

Yes, but for us who have lost him, his loss is irreparable. Mme Rahel could barely say: "*Wäre noch nie ein junger Mann gestorben, hätte man nie Wehmuth gekannt.*" ["If a young man had never died before, melancholy would never have been known."] Both grief and joy flow from the heart of the Creator. *Freude und Leid.* [Joy and sorrow.] Frequently their sounds quiver with their own echoes, and blend; each is incomplete without the other. Now it is the turn of grief. . . .

Farewell, and keep healthy. Write me a word in answer. It seems that I have come to like you even more with the death of Stankevich.

[6]

Marienbad, September 18, 1840

TO ALEKSANDR PAVLOVICH EFREMOV

[. . .] This letter was begun on the 15th, in the morning—and in the evening I received your letter. You can gather from my letters how it staggered and upset me, but as a cast stone does not ripple the surface of a swamp (Goethe's image), so your letter and its consequences, after having moved me for two whole days and two nights, have settled to the soft and gruelly bottom of my life. From boredom, I admit, I am taking my pen in hand and *Hermannanddorotheafying*.[7] How do you like my new word? Listen, *à la* Karamzin:

"Oh sensitive souls! Admit me to your sacred circle! I have found a friend—and I shed tears of joy; I have found a friend—and I thank sagacious providence," etc. "Oh my friend, I said, shedding heated tears," etc. "We embraced, and our tears commingled," etc. A strange fate for tears, you think! They are swallowed like wine, mixed like medicine, shed like water, held back like horses, poured out, spilled; tears deluge and gush forth; they flow in torrents and in streams—even in rivers—happy tears, sorrowful tears, bitter tears, sweet tears, remorseful tears, emotional tears, comforting tears, delightful tears, tears like pearls, tears like jewels, bloody tears, abundant tears, oh tears, tears, teeears [*sic*]—pray to God for us!

I have found a friend—a hound or, if you like, a dog. He is small in stature and very fat, but despite the custom of dogs of his class, he is affectionate and indulgent. And I have named him Philanthropist because

[7] A verb Turgenev invented from Goethe's *Hermann and Dorothea*.

in all Marienbad he is the sole creature to express interest in me, somewhat mixed with tenderness. [. . .]

{ 7 }

[place not given], end of 1846 or start of 1847
TO ALEKSANDR VASIL'EVICH NIKITENKO

[. . .] Yesterday Panaev obtained for me in your name a translation of Byron's *Vision [of Judgment]*, and said you wished to know my opinion of the translation. I read it through yesterday, collated it with the original, and am convinced that the translator knows both the English and the Russian languages badly. [. . .]

{ 8 }

Berlin, March 1, 1847
TO THE *Sovremennik*

. . . You wish to learn some news of Berlin from me. . . . But what can one be expected to say about a city in which people get up at six o'clock in the morning, dine at two, and go to bed much earlier than the chickens; about a city in which, at ten o'clock in the evening, only melancholy and beer-laden night-watchmen wander down the empty streets, while some boisterous and tipsy German goes out of the *Tiergarten* and carefully lights his cigar at the Brandenburg Gate as he "becomes mute before the law"? [8] Joking aside, Berlin is no capital even now; at least, it does not contain even a trace of capital-city life, although you still feel, after having been here for a while, that you are in

[8] A pun in the Russian on *nemets* (a German) and *nemeet* (becomes mute).

one of the centers or focuses of the European movement. Although the appearance of Berlin has not
changed since 1840 (while Petersburg alone grows not
by days but by hours), great inner changes have taken
place. Let us begin, for example, with the university.
Do you remember the rhapsodic descriptions of Werder's[9] lectures, the nocturnal serenade beneath his windows, his speeches, and the tears and shouts of the students? Do you remember? Now, take a good look and
remember it well, because all those innocent escapades
have long been forgotten here. The interest that purely
speculative philosophy had once awakened in young
and old hearts has completely disappeared—at least in
the young hearts. In 1840 they waited for Schelling[1]
with excitement; they hissed Stahl[2] obdurately at his
first lecture; they grew excited at Werder's very name;
they caught fire from Bettina [von Arnim]; they listened to Steffens[3] with reverence. But now no one
goes to Stahl's lectures; Schelling has grown silent;
Steffens is dead; and Bettina has stopped dyeing her
hair. . . . Werder alone is giving his commentaries on
Hegel's logic, without overlooking the opportunity to
bring in verses from the Second Part of *Faust*; but alas!
—before a trio of listeners, only one of whom is a German, and he comes from Pomerania. What am I saying! Even the young, new school, which was then raising its banner so boldly and with such sureness of its

[9] Karl Werder (1806–93), professor of philosophy at Berlin
University and student of Hegel.
[1] Friedrich Wilhelm Joseph von Schelling (1806–54), philosopher named to Academy of Sciences in Berlin in 1841; he
lectured at Berlin University until 1845.
[2] Friedrich Julius Stahl (1802–61), teacher of ecclesiastical
law and polity at Berlin University.
[3] Henrik Steffens (1773–1845), Scandinavian who held
chair in natural philosophy at Berlin University from 1831 until
his death.

own invincibility, even that school has managed to disappear from people's memories. Bruno Bauer still lives here, but no one sees him or hears about him. A few days ago, I met a man at a concert who was sleek, meek, and sad. . . . It was Max Stirner. Moreover, it is understandable why they have been forgotten. Feuerbach is not forgotten; on the contrary! I repeat: the literary, theoretical, philosophical, and fantastic era of German life is, it seems, finished.

Recently, you know, theological disputes have stirred German hearts violently. . . . The legitimate existence of the "German Catholics" (*Deutsch-Katholiken*) has finally been acknowledged; the argument has not yet been decided about the failure of Dr. Rupp (a German Catholic) to be admitted into the Gustavus Adolphus Society (*Gustav Adolf's-[sic] Verein*), which was established to support *Protestant* parishes in Catholic countries, although the general opinion has been in favor of Rupp. . . . Hengsterberg is still concerned with grafting Calvinism upon the Evangelical [Lutheran] faith. . . . Yes. But you would be mistaken if you accepted all these movements, arguments, and disputes as purely theological; other questions are concealed beneath them. . . . A different struggle is at issue. You can easily imagine what ridiculous and strange aspects are sometimes assumed by, to use Hegel's word, the *Logos* (or the Idea, or the Spirit, or progress, or mankind—you have many terms at your disposal), which has been developed conscientiously, painfully, and slowly by German minds . . . but then it is only a step from the ridiculous to the sublime. . . . Everyone here is filled with expectation, especially now.

A few days ago a most ridiculous and ponderous—

but stern and angry—book appeared here by a Mr. Sass. He analyzes Berlin life by parts, and seriously characterizes the main local pastry shops since other "elements or features" of public life are lacking. The first edition of the book has already been sold out. That is a remarkable fact. It indicates the degree to which the Berliners like a critical analysis of their public life, and that they would like a different public life. . . .

Art here—alas! . . . The representatives of art here are all old men (Cornelius, Rauch, the sculptor Schadow, and Begas are already veterans); their works smack of coldness and death—of death because they are almost all busy building and decorating burial vaults, gravestones, and other memorials. A *Campo santo is* being erected near the cathedral in the manner of the Italians (as, for example, in Pisa or Bologna). Frescoes have been ordered from Cornelius. . . . I have seen some of them. They cannot be understood without a special commentary; the composition is sometimes rather successful, but Cornelius *despises* color. Like most artists nowadays, he is an eclectic, an allegorist, and an imitator (although it is evident that he would very much like to be original). *"Ich trinke gern aus dem frischen Quell"* ["I like to drink from the fresh spring"], says Goethe—i.e., I would do better to admire the frescoes of Michelangelo or Orcagna. . . . What is this "captive spirit of imitation" to me? Since my arrival here, the façade of the museum has been decorated alfresco, and rather badly; nothing can be said. They have put Kiss's *Amazon* here; it is a very good group, especially the horse. New buildings are not to be seen in Berlin. The theater has been rebuilt since the fire of 1843, and has been finished very— even too—richly, but it sins against taste in many ways.

Especially unpleasant are the distorted statues *à la*
Bernini which have been placed among the main boxes.
The bluish, mawkishly sweet background of the pictures on the ceiling only damages the general impression. Above the stage are portraits of the four main
German composers: Beethoven; Mozart; Weber; and
Gluck. . . . It is sad to think that the first two lived
and died in poverty (Mozart's grave is not even
known), while Weber and Gluck found asylum in foreign lands, one in England and the other in France.
I have seen and heard Mme Viardot again, and with
great pleasure. Her voice, far from becoming weaker,
has even grown stronger. She is magnificent in the
"Huguenots" and is creating a furor here. The celebrated Mme Cerrito is also here. She is very sweet,
but she is as far from Taglioni, Elssler, or even Car-
lotta Grisi as she is from the stars in the sky. Dreyshock
gave two concerts; he is a drummer, not a pianist, but
his technique is amazing.

There has been an institution here since last year
which is lacking in St. Petersburg. It is an enormous
reading room with 600 (I am saying six hundred)
newspapers and magazines. Of course, two thirds of
them (almost all German) are very bad, but one cannot fail to do justice to the establishment. German
journalism now is really good for nothing.

That is everything interesting I can report to you.
Let me repeat: I have found in Berlin a change that
is major and basic but unnoticeable to the superficial
observer. People seem to be waiting for something
here; everyone is looking forward. But the "beer halls"
(*Bier-Locale* is the name of the rooms in which people
drink that vile and worthless beverage) are filled with

the very same people; the porters wear the very same unnatural hats; the officers are just as fair-haired and tall, and say the letter "r" just as carelessly; it seems that everything is going along in the old style. Only the *Eckensteher* [messengers hired for individual errands] have disappeared; they were famous for their witticisms. Civilization has destroyed them. Beyond that, the omnibuses have multiplied and a certain Mr. Koch is exhibiting a strange, antediluvian monster, *Hydrarchos*, which, in all probability, *fed* on sharks and whales. And something else—I almost forgot! Another individual, by the name of Kroll, has constructed a huge building in the *Tiergarten* where the good Germans gather by the hundreds every week and "have a feast" (*halten ein Festessen*) in honor of some antediluvian event or person: the Battle of Leipzig; the invention of printing; Ronge; the Seven Years' War; the construction of a column; the creation of the world; Blücher, and other antediluvian phenomena.

In my next letter I shall say more about Berlin. I have left out many things . . . but everything cannot be given at once.

[9]

Paris, October 19, 1847

TO PAULINE VIARDOT (NEE GARCIA)

[. . .] You have probably looked through Diderot. One must read his paradoxes to enjoy, refute, and forget. Within his reader he encourages—at his cost— the feeling for the true and the beautiful. Your spirit —so direct, so *open*, and so serious in its delicacy and its grace—must not have relished the capricious, glittering, dilettante prattle of the "French Plato" (never was a man worse nicknamed). Yet, here and there, a person fishes out some new and bold ideas—or rather, some germs of fruitful ideas. His devotion to freedom of the mind and his encyclopedia are what will make him live. His heart is excellent, but when he makes it talk, he lines it with wit and spoils it. The fireworks[4] of paradox will definitely never be worth the *good sun* of the truth. [. . .]

[10]

Paris, November 14/26, 1847

TO VISSARION GRIGOR'EVICH BELINSKI

Why on earth will you not answer, oh father and commander? I sent you a letter four weeks ago, and [there could have been] at least a line in answer. It is not good, by God, it is not good. But, mainly, this is most discouraging for one of us who is ready to reform but demands a pat on the head for his good intentions. [. . .]

I see from the prospectus of the *Sovremennik* that they wish to print my "Lieutenant Pyetushkov." [5] Inasmuch as they are not sending it to me, be magnanimous: mark the weak spots with a pencil, and ask Nekrasov on my behalf to correct them with a few words, to say clearly that Vasilisa became his mistress, etc. etc. I am ashamed to trouble him—he has his hands full, you know, as it is—but nothing can be done. [. . .]

---

[4] This is a pun: the French phrase for "fireworks" (*feu d'artifice*) literally means "fire of artifice."
[5] The final title of the story is simply "Pyetushkov."

[11]

Paris, December 8, 1847

TO PAULINE VIARDOT (NEE GARCIA)

[. . .] The shadow of Shakespeare weighs upon the shoulders of all playwrights; they cannot get rid of their memories; the unfortunates have read too much and have not lived at all. [. . .]

A person can no longer read anything nowadays. Gluck said of an opera that it reeked of music (*puzza musica*). All the works done today reek of literature, craft, and convention. To find a wellspring that is still lively and pure, one must go all the way back. Literary pruritus, twaddle, and the egotism that studies and admires itself are the plague of our times. We are like dogs who return to their vomit.

[12]

Paris, December 19, 1847

TO PAULINE VIARDOT (NEE GARCIA)

[. . .] I am now reading Calderón tenaciously (in Spanish, of course); he is the greatest Catholic dramatic poet who ever lived, as Shakespeare is the most human and the most anti-Christian. His *Devoción de la cruz* is a masterpiece. That immutable, triumphant faith, with no shadow of a doubt or even of a second thought, crushes you with its grandeur and majesty, despite everything repulsive and barbaric in the doctrine. The annihilation of everything that constitutes the dignity of man before the Divine Will, and the indifference toward all that we call virtue or vice with which *grace* is lavished upon His elect, are still a triumph of the human spirit; the being that proclaims its own annihilation with such audacity is elevated to equal even that fantastic Divinity whose plaything that being believes it is. And that Divinity is still the work of His hands. Yet, I prefer Prometheus, I prefer Satan—the model of revolt and of individuality. Only an atom though I am, I am my own master; I want the truth, and not salvation; I expect it from my mind, and not from grace.

Despite everything, Calderón is, above all, a very extraordinary and vigorous genius. As for us, the weak descendants of powerful ancestors, we shall at most attain graciousness in our weakness. [. . .]

{ 13 }

Paris, December 25, 1847

TO PAULINE VIARDOT (NEE GARCIA)

[. . .] Since the last letter I wrote you, I have read still another drama of Calderón's, *La vida es sueño*. It is one of the most imposing dramatic conceptions I know. A savage energy prevails within it, a gloomy and profound disdain for life, a boldness of astonishing ideas, beside the most inflexible Catholic fanaticism. Calderón's Segismundo (the main character) is the Spanish Hamlet, with all the difference between the South and the North. Hamlet is more pensive, more subtle, more philosophic; Segismundo's character is as simple, open, and penetrating as a sword; the one fails to act because of irresolution, uncertainty, and contemplation; the other does act—for his southern blood impels him—but even while acting, he well knows that life is only a dream.

I have now just begun the Spanish *Faust—El magico prodigioso*; I am completely Calderónified. These beautiful works have sprouted naturally on a fertile and vigorous soil; their taste, their bouquet, is simple: the reader does not sense in them the sweat and strain of creative writing. The drama in Spain was the last and the most beautiful expression of a naïve Catholicism and of the society it had formed in its image; whereas in the time of crisis and transition in which we live, all the works of art or literature represent at very most only individual sentiments and opinions, confused and contradictory reflections, the eclecticism of their authors. Life has been scattered; there is no longer any great general movement—except, perhaps, that of industry, which, considered from the viewpoint of the progressive submission of the elements of nature to the genius of man, will perhaps become the liberator and the regenerator of the human race. Moreover, in my opinion, the greatest contemporary poets are the Americans who are going to pierce the Isthmus of Panama and who talk of establishing an electric telegraph across the ocean. Once the social revolution has been consummated, long live the new literature. [. . .]

[14]

Paris, January 5/17, 1848

TO PAULINE VIARDOT (NEE GARCIA)

[. . .] It [George Sand's *François le Champi*] is done in the best manner: simple, true, and poignant. She mixes in, perhaps, a few too many peasant expressions, which sometimes give to her story an air of affectation. Art is not a daguerreotype, and so great a master as Mme Sand could have done without those caprices of a slightly blasé artist. But we can clearly see that she is sick and tired of socialists, communists,

Pierre Leroux, and other philosophers; that they have
worn her out completely, and that she plunges with
delight into the Fountain of Youth of naïve and commonplace art. There are, among others, right at the
beginning of the preface, some marvelous lines describing an autumn day. That woman has a talent for ren-
dering the most subtle and the most fleeting impressions in a firm, clear, and comprehensible manner; she
knows how to depict, even to the perfumes and to the
slightest noises. [. . .]

{ 15 }

Paris, April 30, 1848

TO PAULINE VIARDOT (NEE GARCIA)

[. . .] I have read *Les Provinciales* by Pascal, a
book I confess I had not known and [yet] had spoken
of with a great deal of praise. It is admirable in all
ways. Common sense, eloquence, and comic verve are
all there. And yet, it is the work of a slave—a slave to
Catholicism. "The cherubim, those happy combinations of face and feather," and "those famous winged
visages which are always ruddy and gleaming" of the
Jesuit Le Moine made me guffaw. [. . .]

{ 16 }

*Exact Narrative of What I Saw on Monday,
Paris, May 15, 1848*[6]

TO PAULINE VIARDOT (NEE GARCIA)

I left my house at noon. The appearance of the

[6] A description of this day may be found in Jean Dautry:
Histoire de la Révolution de 1848 en France (Paris: Editions
Hier et Aujourd'hui; 1948) p. 170. Dautry estimates the
crowd at 150,000 as of eleven a.m. His section on May 15 is
entitled: *"L'Assemblée envahie par le peuple de Paris"* ("The
Assembly Invaded by the People of Paris").

boulevards was in no way extraordinary; nevertheless, on the Place de la Madeleine, there were already two or three hundred workers with banners.

The heat was suffocating. Groups of people were speaking excitedly. Soon I saw an old man of about sixty climb up on a chair in the left-hand corner of the Place and give a speech in favor of Poland. I went closer; what he was saying was very violent and very pointless; still, he was greatly applauded. I heard some-one near me say it was the Abbé Chatel.

A few seconds later I saw General Courtois arrive from the Place de la Concorde, mounted on a white horse *à la* La Fayette; he advanced toward the boule-vards while saluting the crowd, and immediately began speaking with vehemence and many gestures; I could not hear what he said. He then returned the way he had come.

Soon the procession appeared, sixteen men abreast, and flags first; about thirty officers of all ranks from the *garde nationale*[7] were escorting the petition. A man with a long beard (who I later learned was Huber) was moving forward in a cabriolet.

I saw the procession unfold slowly before me (I had taken a place on the steps of the Madeleine) and head for the National Assembly. . . . I did not take my eyes off the marchers. The head of the column stopped for a moment before the bridge, off the Place de la Concorde, and then went as far as the grille. From time to time a great cry was raised: "Long live Poland!"—a more mournful cry to hear than that of

[7] The *garde nationale* had been set up to preserve order and to serve as an auxiliary service to the army. Its membership at this time was divided among the hostile factions. (See *La Grande Encyclopédie.*)

"Long live the Republic," the [second] *o* [in *Pologne,*
Poland] replacing the *i* [in *République,* Republic].

Soon one could see men in tunics climb hastily
up the steps leading to the Palace of the Assembly;
people near me said that these were the delegates who
were to be introduced. Still, I recalled that a few days
earlier the Assembly had decreed not to receive *Peti-
tioners at the bar,* as the Convention did; and although
I was completely aware of the weakness and the irresolution of our new legislators, I found this a bit extraordinary.

I came down from my perch and walked alongside
the procession, which had stopped just before the grille
of the Chamber. The entire Place de la Concorde was
mobbed. I heard it said around me that the Assembly
was receiving the delegates at that moment, and that
the entire procession had to march in front of the
Chamber. There were about a hundred *gardes mobiles*[8]
on the steps of the peristyle, without bayonets on the
ends of their rifles.

Overwhelmed by the heat, I entered the Champs-
Elysées for a moment. Then, intending to take Herwegh along, I returned home.[9] I went back to the
Place de la Concorde without having found him; it
was about three o'clock. There was still a huge mob
at the Place, but the procession had disappeared; I
could see on the other side of the bridge only the
rearmost marchers and banners. I had scarcely passed
the obelisk when I saw a hatless man in black clothes

[8] The *garde mobile* (or *garde nationale mobile*) had been
organized on February 25, 1848. It was composed of twenty-
four battalions with 1,000 men in each. Considered as cruel and
most zealous, the *garde mobile* was dissolved in 1849. (See *La
Grande Encyclopédie.*)

[9] Georg Herwegh (1817–75), German poet and revolutionist closely associated with Turgenev in 1848.

come running up, anguish on his face, shouting to the persons whom he met: "My friends, my friends, the Assembly has been invaded, come to our rescue: I am a representative of the people!"

I went forward, as quickly as I could, to the bridge, which I found barred by a detachment of *gardes mobiles*. Incredible confusion suddenly spread in the crowd. Many were leaving; some asserted that the Assembly was dissolved, others denied it. In short, an unimaginable racket.

And still, the outside of the Assembly presented no extraordinary sight; the *gardes guarded* it, as if nothing had happened. One moment we heard the drums beat "to arms"; then everything was silent. (We learned later that it was the President himself who had ordered them to cease beating "to arms"—from prudence or from cowardice.)

Two full hours passed thus! No one knew anything definite, but the insurrection seemed to have succeeded.

I managed to make an opening in the line of guards at the bridge, and took a place on the parapet. I saw a mass of people, but without banners, running along the quays on the other side of the Seine. . . .

"They are going to the Hôtel de Ville," someone near me cried out. "It's February 24 all over again." [1]

I stepped down [from the parapet] to go to the Hôtel de Ville. . . . But at that moment we suddenly heard a long drum roll, and a battalion of *gardes mobiles* appeared near the Madeleine and began to charge us on the double. But as no one offered any resistance

[1] Louis-Philippe had abdicated on February 24, 1848. According to Dautry (p. 79), a popular demonstration on February 25 had involved 200,000 persons.

(except for a handful of men, one of them armed with a pistol), they stopped in front of the bridge after they had taken the rioters to the guardhouse.

Even then, nothing seemed decided; in fact, the faces of the *gardes mobiles* showed uncertainty. For at least an hour before their arrival and a quarter of an hour afterward, everyone believed in the triumph of the insurrection; all we heard were the words: "It's over," uttered in a happy or sad way, according to the way those who uttered them were feeling.

The battalion commander, a jovial and resolute man with an eminently French face, made a short speech to his soldiers which he finished with these words: "Frenchmen will always be Frenchmen. Long live the Republic!" That ought not to compromise him.

I have forgotten to tell you that during the two hours of anguish and waiting, we had seen a legion of *gardes nationaux* move slowly along the avenue des Champs-Elysées and cross the Seine on the bridge opposite the [Hôtel des] Invalides. This was the legion that took the rioters from behind and dislodged them from the Assembly.

The battalion of *gardes mobiles* which had come from the Madeleine was received by the townsmen with joyous rapture. . . . Shouts of "Long live the National Assembly!" began again, with new strength. Suddenly the rumor spread that the representatives had re-entered the hall. The scene was changed before our very eyes. "To arms" burst out on all sides; the *gardes mobiles* (really mobile!) capped their bayonets (which, paren-thetically, produced a prodigious effect) and shouted: "Long live the National Assembly!" A lieutenant colonel of the *garde nationale* ran up panting, gathered some hundred persons around him, and told us what had happened.

"The Assembly is stronger than ever," he exclaimed. "We have crushed the wretches. . . . Oh, gentlemen, I have seen horrors . . . deputies insulted and beaten! . . ."

Ten minutes later all the approaches to the Assembly were crowded with troops; cannon came clattering up as the horses approached rapidly. Troops of the line and lancers also came up. . . . Order and the townsmen had triumphed, this time with reason.

I stayed at the Place until six o'clock. . . . Just before, I learned that the government had been victorious at the Hôtel de Ville also. . . . I did not have dinner that day until seven o'clock.

Of the host of things which struck me, I shall cite merely three. In the first place, an *outward order* never ceased to prevail around the Chamber; the cardboard playthings called soldiers guarded the insurrection as scrupulously as possible; after having let it pass, they closed up again around it. It is true that the Assembly, for its part, showed itself beneath everything that could have been expected of it; it listened to Blanqui's[2] harangue for half an hour without protesting! The President did not put on his hat. The representatives did not leave their seats for two hours, but only when they were chased out. Had this immobility been that of the Roman senators before the Gauls, it would have been superb—but it was not; their silence was the silence of fear; they were in session; the President was

[2] Louis-Auguste Blanqui (1805–81), French revolutionist active in 1830, 1848, and 1871.

presiding. . . . No one protested, except M. d'Adels-
ward . . . and Clément Thomas himself interrupted
Blanqui only to ask seriously for the floor! . . .

I was also struck by the way the hot-chocolate and
cigar vendors moved around the ranks of the crowd.
Greedy, pleased, and unconcerned, they had the look
of fishermen hauling in a heavily laden net.

Third, what I myself found very astonishing was
that I could not realize what the feelings of the people were at such a moment; on my word of honor, I
could not guess what they wished or what they feared,
whether they were revolutionaries, reactionaries, or
simply friends of order. They seemed to be waiting
for the end of a storm. And yet, I frequently spoke to
some workers in smocks. . . . They were waiting. . . .
They were waiting! . . . What, then, is history? . . .
Providence, chance, irony, or fatalism? . . .

[17]

Paris [?], *January* 10, 1849

TO PAULINE VIARDOT (NEE GARCIA)

[. . .] I have met two dogs; one communicative,
merry, giddy, with little or no education, witty, banter-
ing, and something of a rascal, on the best of terms
with everyone, and, to tell the truth, without any
genuine dignity; the other—gentle, dreamy, lazy, and
gluttonous, brought up on readings of Lamartine, ingra-
tiating and disdainful at the same time. They frequent
the same café as I do. The first one belongs (if a dog
can belong!!) to a small army surgeon who is very thin,
very ugly, and very cranky; the second has as its mistress
the lady at the cashier's desk, who is a little old woman
toothless from being good. There are people who affect

you this way. I invited the first to come see me, but he claims that his master would whip him; I was not able to answer him with a good reason, and was content to give him a lump of sugar, which he bit into that very instant, while wagging his tail with politeness and vivacity. [. . .]

[18]

Courtavenel, June 19, 1849

TO PAULINE VIARDOT (NEE GARCIA)

[. . .] The poor Hungarians! An honest man will end up by no longer knowing where to live: the young nations are still barbaric, like my dear compatriots, or else, if they rise up and wish to march, they are crushed like the Hungarians; the old nations are dying and stinking, being already rotten and gangrenous. It would be like singing with Roger: *"Et Dieu ne tonne pas sur ces têtes impies?"* ["And does God not thunder on those impious heads?"] But enough! And anyhow, who said that man is destined to be free? History proves the contrary. It was in no spirit of toadyism that Goethe wrote his famous verse:

> *Der Mensch ist nicht geboren frei zu sein.*
> [Man was not born to be free.]

It is quite plainly a fact, a truth, which he was expressing as the exact observer of nature he was. [. . .]

[19]

Paris, June 1849

TO PAULINE VIARDOT (NEE GARCIA)

[. . .] When one thinks of what bad and useless things there are in the world—cholera, hailstorms, kings, soldiers, etc., etc.!—would God be a misanthrope? [. . .]

{ 20 }

[place not given; perhaps July 1849]
TO PAULINE VIARDOT (NEE GARCIA)

Corbeau, corbeau
Tu n'es pas beau
Mais tu viens de mon pays
Et bien! retourne-z-y.
[Crow, crow,
You are not handsome
But you come from my country
All right, go back there.]

{ 21 }

Courtavenel, July 4, 1849
added July 6, 1849

TO PAULINE VIARDOT (NEE GARCIA)

[. . .] M. Ott [author of *Manuel d'histoire*] is a democrat of M. Bucbez's school—a Catholic democrat. This unnatural alliance can only produce monsters. [. . .]

I have not been able to finish [Delille's French translation of Vergil's *Georgics*]. It is really too flat, and besides, the Alexandrines flow with disgusting ease; it is fluid and insipid, like water. The original is no marvel either; all that Latin literature is forced and cold—really literature of a literary man. [. . .]

Voltaire's *La Pucelle*! Oh well! Do you know that in general it is very annoying, especially the part re-

puted not to be so? But the charming mots, the bold
and witty allusions, the caustic raillery reveal the master. [. . .]

[22]

Courtavenel, July 28, 1849

TO PAULINE VIARDOT (NEE GARCIA)

[. . .] To come back to the stars—you know
that there is nothing more usual than to see them in-
spire religious feelings; at least, that is what one finds
in all the books on raising children. Well! I assure you
that such is not the effect they produce on one who
looks at them plainly and without taking sides. The
thousands of worlds, strewn about profusely in the most
remote depths of space, are nothing but the infinite
expansion of life, of that life which occupies everything, penetrates everywhere and causes the aimless
and needless sprouting of a whole world of plants
and insects in a drop of water. It is the product of
an irresistible, involuntary, and instinctive movement
which cannot behave otherwise; it is no meditated
work. But what is that life? Ah! I do not know at all,
but I do know that for the moment it is everything,
it is at the height of its flowering, it is vigorous. . . .
This indifferent, imperious, voracious, egotistical, and
usurping thing is life, nature—it is God; call it what
you like, but do not worship it. Let us understand
each other: when it is beautiful or good (which does
not always happen), worship it for its beauty or for its
goodness, but do not worship it for either its grandeur
or its glory! [. . .]

For, first of all, it is neither great nor small; second, there is no more glory in the creation than there

is in a falling stone, in running water, or in a digesting stomach; all that cannot behave otherwise than to follow the LAW of its existence, which is LIFE. [. . .]

[23]

Courtavenel, August 16, 1849

TO PAULINE VIARDOT (NEE GARCIA)

[On a "*bore*[3] of the first class"] What an intolerable creature! He must have been born in an old cellar, moist from the loves of an old spider and a paralytic toad. [. . .]

[24]

Courtavenel, May 16, 1850

TO PAULINE VIARDOT (NEE GARCIA)

I am at Courtavenel. I confess that I am as happy as a child to be here. I went out to say hello to all the spots I had said good-by to before leaving. Russia will wait: that immense and somber figure, motionless and masked like the Sphinx of Oedipus. She will gulp me down later. I think I see her coarse, inert look fixed upon me with gloomy attention, as befits eyes of stone. Set your mind at ease, Sphinx, I shall return to you and you can devour me at your leisure if I do not solve your riddle! Leave me in peace for yet a little while! I shall return to your steppes! . . .

It was very nice out today. Gounod spent the entire day walking in the Blondureau woods in search of an idea; but inspiration—as capricious as a woman— did not come, and he found nothing. At least that is what he himself told me. He will take his revenge

[3] English in original.

tomorrow. At the moment he is lying on the bearskin
in labor pains. He has an obstinacy and a tenacity
about his work which arouse my admiration. The void
of this day is making him very unhappy. He utters
sighs as long as an arm and cannot be distracted from
his preoccupation. In his misery, he is blaming the
text. I tried to cheer him up and I believe I have succeeded. It is very dangerous for a person to let himself
get into such a rut; he finally clasps his fingers over his
stomach and says to himself: "Why, all that is atro-
cious!" I heard Gounod's complaints and laughed a
little because I know that the first breeze will disperse
all these little clouds. I am very flattered to be
Gounod's confidant for the minor pains of his creative
activity. . . .

[25]

Paris, June 10/22, 1850

TO ALEKSANDR IVANOVICH HERZEN

I arrived from the country an hour after your departure. You can imagine how annoyed I was; I would
have been so happy to see you once more before returning to Russia. Yes, my friend, I am returning. My
things are all packed; the day after tomorrow I am
leaving Paris, and in a week—next Saturday—I shall
board the steamer at Stettin. You may be sure that
I will deliver all your letters and papers in full and I
shall keep my promises, although you have not honored
me with a communication as to where you are staying.
I will send you books and magazines addressed to Miss
Ern, care of Rothschild, as we have agreed; this very
day I shall drop in on him to tell him about this. God
knows when I shall have a chance to write you again;

God knows what is waiting for me in Russia—*mais le vin est tiré, il faut le boire* [but the wine is drawn, it must be drunk]. In case anything important happens, you can notify me by inserting in the *Journal des Débats* an advertisement *que M. Louis Morriset de Caen* [that M. Louis Morriset of Caen], etc. I shall be reading this journal and will understand what you want to tell me. Farewell, my dear Herzen; I wish you every happiness. I shall embrace all your friends for you. I shall talk with them a great deal about you. I shall also try to send information to you about Ogarev and the others at the same address. Be well, and do what you can. I give your wife a firm handshake, and send kisses to your children. My regards to Herwegh and his wife. Once again, let me embrace you.

[26]

Moscow, January 1/13, 1851
(Postscript of January 3/15)

TO PAULINE VIARDOT (NEE GARCIA)

[. . .] The other [reason I was delayed] was the girl whom my mother had adopted, a real Mme Lafarge—treacherous, spiteful, sly, and heartless.[4] It would be impossible for me to tell you all the evil this little viper has done. She has put one over on my brother,

[4] This is Varvara Zhitova, author of *The Turgenev Family* (translated by A. S. Mills, with an introduction by A. Meyendorf, London: The Harvill Press; 1947). The reference cannot be to Dickens's *Tale of Two Cities* (with its Mme Defarge) because the Dickens novel first appeared in *All the Year Round* in 1859. Turgenev is probably thinking of Mme Marie-Fortunée Cappelle Lafarge (1816–53), a notorious Frenchwoman of the day then serving a sentence at forced labor for having poisoned her husband.

who, in his naïve goodness, took her for an angel; she
has gone so far as to slander loathsomely her own
father, and then, when I managed by sheerest luck to
catch the thread of all the intrigue, she admitted
everything; she defied us with an insolence and an
aplomb that made me think of Tartuffe, hat on
head, ordering Orgon to leave the house. [. . .] My
brother and I have given her a letter of exchange for
60,000 francs payable in three years with six per cent
interest, my mother's entire wardrobe, etc., etc. [. . .]
What an evil and perverse nature at seventeen! It
shows promise. [. . .]

〔 27 〕

St. Petersburg, March 4/16, 1851
March 12/24

TO EVGENI MIKHAILOVICH FEOKTISTOV

[. . .] I am resuming my letter today; all this time
I have been busy and in bad spirits. In the issue of the
Sovremennik sent to Moscow the day before yesterday,
there is a piece of mine[5] about which I would like your
opinion also. Much in the main character is under-
stated *involuntarily*; I would like to know whether you
get the point. As for your remarks about "Bezhin
Prairie," I agree with some, but not some others. For
example, I did not at all wish to make the story fan
tastic; these are not German boys who have come
together, but Russians. The truest remark was made to
me by Dudyshkin, who said that my boys speak like
grown ups. [. . .]

[5] "Kassyan of Fair Springs," later included in A *Sportsman's
Sketches.*

[28]

St. Petersburg, December 3/15, 1851

TO KONSTANTIN NIKOLAEVICH LEONT'EV

I have some unpleasant news to tell you: your
comedy has been banned from start to finish. I admit
I did not anticipate this, even though I did think that
the censor would nibble away at it. [. . .]

[29]

St. Petersburg, December 4/16, 1851

TO IVAN SERGEEVICH AKSAKOV

[. . .] I do not have even a single line ready,
and my reluctance to write about what I told you of
(you remember) in Moscow grows stronger every
day. [. . .]

[30]

St. Petersburg, February 2 [O.S.], 1852

TO SERGEI TIMOFEEVICH AKSAKOV

[. . .] Your idea of continuing *A Family Chronicle*⁶ is excellent. Carry it out. [. . .]

[31]

St. Petersburg, February 21, 1852

TO PAULINE VIARDOT (NEE GARCIA)

[. . .] A very great misfortune has struck us:
Gogol died in Moscow, died after burning everything

⁶ The titles of Aksakov's completed trilogy in English are,
perhaps, best known as *A Russian Gentleman, Years of Childhood,* and *A Russian Schoolboy.*

—everything—the second volume of *Dead Souls,* a host of works finished or begun—in short, everything. It would be difficult for you to appreciate how great this loss is—so cruel, and so complete. There is no Russian whose heart is not bleeding at this moment. He was more than a mere writer to us: he revealed us to ourselves. In more than one sense he was for us the continuator of Peter the Great. These words may strike you as exaggerated and prompted by grief. But you do not know him, you know only the least of his works, and even if you knew them all, it would be difficult for you to understand what he has been to us. One must be a Russian to feel it. [. . .]

[32]

St. Petersburg, March 3/15, 1852[7]

TO IVAN SERGEEVICH AKSAKOV

[. . .] Let me tell you without exaggeration that nothing in my memory has produced such an impression on me as Gogol's death. [. . .] That terrible death is a historical event which cannot be grasped at once; it is a mystery—a formidable and ponderous mystery. Someone ought to try to solve it . . . , but whoever does so will find no consolation . . . —we are all agreed about that. The tragic fate of Russia is reflected upon those Russians who are closest to her vitals; no one person of even the strongest spirit could carry on the struggle of an entire nation by himself, and Gogol has perished! It seems to me, really, that he

[7] This letter was picked up by the censors and preserved by the secret police (the celebrated Third Section) in their Turgenev file.

died because he had decided to do so; he felt like dying, and his suicide began with the burning of *Dead Souls*.[8] As for the impression that his death has produced here . . . , suffice it for you to learn that the Chancellor of the local university, Mr. Musin-Pushkin, has not been ashamed to call Gogol in public a servile writer. That happened a few days ago as a result of the few words I had written for the *Sankt-Peterburgskie vedomosti* about Gogol's death (I sent them to Feoktistov in Moscow). Count Musin-Pushkin could not wonder enough at the audacity of those who felt sorry about Gogol. An honest man should not expend his honest indignation on that! Sitting in mire up to their necks, these people have undertaken to eat that mire to their heart's content. Noble people must now hold on to themselves and to each other more firmly than ever before. Let the death of Gogol at least be useful that way. . . .

[33]

St. Petersburg, May 1/13, 1852

TO LOUIS AND PAULINE VIARDOT (NEE GARCIA)

This letter will be delivered to you by a person who is leaving here in a few days, or else that person will send it on to Paris after having crossed the frontier. So I can talk to you frankly a little, and without fearing the curiosity of the police.

Let me begin by telling you that I have not left St. Petersburg for a month—much against my wish. I am under arrest at a police station, by order of the

[8]Gogol had destroyed a first draft for the second part of his *Dead Souls* in 1846, and the work today, like Dostoevski's *Brothers Karamazov*, is essentially unfinished.

Emperor, for having had an article—some lines on Gogol's death—printed in a Moscow newspaper. That was only a pretext, the article itself being completely innocuous. They were looking askance at me for a long time. They have seized on the first opportunity. I am not complaining about the Emperor; the affair was presented to him so perfidiously that he could not have acted otherwise. They wished to put an end to everything that was being said about Gogol's death; at the same time, to place an embargo upon my literary activity did not bother them.

In two weeks they will send me to the countryside, where I shall have to remain until further developments. As you see, all this is not very pleasant; yet, I must admit they are treating me quite humanely; I have a good room and some books; I can write. I was able to have visitors during the first days. Now this is forbidden because too many came. A man's misfortune does not make his friends turn away from him—even in Russia. The *misfortune,* to tell the truth, is not very great. The year 1852 will be without springtime for me: that is all. What is sadder is that I must bid adieu to all hope of taking a trip abroad. But I never suffered from delusions about that. I was well aware, upon leaving you, that it would be for a long time, if not forever. Now I have only one ambition: to be allowed to move about within Russia. I hope that will not be refused me! The Crown Prince is very kind; I have written him a letter and expect some good to come of it.

You know that the Emperor has left.

They also affixed seals to my papers, or rather, they sealed up the doors to my apartment and opened them again ten days later without having examined anything. They probably knew that nothing illegal would be found.

I must admit I am rather bored in my hole. I am profiting from this enforced leisure; I began studying Polish six weeks ago. I have fourteen more days of confinement. I am counting them—and that's it.

That, my dear friends, is the scarcely pleasant news I have for you. I hope yours will be better. [. . .]

[34]

Spasskoe, October 13 [O.S.], *1852*

TO PAULINE VIARDOT (NEE GARCIA)

Imagine a hurricane, a whirlwind of snow which does not fall but races down, which eddies, which darkens the atmosphere (even though it be white), and covers the land to the height of a man. That is the weather at present, dear Mme Viardot. You Europeans have no idea of what a Russian *metel'* [blizzard] is. Fortunately, it is not very cold—but how many victims [of the weather] there are without that! Two years ago nine hundred persons perished in Tula Province in a *metel'* such as this. No one remembers anything like it. It seems that winter wishes to arrive sooner than usual to console us for the wretched summer we have just undergone. It is the story of the gentleman who marries an ugly, poor woman—but really stupid. And yet I am not sad despite the frightful weather, despite this foretaste of six months of complete isolation in store for me. [. . .]

[35]

Spasskoe, October 28 [O.S.], 1852

TO NIKOLAI ALEKSEEVICH NEKRASOV

I received your letter in answer to my first one.
Please, let us correspond, [then] everything will not
bore me so. Imagine, today there is a blizzard here
such as I have not seen for a long time. The wind is
indescribably vehement and threatens to tear down
everything; there is a turbulent and insane storm in the
air—a howling, and convulsive spasms. . . . The devil
knows what it is! That's living in the village for you!
Today is my birthday; I have turned 34. It is a goodly
number of years. Where have all the years gone, and
for what? Once again, the devil knows. However, I
do not feel especially blue; there will be something
later on. Thanks for your kind description of the Nov-
gorod hunts, etc. I am impatiently awaiting your verses.

You can see from my second letter the impression
Childhood[9] made on me. You are right: this is a real
talent. There is a complete drama in the mere mention
of the woman called *La Belle Flamande* [The Beautiful Fleming], which occurs toward the end of the
story. Write him and encourage him to write. Tell him
—if he should be interested—that I salute him, bow
to him, and applaud him. [. . .]

Hawthorne's novel[1] has been translated very badly;
the style has completely disappeared; it is a shame.
[. . .]

[9] *Childhood* had just been printed in the *Sovremennik* as
Istoria moego detstva. [*The Story of My Childhood.*] It was
the debut in print of its twenty-four-year-old author, Lev Nikolaevich Tolstoy, who signed it with the initials "L.N."
[1] The *Sovremennik* had just printed a translation of Nathaniel Hawthorne's *House of the Seven Gables.*

[36]

Spasskoe, December 12 [O.S.], 1852

TO KONSTANTIN NIKOLAEVICH LEONT'EV

Your letter has made me very happy. I was beginning to think that you had forgotten me. I am granting your request with pleasure and am sending you 100 rubles in silver.[2] I would send you the entire 150, but we have not yet sold our grain because of the low prices. I am impatiently awaiting the story you promised, and shall send it to Kraevski [the editor of the *Otechestvennye zapiski*] as soon as I have read it. Let us hope that the censorship will not be too severe, and that your *Nemtsy* [Germans] will bring you both fame and money. I do not think you will find it unpleasant to learn my real opinion of your work. It seems to me that your talent, despite all its subtlety and early development, lacks—let me not say vigor, but power, and the clarity the Germans call, felicitously, *Heiterkeit*. Incidentally, I am judging from the past, but at your age the past very quickly becomes the distant past. I should very much like to talk to you in writing if not orally, but I do not have the time today. Please do not consider me a Maecenas. People who, despite their external means, cannot become artists become Maecenases; I flatter myself with the hope that I am an artist, and therefore relations between us must be based on comradeship. Compared to you, I have only the unenviable distinction of being older and hence more experienced; I am already applying for retirement while you are just beginning your service.

Send your story along soon. You tell me little

---

[2] A silver ruble at this time was worth considerably more than a paper ruble (*assignatsiia*).

about your health; I conclude, therefore, it is good.
You ask me why I am living in the village. By virtue
of the law according to which water inevitably flows
downhill and does not rise upward.[3] As for the rest, be
healthy and merry. [. . .]

[37]

Spasskoe, December 16 [O.S.], 1852

TO NIKOLAI ALEKSEEVICH NEKRASOV

I am sending you, my dear Nekrasov, the article
about [Sergei] Aksakov's book [on hunting] which I
promised you long ago. Surely the most captious censorship could not find anything inadmissible in it; but
if something were to be struck out, not the article but
the [author's] name would be the cause. Let me ask
you to leave it anonymous, except for the letters "I.T."
I hope you will manage to put it into the first number.
I hope you will not completely dislike it. [. . .]

[38]

Spasskoe, December 28 [O.S.], 1852

TO IVAN SERGEEVICH AKSAKOV

[. . .] I must explain to you why that stupid
passage about Mr. Liubozvonov has remained in my
[*Sportsman's*] *Sketches*.[4] Perhaps you have heard that
the book was printed and published in my absence. I

---

[3] Turgenev had been banished to his estate in "domestic
exile" at this time.

[4] In one of the *Sportsman's Sketches*, "The Peasant Proprietor Ovsyanikov," Turgenev parodied some of Konstantin
Sergeevich Aksakov's traits by having a character talk about
the peculiarities of a Slavophile landowner. (From a note in the
source.)

had scarcely examined the manuscript before I sent it
to Ketcher; I recalled that there was some hint somewhere in the *Sketches* about Slavophilism, I found a
few relevant words in "Hor and Kalinich," and I threw
them out—but, to my great annoyance, the other spot
remained. I can assure you that I was not thinking of
your brother [Konstantin] at all when I wrote it, and
you can easily imagine that in any case I would have
thrown out the passage—if I had remembered it—after
we became friends. I hope your brother will excuse my
absent-mindedness. [. . .]

Now to your letter. I subscribe wholeheartedly to
everything you say about the *Sketches,* and I have already written to your brother. I assure you that sometimes it seems to me as if it was not I who wrote the
book; I am so remote from it. The straining and stiff-
ness, which are too often apparent in it, can partly be
excused by the fact that I was abroad when I wrote it;
surrounded by an element that was not Russian and a
life that was not Russian, I involuntarily used my
pencil twice for each stroke.

In this regard, I am not completely satisfied with
"Mumu"—which is why I would very much like you
to read my latest work, *"Postoialy dvor"* ["The Inn"].
I do not know whether I am mistaken or not—and
there is no one here who could tell me—but I suppose
that in "The Inn" I go to the point more directly and
simply, without being coy or philosophizing, but by
trying to express sensibly what I consider to be the essence. May God grant any author the ability to grasp
and express life when he can philosophize about it or
correct it. "The Inn" has long been ready and copied;
I am waiting for an opportunity to send it to Ketcher
in Moscow, to whom I shall write asking him to give it

to you without fail in a very short time. Let me now ask you, your brother, and [your father] Sergei Timofeevich, to comment on it severely and in detail. You have grasped the idea of "Mumu" so accurately that I would be very much interested in what you have to say about "The Inn."

The isolation in which I find myself is very useful to me. I am working a lot, and, in addition to "The Inn," I have written the first three chapters of a major novel, and also a minor work called *"Perepiska"* ["A Correspondence"]. I would like to read all this to people whose taste I trust; I would very much like to know whether I am following the right or the wrong road. I would give a lot to have the pleasure of seeing you at my place, but I am afraid even to ask you. The trip is not very long. However, I am not a man in good repute,[5] and you too seem to have gone a little astray. But how happy I would be if it were possible! It amounts to going (on the highway) to Mtsensk, and from there it is all of ten versts to my place (Spasskoe-Lutovinovo). [. . .]

In a few days I will send Konstantin Sergeevich a long letter about his article in the *Moskovski sbornik*. It is strange: my views on our people jibe with his, but our conclusions are different.

Your remark about the muzhiks' way of talking is completely accurate.[6] "The Inn" does not contain even a trace of that daguerreotypy. It must all be given up, or, if the writing does not come alive without it, the pen must be given up. [. . .]

[5] This letter was written during Turgenev's period of indefinite exile on his own estate.

[6] Ivan Aksakov had complained about Turgenev's excessive use of localisms in reproducing the speech of the muzhiks; Belinski had once made a similar comment.

[39]

Spasskoe, January 10 [O.S.], 1853

TO PAVEL VASIL'EVICH ANNENKOV

[. . . Konstantin] Leont'ev, the author of the comedy which, you will remember, I had you read in St. Petersburg, has been visiting me for several days. He brought along a good manuscript, which I shall send off to Kraevski in a few days, and is preparing another one for the *Sovremennik*. He has talent, but he himself is quite a worthless little boy—spoiled and egotistical. His voluptuous ecstasy over himself and his reverence for his "gift" (as he himself calls it) far surpass those of the semi-deceased Fedor Mikhailovich [Dostoevski], who made your eyes bulge so.[7] In addition, he [Leont'ev] is ill and whines irritatingly, like a slut.

[40]

Spasskoe, January 16 [O.S.], 1853

TO KONSTANTIN SERGEEVICH AKSAKOV

I have been intending to write you for a long time, but I kept putting it off until I could read your article in the *Moskovski sbornik*.[8] I have now read it with great attention and, as far as I can judge these things, I agree with you about our "patriarchal way of life." This patriarchal way of life, as [Sergei Mikhailovich] Solov'ev and [Konstantin Dmitrievich] Kavelin present it, has always struck me as something artificial and sys-

[7] Dostoevski was then serving his time in Siberia.
[8] Konstantin Aksakov's article was entitled: "O *semeinom byte u slavian voobshche i u russkikh v osobennosti*" ["On Family Life among the Slavs in General and among the Russians in Particular"].

tematic—somehow reminding me of our exercises in philosophy at school in the distant past. Any system— in the good and the bad sense of the word—is not a Russian thing; anything sharp, defined, and delimited does not suit us because, on the one hand, we are not pedants, and on the other . . .

I know Russian history only as a man who has not studied the sources does; my judgment of it stems mainly from an interest in what is now being done in Russian life. [. . .]

My situation now is quite extraordinary. Through the Governor, I asked the Minister of the Interior if I could visit those villages of mine which are not within Orel Province; they answered me a few days ago with a refusal. There is nothing to be done. [. . .]

[41]

Spasskoe, January 22 [O.S.], *1853*

TO SERGEI TIMOFEEVICH AKSAKOV

Yesterday I received the first issue of the *Mosk-vitianin* and read your biography of Zagoskin [in it]. I have never read such a biography in the Russian language! This is a model [biography] for the clear and profound understanding of the character and talent of the man it is devoted to, for the warm sympathy flow-ing in every line, for the sense of inner proportion and exposition of the late master. Some expressions are re-markably exact. I was especially struck by the passage where you say that in reading Zagoskin, "a sense of the national flavor imperceptibly arises from the bottom of one's heart." That is completely correct. I regret only one thing: why did you put in the two excerpts from Zagoskin's works? In addition to Zagoskin's not being a writer who can be judged from excerpts, they (especially the verses) are too insignificant and may create a false impression in the reader.

I have not read *Miroshev*, but I shall certainly do so now; as for [*Iuri*] *Miloslavski*—I used to know it by heart. I remember being at a *pension* in Moscow in 1831 (I was 12 years old) where the supervisor used to tell us the contents of *Iuri Miloslavski* in the evenings. It is impossible to depict the absorbing and absorbed attention with which we all listened; once I jumped up and raced to hit a boy who had begun to talk in the middle of a story. Kirsha, the police constable, Omliash, the boyar Shalonski—all these characters were almost relatives to our whole generation, and even now I remember all the slightest details of the novel. Yes, such a national flavor is enviable, and it is given to few!

In 1832 and 1833 I used to see Zagoskin often in the house of my father, with whom he was very friendly. The impression he made on me scarcely harmonized with the esteem in which I held his novel. However, it was not [really] esteem, but a kind of warm and friendly feeling, as for an older brother (I am speaking about Iuri Miloslavski).

The reason I did not revere Zagoskin himself was twofold: first, he was too plain and too kind—he sometimes even argued with me—and a little boy, such as I was then, cannot revere a man who stands on his own level; second, Zagoskin had a certain good-natured way of boasting about women, which I did not like any the more because on such occasions he was usually changing to French, in completely inaccurate language. But, when I recall all the literary men I have since had occasion to become friendly with (and hardly one of whom is worth a Zagoskin), when I call to mind all their petty irritability, their conceit, and their affectations (I no longer dare mention my own sins in this vein), I cannot wonder enough at the modesty of an author who really, for a certain period, had no equal in love of the nation and who preserved it to the end. The Zagoskin whom I, a thirteen-year-old boy, could treat without any ceremony was an excellent man.

I am sure that you have paid attention to the story of Frol Skobeev in the first issue of the *Moskvitianin*. It is an extraordinarily remarkable work. All the characters are superb, and the naïveté of the style is moving. [. . .] [9]

[42]

Spasskoe, February 5/17 [O.S.], 1853
TO SERGEI TIMOFEEVICH AKSAKOV

I understand very well why you were not quite satisfied with my article;[1] to some extent, I went off on a tangent from your book, but I did not anticipate the merciless behavior that would be shown me by the censors. I no longer remember the multitude of passages which were watered down or rejected. I am sending you a full page and a half which were eliminated—after the words "judgments which they caused" on page 39. Whether the censor suspected this passage of pantheism or whatever it was, or whether my name affected him, I do not know. I wished to talk about

[9] *Frol Skobeev* is a seventeenth-century Muscovite tale about a rogue who brazens his way to success. The Soviet Academy of Sciences History of Russian Literature suggests 1682 as its date.

[1] A review of Aksakov's *Zapiski ruzheinogo okhotnika* [*Notes of a Hunter*].

your book in detail in another article—and I shall probably do so—but, I admit, such a censorship will kill
almost anyone's desire to take pen in hand. [. . .]

[43]

Spasskoe, March 6 [O.S.], 1853

TO EVGENI MIKHAILOVICH FEOKTISTOV

. . . I swear to you on my honor: your idea that I
am bored in the village is pointless. Would I really not
tell you? I am working very hard and, furthermore, am
not alone; I am even happy to be here and not in St.
Petersburg. The past is not repeated and—who knows
—perhaps was distorted. Moreover, a man must know
where to stop; it is time to relax, time to stand on one's
feet. I have not grown older in vain; I have calmed
down, and now I ask somewhat less from life and
somewhat more from myself. And also I have spent
quite a lot of money; it is time to collect the last few
coins, or else, perhaps, there will be nothing to live on
in old age, No, I repeat, I am completely content with
my stay in the village. . . .

[44]

Spasskoe, March 14 [O.S.], 1853

TO PAVEL VASIL'EVICH ANNENKOV

[. . .] A few days ago M. S. Shchepkin read us
Ostrovski's comedy [*Ne v svoi sani ne sadis'*, *Don't Go
Where You Don't Belong*]. He came here on Monday,
and will be leaving tomorrow (i.e., Saturday). What a
sweet old man! He read it very well, and it made a great
impression, but Diderot's *Père de famille* and other
plays (with their strong naturalness and morality) never

left my head; I do not think that *this* path leads to genuine art. Ostrovski does not have the sentimentality that bothers you in Diderot, but sentimentality (thank God) seems to have died forever. In short, the play is extremely clever and reveals the author's remarkable talent as a *playwright*—but, you know, the *tendency* against which you have so justly revolted is reflected here too (or, to speak more precisely, the aspiration toward that [Slavophile] tendency).

Sunday, March 15 [O.S.]

Shchepkin has left, after spending five days with us. I read him my novel—with success, as far as I can judge. In my novel, I have tried to depict as simply as possible what I myself have seen and experienced, without worrying about the lesson to be drawn. [. . .]

[45]

Spasskoe, April 2 [O.S.], *1853*

TO SERGEI TIMOFEEVICH AKSAKOV, AND HIS SONS KONSTANTIN AND IVAN

I returned from a ten-day trip only yesterday. [. . .] [2]

Your analysis of each character in "The Inn," S.T., has really made me swell up; if S.T. has understood so well everything I wished to say, I feel I did not bungle everything. I have already given instructions to have "The Inn" copied for you, and shall send it to you. I shall impatiently await even the least important of your remarks. As for my provincialisms, I unfortunately use them in my own conversation without noticing that I do so; the late critic V. G. B[elinski] always called me

[2] Turgenev had just been to Moscow illegally to see Mme Viardot, who was touring there.

"an Orel man who does not know how to speak Russian." Please point out such expressions to me.

Your *Okhotnichi sbornik* [*Hunting Anthology*] is a brilliant and, I hope, a financially successful idea. Of course I shall contribute my pen and my name to your service. I shall start thinking about the contents of a piece in a few days, and keep you posted. [. . .] [3]

[46]

Spasskoe, May 12 [*O.S.*], *1853*

TO IVAN FEDOROVICH MINITSKI

[. . .] I was very touched by the conclusion of your letter. Yes, Minitski, the best time of a man's life is youth, not only because he sleeps better, eats better, and is stronger, but also because the "sacred flame" is ignited and burns within him—which is mocked only by those in whose hearts it has either been extinguished or has never flared up. Maintain the noble resolution that your words now breathe, and learn that without faith, without a profound and powerful faith, life is not worth living and becomes nasty. Mind you, this is said to you by a man who may be thought permeated with irony and criticizing; but without ardent love and faith, irony is trash and criticism is worse than swearing. If we examine the poetry of evil, incarnated in the character of Satan, we find that even that poetry is based on infinite love; remember [George Sand's novel] *Consuelo*. In any case, our calling is not to be devils— let us be people—and we shall try to be people as long as we can, and walk "with God on the hard road. [. . .]"

[3] The proposed anthology was banned by the secret police (the Third Section).

The author of the charming story *Childhood*—a certain Count L. N. Tolstoy—lives ten versts from Turgenevo, but he is now in the Caucasus.

With the next stagecoach, I shall send you a copy of my [*Sportsman's*] *Sketches* in memory of our stay together. These now impress me as completely immature, but I am pleased with their success just the same. Three months have now passed since the copies were sold out. [. . .]

[47]

Spasskoe, May 12/24, 1853

TO PAULINE VIARDOT (NEE GARCIA)

[. . .] You will receive my letter in London. Do not forget to ask Chorley if he received one from me in February, in which I asked for precise information about a certain author named Chenston[4] (he knows what it is about). [. . .]

[48]

Spasskoe, June 5 [O.S.], 1853

TO SERGEI TIMOFEEVICH AKSAKOV

[. . .] However, I have finished the first part of the novel. I have already sent it off to Annenkov in Petersburg, as I had promised; but it will go to you as soon as he has read it, and I shall then ask you for your opinion (which you know I value highly). Please ask your sons to tell me what *they* think. It is a completely different type of work from "The Inn." Inciden-

---

[4] Aleksandr Pushkin termed one of his playlets in verse an adaptation from Shenstone; Turgenev followed Pushkin's spelling of the name.

tally, the latter has apparently not been fated to reach you quickly. I agreed to the request of one man who wished to transcribe it, but you will receive it soon. Otherwise, there does not seem to be such urgency now. The main thing is that I wish to know what you say about my novel, and whether I have hit upon the tone of a novel. [. . .]

[49]

Spasskoe, June 29 [O.S.], 1853, St. Peter's Day
TO SERGEI TIMOFEEVICH AKSAKOV

[. . .] Have you received the first part of my novel from Ketcher yet? Annenkov read it long ago, and has written me about it; his opinion is quite sensible and fair. I would tell you exactly what he criticizes, but I would like to see whether you agree with him about my being able to do the work. I am impatiently awaiting your judgment.

[50]

Spasskoe, August 30 [O.S.], 1853
TO SERGEI TIMOFEEVICH AKSAKOV

[. . .] I agree with your observations, but will try to justify myself in one thing. *No one* really falls in love with my heroine (whom, by the way, I am completely reworking)—and least of all Dmitri Petrovich, who, on the contrary, even has a capricious hatred of her. To clarify his personality, I shall insert in the first part the chapter of his reminiscences—with which I had planned to begin the second part. The scene of the declaration [of love] will probably now be clearer to you, although apparently it also needs to be changed so as not to leave the reader in doubt. My main characters are Chermak, Dmitri Petrovich, and Glafira. I shall try to express in them, if I can, the contemporary way of life and how it has *degenerated* among us [in Russia]. [. . .]

{ 51 }

Spasskoe, October 12 [O.S.], 1853

TO MRS. SOF'IA ANDREEVNA MILLER (LATER, THE WIFE OF COUNT A. K. TOLSTOY)

[. . .] I would like to begin a war with you about Jean Paul, but that is almost impossible on paper, so I shall postpone it until we meet. I shall be content to ask you whether you know Homer. Take his *Odyssey* (at least in the translation by Voss),[5] and read it or reread it. It has youth and freshness; it is just like a life eternally illuminated by a smiling sun; it has all the charm of poetry's first appearance on the lips of an immortal and happy nation; best of all, it will make you disgusted with the semi-sentimental and semi-ironic intrigues and the sick personality which set Jean Paul apart from all the latest writers. Try it and tell me the results. [. . .]

{ 52 }

Spasskoe, November 20 [O.S.], 1853
section dated November 23 [O.S.]

TO SERGEI TIMOFEEVICH AKSAKOV

[. . .] I just received news that the monarch has seen fit to allow me to leave the village and return to St. Petersburg. I am sure you will share my pleasure

---

[5] Johann Heinrich Voss's German translation.

—but what I find most pleasant is the opportunity to see my friends, of whom you are one of the best. I will be leaving here immediately after December 6. [. . .]

[53]

St. Petersburg, February 10 [O.S.], 1854

TO SERGEI TIMOFEEVICH AKSAKOV

[. . .] The life I have been leading here, while not dissipated, is somehow squandered on a thousand trifles, etc. Incidentally, I have done two good things here: I have persuaded F. I. Tiutchev to publish his collected poetry,[6] and I have helped Fet to revise his translation of Horace and get it into shape.[7] I myself am doing nothing for the present; I hope to get to work in the village.

Today the manifesto about the declaration of [the Crimean] war against England and France has come out here. [. . .]

[54]

St. Petersburg, April 3 [O.S.], 1854

TO KONSTANTIN NIKOLAEVICH LEONT'EV

I received your letter yesterday. While I cannot but thank you for the expressions of interest with which it is filled, I must explain that the matter you mention (my wedding) has no basis in fact. I was especially astonished by the name of my intended bride. I could hardly have been more amazed had I learned that the

---

[6] During 1854 the *Sovremennik* published about 100 of Tiutchev's verses, which were published in book form the same year. Turgenev wrote an article about them.

[7] Fet's translation of Horace came out in 1856.

Emperor of China had made me a mandarin. I cannot understand where this rumor comes from.

The other notions about my life here—which the narrator you speak of has passed along to you—resemble the truth just as little. However, I once really was accidentally introduced to a lady of consequence at a soirée, and I chatted with her for ten minutes; as for the rest, I am living here in very solitary fashion.

You are right in everything you say about marriage; and I shall probably, like everyone else, finally marry some time—but that time has not yet arrived. I do not feel too sorry for you that your suppositions on that score have fallen through; somehow, it seems better to me this way.

I am glad you will soon begin a period of activity, and I wish only that the change in climate will not affect your health.

I intend to spend the summer in the environs of Peterhof; in such times, a man does not wish to go far from the scene of action. But in a few days I will be going to the village for a couple of weeks, and perhaps I shall see you on the way.

Thank you once more for your interest.

[55]

Peterhof, May 31 [O.S.], *1854,* **Whitsunday**
TO SERGEI TIMOFEEVICH AKSAKOV

[. . .] Let us talk a little about the news in literature. First of all, I met [Evgeni] Baratynski's widow (between us, a completely "nutty" woman), and she gave me an album in which she had copied everything left by her husband—letters, etc. Someone could write a rather interesting article. Tolstoy, the author of *Child-*

hood, has sent in a story, a sequel to the first one, entitled *Boyhood*; they say it is superb. A translation of my book [A *Sportsman's Sketches*] has appeared in Paris, with a long preface; it is really, I think, libelous nonsense.

Baratynski is not a poet in the unique sense of a Pushkin, but no one can fail to respect his noble artistic honesty, his constant and unselfish aspirations toward the loftiest aims of poetry and life. Konstantin Sergeevich [Aksakov] would like him despite his Westernism. He has much intelligence, taste, and acuteness—perhaps too much; his every word bears the mark of being chiseled and filed; his verse never hurries, or even flows. [. . .]

The form of Baratynski's verse is an echo of our great and classical epoch.

Nekrasov, whom you dislike so much, has written some good poetry—especially one piece, the lament of an old peasant woman for her dead son. [. . .] [8]

[56]

Peterhof Colony, August 7 [O.S.], 1854

TO SERGEI TIMOFEEVICH AKSAKOV

[. . .] I finally received a French translation of my [*Sportsman's*] *Sketches*, and would have been better off without it! The devil knows what this [translator] M. Charrière has made out of me; he has added entire pages full of his own inventions, and deleted to an incredible extent. [. . .] What an unscrupulous Frenchman! Why must I now, through his kindness, be turned into a fool?

[8] The poem referred to is "V *derevne*" ["In the Village"].

[. . .] I am very glad that you are continuing your *Reminiscences*.[9] Will you not send something to the *Sovremennik?* [. . .]

I am not writing you about political affairs; nothing important has happened recently, except the brilliant repulse of the first French assault on the Aland [islands].[1] The French will finally take the islands—the superiority of their forces is too great—but they will pay high. When the English fleet was nearby, we went to Krasnaia Gorka, fifty versts from here, to see it. [. . .]

{ 57 }

St. Petersburg, August 7/19, 1854

TO THE EDITOR OF *Le Journal de St. Pétersbourg*

Would you be kind enough to insert the following letter? A French translation of my works, published in Moscow two years ago, has just fallen into my hands. This translation, entitled (I am not too sure why) *Mémoires d'un seigneur russe* [*Memoirs of a Russian Nobleman*], has given rise to several articles in foreign newspapers. You will easily understand, Sir, that I do not find it fitting to enter into a discussion with my critics, who are, moreover, much too benevolent toward me. What is really on my mind is to protest against the conclusions some of them think can be drawn from my book. As a writer, as a man of honor, and as a Russian I protest against those conclusions and all deductions that can be made from them; I venture to believe that those

---

[9] Aksakov's reminiscences offer one of the major sources of information about his friend, Gogol.

[1] The Crimean War had already started.

of my compatriots who have read me have done justice
to my intentions; I have never been eager for other approval.

   As for the translation by M. E[rnest] Charrière, on
the strength of which I have been judged, I do not believe that there are many examples of a similar literary
mystification. I am not speaking of the wrong meanings
or of the mistakes with which the translation swarms—a
translation from the Russian cannot avoid them; but
really, the changes, the interpolations, and the additions
which are encountered on every page are unimaginable.
There is no resemblance at all to the original. In all the
Mémoires d'un seigneur russe, there are not four lines
in a row translated faithfully. M. Charrière has taken
special care to embellish my style, which must have
struck him as too shabby and too barren. If I have
someone say: "And I fled," this simple phrase is rendered as: "I fled in a wild and disheveled flight, as if
I had at my heels an entire legion of adders commanded by witches." A hare pursued by a dog becomes,
under the lively pen of my translator, "a squirrel which
climbs to the top of a pine tree, stands up there, and
scratches its nose." A falling tree is transformed into
"a hairy giant which had been laughing at the age-old
assaults of several thousand insects, and which bends
solemnly and without haste towards the earth, its old
nurse, as if to embrace her, as it dies under the bite of
a cutting blade which man has supplied with a handle
made from a fragment of wood which the tree itself
may have furnished"; an old lady "goes from the
chocolate to the saffron, and then to the *café au lait,*
while tufts of yellow, curled hair toss on her forehead
and her eyes blink with as rapid a motion as the run-

ning shaft of the pendulum, which beats sixty times a minute," etc., etc., etc. Can you imagine my astonishment? But here is something even worse. In Chapter xvii, on page 280, M. Charrière introduces a new character, whom he describes, at length and kindly, as a type of peddler selling lucifer matches. . . . What can I say? Well! there is not a word about all that in my book for the good reason that no such person exists in Russia. What is most curious is that in talking about just that chapter in his preface, M. Charrière warns the reader: "The prefatory remarks of the author may seem a bit long for our French impatience."

You understand, Sir, that by using such a method of translating a man can give full rein to his imagination, and M. Charrière has not failed to do so. He trims, he cuts, he changes, he makes me cry and laugh at will, he makes me sneer—and that is what annoys me most. He has a horror of the correct word, and puts a trumpet flourish at the end of every sentence; he improvises all kinds of meditations, pictures, descriptions, and comparisons. All these improvisations may possibly be charming and in very good taste, but I ask M. Charrière himself whether he does not feel that by adding so many beautiful things to my text he deprives himself of the very merit that could recommend him to the attention of French readers—the merit of originality? Let me thank M. Charrière very much for all the friendly statements in his preface, but is it not a bit strange to praise someone else's temper when one has just lent him so much of one's own?

Yours etc.,

P.S. Excuse my adding a postscript to a letter that is already so long. But, among the mistranslations I

have spoken of above, there are two or three so piquant
that I cannot deny myself the pleasure of quoting
them. On page 104, one finds the following sentence:
"The dogs wagged their tails . . . while waiting for a
bobolink." Where does this bobolink come from? The
[Russian] text has *ovsianka*, and the dictionary M. Charrière consulted probably did not tell him that *ovsianka*
also means [oatmeal] *mash for dogs*. On page 380, the
reader is completely surprised to hear (the scene takes
place in the very center of Russia) about "the continual
comings and goings of Negroes, solemnly occupied with
service." *Negroes*! Here is the explanation of the riddle:
M. Charrière has confused the words *arapnik*, a hunting whip, and *arap*, a Negro, and he has composed his
sentence as a result of this. On page 338, we see a
dignitary give his hand to a general to be kissed (!)
. . . Furthermore, I suspect that M. Charrière has
been deceived here deliberately. I am passing by even
better ones, but the time has come for me to stop.

[58]
Spasskoe, October 8 [O.S.], 1854
TO SERGEI TIMOFEEVICH AKSAKOV
[. . .] P.S. They say that the censor has violently
distorted [Tolstoy's] *Boyhood* in the tenth number of
the *Sovremennik*—but read it anyhow and tell me
what you think of it. [. . .]

[59]
Spasskoe, October 29 [O.S.], 1854
TO ELISEI IAKOVLEVICH KOLBASIN
[. . .] I am very glad about the success of [Tol-

stoy's] *Boyhood*. May God grant only that Tolstoy[2] live. I have high hopes that he will astonish us yet; his talent is first-class. I have become acquainted with his sister [Mar'ia] here—a very sweet and congenial woman; her husband is also a Count Tolstoy.

My health is very satisfactory, and my stomach only rarely plays tricks on me. [. . .]

{ 60 }

Spasskoe, November 1 [O.S.], 1854
TO IVAN FEDOROVICH MINITSKI

[. . .] I am very happy you liked my stories. . . . The interest of such persons as yourself serves to remind your brother-scribbler that he is not soiling paper completely in vain. Your observation about *"Zatish'e"* ["The Lull"] is entirely correct and coincides with what Nekrasov, Aksakov, and others have told me. At least I am glad that my gentleman has succeeded, if only somewhat. But, in the tenth issue of the *Sovremennik*, you will find a tale by Lev Tolstoy (the author of *Childhood*) which makes all other efforts seem nonsensical. Here at last is the heir to Gogol—whom he does not resemble in the slightest, as is fitting. It is a pity that the censor has suppressed so much! [. . .]

{ 61 }

St. Petersburg, December 4 [O.S.], 1854
TO COUNTESS MAR'IA NIKOLAEVNA TOLSTOY (NEE TOL-
STOY) AND COUNT VALER'IAN PETROVICH TOLTOY

[. . . Lev Tolstoy's] *Boyhood* has produced a pro-

---

[2] This letter was written on the first day of the bombardment of besieged Sevastopol; Tolstoy was serving as an artillery officei.

found impression here. Lev Nikolaevich [Tolstoy] has, in everyone's opinion, become one of our best writers. And now he has to write another work in order to gain the first place, which is his by right and which is awaiting him. Please give me news of him. [. . .]

[62]

Spasskoe, June 15 [O.S.], 1855

TO PAVEL VASIL'EVICH ANNENKOV

[. . .] I am seeing the Tolstoys[3] rather often. Let me know whether Tolstoy's article "Sevastopol" is good. The issue of the *Sovremennik* containing it will not be here before July 8 or 10. God knows how they do things!

Botkin has sent me Druzhinin's article (in the *Biblioteka dlia chteniia*) about your Pushkin edition. The article is very good, although I am annoyed that he does not notice, or does not wish to notice, Gogol's historical significance. If he says that to expatiate upon that significance is difficult, he should have passed over Gogol in complete silence. But still, there are many good things in the article. [. . .]

[63]

Spasskoe, June 17 [O.S.], 1855

TO VASILI PETROVICH BOTKIN

[. . .] I have read [Druzhinin's] article on Pushkin with great delight. It is noble, warm, sensible, and accurate. It is the best thing Druzhinin has written.

---

[3] Lev's sister Mar'ia and some of his other relatives. The reference is to Tolstoy's *Tales of Sevastopol.*

But he is wrong about Gogol . . . , i.e., he is completely right in what he says, but because he cannot say *everything*, the truth comes out as a falsehood. There are periods when literature cannot be art *alone*, and there are interests above poetic interests. The moment of self-knowledge and criticism is every bit as necessary in the development of a nation's life as it is in a person's—you know what I mean. But just the same, the article is excellent, and when you write Druzhinin, give him my sincere thanks. Our present literary men should take to heart much of what he says, and I am the first to know *où le soulier de Gogol blesse* [where Gogol's shoe hurts]. [. . .]

[64]

Spasskoe, July 9 [O.S.], 1855

TO VASILI PETROVICH BOTKIN

[. . .] They say that you have taken up residence at Kuntsovo, with Nekrasov. How is his health? Tell me about your way of life. His verses *"Russkomu pisateliu"* ["To a Russian Writer"] are not bad, but it would have been better if V*las* had not been printed. [. . .]

[65]

Spasskoe, July 10 [O.S. (?)], 1855

TO NIKOLAI ALEKSEEVICH NEKRASOV

Your letter has found me here, my dear Nekrasov, thanks to the cholera, which is raging just where I wished to go after grouse—in the Zhizdra District. My rangers have returned, and are talking about the wonderful spots there. . . . What is to be done! I love hunting passionately, but I fear the cholera even more. I am now sitting here and working on a major story[4] (120 pages are done), and I do not know what the result will be. Your verses "To——" are simply Pushkinesque in their quality; I immediately committed them to memory. Do me a favor and send me your tale in verse; I am sure that it contains wonderful things.[5] Let me wholeheartedly encourage your intention to write an autobiography; your life is really one of those which, all conceit aside, must be told, because it offers much that many a Russian heart will respond to profoundly. I thank you in advance for the dedication to me, but I hope that the public will not find out about it soon. (By the way, I am also flattered by Tolstoy's dedication.[6] How superb his Sevastopol is!)

To my extreme annoyance, I left my copy of [Robert] Burns in St. Petersburg. May I ask you to have good Vasili [Botkin] drop into a book store and buy and send me a copy (finding one is quite easy). I am sure you will be enraptured by Burns. I will translate him with delight. I promise to make an excellent selection, and to adopt the meter; Burns is a pure wellspring of poetry. For the present, try writing something in the following stanza, which was his favorite:

To you, my friend, I cannot say
For whom your muse should work and play
But I cannot conceal today
    From those I greet

---

[4] *Rudin*.

[5] The first poem is *"Davno otvergnuty toboi"* ["Having Long Been Rejected by You"] and the second is *"Sasha."*

[6] Tolstoy had dedicated his "Wood Cutting" to Turgenev.

STANDING (left to right): Lev Nikolaevich Tolstoy, Dmitri Vasilievich Grigorovich

SEATED (left to right): Ivan Aleksandrovich Goncharov, Ivan Sergeevich Turgenev, A. V. Druzhinin, Aleksandr Nikolaevich Ostrovski. (Photograph, 1856; *The Bettmann Archive*)

That on me has begun to weigh
  The cruel heat.[7]

Understand? This stanza is suitable for elegiac and melancholy works. This is the stanza of so famous a poem of Burns's as the one to a field flower he cut while plowing.[8] Please do send me the Burns.

Thanks for your encouraging exhortation. As you say, I have really been and partly still am in a mood, if not of decay, then of self-doubt. I see all too clearly what my shortcomings are, and my sureness of myself has disappeared together with my self-confidence. However, I shall strain as hard as I can, if only to live up to my friends' good opinion of me. [. . .]

{ 66 }

Spasskoe, July 10 [O.S.], 1855

TO IVAN IVANOVICH PANAEV

The cholera is so virulent everywhere (especially

[7] As a *jeu d'esprit*, I asked Dr. David Daiches to put Turgenev's lines into Scots from a prose translation. He answered: "Turgenev's lines are surely too few to fit into a whole Burns stanza, but here is the best I can do:

'I canna tell ye whom tae choose
As subject for your rhymin' Muse,
But och, I hae tae tell ye news
  Will bide nae mair:
The lowe that starts to fash me noo's
  A skaith richt sair.' "

Dr. Daiches has even been kind enough to translate this version back into English:

"I cannot tell you whom to choose
As subject for your rhyming muse,
But ah, I have to tell you news
  [That] will wait no longer:
The flame that is beginning to trouble me now
  Is a harm right sore."

[8] "To a Mountain Daisy, on Turning One Down with the Plough, April —, 1786."

where I wanted to go hunting) that I am involuntarily [sic] staying home and having a spell of the blues. But I am also working. [. . .] Chernyshevski's book, that rotten corpse, that result of malicious stupidity and of blindness, should not have been analyzed in Mr. Pypin's manner. Such a trend would be ruinous, and the *Sovremennik*, more than any other [periodical], ought to rise up against it. Fortunately, the book is so dry and lifeless that it cannot do much damage.[9] Tolstoy's piece about Sevastopol is a marvel! I shed some tears while reading it—and shouted hurrah! I am very flattered that he wishes to dedicate his new story ["The Wood Cutting"] to me. I saw a notice about the *Sovremennik* in the *Moskovskie Vedemosti*. Good: may God enable you to keep your promises—i.e., that articles arrive, that Tolstoy does not get killed, etc. All this would help you a great deal. The Tolstoy piece produced a general furor here. The summer editions of the *Sovremennik* have been good so far—interesting and sensible. [. . .]

[67]

Spasskoe, July 25 [O.S.], 1855

TO VASILI PETROVICH BOTKIN AND NIKOLAI ALEKSEEVICH NEKRASOV

[. . .] As for Chernyshevski's book,[1] my chief objection is this: in his eyes, art is (as he himself expresses it) only a surrogate for reality, for life, and is essentially fit only for immature people. No matter how you look at it, this idea of his is at the basis of every-

[9] Part of the *Tales of Sevastopol* had just appeared.
[1] Chernyshevski's *Esteticheskie otnoshenia iskusstva k deistvitel'nosti* [*The Aesthetic Relationship of Art to Reality*].

thing. But, in my opinion, this idea is nonsense. There is no Shakespearean Hamlet in life, or, if you like, there is one, but Shakespeare discovered him and made his accomplishment public.

Chernyshevski is taking a lot on himself if he imagines that he himself can always penetrate to the heart of life you talk about. I can just imagine him extracting poetry from reality for his own use and as a pastime! No, my friend, his book is false and harmful; some time you and I will talk about this at length.

I have made use of my inability to go hunting: yesterday I finished a major tale seven signatures long.[2] I have written it with love and care; what the result is, I do not know. I shall leave it alone for a while, then reread it, correct it, and send it to you after it has been copied—what do you say? [. . .]

[68]

Spasskoe, July 25 [O.S.], 1855

TO PAVEL VASIL'EVICH ANNENKOV

[. . .] As a result of having nothing to do, I set to work and yesterday finished a very long story over which I had labored as never before in my life.[3] I have no idea whether I succeeded. The idea is good, but the execution—that is the main point. I shall read it to you if you come to see me in September and do not trick me, as usual. [. . .]

[2] *Rudin.*
[3] *Rudin.*

[69]

Pokrovskoe, October 3 [O.S.], 1855[4]

TO COUNT LEV NIKOLAEVICH TOLSTOY

I have long been planning to meet you, even if only in writing (as nothing else is possible for the time being). [. . .]

First of all, let me thank you from my heart for having dedicated your "Wood Cutting" to me: in my entire literary career, nothing has yet so flattered my vanity. Your sister has probably written you about my high opinion of your talent and about how much I am expecting from you; recently I have been thinking about you very often. I am terrified when I think of where you are. Although I am really glad about all your new emotions and experiences, there is a limit to everything, and there is no need to tempt a fate that would like so much to harm us at every step, especially now. It would be good if you could manage to get away from the Crimea. You have demonstrated sufficiently that you are not a coward. However, yours is not a military career; your purpose is to be a literary man, an artist of ideas and words. I decided to say this because in your last letter (which was received today) you hint at the possibility of a leave; furthermore, I love Russian literature too much not to nurse the desire to see you out of reach of stupid, indiscriminating bullets. If you really get a chance to come to Tula Province even for

[4] The source gives the date for this letter as October 3 [O.S.]. This is surprising because M. K. Kleman (*Letopis' zhizni i tvorchestva I. S. Turgeneva* [*Chronicle of Turgenev's Life and Work*], Moscow-Leningrad, Academia, 1934, p. 79) states that Turgenev was in Moscow, not Pokrovskoe, on October 9. Kleman adds that, in Turgenev's handwriting, 9 frequently looks like 3.

a short while, I would come from St. Petersburg to meet you; this will be no great attraction for you, but really, come for your own sake and for that of literature. Let me repeat to you: your weapon is the pen and not the sword, while the Muses not only cannot stand vanity, but are even jealous [of other activities].

We would meet, talk to our hearts' content, and, perhaps, our acquaintanceship would be profitable for both of us.

I would like to say a lot about you and your works, but that is impossible on paper—especially in this letter. I am postponing all that for a personal meeting, of which I do not despair.[5]

During the course of the summer, I have been seeing your relatives frequently, and I really like them. How much all of us regret the departure of [your brother] Nikolai Nikolaevich! I am really annoyed when I remember that we are meeting so late, although we are such close neighbors.

An answer from you would make me very happy. My address is: Stepanov's house at the Annichkov Bridge, on the Fontanka, St. Petersburg.

Let me send you friendly greetings, my dear Lev Nikolaevich, and wish you everything good, starting with health. I remain one who genuinely esteems you.

[70]

St. Petersburg, December 3 [O.S.], 1855
TO VASILI PETROVICH BOTKIN

[. . .] You already know from Nekrasov that

---

[5] The meeting finally took place in St. Petersburg on November 21/December 3, 1855.

Tolstoy is here and is staying at my place. I would very much like you to meet him. He is a congenial man, original to the highest degree.

The one you would not recognize is me, your humble servant. Imagine me making the rounds of suburban dances, with coquettes present, in love with a charming Polish woman, giving her silver plate, and spending my nights with her until eight in the morning! How unexpected and unlike me that is—is it not? But that is the way things are, anyhow. I have a belly full now, and wish to get back to my routine, live as a philosopher, and work—for to make a fool of oneself at my age is a shame! [. . .]

[71]

St. Petersburg, December 9 [O.S.], 1855

TO PAVEL VASIL'EVICH ANNENKOV

[. . .] Just think, Tolstoy (L.N.T.) has been staying with me for over two weeks, and what I would give to see the two of you together! You cannot imagine what a sweet and remarkable person he is, although because of his savage fervor and his buffalo-like stubbornness, I have named him the Troglodyte. I have a strange, almost fatherly feeling for him. He read us the beginning of his *Youth* and the beginning of another novel.[6] Oh, these are magnificent works! In general, literature is now *en grand complet* [in full swing]. [. . .]

---

[6] *The Novel of a Russian Landlord*, which Tolstoy never finished; his "Morning of a Landlord" is an excerpt from it.

[72]

St. Petersburg [end of 1855, start of 1856]
TO NIKOLAI ALEKSEEVICH NEKRASOV

[. . .] I am sending you the proofs of *Rudin*,
my dear Nekrasov; there has been a misunderstanding
with the Turgenevs; I did not give them that item to
read at all, but kept it myself. [. . .]

[73]

Spasskoe, June 10 [O.S.], 1856
TO COUNTESS ELIZAVETA EGOROVNA LAMBERT

[. . .] When I look back at my past life, it seems
that I have done nothing more than pursue trifles. Don
Quixote, at least, believed in the beauty of his Dulcinea, but the Don Quixotes of our times realize that
their Dulcinea is an ugly hag and keep running after
her anyhow.

We have no ideal; that is the trouble. But an ideal
is given only by a strong and civic way of life, by Art
(or Science) and Religion. Not everyone is born an
Athenian or an Englishman, an artist or a scholar, and
religion is not given immediately to everyone. Let us
wait, and have faith, and keep in mind that meanwhile
we are making fools of ourselves. To know this may
at any rate be useful. [. . .]

[74]

Courtavenel, September 22, 1856
TO ALEKSANDR IVANOVICH HERZEN

[. . .] I finished reading your memoirs in the second part of *Poliarnaia Zvezda* [*The North Star*]. They

are charming; the only thing to be regretted is the in-
accuracies of the language. But you must certainly continue these stories: they contain a certain courageous
and artless truth, while merriness and freshness burst
through their sad tones, as if involuntarily. I liked all
this enormously, and ask you again to go on without
being ashamed of anything. This is strange business! In
Russia I tried to induce old [Sergei] Aksakov to continue his memoirs; and here—you! And that is not so
contradictory as the first glance would indicate. Both
his memoirs and yours are truthful pictures of Russian
life, only at two extremes and from two different view-
points. But our land is not only great and abundant, it
is also wide and includes many things that seem to be
alien to one another. [. . .]

{ 75 }

Courtavenel, September 18/30, 1856

TO VASILI PETROVICH BOTKIN

[. . .] She [Turgenev's daughter] has completely
forgotten Russian and I am glad. She has no reason to
remember a strange language to which she will never
return. [. . .]

{ 76 }

London, September 4, 1856

TO HIS DAUGHTER, PAULINE

[. . .] You complain about being bored. At your
age, my child, to admit being bored is every bit as
shameful as it would be to confess having stolen something. You are, in fact, committing a robbery against
yourself—an irretrievable theft. You are robbing your-

self of time and everything you would have been able to fill it with. [. . .]

【 77 】

Paris, November 11, 1856

TO ALEKSANDR VASIL'EVICH DRUZHININ

[. . .] I am very glad that you liked my story "Faust." Your approval is my guarantee: I believe in your taste. You say that I could not linger over George Sand; of course I could not linger over her—just as, for example, over Schiller. There is this difference between us: for you, the entire tendency is an error that ought to be uprooted; for me, that tendency is the imperfect truth, which, in an age when the complete truth is still inaccessible to human beings, will always find followers. You think that the time has already come to erect the walls of the building; I suggest that digging the foundations is still before us.

I can say the same about Chernyshevski's articles. I am annoyed with him because of his dryness and stale taste—and also because of his lack of courtesy in dealing with living people (as, for example, in the September issue of the *Sovremennik*). But I do not find him a "carcass"—on the contrary; I sense a vital stream in him, although not the one you would like to meet in criticism. He understands poetry poorly; but, you know, there is no great harm in that; a critic does not make poets, and he does not kill them. But [Chernyshevski] understands—how could this be expressed?—the demands of reality, of contemporary life, and in him this is no manifestation of a disordered liver (as dear Grigorovich once said), but the very root of his entire existence. However, enough about that; I consider Chernyshevski useful; time will show whether I was right. Moreover, you and your magazine [*Biblioteka dlia chtenia*] will "counterbalance" him; let me rejoice about that in advance. You remember that I, an admirer of Gogol's and his least important follower, told you once about the need to return to the Pushkin element (as a counterbalance to the Gogolian). A striving for impartiality and the entire truth is one of the few good qualities I am grateful to nature for having given me. [. . .]

I am awaiting your [translation of Shakespeare's] *King Lear* impatiently. To translate [Shakespeare's] *Coriolanus* is a wonderful idea. It would really suit your taste, oh you, sweetest of conservatives! [. . .] [7]

[78]

Paris, November 16/28, 1856

TO COUNT LEV NIKOLAEVICH TOLSTOY

[. . .] French phrase-making is every bit as repulsive to me as to you, and never has Paris seemed so prosaically insipid to me. Contentment does not suit Paris; I have seen the town at other moments and liked it better. What keeps me here are old and indissoluble ties with a single family [the Viardots], plus my daughter (whom I love very much), a sweet and intelligent girl. [. . .]

Fet is now in Rome with [Nekrasov]. Yes, my friend, he was in Paris—but you cannot imagine a more

[7] Druzhinin's version of *King Lear* was printed in the *Sovremennik* during 1856; his translation of *Coriolanus* appeared in the *Biblioteka dlia chtenia* in 1858.

unhappy and forlorn creature. He was so bored that one could have screamed. He saw no one but his French servant. He came to visit me (i.e., at M. Viardot's) in the country, and left (between us) an unpleasant impression. An officer *endimanché* [in his Sunday best], with rings on his fingers and the ribbon of St. Anna in his buttonhole, he told the most stupid stories in broken French, and the humor disappeared entirely; his eyes were wide open, his mouth rounded, a senseless astonishment on his face—but let us drop the subject. I so argued with him in my room that the entire house groaned with the wild sounds of Slavic speech; in short, it was awful. However, he has written some graceful verses and some detailed travel notes, which contain much that is childish, but also many intelligent and sensible remarks which create a touchingly open-hearted and sincere impression. He is really a "nice fellow," as you call him. [. . .]

You have finished the first part of *Youth*—wonderful! How ashamed I am that I cannot hear it! If you do not lose your way (and there is no reason to suppose that you should!), you will go very far. Let me wish you health, activity, and freedom—spiritual freedom.

As for my "Faust," I do not think you will like it very much. My works could please you—and perhaps had a certain influence on you—only until you began to depend on yourself. I have nothing to teach you now; you see only a difference in manner; you see the blunders and the omissions. All you can do is to study man, his heart, and the really great writers. But I am a writer of a transitional period, and I am fit only for people who are in a transitional state. [. . .]

[79]

Paris, November 25/December 7, 1856

TO VASILI PETROVICH BOTKIN

[. . .] It strikes me that the main shortcoming of our writers (and especially of myself) is that we have little contact with real life—i.e., with living people; we read too much and think abstractly; we are not specialists, and hence we do not produce anything special. [Johann Heinrich] Merck says, with complete accuracy: "*Alles* (among the ancients) *war local, für den Moment—und dadurch ward's ewig. Wir schreiben in's weite Blaue, für alle Menschen und für die liebe Nachwelt—und eben dadurch für niemand.*" ["Everything (among the ancients) was local and for the moment—and that is why it became eternal. We write at complete random, for all men and for dear posterity, and that is precisely why we write for no one."]

If one of us pays attention *auf das Locale* [to what is local], he immediately tries to make it general—i.e., to give general significance to what he has created—and this results in nonsense.

I mentioned Merck. I am now very busy with him and intend to introduce him to the Russian public. He was a very great critic, who can perhaps be compared only to Lessing. Those who know about him (and they are very few in number) think that Goethe took his Mephistopheles from him and that is all. That is partly accurate—and to be original in such a way is very honorable—but there was more to Merck than one ironic negation. I have finally obtained his selected works[8]—a small book of 350 pages (with his biogra-

[8] *Johann Heinrich Merck*: Ein Denkmal, *herausgegeben von Dr. Adolf Stahl, Oldenburg, Schulze'sche Buchhandlung,* 1840. (Turgenev's note.)

phy)—and I have found a multitude of superb things
there. Can anything be better, for example, than the
following dictum? He once told Goethe: *"Dein Bestre-
ben, deine unablenkbare Richtung ist: dem Wirklichen
eine poetische Gestalt zu geben; die andern suchen das
sogenannte poetische, das Imaginative zu verwirklichen
—und das gibt nichts wie dummes Zeug."* (Your efforts,
your inevitable tendency is to give poetic shape to reality; others seek to give reality to the so-called poetic,
the imaginative, and that results in nothing but stupid
trash.) [. . .]

I recently also read [Thomas de Quincey's] *The
Confessions of an English Opium Eater*—a marvelous
thing. I have never seen anything like it. [. . .]

[. . .] I have read Suetonius, Sallust (whom I
hated because of his artificial style), and Tacitus, and
I have begun Titus Livius. I find these writers—especially the first ones—strikingly modern. [. . .]

[80]

Paris, December 5/17, 1856

TO ALEKSANDR VASIL'EVICH DRUZHININ

I am answering your letter, oh sweetest of conservatives! First of all, I must tell you that I have done
a lot of work on the story I plan to send to the *Biblioteka dlia chtenia,* and which will be entitled "A Tour
in the Forest"—an unpublished selection from *A
Sportsman's Sketches,* about three signatures long. As
soon as I finish it, I shall immediately copy it and send
it off—and let Annenkov smite himself on the thighs
and expatiate about his disbelief in my working, but
the piece will have been sent! Rumors are coming to
me from all sides about the magnificent regeneration

of the *Biblioteka dlia chtenia*, and I applaud and rejoice. Please support poor Pisemski and give him some work. I received a letter from him which has moved me (I have already answered him). [. . .]

M. N. Longinov has informed me of the *Russki vestnik's* advertisement for 1857 (in the *Moskovskie vedomosti*) and its sally against me.

This sally (between you and me) almost made me happy, despite its worse than unceremonious tone. I now consider myself free from any obligation to give him anything. I have already sent the *Moskovskie vedomosti* a letter, written in the most measured tones, about the affair.[9] This dirty gossip is a little ridiculous, and it is unpleasant to inflict oneself on the public, but nothing else can be done. . . .

You write that I will end up editing a magazine. I do not know what the future has in store for me—but there would be so many difficulties, both internal and external! I am condemned to lead a gypsy's life, and apparently I am never going to build myself a nest anywhere! And without a permanent nest, I could not run a magazine. [. . .]

Incidentally, inasmuch as you chase so after literary ladies, you will be pleased to know that I was introduced to Mrs. [Harriet] Beecher Stowe. She is a kind, plain, and—imagine!—shy American woman; she had her two redheaded daughters with her, in red burnooses and fierce hoop skirts—very strange figures. [. . .]

They say you have been seeing a lot of Tolstoy and that he has become sweet and serene. I am very

[9] Katkov, the editor of the *Russki vestnik*, had hinted that Turgenev's "Phantoms" (which the author had promised to *Russki vestnik* earlier) was probably quite similar to the story Turgenev promised to the *Sovremennik* as "Faust." Turgenev thereupon broke off relations with Katkov's magazine.

glad. When that young wine ferments, a drink worthy
of the gods will appear. [. . .]

[81]

Paris, December 8/20, 1856

TO COUNT LEV NIKOLAEVICH TOLSTOY

Yesterday my good fairy took me by the post
office [. . .] and there I found your letter about my
"Faust." You can easily understand how happy I was
to read it. Your interest has made me sincerely and
profoundly happy. And furthermore, the whole letter
radiated something gentle and serene, a friendly tranquility. All I can do is to hold my hand out to you
across the "ravine," which has recently turned into a
barely noticeable crack—but let us not even recall it;
it is not worth recalling. [. . .]

I am impatiently awaiting the arrival of the *Biblioteka dlia chtenia*; I would like to finish [Druzhinin's]
article about Belinski (although I shall probably not
like it much). That the *Sovremennik* is in bad hands
is beyond any doubt. Panaev was writing me frequently;
he asserted that he would not act "giddily"—and un-
derlined the word. But now he has grown tame and is
as quiet as a child who has dirtied his pants at the
table. I wrote about everything in detail to Nekrasov
in Rome, and quite possibly this will force him to
return earlier than he had planned. Write me in what
issue of the *Sovremennik* your *Youth* will appear, and
by the way, tell me your final impression of *King Lear*,
which you have probably read, if only for the sake of
Druzhinin [who translated it].

I am much comforted by your intention to work,
as you say, "with clenched teeth." That is respectable,

but I, sinner that I am, am (between us) doing nothing here. I hope to finish shortly a story for Druzhinin, but nothing for the [*Sovremennik*] "coalition" (which does not really offer anything "sublime"). My illness is disturbing my routine, alas! it is no longer gastritis, which is easy to get along with, but a prosaically undeniable pain in the bladder. In addition, like a frozen fish in the thaw, I am decomposing in this alien air. I am too old not to have a nest, and not to stay at home. I certainly shall return to Russia in the spring— although, with my departure from here, I shall have to say farewell forever to my dream of so-called happiness. [. . .]

[82]

Paris, December 16/28, 1856

TO COUNT LEV NIKOLAEVICH TOLSTOY

[. . .] Chernyshevski goes much against your grain, but here you are exaggerating a little. Let us assume that his "fetishism" [about Belinski] does repel you, and that you are indignant with him for having dug up old times, which, in your opinion, ought to have been left alone; remember, however, that we are discussing a man who was his entire life I will not say a martyr (you do not like fine words) but a toiler, an employee whose merits were frequently usurped and whose hands were used by a speculator to rake in money.[1] (I myself have witnessed this more than once.) Remember that poor Belinski never in his life knew happiness, peace, or even the most ordinary pleasures or comforts; that for expressing ideas which have now

[1] Andrei Aleksandrovich Kraevski, publisher of the *Otechestvennye zapiski*.

become commonplace, he was spattered with mud, stones, epigrams, and denunciations from all sides; that he escaped what might have been a very bitter fate only through death. After all that, do you find that two or three articles in his praise, which may have been written somewhat dithyrambically, are really too great a reward, that they cannot be tolerated—and that they are "rotten eggs"? So that you may understand my feelings about these articles, I suggest that we arrange a meeting ten years from now; I shall then see whether you will be happy if you are forbidden to say a word of love for a friend of your youth, for a man who rejoiced, suffered, and lived by virtue of his convictions. . . . But such a man will hardly exist in your memories. [. . .]

[83]

Paris, December 16/28, 1856

TO IVAN IVANOVICH PANAEV

I received your letter today and am answering it immediately. My stupid illness has really interfered with my work. I am in no state to finish my long story for the second number of next year's *Sovremennik*. Anticipating this misfortune, I had already set the story aside and begun working on "Hamlet and Don Quixote," which I certainly shall send off in a few days. Beyond that, I am trying to write at least a little story—the idea is ready in my head. And I do not guarantee this—but as for "Hamlet and Don Quixote," you can be completely at ease: you will have it at the beginning of January, I give you my word of honor. [. . .]

In answer to Katkov's escapade, I sent Longinov

a letter for the editor of the *Moskovskie vedemosti*.
It is written in completely measured tones; I limited
myself to saying that I feel free of any obligation to
give them a story. I shall now finish "Phantoms" and
place it in the *Sovremennik*, if only to show Mr. Katkov
that "Phantoms" is not [my] "Faust." I ask you to
reprint the letter (after it has been printed in the
Moskovskie vedomosti) in the *Sovremennik* without any
special commentary (in "Notes from the Magazines").

I am glad that [Tolstoy's] *Youth* has appeared, and
that he himself is at peace. This is very good. But that
the other contributors are idle is bad. I assure you I
would have been pulling like a horse had the abomina-
tion not hit me like a bolt from the blue. But fortunately things seem to be getting better now, and I
shall try to make up for lost time. [. . .]

[84]

Paris, January 6, 1857

TO COUNTESS MAR'IA NIKOLAEVNA TOLSTOY
(NEE TOLSTOY)

[. . .] I am very glad that you liked [my]
"Faust." What you say about the other man within me
is completely true, but you may not know the reason
for this duality. I too shall be frank with you. You
see, I have been finding it bitter to grow old without
having known complete happiness, and without having
built myself a peaceful nest. My heart was still young,
and yearning, and languishing, but my head had grown
calm from experience, and rarely gave way to my
heart's outbursts, and took out its own weakness, bitterness, and irony on my heart. But when my heart in

turn asked my head just what the *latter* had done,
whether my head had arranged a reasonable and correct life, my head was forced to grow ashamed and
silent. And then they each—heart and head—tried to
outdo each other in melancholy. All this has changed
now. . . . When you knew me, I was still dreaming
of happiness; I refused to part with hope; now I have
finally waved good-by to all that. Everything has become quiet; the rough spots have disappeared; the inner
reproaches have been stilled. Why blow on the ashes?
The flames will not blaze up anyhow. Why all this
happened is a long story; among other things, the years
have taken what is theirs. You will wonder at my
égalité d'humeur [even temper]. Why dig down to
whatever bitterness has set in? A person must not dig
to the bottom of any man. "Faust" was written during
a crisis, during a turning point in my life; my entire
heart flared up in a final blaze of reminiscences, hopes,
and youth. . . . All this should not be repeated. But
you speak in vain of my happiness; the grass on the
other side of the fence is greener, and someone else's
lot is enviable. Enough about that. [. . .]

I am in rather frequent correspondence with your
brother Lev. I think that he is changing for the better.
May God grant that he grow calm and mellow. He
will (without exaggeration) be a great writer and an
excellent person. He is now in very close contact with
Druzhinin; I would wish him a different comrade, but
you know that pleasing your brother is difficult. Until
he is torn away from a dish (excuse the coarse expression), he will not stop eating and praising it, and he
will continue praising it even after he has begun to
feel a pain in his stomach. With all that, Druzhinin is
a very good man—but not for your brother. [. . .]

[85]

Paris, January 8, 1857

TO SERGEI TIMOFEEVICH AKSAKOV

[. . .] A certain [Henri-Hippolyte] Delaveau, a
local literary man who knows Russian well, has written
an article about your *Family Chronicle;*[2] I have helped
him and made a few comments to him. The article
ought to appear soon in the *Revue des deux mondes.*

Your idea of writing a children's story about a
child is a fine one, and I am sure you will carry it out
in the best possible way, with the epic clarity and
simplicity that is your specialty among the entire writing fraternity.[3] [. . .]

[86]

Paris, January 3/15, 1857

TO COUNT LEV NIKOLAEVICH TOLSTOY

I do not know if my letters make you very happy,
but yours comfort me. A change is apparently taking
place in you—a completely felicitous one. (Excuse me
if I seem to be giving you a pat on the head; I am all
of ten years older than you, and I even feel as though
I were becoming your uncle and crony.) You are
calming down, brightening up, and—the main thing
—growing free, free from your own opinions and preju-
dices. Looking to the left is every bit as pleasant as
looking to the right; the world is certainly big enough;
everywhere there are "perspectives" (Botkin stole that
word from me); a person need only open his eyes. May

---

[2] In Duff's translation, this work is entitled A *Russian Gentleman.*

[3] Aksakov published *Years of Childhood* (as Duff calls it)
the following year.

God grant that your horizons grow with every day! Only those people who do not have their hands on the entire truth and wish to grab it by the tail value [philosophical] systems; a system is just like the tail of the truth—but the truth is like a lizard; it leaves its tail in your hand and runs away: it knows that it will shortly grow another one. [. . .]

[Your sister] also liked my "Faust." That work has had a strange fate! It is not at all to the taste of some people (among them, to my extreme regret, even Mme Viardot). By the way, what ridiculous rumors are circulating among you [in Russia]! Her husband could not be in better health, and I am just as far from marriage as, for example, you are. But I love her more than ever and more than anyone else in the world. That is right.

Your *Childhood and Boyhood* is the rage among the local Russian ladies. The copy sent to me is being read extremely quickly—and I have already been forced to promise some of them that I shall introduce them to you. They ask me for your autograph; in short, you are in vogue—more so than hoop skirts. I am telling you this because no matter what a man says, there is a little spot somewhere in the heart which is tickled by such praise (and by any other). Let it be tickled—and here's to you! [. . .]

Your acquaintance with Shakespeare, or, to speak more correctly, your proximity to him, makes me happy. He is like Nature; sometimes, you know, she has a very vile appearance (just recall a lachrymose, slimy, October day on the steppes), but even then she is indispensable, truthful, and (prepare yourself; your hair will stand on end) purposeful. Do become acquainted with *Hamlet, Julius Caesar, Coriolanus, Henry IV, Macbeth,*

and *Othello* also.[4] Do not allow the outer absurdity to
antagonize you. Get to the core, to the heart of the
work, and you will wonder at the harmony and profound truth of that great mind. I can see you from here,
reading these lines and smiling, but just think, *perhaps*
even Turgenev is right. Anything can happen!

I am not speaking to you about my acquaintances
here; I have met only one sweet girl (and she is a
Russian) and one very intelligent man (and he is a
Jew). The Frenchies are not to my taste; perhaps they
are excellent soldiers and administrators; their heads
all have a single track, and the selfsame ideas (which
have been accepted once and for all) race around it.
Everything that is not theirs strikes them as wild—and
stupid. "*Ah! le lecteur français ne saurait admettre
cela!*" ["Oh! The French reader will not know how to
allow that!"] Having uttered these words, a Frenchman cannot even imagine that you will object. God
be with them!

Well, farewell, dear Tolstoy. Expand in breadth
as you have hitherto grown in depth, and, in time,
we shall sit in your shade and even praise its beauty
and coolness.

[87]

Paris, January 12/24, 1857

TO IVAN IVANOVICH PANAEV

I know that my letter will make you sad. You
have lost a pound of candy—and I cannot send anything for the second issue of the *Sovremennik*. The
only thing that consoles me, although bitterly, is that

---

[4] Tolstoy had already read Druzhinin's translation of *King
Lear*.

the responsibility for this negligence is not mine but my illness's. I know that not all of you will believe either my ailment or my love for hunting; unfortunately, my illness is all too real. My bladder began disturbing me as soon as I reached Paris, and recently the doctors have discovered spermatorrhea, i.e., the involuntary flow . . . an exceedingly nasty and persistent illness, which has already forced me to undergo an operation, etc., etc. This illness has the terrible peculiarity of affecting the nerves and the moral condition of the soul, and I am as little able to write now as I am to sing or walk a tightrope. [. . .]

[88]

Paris, January 13 [O.S.], 1857

TO ALEKSANDR VASIL'EVICH DRUZHININ

[. . .] I read your [translation of] *King Lear* and was touched, but I was especially moved by your introductory article. It is charming! One must admit that if you were not a conservative, you could never have seen Kent as such a "great and loyal subject." I *à la lettre* [literally] shed a few tears. All the characterizations and all the attitudes are truthful, profound, on a broad scale, and full of love and freedom. You have made me very, very happy. Thank you. [. . .]

Tolstoy writes me that he is preparing to come here and go on to Italy in the spring; tell him to hurry if he wishes to find me here. Moreover, I shall write him myself. I see from his letters that the most felicitous changes have taken place in him, which delights me thoroughly. I read his "Morning of a Landlord," which pleased me very much by its sincerity and the almost complete freedom of outlook; I say "almost" because

a certain prejudice remains concealed in the way he
attacked the problem. Perhaps he himself is not conscious of that. The chief moral (I am not speaking
about the artistic) impression of the story is that as
long as serfdom exists, there will be no opportunity for
friendship and understanding on either side, despite
the most disinterested and honest readiness for friendship—and that impression is good and true. But with
all this, there exists something collateral and concom-
itant—to wit, that educating the muzhik and improving his way of life in general does not lead anywhere
—and this impression is unpleasant. But the mastery
of language, of narration, and of characterization is
great. [. . .]

[89]

Paris, February 17/March 1, 1857

TO VASILI PETROVICH BOTKIN

   [. . .] Tolstoy is here, and he looks at everything in silence, his eyes bulging. But he is still ill at
ease with himself and hence not quite comfortable
with others. I rejoice in looking at him; to tell the truth,
he is the sole hope of our literature. [. . .]

   [. . .] Mr. Shchedrin is taking my place as a
writer with an ax to grind; the public now needs coarse
and piquant things. But a poetic and complete nature
such as Tolstoy's will finish and present clearly and
completely what I have merely hinted at. [. . .]

   Because I have a fair knowledge of Russian [*sic*]
I intend to undertake the translation of *Don Quixote*,
if I am healthy. You will probably think that I exag-
gerate, and will not believe me. I hope you realize that

I have never spoken more seriously or more sincerely.
[. . .]

{ 90 }

Paris, March 5, 1857

TO ALEKSANDR IVANOVICH HERZEN

[. . .] I gave your regards to [Lev] Tolstoy; he
was very happy to receive them, and instructs me to
tell you that he has long wished to become acquainted
with you, and that even now he likes you as a person
just as he has liked your works. [. . .]

{ 91 }

Paris, March 7, 1857

TO VLADIMIR NIKITICH KASHPEROV

I was just preparing to answer your letter, when
suddenly the sad news of [Mikhail] Glinka's death
arrived. Although not much could have been expected
from him, I am nevertheless very, very sorry, especially
when I think of how much the man was able to do
and how little he has left. But let us be grateful for
that little. His name will not be forgotten in the history
of Russian music, and if that music is destined to
develop at some time, it will be traced back to him.

{ 92 }

Paris, March 6/18, 1857

TO IVAN IVANOVICH PANAEV

[. . .] Yesterday I received a letter from Vol'f,
saying that they [the censors] have passed the comedy

Nakhlebnik [*The Parasite*]. I am very happy. [. . .]
I am in no state to work at all. But you are wrong to
assume that my article "Hamlet and Don Quixote" has
not even been started; on the contrary, it is almost
done, and if I could count on at least a short let-up,
I would soon send it off. I cannot in my condition
promise anything, but I will try. [. . .]

[93]

Paris, April 3/15, 1857

TO PAVEL VASIL'EVICH ANNENKOV

I am still here, but I am alone now; Tolstoy has
suddenly left for Geneva. He has written me a most
remarkable letter from there; he speaks of Paris as
Sodom and Gomorrah, and compares himself to a
stone in a river—a stone that gradually becomes covered with slime and is bound to break suddenly loose
and seek a different river which may contain less slime.
Paris is really not at all suited to the structure of his
mind. He is a strange man. I have never met such a
person, and I do not understand him at all. . . . He
is a blend of poet, Calvinist, fanatic, and landowner's
son—somewhat reminiscent of Rousseau, but more
honest than Rousseau—a highly moral and, at the
same time, uncongenial being. [. . .]

You have bestowed unusual praise on Ostrovski's
inert, stupid, and bad comedy [*Dokhodnoe mesto* (*A
Profitable Spot*)], in which (except for Iusov, and him
only in Act III) everything is insufferably coarse and
lifeless. The play is just like the frozen carcass of a hog.
Relying on you, I took a notion to read it aloud to a
very sweet and intelligent Russian family. . . . We
grew numb, we ached, and we howled from boredom

and pain. Everything I have said here I am ready to sign in blood, and henceforth I do not believe in Ostrovski's future. [. . .]

Not on a single one of my stays in Paris have I met so many people as on this one. I shall be visiting [Alexandre] Dumas [*fils*] before my departure, but such acquaintanceships have not brought me any pleasure —even my curiosity has not been satisfied, perhaps because a man does not observe or study when he is in a bad mood. Prosper Mérimée, at whose house I have dined, is a perfect Druzhinin *en grand* [on a large scale]; he is just as cold, and loves all kinds of obscenity. I have not met a single remarkable or attractive person; they are all dry, sleek, narrow, and concise. [. . .]

There is no news of the theater. [. . .] [Dumas's] *Question d'argent* [A *Question of Money*] is clever but rather boring prattle. The French have lost the talent for truth in art; their art is dying out. [. . .]

[94]

Sinzig bei Remagen am Rhein, July 17, 1857

TO ALEKSANDR IVANOVICH HERZEN

[. . .] Prince Dolgorukov, who has replaced Orlov, is turning out to be a very great obscurant; the gendarmes are again interfering with private life, family affairs, etc.

[95]

Boulogne, August 4, 1857

TO VASILI PETROVICH BOTKIN

[. . .] I read his [Lev Tolstoy's] short piece ["Lucerne"], written in Switzerland, but I did not like it. It is a mixture of Rousseau, Thackeray, and the Short Orthodox Catechism. He stands like Hercules at the crossroads; may God grant that he take the right way. [. . .]

[96]

Rome, November 22/December 4, 1857

TO NIKOLAI ALEKSEEVICH NEKRASOV

I hasten to inform you that a few days ago I finally finished for the *Sovremennik* a story of three and a half or even four signatures in length, and to preclude your doubting my words, I am appending a certificate by Botkin, to whom I have read the work. All that remains to be done are a few corrections and transcriptions. [. . .] Excuse the shortness of this note; my time is all going into the transcribing of "Acia"—the tale is called "Acia." [. . .] [5]

[97]

Rome, November 25/December 7, 1857

TO COUNT LEV NIKOLAEVICH TOLSTOY

[. . .] Botkin has highly praised the beginning of your novel [*The Cossacks*] about the Caucasus. You write that you are very pleased you did not follow my advice and make yourself only a literary man. I am not arguing. Perhaps you are right, but I (sinner that I am), no matter how I rack my brains, cannot think of just what you are if not a literary man: an officer? a landowner? a philosopher? the founder of a new religious

[5] The letter contains the following remark signed by V. Botkin: "I hereby certify that Turgenev has really read me the finished story 'Acia'."

doctrine?[6] a civil servant? a businessman? Please extricate me from my difficulties and tell me which of these suppositions is correct.

I am joking. [. . .]

[. . .] Of the other Russians [here], the only artist is [Aleksandr Andreevich] Ivanov, a remarkable and intelligent person; our other artists are fools infected with *Briulovism*[7] and are ungifted—i.e., not that they are ungifted (they all have talent), but they do not know what to do with it. They live with strumpets, they curse Raphael—and that is all. There is no Russian art yet. [. . .]

[98]

Rome, January 1/13, 1858

TO IVAN IVANOVICH PANAEV

[. . .] I have now set to work on a major story,[8] which I hope to bring with me to Russia in May, along with the interminable "Hamlet and Don Quixote."

[99]

Rome, January 17/29, 1858

TO COUNT LEV NIKOLAEVICH TOLSTOY

[. . .] You would be right if, in having suggested that you be a literary man, I had restricted the significance of a literary man to lyric twitterings; our period has no time for birds singing away on a branch. All I wished to say was that every man, without ceas-

---

[6] This letter antedates the publication of Tolstoy's *Confession* by about a quarter of a century.

[7] Karl Pavlovich Briulov was the Russian who painted *The Last Day of Pompeii*. He was a pet *bête-noire* to Turgenev.

[8] Apparently *A House of Gentlefolk*.

ing to be a man, ought to be a specialist; specialism ex-
cludes dilettantism (excuse all these "isms"), and to be
a dilettante means to be impotent. In what you have
done thus far, the dilettante has been apparent—an
unusually gifted one, but a dilettante; I would like to
see you at a workman's bench, in a workman's apron,
with your sleeves rolled up.

I find it strange, however, that Nekrasov has rejected [your] "Muzykant" ["The Musician"].⁹ What
did he dislike—the very musician who has trouble with
himself? Botkin has remarked that the character of the
musician lacks the attractive charm which is insepara-
ble from a man's artistic power; perhaps he is right; an
author must not limit himself to stating the charms if
he wants the reader to feel part of the charm a musician exerts by *sounds*.

The same Botkin has told me about your intention to begin a magazine with Fet, dedicated exclusively to art; will this not be a *pendant* [counterpart] to
your exclusively military magazine? Wait for our return
before you embark on this business; we shall have a
good talk, and will perhaps work something out—I
understand the motives behind such a project. I hope
you find what you are looking for in Moscow society. [. . .]

{ 100 }

Vienna, April 8, 1858

TO COUNT LEV NIKOLAEVICH TOLSTOY

[. . .] I know that you are dissatisfied with my
last story, and you are not alone: many of my good
friends do not praise it. I am convinced that all of you

⁹ An early version of "Albert."

are right—but, for all that, I wrote it very heatedly, almost with tears; no one can know what he is doing. If I had been told that "Acia" came out very well, I would have wondered—knowing the state of mind I was in when I wrote the story—but I would have believed the information; now, however, I believe and even seem to realize for myself that the tale was poor and unsuccessful. No matter what a man says, if there is no major and healthy talent, writing is a lottery every time. [. . .]

Botkin has shown me your letter, in which you talk with such fire about your intention to found a *purely artistic* magazine in Moscow. You find political intrigues repulsive—really dirty, dusty, banal business— but you know there are dirt and dust in our streets, and yet we cannot get along at all without cities. [. . .]

Oh, my dear Tolstoy, if you knew how difficult I find things and how sad I am! Take a lesson from me: do not let life slip through your fingers. May God spare you the feeling that life has passed by and at the same time has not begun yet, that everything is before you— an infinity of youth with all the fruitless emptiness of old age. I do not know how you should act to avoid falling into such a misfortune; perhaps you are not destined to fall into that misfortune. At least accept my sincere wishes for sound happiness and a sound life. This is wished you by a person who is profoundly and deservedly unhappy. [. . .]

{ 101 }

Spasskoe, June 25/July 7, 1858

TO PAULINE VIARDOT (NEE GARCIA)

[. . .] He [Lev Tolstoy] is seriously and in all

earnest a first-rate talent, and I do hope to convince you of this someday by translating his *Childhood* for you. [. . .]

[102]

St. Petersburg, December 27 [O.S.], *1858*
TO AFANASI AFANAS'EVICH FET

[. . .] Why is Tolstoy not coming? Druzhinin is waiting for him with melancholy impatience. Are you sure the bears [which Tolstoy was hunting] really have not eaten him?

[103]

St. Petersburg, February 11 [O.S.], *1859*
TO COUNT LEV NIKOLAEVICH TOLSTOY

I received your kind letter with its geographic patterns and its very true (although confusedly expressed) ideas. It made me wish to see you, as you say, eating thick pies at my table under the pensive glance of Zakhar.[1] Fine—come! We shall chat, and argue a bit (as we cannot avoid arguing); you will see new faces, hear good music, and then, with a clear head and soothed nerves, you will return to your novel [*Family Happiness*] (about which, Fet tells me, you are constantly racking your brains). I would like to listen to [your reading of] your novel and tell you my opinion of [your story] "Three Deaths"; most people here like the story, but they find the ending strange, and do not quite understand the connection between this and the

[1] Zakhar was Turgenev's personal servant; at this time he was still a serf.

two preceding deaths, while those who do understand
are not satisfied. I have seen [your cousin] Countess
[Aleksandra] Tolstoy twice—but I will not tell her
what you wrote me. There is something strange. She is
a very good and intelligent woman; to associate with
her must be very "healthy" for the soul, but there is
a certain sharp finish to her convictions, her words, and
even her movements which rather disturbs me. I have
found two or three women here who are more to my
liking.

So, come with Botkin, and I shall later accompany
you both to Moscow and spend a week or so there.

Regards to all of yours and to [your sister] Mar'ia
Nikolaevna. [. . .] Give the children a kiss for me.

[104]

Spasskoe, March 27 [*O.S.*], 1859

TO COUNTESS ELIZAVETA EGOROVNA LAMBERT

[. . .] Death is carrying people off without looking. We are all in its debt, and debtors cannot tell the
creditor precisely on whom to call first. [. . .]

[105]

Spasskoe, April 7, 1859

TO IVAN ALEKSANDROVICH GONCHAROV

I cannot conceal that I am taking up my pen this
time against my custom and with little pleasure. For
what pleasure is there in writing a man who considers
one the usurper of others' ideas (*plagiaire* [plagiarist]),
a liar (you suspect that there is another obstacle to the
plot of my new story, and that I only wish to distract

you from it), and a chatterbox (you suppose I repeated our conversation to Annenkov). You will agree that, whatever my "diplomacy" may be, to smile and pay compliments upon receiving such pills is difficult. You will also agree that at half—what am I saying! at one tenth—of such rebukes, you would really get angry. But I—call it weakness or pretense, as you like—I merely thought: "He has a really good opinion of me," and only wondered that you were able to have found something in me you could like. And thanks for that!

Let me say without false humility that I completely agree with what your "teacher" said about *A House of Gentlefolk*. But what on earth do you wish me to do? I can certainly not repeat *A Sportsman's Sketches ad infinitum!* And I do not feel like giving up writing, either. All that remains is to write stories in which, without my pretending to wholeness, to vigor in the characters, or to a profound and thorough penetration of life, I can express whatever comes into my head. There would be seams that have only been basted. How can this misfortune be helped? Whoever needs a novel in the epic sense of the word does not need me; but I think just as much about writing a novel as I do about walking on my head. Whatever I may have written, I shall write a number of sketches. *E sempre bene!* But you will see only diplomacy in this admission. Why, Tolstoy thinks that I even sneeze, drink, and sleep for the sake of phrase-making. Take me as I am or do not take me at all—but do not ask me to re-educate myself and especially into such a Talleyrand—ouch! But enough of this. All these intrigues do not get us anywhere; we shall die, and stink after our deaths. [. . .]

{ 106 }

Spasskoe, April 12 [O.S.], *1859*

TO VASILI PETROVICH BOTKIN

[. . .] I have closed all my accounts with [Lev] Tolstoy; as a person he no longer exists for me. May God grant all the best to him and his talent. But if I were to say hello to him, I would inevitably feel like saying farewell—and without a further appointment. We were created at opposite poles. If I am eating soup and like it, *for that reason alone* I am sure Tolstoy finds it repulsive, and vice versa. [. . .]

{ 107 }

Vichy [*received on June 10/22, 1859*]

TO PAVEL VASIL'EVICH ANNENKOV

[. . .] Sollogub has taken a notion to translate *A House of Gentlefolk* [into French] for the *Revue contemporaine*—a foul little magazine—but I have declined so great an honor. For me, everything French stinks and, if a man must choose, to deal with French *épiciers* [philistines] is better than to deal with French *beaux esprits* [wits]. I am living in a modest Vichy hotel, where I see several French *épiciers* at the *table d'hôte;* one of them is especially captivating. He is convinced that Russian muzhiks sell their children *pour le sérail du Grand Kan des Tartares, monsieur* [for the harem of the Great Tatar Khan, sir]! And he adds: "Ah, *monsieur! quelle sale chose que la réligion de Mahomet!*" ["Oh, sir, what a dirty thing the religion of Mohammed is!"] I, of course, did not disillusion him. The local peasants swear violently and use extraordinarily complicated expressions. [. . .]

[108]

Vichy, June 26, 1859

TO HIS DAUGHTER, PAULINE

I received your letter and am answering it without losing any time, as you see. I am happy that you have been to church and also that Father Vasiliev has made an impression on you, but—to speak to you *seriously*, as you say—I am very displeased with the rest of your letter. A tone prevails in it with regard to Mme Viardot which I can neither admit nor permit. You are forgetting a bit too much everything you owe her. You must realize that I do not want you to give the impression that you are trying to set me against her—which, moreover, would be futile, for I would find her to be right ten times out of ten. Not to mention anything else, how can you wish her, for example, to be wrong about your singing lessons? What could she possibly have in mind if not your interests? Let me tell you again: you owe her complete obedience and—you can believe me —you would be most unfortunate if she ceased to be interested in you and she abandoned you to certain instincts that exist within you and must be uprooted. You are egotistic and sensitive, and you do not love those who are deserving, but those who show affection for you or who spoil you. So, my child, no more of these things; stop telling me I should go to Courtavenel; I will go, so we shall most likely spend our vacation there instead of gadding about. [. . .]

This letter will not make you very happy—but if you think over what I am saying to you, you will find it very useful; if I did not tell you the truth about yourself, who would? I am telling this to you because I love you with all my heart. [. . .]

[109]

Courtavenel, July 16 [O.S.], 1859[2]

TO AFANASI AFANAS'EVICH FET

[. . .] My warmest greetings to Nikolai Tolstoy, and my regards to Lev—also to his sister. His postscript is correct: I have *no reason* to write him. And I know he does not like me much, but I do not like him, either. The elements in us are too different, but the world is big; we hardly wish to disturb each other. [. . .]

[110]

[France, summer 1859] [3]

TO COUNTESS ELIZAVETA EGOROVNA LAMBERT

[. . .] I know that something has died within me; why stand and look at a closed grave? What has died within me is not my emotions, no, but the opportunity to satisfy them. I look at *my* happiness as I look at *my* youth—as someone else's youth and happiness. I am here, but all that is there—and between the *here* and the *there* is an abyss that nothing can ever fill. The only thing left for a person is to let himself be carried on the waves of life for the time being, and think about port after he has found a sweet and dear comrade, such as you—a comrade in emotions, in ideas, and, the main thing, in attitude (you and I both expect very little for ourselves)—to hold his hand firmly, and float together. [. . .]

[2] Written in blank verse.

[3] Although this letter is undated and bears no place of origin in the source, it is printed there between the letters of June 24, 1859 (from Vichy), and August 4, 1859 (from Bellefontaine near Fontainebleau).

{ III }

Courtavenel, August 1/13, 1859

TO PAVEL VASIL'EVICH ANNENKOV

[. . .] I know that a great Praetorian festival is taking place in Paris tomorrow.[4] All the streets of Paris have been blocked off; triumphal arches, Venetian masts, statues, emblems, and columns have been erected everywhere; flags and flowers have been put up everywhere; the Emperor, in the spirit of the Caesars and Rome, will deliver an *allocutio militibus* [allocution to the soldiers]; so that *maxima similitudo invenire debet* [the greatest similarity must arise] between *Galliam huius temporis et Romam Trajani necnon Caracallae et aliorum Heliogabalorum* [the Gaul of these times and the Rome of Trajan—and also of Caracalla and the other Heliogabali]. I am afraid to go on with this Latin; I do not know whether you, my learned friend and antagonist of liberalism, will understand. Of course, I fled from Paris at a time when hundreds of whistling and roaring trains were hurrying thousands of guests from all over Europe to the *center* of the world; any military celebration *ist mir ein Gräuel* [is loathsome to me], all the more so because there will be bayonets, uniforms, shouts, bold *sergents de ville* [*policemen*], and sweat-drenched adjutants; the weather will be hot, sultry, and fetid—*connu, connu* [that is an old story]! . . . A man is better off sitting at the closed window and looking at the motionless garden, slowly mingling the images of his fancy with reminiscences of his distant friends and the far-away homeland. The room is cool

---

[4] The war between Austria, on the one hand, and France and Sardinia, on the other had just been concluded.

and quiet; the voices of children are heard in the hall; the sounds of Gluck float down from above. . . . What more can a man wish for? [. . .]

{ 112 }

Spasskoe, October 9 [O.S.], 1859

TO AFANASI AFANAS'EVICH FET

I chatted peacefully with Tolstoy and we parted on friendly terms. Misunderstandings between us appear impossible because we understand each other clearly and realize that we cannot become close friends. We are formed of different clay.

{ 113 }

Spasskoe, October 14 [O.S.], 1859

TO COUNTESS ELIZAVETA EGOROVNA LAMBERT

[. . .] The idea recently entered my head that the fate of almost every person contains something tragic—but the tragedy is frequently concealed from the person himself by the banal superficiality of life. Whoever remains on the surface (and many do) frequently does not even suspect that he is the hero of a tragedy. A certain young lady regrets that her digestion is bad, but does not know that these words mean her entire life has been smashed. Here, for example, everything is quiet around me, and existence is peaceful, but once you get used to the idea, tragedy is apparent in each development of a nation—either the country's own tragedy or what history has imposed upon it. And in addition we are all sentenced to death. What further tragedy is needed? [. . .]

{ 114 }

[Perhaps Spasskoe or Moscow, November or December 1859] [5]

TO COUNTESS ELIZAVETA EGOROVNA LAMBERT

[. . .] It is always good for a person to reveal his soul to someone else—good for himself and for the other person. But there is no point in your accusing me of behaving like a coquettish author. If I could not write you more than ten lines, then I could not write more than two words for the public in my present state of mind. Work has been imposed upon me, but I am in no condition to do it. I am not bored or sad; rather, I feel a terrible, indefinable wish for my own nest, for a *home*,[6] and realize that to fulfill my dream is impossible. At the same time, I am constantly aware that everything earthly is vain, while *something* I have no name for is near. The word "death" alone does not express that *something* completely—and hence the turning to God, together with a longing for the forbidden green meadows. But the lamp must flare up once more before the end. And let it.

I find that man is too much inclined in general to pity himself. I am sitting with a full stomach in a warm and smoky room, and am whimpering—while there are so many poor. I am even ashamed to finish talking about all this. [. . .]

[5] Judged from where it appeared in the chronology of the source.
[6] English in the original.

[115]

St. Petersburg, Febuary 16 [*O.S.*]*, 1860*

TO KONSTANTIN NIKOLAEVICH LEONT'EV

I have not answered you before because I wanted to say something positive about your story both from the standpoint of its intrinsic value and that of its extrinsic (magazine) appraisal. Mind you, your story is not bad; it reads easily, but that is all; it is intelligently conceived, and strives for simplicity and clarity; the characters are truthful. But it has little life, beauty, or motion; all these have been replaced by some kind of playful and frequently pretentious cunning of the author's; apparently the author sketches something and makes an attempt—while he himself scoffs. As a result, what emerges is cold, pale, and bloodless. Your brain has done a great deal of work; apparently you have gone through a rather variegated spiritual experience and have matured—but are you an artist? With my hand on my heart and weighing my words, I cannot answer this question by either yes or no. I would be very sad were my words to discourage you from writing; I would not ask that of myself. Continue to work: perhaps you will finally master yourself and your powers, and will clearly understand your calling. Subtleties, clever remarks, or observations will not help unless you create living characters. Why do you not try to write critical and aesthetic studies? I am sure you have all the material for doing so. [. . .]

Every reader who begins your story will certainly read it to the end and think: you know, this is written interestingly and well—but that will be the limit of his impressions. That is not enough for you. I know that perhaps in time you will succeed in doing even more.

[. . .] Please do not let my letter grieve you; the opinions I have expressed are most likely sharper than they ought to be, but you are not a boy and can stand firmly on your own feet. Go forward, and you will get there.

{ 116 }

St. Petersburg, February 22 [O.S.], *1860*

TO AFANASI AFANAS'EVICH FET

[. . .] And Lev Tolstoy continues to behave strangely. Apparently such conduct was ordained for him at his birth. When will he turn a handspring for the last time and stand on his feet?

{ 117 }

Courtavenel, July 19/31, 1860

TO EVGENI MIKHAILOVICH FEOKTISTOV

[. . .] Although I do not have a line yet, I still hope to deliver my article to you at the end of the fall. But not "Kol'tsov and [Robert] Burns." My chief reason for this is that I do not wish any repetition of the affair with the *Russki vestnik*, because the article was promised to the magazine and not to Khmel'nitski personally. Furthermore, "Kol'tsov and Burns" has not even been begun; consequently, I can just as easily write something else. Various plans are wandering about in my head; I do not yet know which one I shall consider, but I have high hopes of keeping my word. [. . .]

[118]

Paris, September 8 [O.S.], 1860

TO AFANASI AFANAS'EVICH FET

[. . .] There is no news whatever about Lev Tolstoy, but I, I confess, am not too interested in knowing anything about a man who is himself interested in no one. [. . .]

[119]

Courtavenel, October 3, 1860

TO KONSTANTIN NIKOLAEVICH LEONT'EV

. . . Your weakness, as always happens, lies in the very same place as your strength; your devices are too subtle and too preciously clever—often to the point of being obscure. A poet must be a psychologist—but a secret one; he must know and feel the roots of phenomena, but only present the phenomena themselves— in bloom or in decline. . . .

[. . .] Reading your opinion of "First Love" was a pleasure for me. To change would be difficult for a veteran on the eve of complete retirement; whatever has come out badly will not be corrected; whatever succeeds will not be repeated. There remains but one thing for us to think about: to know how to be silent in season. Meanwhile, all my work is not yet finished; and now I have been thinking of a rather long piece. And that, as you say, I have been sad for a while is not surprising; I shall soon be 42, and I have not built myself a nest; I have not settled down in any spot on the earth; there is little to be happy about. [. . .]

{ 120 }

Paris, October 12, 1860

TO PAVEL VASIL'EVICH ANNENKOV

[. . .] Give the enclosed note to Ivan Ivanovich Panaev. If he would like to learn the real reason why I wish no longer to contribute to the *Sovremennik*, ask him to read the third line of p. 240 in the June issue of the current year, where Mr. Dobroliubov[7] accuses me of having deliberately caricatured Rudin to please my rich literary friends, who look on any poor person as a scoundrel. That is really going too far. No decent person can contribute to such a magazine. [. . .]

{ 121 }

Paris, October 1/13, 1860

TO IVAN IVANOVICH PANAEV [8]

Although, if my memory is correct, you have stopped publishing [the names of] your contributors in the *Sovremennik*, and even though, from your reviews, I must conclude that you no longer need me, still, for the sake of the truth, I ask you not to include my name in the list of your contributors—especially because I have nothing ready and because the big thing I have just begun to work on and will not finish until next May has already been promised to the *Russki vestnik*.[9]

As you know, I have taken up residence in Paris for the winter. I hope you are healthy and happy. [. . .]

[7] The article was written not by Dobroliubov, but by Chernyshevski.

[8] According to Annenkov, Turgenev sent this letter to him for forwarding, which Annenkov did not do.

[9] *Fathers and Children.*

{ 122 }

Paris, November 4, 1860

TO ALEKSANDR IVANOVICH HERZEN

[. . .] Apparently Heidelberg is distinguished for creating gossip: they are saying there that I am keeping a serf-mistress with me by force, that Mrs. [Harriet] Beecher Stowe (!) publicly reproached me and that I cursed her out. *Eine schöne Gegend* [a beautiful region]. [. . .]

{ 123 }

Paris, January 9, 1861

TO ALEKSANDR IVANOVICH HERZEN

[. . .] I have broken off all relations with the *Sovremennik* and Nekrasov. This, by the way, has been caused by the curses *à mon adresse* [at me] in every issue. I instructed them not to put my name among the contributors, but they took it and placed it at the very end [of the list] among the scoundrels. What is to be done now? [I do not wish] to revive the Katkov business in the newspapers at all. [. . .]¹

{ 124 }

Paris, January 8/20, 1861

TO COUNTESS ELIZAVETA EGOROVNA LAMBERT

[. . .] I feel as if I had died long ago, as if I belonged to an existence long past, but an existence that has essentially preserved a lively love for the Good and the Beautiful. But there is no longer anything per-

¹ Katkov earlier claimed that Turgenev's "Faust" had been specifically promised to him, which Turgenev denied.

sonal in this love; whenever I look at any beautiful young woman, I think little about her in regard to myself, to possible contacts between her and me. I feel as if I were a contemporary of Sesosthris, by some miracle still moving on the earth among the living. A man's ability to experience his own death within himself is, perhaps, one of the most indubitable proofs of the immortality of the soul. Here I am, dead, and for all that, I am alive and perhaps have even become better and purer. What next? [. . .]

[125]

Paris, January 19/31, 1861

TO PRINCESS OLGA DMITRIEVNA KHILKOVOI

[. . .] For the most part, I have been staying home and doing nothing. [. . .] You have given me a just reprimand, in your letter, for spending time uselessly. [. . .]

I am getting acquainted with the young Frenchmen, but find they have little taste. All I am thinking of is returning to my beloved Mtsensk district in the spring. How pleased I shall be to see that old stuff; nothing is superior to it for your fellow steppe-dweller. St. Egor's Day,[2] the nightingales, the smell of the straw and of the birch buds, the sun, and the puddles on the roads—these are the things my soul thirsts for. [. . .]

---

[2] St. Egor's Day is linked with St. George's Day. A church calendar gives this date as April 23, but Ushakov's dictionary gives it as November 26 (both Old Style). From the context, the spring date seems more likely.

[126]

Paris, February 15/27, 1861

TO PAVEL VASIL'EVICH ANNENKOV

[. . .] A few days ago Lev Nikolaevich Tolstoy came here from Italy—not without his eccentricities, but pacified and mollified. The death of his brother [Nikolai] has affected him strongly. He read me some selections from his new literary works, from which we may conclude that his talent is far from exhausted and that he has a great future. [. . .]

[127]

Paris, February 16/28, 1861

TO COUNTESS ELIZAVETA EGOROVNA LAMBERT

I am returning Mr. G's letter to you. He must be right (my friend [Louis] Viardot has exactly the same opinion of "First Love");[3] to say that I in no way imagined that the plot I had chosen would be immoral is no excuse, but rather *une circonstance aggravante* [a damaging circumstance]. However, let me take the liberty of protesting against one thing: I did not write at all with the aim of producing, as they say, a striking effect; I did not think up this story; life itself gave me the whole tale. I hasten to add that this does not justify me; I probably should not have touched the story at all. I say "probably" because I do not wish to lie. If anyone were to ask me whether I would agree to having the story destroyed, I would say no. But I do agree willingly never again to speak or think about it. [. . .]

[3] "First Love" deals with a boy who falls in love with a girl, only to discover that his father is her lover.

{ 128 }

Paris, March 9, 1861

TO ALEKSANDR IVANOVICH HERZEN

[. . .] Say a couple of words in the *Kolokol* about [Taras] Shevchenko's death. The poor fellow killed himself by the immoderate use of vodka. Not long before his death, a remarkable incident happened to him: a district police officer (in Chernigov Province) arrested him and sent him as a prisoner to the capital of the province because Shevchenko *had declined to paint his full-length portrait in oils. This is a fact.* [. . .]

{ 129 }

Paris, March 10/22, 1861

TO COUNT LEV NIKOLAEVICH TOLSTOY

You did not like the English. [. . .] I rather expected that. I think you had neither the time nor the chance to penetrate to the heart's blood, which pulsates, for example, in many of the characters in Dickens's novel, and which flows quite deeply—especially in every individual Englishman. One must not forget that they are as as shy as they are haughty, and do not know how either to speak out or to assert themselves. [. . .]

{ 130 }

Paris, March 14/26, 1861

TO VARVARA IAKOVLEVNA KARTASHEVSKI
(NEE MAKAROV)

[. . .] The news of Shevchenko's death has

grieved me; the poor fellow did not use his freedom long.[4] I can imagine the impression this has produced upon the entire Little Russian world. We here sang a *Te Deum* in honor of the emancipation [of the serfs].[5] The priest gave a little speech which moved us all to tears. We prayed from our hearts for the Tsar. [. . .]

{ 131 }

Spasskoe, May 21 [*O.S.*], *1861*

TO IAKOV PETROVICH POLONSKI

[. . .] I saw Fet on May 9, the very day of my arrival here, and I shall shortly see him again with Lev Tolstoy; we are going to Tolstoy's village (sixty versts from here), which is absorbing Tolstoy completely from head to foot. He has now made himself an agronomist—a landed proprietor to the point of *hopelessness*; he has let his beard grow to his loins, with tufts of hair *behind* and *under* his ears; he does not wish to hear about literature and curses the magazines with enthusiasm. However, I shall give him your letter and your verses; he really likes you. His nose, in which you are so interested, now reminds me of the lines from Derzhavin's ode: "Dark purple, amber-colored," etc. Judging from the aforesaid, you will see that this is not the time to *interrogate* Fet. But I will pass your wish on to Tolstoy—or, I had better say, the wish of the times for which I too shall work as soon as I have got rid of my novel for the *Russki vestnik*. You

[4] Shevchenko had been in exile from 1847 to 1857, and, after a brief period away from direct surveillance, was arrested again in 1859. His offenses were political. He died on February 26/March 10, 1861.

[5] February 19 [O.S.], 1861.

have not told me where the three chapters of your own novel in verse will appear, have you?

I am busy with both economic and literary affairs. The business with my peasants is going well for the present—because I have made them every possible concession—but there are difficulties ahead. Many of them do not wish to go on quitrent, and without quitrent, redemption (which is, after all, the main object) is impossible. [. . .]

[132]

Spasskoe, May 27 [O.S.], 1861

TO COUNT LEV NIKOLAEVICH TOLSTOY

Sir,

In answer to your letter, I repeat only what I myself considered my duty to tell you at Fet's house; carried away by a feeling of involuntary hostility whose reasons this is not the place to go into, I insulted you without your having given me positive cause, and then requested your pardon. I am now ready to repeat just that in writing, and am requesting your pardon for the second time. What occurred this morning clearly showed that any attempts at close friendship between such antithetic natures as yours and mine cannot lead to anything good, and I am fulfilling my duty to you even more willingly [than otherwise] because this is probably the final manifestation of relations between us. From my heart I hope this [note] will satisfy you, and I agree to any use you might care to make of it.

With complete respect, I have the honor to remain, my dear Sir, your most humble servant.

Iv. Turgenev.

{ 133 }

Spasskoe, June 7/19, 1861

TO PAVEL VASIL'EVICH ANNENKOV

[. . .] We are having a talk with the muzhiks, who have expressed their good will to me; my concessions are almost abject. But you yourself know, and will probably find out even more in the village, what sort of a bird the Russian muzhik is; to rely on him for the redemption business is madness. They do not even go over to quitrent without in the first place getting "all tied up," and second, without depriving themselves of the opportunity to perform their three-day *barshchina* in a very poor way.[6] Any reasoning is now useless. Even if you show them 100 times that they lose 100% on the *barshchina*, they will answer you just the same: "Folks say they don't go along." The ones on quitrent even envy the ones on *barshchina* because "they have favors, and we don't." Fortunately, the muzhiks here in Spasskoe have been on quitrent since last year. [. . .]

An unpleasant occurrence took place in the same village [which Fet owns]. . . . I finally quarreled with Lev Tolstoy (the affair, *entre nous*, hangs a hair's breadth away from a duel—and the hair is now far from broken). *It was my fault*, but [my] outburst was, to speak in learned language, occasioned by the long-standing hostility and antipathy between our two natures. I felt that he hated me, and did not understand why, after periods without contact, he would turn to me again. I would have kept my distance, as before,

---

[6] *Barshchina* was payment by a serf to his master in time and labor, as contrasted with *obrok*, which was payment by a serf to his master in kind or money (and which has here been translated "quitrent").

but I tried to get close to him—and have almost closed
with him at the barrier [in a duel]. *And I never liked
him*—why on earth was not all this understood long
ago. [. . .]

[134]

Spasskoe, June 7/19, 1861

TO COUNTESS ELIZAVETA EGOROVNA LAMBERT

[. . .] I have been in a rather strange position
these days. I (between you and me) almost fought a
duel with Count Lev Tolstoy, the writer. I must tell
you that a long-standing antipathy has existed between
us. I avoided him in every way, yet he, without ceasing
to hate me, constantly sought me out and tried to get
close to me. I do not wish to say anything bad about
him. In any case, his temperament is self-tormenting
and completely alien [to me]. He met me as if in order
to tease me and enrage me. Because of a completely
irrelevant conversation (the subject was philanthropy),
I, being furious inside, told him something coarse and
impertinent. I expected an immediate challenge, but
he was at first extremely mild and polite, and vexation
blazed up within him only after I had apologized in
writing. In short, unpleasant business has come up and
has stretched out for several days, during which I was
convinced that a duel was inevitable. Somehow, things
have been patched up, but we have now broken off
forever. I do not regret this because a close friendship
between us was never possible. But I am annoyed with
myself; how could I have lost my self-control to such an
extent? It turns out that no one can guarantee anything and that, really, as they say before the sacrament,
"I am the first sinner. [. . .]" [7]

[7] Quoted in Church Slavic.

[135]

Spasskoe, June 14 [O.S.], *1861*

TO DMITRI IAKOVLEVICH KOLBASIN

As for the rest, everything is quiet around here. Hunting has not yet begun, but I am getting ready and shall go with Fet and Afanasi, who has got very old but is keeping up his spirits anyhow. [. . .] [8]

[8] At this point "E. K.", the editor of the Russian volume from which this letter was taken, adds a note: "Afanasi was Turgenev's former serf, introduced into *A Sportsman's Sketches* as Yermolai. He figures throughout the tale 'Yermolai and the Miller's Wife,' which was based in its entirety on an actual occurrence. When Turgenev went to Spasskoe, his village, he would know in advance that Afanasi, known as the serf and hunter, Yermolai, would come to him the next morning, because Afanasi's responsibility, back in the days of the old mistress, had been to supply game for the owner's table. I remember even now the tall, graceful muzhik in a rather short, homespun coat which reached only to his knees and with a cord for a belt, monotonously reporting to Turgenev about the broods of land rails, great snipe, etc. Turgenev would listen to him attentively, without interrupting his flowing speech, take money out of his purse, and say: 'Now take care of me, Afanasi; you know how.' The charming tale about the 'nightingales' was not the work of Turgenev, but was literally taken from the words of Afanasi, who was a great specialist in all kinds of hunting and fishing, from bear to carp. He would talk in such detail about angling that one could have written an entire book from his comments. I still remember an amusing incident with Afanasi on a hunt; after a long and hard walk through the swamps and over the steppe, the hunters lost their way and came upon a hut in some settlement they were not familiar with; they were terribly hungry, but the woman of the hut did not have a samovar, or anything edible, except fresh mushrooms. Turgenev greedily attacked his favorite dish, but immediately stopped eating as he discovered that the mushrooms had been poorly prepared and were quite underdone. Afanasi devoured the entire bowl of mushrooms in silence, ordered some more, and then, crossing himself in front of the icons, gave his hostess a harsh look and said: 'But the mushrooms were raw, dearie.' Turgenev would recall the episode very frequently, asserting that his Afanasi could even digest bullets. Incidentally, Turgenev said the same thing about the stomach of I. I. Panaev."

[136]

Spasskoe, July 8/20, 1861

TO HIS DAUGHTER, PAULINE

[. . .] Mme Innis [Pauline's governess] knows
that she has only to turn to M. and Mme Viardot in
case money is needed. And, on that subject, I must tell
you I am very displeased that you have not written
a single word to Mme Viardot since your trip. You continue to appear ungrateful, and even if you believed
that you had no obligations to her, how could you fail
to respect a person whom your father loves and respects
more than any other person in the world! [. . .]

[137]

Spasskoe, July 10 [O.S.], 1861

TO PAVEL VASIL'EVICH ANNENKOV

[. . .] The [peasant] business is growing, spreading, and moving across the entire expanse of Russian
life, and taking, for the most part, monstrous forms.
And to try to give any kind of sensible *résumé* of it now
would be madness; nothing at all can be foreseen so
long in advance. We are all surrounded by these waves
and they are carrying us. Meanwhile, I can only say that
everything is quiet here, the volosts have been established and the village elders introduced, but the peasants have understood one thing—that they must not
be beaten, that the landholders' power has, in general,
been weakened, and, as a result, a man "must look out
for himself." The small gentry are howling, and the
district police officers are using the lash daily, but only
a little. The general picture, with the poor harvest to be
expected, is not very beautiful—but there have been

even worse. The peasants are not going on quitrent, and regard their new powers with bewilderment; but meanwhile there is no shortage of farm hands, and that is the main thing. [. . .]

{ 138 }

Spasskoe, July 19 [O.S.], 1861

TO COUNTESS ELIZAVETA EGOROVNA LAMBERT

[. . .] Essentially, because life is an illness, everything that we call philosophy, science, morality, art, poetry, etc., etc., is nothing but soothing medicine, *des calmants ou des palliatifs* [sedatives or palliatives]. [. . .]

{ 139 }

Paris, second half of September 1861

TO [COUNT] LEV NIKOLAEVICH TOLSTOY

Before my departure from [St.] Petersburg, I learned that you have been circulating in Moscow a copy of your last letter to me, and that you are calling me a coward unwilling to fight you, etc. I was unable to return to Tula Province, and I continued my trip. But because, *after all that I have done to smooth over the phrase that had escaped me,* I consider your *conduct* both insulting and dishonest, I am warning you that this time I will not allow it to remain unnoticed and, upon my return to Russia next spring, I shall demand satisfaction from you. I must notify you that I have informed my friends in Moscow of my intention so that they might counteract the rumors that you have been spreading.

{ 140 }

St. Petersburg, October 26/November 7, 1861

TO PAVEL VASIL'EVICH ANNENKOV

[. . .] I received a letter from Lev Tolstoy in which he informs me that there is not a word of truth to the rumor that he has been circulating the copy of a letter in which he insults me. Hence, my challenge becomes inoperative and we will not fight [a duel], about which I, of course, am very glad. Please tell Kolbasin —and let him believe his friends less.

{ 141 }

Paris, October 30/November 11, 1861

TO MIKHAIL NIKIFOROVICH KATKOV

I wrote you recently, but, after receiving your letter yesterday, I feel I must write you a few words in answer. I agree with your observations—almost all of them—especially about *Pavel Petrovich* [*Kirsanov*] and Bazarov himself.[9] As for Mme Odintsov, the unclear impression she produces shows me that she also needs more work. (Incidentally, the *argument* between Pavel Petrovich and Bazarov has been completely reworked and abridged.) You will agree that the story must obviously be set aside for now, both because of present circumstances and because of its internally unfinished state. I am very sorry that things have worked out this way, but with such a subject one must appear completely armed (as far as possible) before the reader. I want to look the whole thing over without hurrying and plow it again. I suppose that all the difficulties ex-

[9] Pavel Petrovich Kirsanov, Bazarov, and Mme Odintsov are characters in *Fathers and Children.*

isting *now* (internally and externally) will disappear toward the time of my return to Russia—that is, toward spring (toward April)—and we shall at last allow the brain-child to walk around in the world.

I can agree with only one thing: Mme Odintsov ought not to be ironic, nor should the muzhik stand above Bazarov, although the latter is himself empty and barren. . . . Perhaps my attitude toward Russia is more misanthropic than you suppose; in my eyes, Bazarov is the real hero of our times.[1] A fine hero and fine times, you will say. . . . But that is how things are. [. . .]

{ 142 }

Paris, November 8 [O.S.], *1861*

TO AFANASI AFANAS'EVICH FET

Incidentally, "one more and final story"[2] about the unfortunate affair with Tolstoy. Upon going through [St.] Petersburg, I learned from *trustworthy persons* (I have more than enough of such trustworthy persons!) that copies of Tolstoy's last letter to me (the letter in which he "despises" me) were being circulated in Moscow—copies that seem to have been released by Tolstoy himself. That infuriated me, and I sent him a challenge from here to be effective upon my return to Russia. Tolstoy answered me that the circulation of copies is a pure fabrication and then sent me a letter in which, after repeating that I had insulted him, *he apologized and declined the challenge.* Of course, this must put an end to the affair, and all I ask of you is to tell him (be-

---

[1] Perhaps a reference to Lermontov's great novel, A *Hero of Our Times.*

[2] The Russian for this is a famous phrase from Pushkin's *Boris Godunov.*

cause he writes me that he will consider any further communication from me an insult) that I myself withdraw the challenge, etc., and hope that all this will be buried forever. I have destroyed his letter (of apology), and I have never received the other letter, which, he says, was sent to me through Davydov, the bookseller. And now, *de profundis* about the entire business.

[143]

Paris, December 11/23, 1861

TO PAVEL VASIL'EVICH ANNENKOV

[. . .] The [French] government is waiting and hoping for war with America. A few days ago a Protestant pastor whom I know was summoned to the Ministry and threatened *thereat* for having placed an article about involuntary servitude in his little magazine (which is called *Piété-charité*). (The article contains four little pages and was written by the *daughter* of Nikolai Ivanovich Turgenev.) They announced to him that people must not dare to attack slavery because war is expected. And Mr. [Eugène] Pelletan has been sentenced to three months in jail for having wished France the freedom that Austria enjoys. How can one remain unmoved now! [. . .]

[144]

Paris, December 29, 1861

TO FRIEDRICH VON BODENSTEDT

[. . .] At the time of my passage through St. Petersburg, I did not see the editors of the *Sovremennik*. You ought to be told that this year a sort of disagreement has arisen between us, caused in part by the divergence of our political opinions and in part because I have given my works to a Moscow magazine (the *Russki vestnik*) that is opposed to the *Sovremennik*. [. . .]

{ 145 }

Paris, December 26, 1861/January 7, 1862

TO FEDOR MIKHAILOVICH DOSTOEVSKI

Your letter greatly astonished me. You seem to infer that I ascribed to you the circulation of the rumors about my story, but such an idea never even entered my head; how could such a thing have been implied in my letter? As if a man must seek a special explanation for any gossip! It prevails in our literary life, especially in the backyards where they publish such things as the *Knizhny vestnik*.[3] However, the whole matter is not important; I am only sorry that it could have disturbed both you and Katkov. I am afraid that the readers, upon reading *Fathers and Children*, will say: what was all the fuss about? In short, I wished to postpone publication until spring for many reasons, but the merchant keeps demanding the goods he purchased; nothing can be done; I have to let him release the work *tel quel* [as it is].

I am extremely interested in Ostrovski's *Minin*. Please tell me your impression. It is a new and bold effort! May God grant it success! But even if it is not successful, I am still sure that a *failure* of Ostrovski's may be more interesting than the *success* of many others. Give him my greetings.

[3] The *Knizhny vestnik* had declared that *Fathers and Children* would be published in V*remia* rather than in the *Russki vestnik*.

The story ["Phantoms"] intended for [your magazine] *Vremia* has been making progress recently, and I have high hopes that it will be ready for the second issue, but you yourself know that this is capricious business.

I am very grateful to you for having sent me the two numbers of *Vremia,* which I am reading with great pleasure. Especially your *Memoirs from the House of Death.* The picture of the steam bath is altogether Dantesque, and your characterizations of various persons (such as Petrov, for example) contain much subtle and accurate psychology. I sincerely rejoice in the success of your magazine and, I repeat, I am ready to collaborate on it in every way. Greetings to your wife and all your friends. [. . .]

[146]

Paris, January 7 [O.S.], *1862*

TO AFANASI AFANAS'EVICH FET

[. . .] You can write him [Tolstoy] or tell him (if you see him) that I, without making speeches or playing with words, like him very much, respect him, and follow his career—*from a distance,* but that everything appears different when we are near each other. What is to be done? We ought to live as though we existed upon different planets or in different centuries.

[147]

Paris, February 4, 1862

TO AFANASI AFANAS'EVICH FET

[. . .] Just as Tolstoy's fear of phrase-mongering has driven him to the most desperate phrase-mon-

gering, so your aversion to the *mind* in art has led to
the most precious philosophizing and has deprived
you of the same naïve emotion about which you make
such a fuss. [. . .] However, this is an interminable
argument between us; I say that art is so great a matter
that a whole man will barely grasp it with all his facul-
ties (including the mind, by the way). You ostracize
the mind, and see in a work of art only the unconscious
whisperings of a sleeping person. I must call that attitude Slavophile because it contains the features of that
school—"Everything is black here, but there everything
is white"; "the entire truth is on one side." But we,
sinners that we are, suggest that a man just amuses
himself by swinging the ax from the shoulder like that.
However, it is of course easier that way, and then, once
a man acknowledges that the truth is both here and
there, that there is no sharp boundary to be drawn,
he has to exert himself after he weighs both sides, etc.
And that is boring. It is pleasanter to bark things out
in military style. "Attention! Brain—column right,
march! Halt! Dress right, dress! Art—column right,
march! Halt! Dress it up!" Marvelous! The only thing
left is to write a report that everything is present or
accounted for. But here one must say with (clever or
stupid, what do you think?) Goethe:

Ja! Wenn es wir nur nicht besser wüssten! [*sic*]
[Indeed! If only we did not know better!]

And that is your ideal. [. . .]

{ 148 }

Paris, February 11, 1862

TO ALEKSANDR IVANOVICH HERZEN

[. . .] *Et tu, Brute!* You, you are reproaching me for giving my work to the *Russki vestnik?* But why on earth did I quarrel with the *Sovremennik,* incarnated in the person of Nekrasov? In their prospectus they assert that they have rejected me as outdated; *mais tu n'es pas dupe* [but you are not fooled], I hope, by this maneuver, and you know very well that I discarded Nekrasov as dishonest. Where on earth was I to place my work? In the *Biblioteka poit?* And, after all, the *Russki vestnik* is no longer such trash (although a good deal in it repels me to the point of nausea).
[. . .]

{ 149 }

Paris, March 10, 1862

TO VASILI PETROVICH BOTKIN

[. . .] I am sending you, under separate cover [Ostrovski's play], *Minin,* which I received (and read) this very day. I do not know what sort of an impression *Minin* will make on you, but it struck me as an impotent and sluggish work written in the most sublime language, with several charming rays of *lyricism* —such as, for example, the song of the servant girls in the second act—but no trace of drama; the characters are not alive, and *Minin* in general smacks of Karamzin and Zagoskin. I may be mistaken, but this is not what I was expecting from Ostrovski. [. . .]

It is flabby, without any flesh and blood. . . . You

will see for yourself. But the language, I repeat, is a model. None of us has written like that before. [. . .]

{ 150 }

Paris, March 5/17, 1862

TO AFANASI AFANAS'EVICH FET

[. . . Ostrovski's] *Minin* has not come off because of mind—but mind is irrelevant here; there was plainly not enough power or talent. Has not *Minin* been produced entirely with the outlook that caused Ostrovski to create Rusakov in *Ne v svoi sani ne sadis'* [Don't Go Where You Don't Belong]? And at that time he was not yet listening to the professors. Mind could hinder but not help a bit in the writing of a rather poor chronicle with a piously national tendency, with the usual tender lyrical emotions, and in a beauful, tender, and subdued style. The Achilles' heel of Ostrovski has been revealed, and that is all. [. . .]

{ 151 }

Paris, March 18/30, 1862

TO FEDOR MIKHAILOVICH DOSTOEVSKI

I have something to tell you: the extent to which your opinion about *Fathers and Children* has made me happy. The point is not that you have gratified my egotism, but that you have not been mistaken and did not altogether miss the mark—and that therefore the work has not been in vain.[4] This has been all the more important to me because people I trust (I am not talking about Kolbasin) have seriously advised me to throw

---

[4] Dostoevski's comments have been lost.

my work into the fire, and a few days ago Pisemski (this is between you and me) wrote me that the character of Bazarov was a complete failure. How can you tell me not to have doubts or be confused? It is difficult for an author to sense *immediately* the extent to which his idea has been brought to life, whether it is true, whether he has mastered it, etc. His own works are like a forest to him.

You yourself have most probably experienced that more than once. And hence, thanks again. You have so completely and subtly grasped what I wished to express through Bazarov, that all I could do was to throw up my hands in wonder—and in pleasure. May God grant that this indicates not only the perspicacity of a master, but also the comprehension of the average reader, i.e., may God grant that everyone will see at least part of what you have seen! Now I am calm about the fate of my story; the thing is done with, and I have no cause for regret.

Here is further proof for you of how well you have understood the character: in the meeting between Arkadi[5] and Bazarov, in the passage where you say something is lacking, Bazarov talks about the duel, mocks *cavaliers*, and Arkadi listens to him with horror, etc. I have cut this out and now regret having done so. In general, I have scribbled and reworked much under the influence of unfavorable comments and this, perhaps, caused the sluggishness you observed. [. . .]

[5] Arkadi, like Bazarov, is a character in *Fathers and Children*.

[152]

Paris, April 6/18, 1862

TO AFANASI AFANAS'EVICH FET

First of all, thanks for the letter—and the thanks would be greater if you had not felt obliged to put on kid gloves before massacring me. Believe me, I have borne and know how to bear the most caustic truth from my friends. So, despite all your euphemisms, you do not like *Fathers and Children.* I bow my head, for nothing can be done. Still I wish to say a few words in my defense, although I know how unseemly that is— and how pointless. You blame all the trouble on *ax-grinding,* on *contemplation*—in short, on the mind. But, really, all you needed to say was that the work lacked craftsmanship. I am apparently more naïve than you suggest. Ax-grinding! And what is the purpose of the ax-grinding in *Fathers and Children?* Did I wish to abuse Bazarov or to extol him? *I myself do not know* because I do not know whether I love him or hate him! Katkov has censured me because Bazarov emerged as an apotheosis. You also mention *parallelism,* but where is it?—and where are the believing and unbelieving *pairs?* Does Pavel Petrovich believe or does he not? I do not know, for I merely wished to present what the Stolypins, the Rossets, and other Russian ex-lions typify. Strange business; you reproach me with parallelism, while others write me: Why does Anna Sergeevna not have a lofty nature to show more fully her contrast to Bazarov? Why are Bazarov's parents not completely patriarchal? Why is Arkadi banal? Would not presenting him as an honest and instantly attractive young man have been better? What is the point of [introducing] Fenichka, and what inference is to be

drawn from her character? Let me say one thing: I
sketched these characters as I would have sketched
mushrooms, leaves, or trees; they hurt my eyes and I
began to draw. But to free myself from my own impressions merely because they resemble ax-grinding
would be strange and ridiculous. I do not wish to
imply that this makes me a fine fellow. On the contrary, what may be inferred from my words is even
more to my shame: not that I have tried to outsmart
myself, but that I did not know how [to fulfill my in-
tentions]. But truth comes first. And, moreover, *omnia
vanitas*.

{ 153 }

Paris, April 12/24, 1862

TO VASILI PETROVICH BOTKIN

[. . .] You are listening to Liszt's papal choir
in Rome, while here Schumann is in style, thanks to
the appearance of his wife, who is giving concerts.
I admit that his music is not to my taste at all. Sometimes it is charming, with much imagination and mys-
terious perspectives, but it has no form, no design, and
we old men find this *à la longue* [in the long run]
intolerable. This is really the music of the future; it has
no *present*; it is all only *Ahnungen* [presentiments],
Sehnen [yearning], etc. [. . .]

{ 154 }

Paris, April 14/26, 1862

TO KONSTANTIN KONSTANTINOVICH SLUCHEVSKI

I hasten to answer your letter, for which I am very

grateful. One cannot fail to value the opinions of young people; in any case, I would very much like to avoid all misunderstandings about my intentions. Let me answer you seriatim:

1) The first reproach recalls the accusation made against Gogol and others: why did they not introduce *good* people among the bad ones? Moreover, Bazarov dominates all the other characters in the novel. (Katkov believes that I have presented him as the apotheosis of the *Sovremennik*.) The traits he was endowed with are not accidental. I wished to make a tragic figure of him—but this was no place for tenderness. He is honest, truthful, and a democrat to the marrow of his bones—and you do not find *good* sides to him? He recommends [Karl Ludwig Büchner's] *Kraft und Stoff* [*Energy and Matter*] precisely because it is a *popular*—and hence a frivolous—book; the duel with Pavel Petrovich is introduced precisely to indicate more graphically the idleness of the elegant and noble gentry (presented in a way that is almost exaggeratedly comic); and if he had declined the duel, you know that Pavel Petrovich would have killed him [Bazarov]. In my opinion, Bazarov constantly gets the better of Pavel Petrovich, not vice versa, and if he is called a "nihilist," you must read "a revolutionary."

2) What has been said about Arkadi, about the rehabilitation of the fathers, etc., merely shows that I have not been understood—which is my own fault! *My entire story is directed against the gentry as the leading class.* Look at the characters of Nikolai Petrovich, Pavel Petrovich, and Arkadi. They are weak and faded, or limited. A feeling for aesthetics has compelled me to take the best representatives of the gentry

so as to show my theme more faithfully: if the cream
is bad, what then is the milk like? To have taken civil
servants, generals, robbers, etc. would have been a
crude *pont des ânes* [way out]—and an inaccurate one.
All the real *negators* whom I have known—Belinski,
Bakunin, Herzen, Dobroliubov, Speshnev, etc.—came
without exception from comparatively kind and honest
parents. And this contains a great idea: it removes any
shadow of *personal* indignation, of personal irascibility
from the *doers*, the negators. They go their way only
because they are more sensitive to the demands of
national life. Countess Sal'ias is incorrect in saying that
such characters as Nikolai Petrovich and Pavel Petrovich are our grandfathers; Nikolai Petrovich is myself, Ogarev, and thousands of others; Pavel Petrovich
is Stolypin, Esakov, and Rosset—who are also our
contemporaries. They are the best of the gentry, and
that is just why I have chosen them to show its insol-
vency. To present grafters on the one hand and an ideal
young man on the other is a picture others may draw.
. . . I wanted more. In one spot my Bazarov told
Arkadi (but I cut this out because of the censorship)
—the same Arkadi in whom your Heidelberg friends
see a *more successful character:* "Your father is an
honest fellow, but if he were the most out-and-out
grafter, you would not go beyond noble submissiveness
or effervescence because you are a little gentleman."

    3) O Lord! Mme Kushkin—that caricature—you
find *most successful of all!* Even to answer that would
be impossible. Mme Odintsov is as little *in love* with
Arkadi as with Bazarov—how is it you do not see
this! She is just the representative of our cold, idle,
dreaming, curious, and epicurean ladies, of our gentle-
women. Countess Sal'ias has understood this character

perfectly clearly. [Mme Odintsov] would like first to pat the fur of the wolf (Bazarov)—if only he does not bite—and then to stroke the little boy's curly hair, and continue reclining, all clean, on her velvet.

4) In my opinion Bazarov's death (which Countess Sal'ias calls *heroic* and therefore criticizes) was needed to place the final touch on his tragic figure. And your young people find it too accidental! Let me finish with the following observation: if the reader does not love Bazarov in all his coarseness, heartlessness, pitiless dryness, and causticity, if, let me repeat, the reader does not love Bazarov, the fault is mine and I have not attained my goal. But I did not wish (to use his words) to "sugar-coat" him, although by doing so I probably could have won over the young people to my side immediately. I did not wish to buy that kind of popularity with concessions. Better to lose the battle (and I seem to have done so) than to win by subterfuge. I was dreaming of a gloomy, savage, and large-scale figure half sprung from the soil, strong, malicious, honest—and for all that condemned to perish because for all that he stands at the threshold to the future; I dreamed of a strange *pendant* [counterpart] to Pugachev, etc. And my young contemporaries tell me, shaking their heads: "You, my friend, have made a fool of yourself and have even offended us. Your Arkadi has come out more purely—too bad you did not labor over him some more." I ought now, as the gypsy song has it, "to take my cap off and bow low." So far, only two persons—Dostoevski and Botkin—have completely understood Bazarov, i.e., grasped my intentions. I shall try to send you a copy of my story. And now *basta* [enough] about it. [. . .]

[155]

Paris, April 28, 1862

TO ALEKSANDR IVANOVICH HERZEN

I am answering your letter immediately, not to defend myself, but to thank you and at the *same* time to declare that, in creating Bazarov [in *Fathers and Children*], I not only was not angry with him, but felt an "attraction, a kind of ailment" for him—so Katkov became horrified at first, saw in him an *apotheosis* of the *Sovremennik*, and consequently persuaded me to drop quite a few mollifying features, which I regret. At least he did not suppress "the man with the perfumed moustache" and the others! This is the triumph of democratization over the aristocracy. With my hand on my heart, I feel no guilt toward Bazarov and could not have given him needless sweetness. If they do not like him as he is, with all his ugliness, then I am guilty of not knowing how to cope with the character I had selected. To present him as an ideal would have been no great trick; but to make him a wolf while nevertheless justifying him—that was hard, and I have probably not succeeded; I wish only to turn aside the reproaches caused by irritation at him. On the contrary, I think the opposite of irritation shines in everything, in his death, etc. But *basta cosi* [enough as it is]; when we see each other, we shall chat some more.

I have never been addicted to mysticism, and I never will be; in respect to God, I maintain the opinion of Faust:

> *Wer darf ihn nennen,*
> *Und wer bekennen:*
> *Ich glaub' ihn!*
> *Wer empfinden*

Und sich unterwinden
Zu sagen: ich glaub' ihn nicht!
[Who has the right to name Him,
Who, to claim,
"Yes, I believe in Him!"?
Yet who can truly feel
And dare to say,
"There is no God."?]

By the way, this emotion of mine has never been a secret to you. . . .

{ 156 }

Baden-Baden, September 28, 1862

TO "MARKO-VOVCHOK" (PEN NAME OF MAR'IA ALEKSANDROVNA MARKOVICH)

. . . You ask what sort of a man [Mikhail] Bakunin was. I presented a rather faithful portrait of him in Rudin; now [Bakunin] is a Rudin who was not killed on the barricades. Between us, he is a wreck. He will potter around for a while longer and try to stir up the Slavs, but nothing will happen. I feel sorry for him: for an outdated agitator who has lost his touch, life is a painful burden. That is my frank opinion of him, but do not gossip about it. [. . .]

{ 157 }

Baden-Baden, October 8, 1862

TO ALEKSANDR IVANOVICH HERZEN

[. . .] Our chief disagreement with O[garev] and H[erzen] and with Bakunin, too, consists precisely in the fact that they, despising the educated class in

Russia and almost trampling it in the mud, presuppose
revolutionary or reforming principles within the *people*;
as a matter of fact, quite the opposite is true. Revolution, in the real and living sense of the word—I could
have added: in the broadest sense of the word—exists
only within a minority of the educated class. If only
we do not wipe each other out, that is enough for its
[the revolution's] triumph. [. . .]

{ 158 }

Baden-Baden, October 8, 1862
[second letter to Herzen so dated]

TO ALEKSANDR IVANOVICH HERZEN

[. . .] As for my answer to the letters in the
Kolokol,[6] several pages have already been drafted. I
shall show them to you, but, because everyone knows
that you are writing me, I have held off a while (especially because I received, incidentally, a *semi-official*
warning against getting printed in the *Kolokol*). The
loss to the public is not great, but all this is important
to me. My main objection is that, in regard to me
particularly, you stated the question incorrectly: not
because of Epicureanism, not because of my weariness
and laziness have I withdrawn, as Gogol says, to the
canopy of the stream of European principles and institutions. If I had been twenty-five, I would not have
acted differently—not so much for my own advantage,
as for the people's. The role of the *educated* class in
Russia is to transmit civilization to the people, so that
the people can decide for themselves what to reject or

⁶ The *Kolokol* was Herzen's Russian-language periodical
published in London; it could not legally be sent to the general
public in Russia because of the censorship.

accept; this is, in essence, a modest role, although Peter the Great and [Mikhail] Lomonosov have assumed it. In my opinion, this role is not yet nearly completed, although revolution does bring it to action. But *you* gentlemen have, on the contrary, a German method of thinking; so do the Slavophiles. You are abstracting, from the barely intelligible and comprehensible substance of the people, the principles upon which you propose they construct their life. You are whirling around in a fog. What is most important is that essentially *you are repudiating revolution* because the people whom you kneel before are conservative *par excellence*. The people carry within themselves the embryos of just such a bourgeoisie [as you have depicted]; it is in their coats of tanned sheepskin, their warm and filthy huts, their bellies stuffed to the point of heartburn, and their aversion to every civic responsibility and independent action. All this goes far beyond the traits to which you have referred in your letters to characterize the western bourgeoisie accurately and faithfully. There is no need to go far afield—look at our merchants. I have not used the word "abstracting" for nothing. The *zemstvo*, about which you bent my ear in London—the celebrated *zemstvo*—has in reality turned out to be just such a theoretical and contrived thing as Kavelin's "patriarchal way of life," etc. I labored (really labored!) over Shchapov[7] during the summer, and nothing will change my convictions now. *Zemstvo* either means exactly the same as does any Western word of equal strength, or it means nothing, and, in Shchapov's meaning, it is absolutely unintelligible to 100 muzhiks out of 100. You have to seek

[7] Shchapov had just written an article entitled "*Zemstvo i raskol*" ("Zemstvo and Schism").

a different trinity from the one you have found—
"zemstvo, artel, and mir"—or to admit that the special
structure which will be imparted to state and social
forms by the efforts of the Russian people has not yet
been so clarified that reflective persons such as ourselves can categorize it. Or else danger is in the offing:
a man will throw himself down before the people,
corrupt them, call their convictions sacred and lofty,
or else brand those convictions unfortunate or mad—
all of which Bakunin has done on one whole page of
his last pamphlet. Incidentally, about him: on p. 21
he says: "In 1863, there will be a terrible misfortune
in Russia if the Tsar does not decide to summon a
national duma of the zemstvos." If Bakunin wishes,
I offer him any kind of bet he likes: I assert that the
Tsar will summon nothing and that 1863 will pass
extremely peacefully. *Es gilt?* [Is it on?] I am sure that
here too my prophecy will be fulfilled, as was, you remember, the one I made about the *ustavnye gramoty* [8]
in London during the spring. I was mistaken only in
that I thought that half of them would be introduced
toward the end of the year, and they have almost all
been introduced by now.

Ah, my old friend, believe me: Only the educated
class, a minority that Bakunin calls rotten, uprooted
from the soil, and traitorous, supports revolutionary
propaganda. In any case, *you* have no other public.

---

[8] The *ustavnye gramoty* were the complicated regulations
governing relations between landlords and their former serfs
after the emancipation of 1861.

[159]

Paris, November 8, 1862

TO ALEKSANDR IVANOVICH HERZEN

[. . .] The present letter has been evoked by
your last letter to me in the *Kolokol*. [. . .] You
diagnose contemporary mankind with unusual subtlety
and sensitivity, but why on earth must this be *Western*
man and not *bipèdes* in general? You are just like a
physician who, having examined all the symptoms of
a chronic illness, declares that the whole trouble comes
from the patient's being a Frenchman.

An enemy of mysticism and absolutism, you bow
down mystically before the Russian sheepskin coat,
and see in it the grace, novelty, and originality of future
social forms—*das Absolute*—in a word, the very same
Absolute at which you jeer in philosophy. All your idols
are smashed, but a man cannot live without an idol,
so let an altar be erected to the new and unknown god
(inasmuch as almost nothing is known about him),
and you will be able again to pray, to believe, and to
wait. The god does the complete opposite of what you
are expecting from him; you think this is temporary,
accidental, and forcibly grafted on to him by external
power. Your god loves, to the point of adoration, what
you hate and he hates what you love; he accepts just
what you reject in his name; you turn your eyes aside,
close your ears, and, with the ecstasy peculiar to all
skeptics who have grown tired of skepticism—with
that specific, ultra-fanatic ecstasy—you keep talking
about "vernal freshness, beneficial tempests," etc. History, philology, and statistics are nothing to you; facts
are nothing to you even though, for example, it is undeniable that we Russians, both by language and by

nature, belong to the European family—the *genus
Europaeum*—and, consequently, by the most immutable delvings of physiology, must take the same road.
I have never yet heard of a *duck*, belonging to the family of *ducks*, that breathed with gills like a fish. And
meantime, because of your mental illness, your weariness, your thirst to place a fresh crystal of snow on a
withered tongue, you attack everything that should be
dear to every European, and therefore to us, too—
civilization, legality, finally revolution itself. And, having filled young heads with your social and Slavophile
home-brewed and unfermented beer, you allow [these]
intoxicated and befogged [people] into a world where
they will stumble at their first step. I do not doubt that
you will do all this in good faith, honestly, and sorrow-
fully, with heated and sincere self-denial . . . but this
does not help. [Do] one of two things: either serve
revolution and European ideals as you did before, or—
if you have reached the conclusion that they are worthless—have the spirit and the courage to look the devil
in the eye, and say [you are] *guilty*[9] to *all European
mankind*—and not with evident or implied exceptions
in favor of a Russian Messiah who is expected at any
moment, and in whom you really and personally believe
as little as you do in the Hebrew one. You will say:
that is frightening—one can lose both popularity and
the chance to continue one's activities. I agree, but
on the one hand, to act as you are acting now is also
fruitless; on the other, I am assuming in spite of you
that you have enough spiritual strength to accept the
consequences of your saying what you consider to be
the truth. We shall wait a while, but for now this is
enough. [. . .]

[9] English in original.

[160]

Paris, December 10, 1862

TO THE EDITOR OF THE *Severnaia pchela*

The following sentence appeared in a feuilleton of the November 22 (No. 316) issue of your newspaper, over the signature "A. Iu."

"Let . . . Mr. Nekrasov [editor of the *Sovremennik*] *sacrifice* . . . Messrs. Turgenev, Druzhinin, Pisemski, Goncharov, and Avdeev and issue the *Sovremennik!*"

I have more than once met in print the opinion Mr. A. Iu. expresses. It has even entered the prospectus of the magazine Mr. Nekrasov edits. I have not thus far considered it necessary to pay attention to such "declarations," but because the words of Mr. A. Iu. force me to conclude, despite myself, that silence (especially when prolonged) could be taken as a sign of consent, I tell you in a few words how *my* alienation from the *Sovremennik* really developed.

I shall not go into the details of when and why it started. In January 1860, when the *Sovremennik* published another piece of mine ("Hamlet and Don Quixote"), Mr. Nekrasov offered me, in the presence of witnesses, a rather substantial fee for a story that had been promised to the *Russki vestnik*; in the spring of 1861 the same Mr. Nekrasov sent a letter to me in Paris in which he complained with great emotion about my coolness, renewed his flattering offers, and, incidentally, informed me that he dreamed of me almost every night.

I answered Mr. Nekrasov immediately with an *absolute refusal*, informed him of my firm decision to sever my relations with the *Sovremennik*, and added:

"Henceforth the magazine need not stand on ceremony in its opinions of me."

And Mr. Nekrasov's magazine immediately did stop standing on ceremony. Malevolent hints appeared right away, and with the speed peculiar to all Russian progress, they became out-and-out attacks. All this was in the nature of things, and I probably deserved those attacks; but now I leave it to your own readers to judge how just the opinion of Mr. A. Iu. is. Alas! Mr. Nekrasov did *not* sacrifice me for his convictions; and remembering the names of his other sacrifices as listed by Mr. A. Iu., I am almost ready to reproach the editor of the *Sovremennik* for the exception. But, moreover, have Messrs. Druzhinin, Pisemski, Goncharov, and Avdeev really fallen under his sacrificial knife? It seems to me that Mr. Nekrasov has been much less of a *zhrets*[1] during the course of his career than Mr. A. Iu. assumes.

[161]

Paris, December 3/15, 1862

TO IVAN PETROVICH BORISOV

The news about Tolstoy's wedding has made me very happy, and so does what you write about his wife. I remember having seen her at the house of her father, Andrei Evstaf'evich Bers, when she was barely more than a child. I wish Tolstoy peace, calm, and happiness. I would not care to meet him, but I have never ceased to take the most lively interest in everything that concerns him. I have learned with particular pleasure that

---

[1] In Russian a *zhrets* is a pagan priest whose chief duty is to preside over sacrificial rituals. (Ushakov.)

he has once again turned to literature: he never should have left it.

The news you have given me about the progress of the peasant business[2] is, on the whole, comforting, and jibes with the news from other sources. I hope that by spring everything will have calmed down for good, and when I show up at Spasskoe during May, the deed will have been done and the new life begun. But the old one will not be forgotten either, to wit: trips to Novoselki, Stepanovka, Rederer, etc.

{ 162 }

Paris, January 19/31, 1863

TO PAVEL VASIL'EVICH ANNENKOV

[. . .] Everything is quiet here. I was present at three readings by [Charles] Dickens and went into ecstasies over them. All our [public] readers—Pisemski, Ostrovski—become something less than the common fly before this genius. What merriment, power, grace, and profundity! To convey my impression is impossible. Even Botkin became excited, and he is preparing an article in our magazine.

[Louis] Viardot and I have translated [Pushkin's *Eugene*]*Onegin* [into French] and it will be printed. [. . .]

---

[2] The announcement that the serfs would be freed had come in February 1861, but arrangements to carry out the relevant decrees were slow, cumbersome, and accompanied by disorders.

[163]

Paris, February 12, 1863

TO ALEKSANDR IVANOVICH HERZEN

[. . .] Can you imagine: the Third Section[3] *is summoning* me—me, your antagonist—to Russia, with the usual threat of confiscation, etc., in case of disobedience. How do you like that? You know, this is comic in the highest degree, after all. I answered with a letter to the Sovereign in which I asked him to have the points in question sent me. If my answers will be satisfactory [to the authorities], so much the better; if not, I shall not go. Let them hurry and *deprive* me of my civil-service titles, etc.

[164]

Paris, April 7/19, 1863

TO AFANASI AFANAS'EVICH FET

[. . .] My *case* seems to have ended well. They sent me questions of extremely little importance; I answered immediately, and now, I think, everything has been filed in the archives.[4]

I read [Tolstoy's] *Cossacks* and went into ecstasies over it. (And so did Botkin.) Only the character of

[3] The Third Section of the Imperial Chancellery was an organization of the ubiquitous state police.

[4] Turgenev's answer in writing to the list of questions sent him in February 1863 by the Senate (in its capacity as a supreme court) did not end his involvement in the case of "persons accused of connections with [Herzen's] London propagandists." A second subpoena followed in September, and Turgenev gave his testimony orally to the Senate in St. Petersburg the following January. By an edict of January 28/February 9, 1864, he was allowed to leave Russia. On the following June 1/13 the Senate cleared him completely.

Olenin spoils the generally magnificent impression. There was no need again to bring in a troubled, boring, and useless creature so as to contrast civilization with unsullied, primitive nature. How come Tolstoy will not get rid of this nightmare! And, incidentally, how about Chernyshevski's little novel [*What to Do*] in the *Sovremennik?* It is really charming!

Everything seems quiet with you, as it ought to be. And thank God! I am in no mood to tell you the degree to which Polish affairs are tormenting me. . . .[5] Everyone here is preparing for war. [. . .]

{ 165 }

Baden-Baden, April 27/May 9, 1863

TO COUNTESS ELIZAVETA EGOROVNA LAMBERT

[. . .] The convictions of my youth have not changed. But I never have been and never will be occupied with politics; it is alien and uninteresting to me. I pay attention to politics only insofar as a writer, who is called upon to depict contemporary life, must. But you do wrong to demand from me in *literature* what I cannot give—fruits that do not grow on my tree. I have *never written for the people*. Beginning with *A Sportsman's Sketches* and finishing with *Fathers and Children*, I have written for that class of the public to which I belong. I do not know how useful I have been, but I do know that I have steadily moved toward one and the same goal, and deserve no reproach about that. [. . .]

---

[5] On January 22, 1863, the Polish National Committee had declared a state of insurrection against Russia.

[166]

Baden-Baden, September 15/27, 1863

TO PAVEL VASIL'EVICH ANNENKOV

[. . .] I wish to say a few words about the enclosed fantasy. It was copied over a month ago and
has been in my house ever since. Would you please
read the junk attentively and decide whether the piece
is worth printing at present or whether its publication
ought to be postponed for more peaceful days? If
you decide to have the piece printed, then give some
thought as to how. I promised "Phantoms" to the
editorial board of V*remia*, but since that time V*remia*
has become a phantom itself.[6] Dostoevski (who visited
me a few days ago in Baden) has asked me to wait
until October in the hope that his journal might be
permitted again; in that case, of course, my piece will
have to appear there. [. . .]

[167]

Baden-Baden, November 26/December 8, 1863

TO VASILI PETROVICH BOTKIN

[. . .] That you were bewildered by "Phantoms" makes me think we had better wait a while
before having it printed. It contains absolutely no
allegory of any kind; I myself understand Ellis as little
as you do. It is a series of mental *dissolving views*,[7]
provoked by the transitional and genuinely ponderous
and obscure state of my *I*. There is no doubt that I

[6] Fedor Dostoevski was the unofficial editor of V*remia*, a
magazine that was suppressed by the Russian government after
it had run an article by Strakhov on the Polish insurrection of
1863, which piece was intended to be favorable to the Russian
government.
[7] English in original

shall either stop writing entirely, or write something completely different from what I have been writing. Probably the first, but we shall talk over the whole business. [. . .]

{ 168 }

Baden-Baden, December 9/21, 1863

TO PAVEL VASIL'EVICH ANNENKOV

[. . .] Incidentally, ask Dostoevski not to print "Phantoms" before my arrival. I may rework it considerably. Everything indicates that we had better wait a while. [. . .]

{ 169 }

St. Petersburg, January 25, 1864

TO AFANASI AFANAS'EVICH FET,

[. . .] After your departure, I read Tolstoy's "Polikushka" and was amazed at the power of his mighty talent. But so much material is wasted. He even drowns the son for no reason; that comes off horribly. However, at the same time the story has pages that are truly amazing! He even makes your blood curdle, and you know ours is so thick and coarse! A master! A master! [. . .]

{ 170 }

Baden-Baden, March 15, 1864

TO HIS DAUGHTER, PAULINE

[. . .] I have often repeated to you that I have never wanted you to marry except for love. If love is lacking, all the rest is nothing. [. . .]

[171]

Paris, March 21/April 2, 1864

TO ALEKSANDR IVANOVICH HERZEN

I have been vacillating for a long time, after returning from Russia, as to whether to tell you of the remark in the *Kolokol* about a "gray-haired Magdalene of the masculine sex whose hair and teeth are falling out from repentance," etc. I admit that this remark, which evidently refers to me, has grieved me. That Bakunin, who has borrowed money from me, should have put me in a most unpleasant position through his old wives' tales and his light-headedness (he has ruined others entirely), that Bakunin, I say, has been spreading the most banal and foul slander about me—this is only natural, and, having known him a long time, I did not expect anything else from him. But I did not expect you in just the same way to fling mud at a man you have known for almost twenty years—solely because his convictions differ from yours. You have not lagged far behind the late [Tsar] Nikolai [I], who also condemned me without even asking me whether I was really guilty. If I could show you the answers I wrote to the questions sent,[8] you probably would become convinced that, without concealing anything, I not only did not abuse any of my friends, but did not even think of disowning them; I would have considered such an action beneath my dignity. I admit, not without some pride, that I remember the answers that, despite their tone, caused my judges to respect and believe me.
[. . .]

---

[8] See above, Letters #163 and #164.

{ 172 }

Baden-Baden, June 1/13, 1864

TO PETR ALEKSANDROVICH PLETNEV

[. . .] There are enough Russians here—but not one whom I like. There is no one with whom to discuss what one likes—poetry and Pushkin. [. . .]

{ 173 }

Baden-Baden, June 5/17, 1864

TO IVAN PETROVICH BORISOV

[. . .] A few days ago I reread Lev Tolstoy's novel *The Cossacks* and again went into raptures. It is indeed a wonderful thing and has extraordinary power. What is he doing? Write a few words about him. Although he and I are Montague and Capulet, I take a great interest in him and would be glad to learn that he is well. [. . .]

{ 174 }

Baden-Baden, July 12, 1864

TO FRIEDRICH VON BODENSTEDT

[. . .] Perhaps you might add that I spent 1852 and 1853 in [domestic] exile. It was not very annoying. I had incurred the penalty after the appearance of my article on Gogol's death. The real reason [for this penalty] was the appearance of my *Sportsman's Sketches*. My exile ended upon the intercession of the Crown Prince and present Emperor [Aleksandr II]. Most of the sketches were written abroad—in Paris— during 1847–9, and hence had an almost melancholy tone. For a long time I was of two minds as to whether

I should stay abroad for good. Fortunately, I did not.
[. . .]

[175]

Baden-Baden, September 3 [O.S. (?)], *1864*
TO [COUNTESS] ELIZAVETA EGOROVNA LAMBERT

[. . .] I will not expatiate on the first point; I
am not a Christian in your sense and perhaps not in
any sense, and therefore let us put the whole thing
aside. This can only lead to severe misunderstandings.
[. . .]

[176]

Baden-Baden, January 10, 1865
TO MISS INNIS [HIS DAUGHTER'S GOVERNESS]

I am writing you this short note to inform you of
the following: I have learned that Prince Trubetskoi
and other persons intend to be present at the ceremony
of my daughter's conversion [to Roman Catholicism,
before her marriage to a Frenchman]. I am strictly
opposed to this. If you do not wish to bring the most
serious unpleasantness down upon me, see that the
ceremony is performed *as quietly and as secretly* as
possible. I do not doubt that this note will suffice.
I trust your discretion completely. Besides, I am writing
the Prince about it. A thousand regards.

[177]

Paris, January 28/February 9, 1865
TO IVAN PETROVICH BORISOV

[. . .] I have come to Paris to attend the wedding of my daughter, who on February 25 will become the wife of a good, young Frenchman, Gaston Bruère. After many unsuccessful efforts, this one has been crowned with success. Now I am glad there was no hurry; the match is satisfactory in all regards. I am extremely busy; getting a girl married in France involves almost as many formalities as a criminal case, and my daughter's abnormal [illegitimate] situation complicated the difficulties tenfold. However, everything has been settled, and, except for illness or something even worse, no obstacles are to be feared. You can easily imagine how pleased I am. [. . .]

The news about Tolstoy has grieved me very much. I hope that he has recovered and has been working for a long time. He knows best. If only the man were not so cunning and surrendered to his talent—oh, Lord God, how far he would go! His life is just beginning—how young an age is 36!—and what powers he has! I am impatiently awaiting his new novel. [. . .]

[178]

Paris, February 16, 1865

TO PAULINE VIARDOT (NEE GARCIA)

[. . .] I was present at the opening of the Chambers in the Great Hall of the Estates at the Louvre. We were squeezed in like sardines. Three things struck me: the exclusively *military* character of the ceremony (the only passage applauded was the reference to constructing a new Arch of Triumph); the complete and absolute absence of pretty women; and the sound of the Emperor [Napoleon III's] voice. If a person could categorize voices as he sketches heads, he would say that a Swiss professor was talking—a professor of botany or of numismatics. The speech itself was quite innocuous, very peaceful—and ambiguous, that goes without saying. [. . .] There is nothing more ridiculous than certain cowled figures rigged out in uniform: the red, yellow, motley, and gilded toques of the lawyers and the judges had such a counterfeit oriental appearance that one could have died laughing. What ribbons, badges, gilt, helmets, and plumes! Good Lord! And to say that all this frippery makes an impression! What am I saying? It rules the world. . . .

[179]

Baden-Baden, February 21 [O.S.], *1865*

TO FEDOR MIKHAILOVICH DOSTOEVSKI

I hasten to inform you that I have received your note for 300 rubles. Thank you. Of course, I would not have troubled you had not the wedding of my daughter, with all its foreseen and unforeseen expenses, forced me to knock on every door. I hope that the payment did not bother you too much. What you say about your work simply frightens me—a Baden bourgeois grown lazy! I am very sorry that your health is unsatisfactory; look after it and do not strain yourself! You would do better to hire a young industrious helper for the administrative part. The expense will be repaid with interest. I have decided not to publish "*Sobaka*" ["The Dog"], not because it is a minor work, but because, as most of my friends agree, it did not come off. Being silent is better than speaking badly! I see from Annenkov's letters that literature seems to have come to life recently; he writes me about Tolstoy's novel [9] and

---

[9] *War and Peace.*

Ostrovski's drama.[1] I would like to read them, but it seems that I must postpone this until after my return, which will not be later than April 15 or 20. At that time I will also acquaint myself with your magazine. I wish you everything good, beginning with good health, and I send you friendly greetings.

[180]

Baden-Baden, March 16/28, 1865

TO IVAN PETROVICH BORISOV

[. . .] Since your letter arrived, I have managed to read Ostrovski's play, V*oevoda*, and the opening of Tolstoy's novel.[2] To my sincere grief, I must admit that the novel strikes me as absolutely poor, boring, and unsuccessful. Tolstoy has not stuck to his last [*sic*], and all his shortcomings are breaking through the surface. Against the canvas of a historical novel, how paltry are all these little tricks, craftily brought in and pretentiously presented—the petty psychological observations which, under the pretext of "truth," he hunts up from the armpits and other dark places of his characters. And he places this unfortunate effort above his *Cossacks*! If he says so sincerely, so much the worse for him. And how cold and dry it all is; how one feels the author's lack of imagination and naïveté; how fatiguingly a memory works upon the reader—the memory of what is banal, accidental, and needless! And what young ladies! They are always scrofulous and affected. No, that must not be the way; that is the way

---

[1] V*oevoda*.
[2] The first twenty-eight chapters of W*ar and Peace* had just appeared in the January (1865) issue of the *Russki vestnik* under the title *1805*.

to fall—even with his talent. I find this very painful, and would like to be mistaken.

But Ostrovski's *Voevoda* moved me. No one before him has written in such glorious and pure Russian with such taste! The last act is bad (especially where the Voevoda chases his bride *to kill her by tickling her*); but Acts II and III are perfection. What fragrant poetry some spots have—like our Russian groves in the summer! At least in the wonderful scene with the *Domovoi*.[3] Ah—he is a master, that man with a beard [Ostrovski], a master! [. . .]

[181]

Baden-Baden, August 5/17, 1865

TO IVAN PETROVICH BORISOV

[. . .] Tolstoy's suggestion again smacks of him [Fet]: Tolstoy occupies no such position in my view. And we would probably not meet; as for his sister [Mar'ia], I certainly have no reason to avoid her. I wish him and his (from all reports) sweet wife all the best, but he has hardly ceased to complicate matters. At the very time when, in your words, he was inquiring about me with interest, he was writing Fet that he hates me more every day. And that is why even his opinion about [his] uncle rather indicates that he is more concerned about his own impressions than about people who arouse those impressions. I am glad that he goes on working, and I hope that the later parts of his novel [*War and Peace*] will be better than the early ones. [. . .]

---

[3] In Russian folklore the *Domovoi* is a supernatural spirit that inhabits houses.

{ 182 }

Baden-Baden, December 19, 1865/January 1, 1866
TO PAVEL VASIL'EVICH ANNENKOV

[. . .] Please get me the works of Sleptsov, published by the *Sovremennik* office. This youth has more
talent than all the other "young fellows. [. . .]"

{ 183 }

Baden-Baden, January 17/29, 1866
TO PAVEL VASIL'EVICH ANNENKOV

[. . .] Sleptsov's works are not so interesting in
themselves as instructive as a phenomenon. They reek
strongly of moldy underdrawers—*fond de culottes*—
which is peculiar to our contemporary literature. What
poverty and emptiness of content there is, but there is
talent. [. . .]

No book yet has so offended the French public as
Edgar Quinet's *La Révolution*. All parties are grinding
their teeth; they cannot forgive him his despicable disbelief in the future, the power, and the intelligentsia
of the Latin races in general and of the French nation
in particular. The book is wonderful, and your mention
of Belinski's name is completely appropriate. [. . .]

{ 184 }

Baden-Baden, February 9/21, 1866
TO PAVEL VASIL'EVICH ANNENKOV

[. . .] I have a translation of a short (but excellent) tale by Cervantes—*Rinconete and Cortadillo.*
[. . .] I do not know whether I told you about my

translation of [Charles] Perrault's tales [into Russian] for the bookseller M. O. Vol'f, who bought illustrations from Doré. The translation was printed in Leipzig and will probably appear in [St.] Petersburg toward Easter. [. . .]

[185]

Baden-Baden, February 17/March 1, 1866

TO PAVEL VASIL'EVICH ANNENKOV

[. . .] I suggested to Mme Viardot that she read (together with me) Tolstoy's *Childhood* in Russian, as a work that is a classic in its own way. I began to read it, and suddenly became convinced that this celebrated *Childhood* is simply bad, forced, boring, pettily detailed, and incredibly outdated. My discovery grieves me; has *Childhood* too become a mirage? And when will there be an end to mirages? Or perhaps I have grown old and dim-witted. [. . .]

[186]

Baden-Baden, March 25/April 6, 1866

TO PAVEL VASIL'EVICH ANNENKOV

[. . .] In the second part of *Crime and Punishment*, the dam you were speaking of broke, and a lot of nonsense poured out. The work reeks of the putrid and sour-tasting state of mind that belongs in a hospital. I did not like the continuation of Tolstoy's *1805*, either, [because of its] pettiness and a certain capricious preciosity in the separate brush strokes. There are also the eternal repetitions of the same internal racket: what am I, he says, a coward or not, etc. It is a strange historical novel. [. . .]

{ 187 }

Baden-Baden, April 21, 1866

TO LUDWIG PIETSCH

[. . .] The older a man gets, the faster life slips through his fingers. [. . .]

{ 188 }

Baden-Baden, March 25/April 6, 1866

TO AFANASI AFANAS'EVICH FET

Of the two poems that were sent, the one (the printed one) to Tiutchev is beautiful; it radiates the old (I had better say "the young") Fet. The other is unsatisfactory. "Why?" you ask?

[. . .] All your personal, lyrical, and love poems —especially the passionate ones—are weaker than the others. They sound as if you had written them without the object of your verses ever having existed. And with that you can take a shoe and really hit me over the head. [. . .]

The first part of Dostoevski's *Crime and Punishment* is wonderful; the second part smacks of moldy, petty introspection.

The second part of *1805* is also weak. How banal and crafty it all is, and has Tolstoy really not become thoroughly bored by those eternal meditations—"Am I a coward," he says, "or am I not"—and the pathology of battle? Where are the characteristics of the age? Where is the historical coloration? The character of Denisov is boldly delineated, and would have been good as a figure against a background; but there is no background. [. . .]

[189]

Baden-Baden, June 27 [O.S.], 1866

TO AFANASI AFANAS'EVICH FET

Tolstoy's novel [*War and Peace*] is bad, not because it is infected with "being sensible"—that gives
no cause for fear—but because he has mastered nothing, knows nothing, and is offering, under the names of
Kutuzov and Bagration, servile copies of minor contemporary generals.

[190]

Baden-Baden, September 30/October 12, 1866

TO IVAN PETROVICH BORISOV

[. . .] But I have refused to read Dostoevski's
Crime and Punishment; it is something like a prolonged
colic; Lord have mercy in time of cholera! [. . .]

[191]

Karlsruhe, January 12/24, 1867

TO IVAN PETROVICH BORISOV

[. . .] In the first issue of the V*estnik Evropy*,
I read the beginning of Goncharov's new novel [4] and
am completely dissatisfied with it; the verbosity is intolerable and senile, and there is a great deal that is
mechanically conventional, philosophizing, and rhetorical. One must admit that after the TRUTH of Lev Tolstoy, all the elderly literature about civil servants
smacks very much of what is false—sourly and unpleas-
antly false. The only good scenes are in the village and
in the district seat. I do not know anything more repul-

⁴ *Obryv* [*The Precipice*].

sive than Mme Belovodov—a kind of lady chief of the unassessed-taxes department. But maybe you look at all this in a different light, and even like it. [. . .]

[192]

Moscow, March 25/April 6, 1867

TO PAULINE VIARDOT (NEE GARCIA)

[. . .] I have just had another long conversation with Katkov. After some random compliments about my novel [*Smoke*], he finally told me that he is afraid lest a certain person be recognized in Irena. He therefore advises me to *abridge* the character. I refused for two reasons: first, his idea lacks common sense and I do not wish to spoil an entire piece of work only to please him; and, second, the proofs are corrected and checked, and to do them all over again would be quite a job and take another ten days. Enough of Moscow as it is! I swear I feel here as though I were in jail. [. . .]

[193]

Moscow, March 28/April 9, 1867

TO PAULINE VIARDOT (NEE GARCIA)

[. . .] More trouble: Mr. Katkov is making so many major difficulties for my unfortunate novel [*Smoke*] that I am beginning to believe he will not be able to publish it in his magazine. Mr. Katkov wishes at any cost to make a virtuous matron of Irena, and exemplary citizens of the generals and other gentlemen who figure in my novel; you see that we are not close to understanding each other. I made some concessions, but today I finally said: "Stop there!" Let us see if he yields. [. . .]

{ 194 }

Moscow, April 10, 1867

TO PAULINE VIARDOT (NEE GARCIA)

[. . .] Since this morning a blizzard has been blowing, whining, moaning, and howling through the desolate streets of Moscow; branches strike one another and writhe like people in desperation. Bells are tolling sadly everywhere: we are in the middle of Lent. What nice old weather! What a charming country. [. . .]

The Katkov affair has been settled; I have sacrificed one scene, but, more important, I have saved the rest [of *Smoke*]. The main part remains intact. But this is really the other side of the coin in literature. [. . .]

{ 195 }

Baden-Baden, April 10/22, 1867

TO PAVEL VASIL'EVICH ANNENKOV

From my note to Botkin, you probably already know about my safe arrival in my *homeland* or, at least, in my *nest*. I have found everything in order. The view from my windows is just as green and golden here as it was dim and white in Moscow. The sun is shining, the lilac is in flower, the blackbirds are singing, and the French are threatening from across the Rhine—the first occupant of my house may well be a French general. But we cannot help that misfortune, and if the storm breaks, we will merely curl up in the corners. Everyone here is now afire with patriotism—what next? I am impatiently waiting for news from you. Are you doing anything? Is Glafira Aleksandrovna [Annenkov's wife] recovering?

Have any rumors started because of the reading,[5] and [if so] what are they about? Of course, all this interests me very much. It looks as though I will soon buckle down to work again; the literary vein has begun to flow and has not calmed down yet. My leg is better[6] and I have even begun to hobble about the streets.

The Viardot family sends regards; they regret very much that you cannot come.

Do you remember the snowstorm in [St.] Petersburg on the day of my departure? Everything was buried beneath snowdrifts. The snow began to disappear after Pskov, but there was not a blade of grass before [I reached] the frontier. Some grass came into sight around Königsberg, and it grew more and more common—right up to Frankfurt [am Main], while south of Frankfurt, spring was already beaming. And perhaps you have snow even now. [. . .]

{ 196 }

Baden-Baden, May 22, 1867

TO ALEKSANDR IVANOVICH HERZEN

[. . .] Potugin [in *Smoke*] annoyed you, and you regret that I did not delete half his speeches. But imagine, I don't think he talks enough, and my opinion is confirmed by the general fury this character has aroused against me. Josef II said to Mozart that there were too many notes in [one of] his operas. *"Keine zu*

---

[5] While still in St. Petersburg, Turgenev had given a public reading of selections from *Smoke*, which was still unfinished.
[6] Turgenev had had an attack of gout.

viel" ["Not one too many"], answered the latter. I am
even less a Mozart than you are a Josef II, but I dare
to think that in it [*Smoke*] there is *"kein Wort zu viel"*
["not one word too many"]. Whatever is attacked
abroad as a commonplace can, among us, produce a
rage because of its novelty. [. . .]

It seems as though you are making too many
Kratzfüsse vor den Slavophilen [bowings and scrapings
before the Slavophiles], whom you carry in your heart
out of habit. It seems to me that if you were to sniff
the vegetable oil they all smell of [. . .] you would
somewhat restrain your emotions. [. . .]

[197]

Baden-Baden, May 23/June 4, 1867

TO ALEKSANDR IVANOVICH HERZEN

[. . .] I sent you a copy of *Smoke* at the same
time as my letter. I read the review in the *Golos* and
also know that everyone is cursing me—reds, whites,
from above, from below, and from the side, especially
from the side. Even indignant verses have appeared.
But somehow I am not embarrassed—not because I
imagine myself impeccable, but because it is like water
off a duck's back. Imagine, I even rejoice that my
limited Westerner, Potugin, turns up at the very time
of the pan-Slavic dance and *prisiadka,*[7] where Pogodin,
under the overshadowing right hand of Filaret, so dash-
ingly turns a step to the harmonica.

---

[7] This is a Russian dance characterized by squatting; Americans call it a *kazatsky.*

[198]

Baden-Baden, May 23/June 4, 1867

TO PAVEL VASIL'EVICH ANNENKOV

[. . .] It seems to me that at no time has anyone been so unanimously cursed as I have been for
Smoke. Stones are flying from all sides. Fedor Tiutchev
has even written indignant verses. And just think—I
am not embarrassed at all. [. . .] On the contrary,
I am very happy that my downtrodden Potugin, who
believes solely in European civilization, appears with
castanets at the very climax of the Pan-Slavic fandango,
and Pogodin so amusingly turns handsprings in the
midst of this. [. . .]

[199]

Baden-Baden, May 23/June 4, 1867

TO DMITRI IVANOVICH PISAREV

[. . .] You, like almost all other Russian readers, do not like *Smoke*. In view of such unanimity, I
cannot help wondering about the value of my brain-
child—but your arguments do not strike me as accurate.
You remind me of Bazarov [in *Fathers and Children*]
and invoke me: "Cain, where is Abel, thy brother?"
But you have not considered that even if a Bazarov existed (which I do not doubt), he could not be dealt
with in literature. He ought not to be treated from a
critical standpoint—but to treat him from any other
would be inappropriate. All he can do now is to *declare*
why he is a Bazarov. It would be completely fanciful
and even fraudulent to talk about him or in his name
until he has declared himself. Hence the "tower" is of
no use; still, I do not think I chose so low a hillock as

you presume. One can still survey all of Russia from the heights of European civilization. You believe that *Potugin* (you probably mean *him* and not *Litvinov*) is the Arkadi [of *Fathers and Children*]. Here, however, I must say that your critical sense has betrayed you; the two characters have nothing in common; Arkadi has no convictions of any kind, while Potugin will die an avowed dyed-in-the-wool Westerner. If the smoldering but inextinguishable fire within him is not felt, my efforts have been in vain. Perhaps [Potugin] is dear to me alone, but I rejoice that he has appeared and is being cursed right now, at the very time of the Pan-Slavic drinking party everyone is surrendering to at home. I rejoice that even now I have succeeded in displaying the word "civilization" on my banner—let them hurl filth at it from all sides. *Si etiam omnes, ego non.* [Even if everyone else does so, I will not.] And there is nothing to say about Litvinov, either, he too is no Arkadi; he is an ordinary honest man, and that is all. I could easily have inserted such a sentence as: "However, we really have clever and strong workers toiling in silence." But from respect for both the workers and the silence, I have preferred to do without that phrase; young people do not need honey smeared on their lips—at least I don't think so. [. . .]

[200]

Baden-Baden, June 16/28, 1867

TO PAVEL VASIL'EVICH ANNENKOV

[. . .] As for *Smoke*, I assure you that here too I agree, as always, with Goethe's saying:

Mit keiner Arbeit hab' ich geprahlt,
Und was ich gemalt hab', hab' ich gemalt.

[Of no work have I ever boasted
And what I have portrayed, I have portrayed.]

But it is the public that will finally decide. You cannot please everyone. [. . .]

{ 201 }

Baden-Baden, June 16/28, 1867

TO IVAN PETROVICH BORISOV

[. . .] You do not like *Smoke*; everything indicates that no one in Russia does. However, I am such a confirmed sinner that not only do I not repent, I even persist. I will add a preface to the separately published edition of the novel in which I will indicate even more strongly that we Russians must learn, as we once did, from the Germans, just as the Germans learned from the Romans, etc. Whether they curse me in all the churches or simply throw me into a mud puddle is no longer any headache of mine. [. . .]

{ 202 }

Baden-Baden, September 24/October 6, 1867

TO VASILI PETROVICH BOTKIN

[. . .] Mr. Eugene Schuyler, my American translator, was passing through here and handed me four copies of *Fathers and Children*. Hence, there is no need to be concerned about them. The translation shows that he worked from the French, and that his knowledge of Russian is somewhat limited. He has been appointed American consul in Moscow and has already gone there. [. . .]

[203]

Baden-Baden, October 7/19, 1867

TO PAVEL VASIL'EVICH ANNENKOV

A French writer is living here, a M. Ducamp, whom I am friendly with and, to a certain degree, indebted to. He has written a novel, *Les Forces perdues*, and, upon learning that I liked it, asked me to help get it translated into Russian, which I did promise. (All this happened last winter.) In March I saw Mme E. N. Akhmatov, the publisher of *Sobranie perevodov* [*Collected Translations*], etc., and I agreed to write a preface for the translation to appear in her series; as far as I know, it has long been ready. But because of my peculiar laziness, I finished the preface only today (blushing inwardly, I told Ducamp that I had sent it off long ago), and I am now forwarding it to you. Read the product, correct it if necessary, take it to Mme Akhmatov, and hand it to her with great apologies from me. I, for my part, am writing her [both] about the preface and about my giving you the right to make the necessary changes. Do not lose any time, and ask Mme Akhmatov to rush the printing because I am dying of shame here before M. Ducamp. You would be obliging me very, very much by doing this. [. . .]

[204]

Baden-Baden, December 12, 1867

TO ALEKSANDR IVANOVICH HERZEN

[. . .] According to my understanding, Europe is neither so old nor Russia so new as you imagine. We are in the same boat, and no especially new message is expected after us. But if God grants you a hundred years of life, you will die the last Slavophile and will write learned, amusing, profound, and paradoxical articles that [. . . every reader will find] impossible not to read through. I regret only that you feel obliged to deck yourself out in clothing that does not quite fit you. Believe me or not, but all your articles are useless for *influencing* the European public. . . . For example, just one great Russian painter's work would be better propaganda than thousands of dissertations about the artistic potential of our breed. People in general are crude, and do not in any way need justice or impartiality; but a blow between the eyes or at the pocket is something else again. [. . .]

[205]

Baden-Baden, December 13/25, 1867

TO ALEKSANDR IVANOVICH HERZEN

[. . .] Your son, as a steady and practical person, believes only in science—i.e., he reckons upon it alone—but you, a romantic and an artist, believe in the people, in a special breed of people, in a famous race. . . . And all this thanks to what has been contrived by gentlemen and fastened on the people; democratic social tendencies of the "mir" and "artel" type are completely alien to the people. Russia does not know how to avoid the mir, and as for the artel, I shall never forget the expression on the face of a commoner as he told me [some time] this year: "A man who has not known the artel does not know the noose." I hope to God that the inhuman, exploiting principles on which our artels act are never adopted on a broader scale. [. . .] You point out some Petr to me and say: "Look, Petr is dying: he is scarcely breathing." I agree!

But that scarcely implies that Ivan is healthy. Especially if you take into account that Ivan has precisely the same complexion as Petr has, and has the same illness. No, my friend, no matter how you look at it, old Goethe is right "*Der Mensch (der europäischer* [*sic*] *Mensch) ist nicht geboren, frei zu sein.*" ["Man (European man) was not born to be free."] Why, the question is physiological, and a slave society with subdivisions into classes is encountered at every step in nature (the bees, etc.). Of all the European nations, the Russian itself needs freedom least. The Russian, left to himself, *inevitably develops into an Old Believer:* that is where he is being driven and pushed. Have you yourself not been sufficiently burned by this question to realize the denseness, darkness, and tyranny that exist? I answer as Scribe does, "*prenez mon ours.*" Take science and civilization and treat them with homoeopathy bit by bit. And then, perhaps, like Ivan Sergeevich Aksakov, you will reach the point of recommending Orthodoxy as a cure-all to Europe. Faith in the people is, in its own way, a religion, too. You are an inconsistent Slavophile (which, incidentally, makes me personally very happy). And things turn out so that each of us is astonished at the other's *failure to see* what seems so clear. [. . .]

{ 206 }

Baden-Baden, January 13 [O.S.], *1868*
TO IAKOV PETROVICH POLONSKI

[. . .] You are thanking me needlessly for my frankness; how could I fail to be frank with you when in our time the sacred flame of poesy burns within you alone? I am not counting Aleksei [Konstantinovich]

Tolstoy or Maikov! Fet has lost the last particle of his touch, and the Minaev gentlemen and their ilk cannot be discussed. Even their teacher, Mr. Nekrasov, is a poet of strainings and tricks; I tried to read his collected poems again a few days ago. . . . No! Poetry did not even spend a night there—and I threw that chewed-up papier-mâché with its strong vodka sauce into the corner. You alone can and must write verses. [. . .]

[207]

Baden-Baden, February 14/26, 1868

TO PAVEL VASIL'EVICH ANNENKOV

[. . .] I read both Tolstoy's novel [8] and your article about it. Without flattery I tell you that not in a long time have you written anything more intelligent and sensible; the whole article testifies to its author's truthful and delicate critical sense. Only in two or three spots are a lack of clarity and a seeming confusion of ideas noticeable. The novel itself aroused my most lively interest. Dozens of pages in a row are wonderful and first class—such as everything descriptive, or dealing with everyday life (the hunt, the drive in the night, etc.). But the historical supplement (which has really made the readers rapturous) is a puppet show and a fraud. Just as Voroshilov in *Smoke* throws dust into people's eyes by quoting the latest word on science (without knowing the first or the second thing about it —which the honest Germans cannot even conjecture), so Tolstoy startles the reader with the tip of [Tsar] Aleksandr's shoe, or with Speranski's laugh, making one

[8] Only three of the six volumes of *War and Peace* had come out so far in the first edition.

believe that the author, having deciphered such trifles, knows *everything*. But all Tolstoy knows are these trifles. This is a trick and nothing more, but the public has fallen for it. A lot could also be said about Tolstoy's so-called psychology. Not a single character is genuinely developed (as you, by the way, have so excellently observed). What he mercilessly places on the lips and within the perception of his every character—giving the vacillations and the vibrations of one and the same emotion or situation—is the old mannerism: "I love," he says, "but really, I hate," etc., etc. How sickening and boring all these quasi-subtle reflections, meditations, and observations of his own emotions are! Tolstoy does not appear to know any other psychology, or else he deliberately ignores it. And how agonizing are the premeditated and stubborn repetitions of one and the same brush stroke—the downy upper lip of Princess [Lise] Bolkonski, etc.

For all that, the novel does contain things that in the whole of Europe no one but Tolstoy could have written, and that make me break out in goose pimples and a fire of enthusiasm. [. . .]

[208]

Baden-Baden, February 27/March 10, 1868
TO IVAN PETROVICH BORISOV

[. . .] I read Tolstoy's novel with great delight, although it contains much I am not completely satisfied with. Everything dealing with mores and war is wonderful. Things are there which will not die as long as the Russian language exists. But the entire *historical* side is—excuse the expression—a puppet show. I shall not even mention that there is no trace of a genuine depiction of the period. What do we find out about [Tsar] Aleksandr, Speranski, and the others, except the merest trifles, selected capriciously by the author and elevated into character traits? This is a fraud in its own way. [. . .] Read Annenkov's very intelligent (but, as usual, somewhat obscure) article about Tolstoy's novel in the *Vestnik Evropy*. There is no genuine development of the characters; they all move forward by jumps. Furthermore, there is an enormous amount of the old psychological hubbub ("What," he says, "am I thinking? What are they thinking about me? Am I in love, or can I not stand it?" etc.) that positively constitutes Tolstoy's monomania.

But, for all that, the novel has so many first-rate beauties, so much vitality, truth, and freshness, that one cannot help but admit that, with the appearance of *War and Peace*, Tolstoy has taken the top place among all our present writers. I am awaiting the fourth volume impatiently. [. . .]

[209]

Baden-Baden, March 6 [O.S.], 1868

TO IAKOV PETROVICH POLONSKI

Your last letter is permeated with such despair that I think I would pay to find words of encouragement to cheer you up.

I would like to tell you one thing: just as, in the long run, no one can pass himself off as being greater than he really is, so anything that really exists cannot fail to be acknowledged . . . in due time. You did not invent your talent; it really exists and, hence, will not be lost. And that you sometimes come out badly in our anti-poetic time is something about which nothing can be done; but you ought not to despair. If a man does not destroy himself, no one will destroy him.

Look, you must try to get a little more out of Vol'f. Sitting there by the sea, you must wait for good weather—without folding your arms—and continue to work. Whatever they say, you are the author of—well, at least *Kuznechik* (*The Grasshopper*), and *Kuznechik* will be read when many of the present day's profound names and works have been engulfed by oblivion.

I am very glad that in connection with my *Istoriia* (*History* [*of Lieutenant Ergunov*]) you trusted your own impression rather than the judgment of Mr. P. K. After the death of a certain Russian emigrant (V. I. K.), Mr. P. K. (and I do not say this because he criticizes me, but because I observed him) went to great labors to fill the post with the *most stupid* of our contemporaries. A real department-head *dunce* of the first class, with the picture of the goddess *Idiocy* in his buttonhole![9] In any case, he has in his usual way crawled into the mud, asserting that I wrote my trifle in a hurry and in feuilletonistic style; actually, I never worked so hard on a piece; I rewrote the darned thing three times! But enough of that.

There is no review of *War and Peace* by Annenkov in the *Russki vestnik*—but there is one in the *Vestnik Evropy*. Whatever he says is very intelligent and sensible, although there are some confusing expressions. Tolstoy's novel is an astonishing work, but its weakest part is precisely what has enraptured the public: the historical part and the psychology. His history is a trick that drives fine trifles into your eyes; his psychology is a

[9] A pun on *deistvitel'ny tainy sovetnik*, the civil-service equivalent of a full general, and *deistvitel'ny tainy*, meaning "genuine [and] secret."

capricious and one-sided racket about always the same emotions. Everything dealing with the day-to-day life and war, everything descriptive is first class—and we have no masters like Tolstoy.

The lines you wrote about me can also serve you as a positive example: a certain gentleman, not embarrassed in the slightest, asserts that, out of my hurt egotism, I have sacrificed . . . honor, just as Chernyshevski declared in print that I was *bribed with money* to change Rudin's character for the worse. What about all that? It is all like spring freshets; it will run off and not a trace will remain. And it is no reason to cause you grief.

I send you friendly greetings and wish you everything good, starting with a courageous spirit.

[210]

Baden-Baden, March 13, 1868

TO HIS DAUGHTER, PAULINE

[. . .] If my uncle had not acted so infamously toward me, I would have been in a position to give you 50,000 francs. However, I have just spent 75,000 to buy back the bills of exchange I gave him eleven years ago (without actually receiving a sou) to be presented upon my death. And not only did he present them now, with me alive, but he is also having himself paid with compound interest!!—that is to say, more than twice the principal. This has come as a blow to me, and with the present state of affairs in Russia, my fortune is pretty well shaken. [. . .]

{ 211 }

Baden-Baden, February 12/April 12 [sic], 1868
TO AFANASI AFANAS'EVICH FET

I have just finished the fourth volume of W*ar and Peace*. It contains intolerable things and astonishing things, and the astonishing things, which essentially predominate, are magnificent; none of us [Russians] has written anything better, and rarely has anything so good ever been written. The fourth and the first volumes are weaker than the second and especially the third; the third volume is almost a *chef d'oeuvre*. [. . .]

{ 212 }

Baden-Baden, April 8/20, 1868
TO IVAN PETROVICH BORISOV

[. . .] I received the fourth volume of Tolstoy [W*ar and Peace*], but I have not managed to finish it yet. Judging by the magazine reviews, I am afraid he has devoted himself too much to philosophy and, as sometimes happens to him, has taken the bit between his teeth and rushed off to fight and kick for nothing. [. . .]

{ 213 }

Baden-Baden, April 13/25, 1868
TO PAVEL VASIL'EVICH ANNENKOV

[. . .] Tolstoy's fourth volume has been delivered to me. . . . It contains a lot that is beautiful, but its deformities cannot be overlooked, either. A misfortune ensues when a self-educated man, even a Tolstoy, undertakes to philosophize. He inevitably saddles his hobby horse and thinks up some sort of a system, such as, for example, historical fatalism, and then begins to write. Wherever he touches the earth, he is like Antaeus, and regains all his powers: the death of the old Prince [Nikolai Andreevich Bolkonski], Alpatych, the revolt in the village—all that is highly impressive. Natasha, however, is turning out rather weak. [. . .]

{ 214 }

Spasskoe, June 13/25, 1868

TO PAULINE VIARDOT (NEE GARCIA)

[. . .] The impression Russia makes on me now is disastrous. I do not know whether it all comes from the recent famine—but it seems to me that I have never seen the dwellings so miserable and so ruined, the faces so wan and so sad, with taverns everywhere and incurable poverty. Spasskoe is the only village I have seen thus far in which the thatched roofs are not open, and God knows that even Spasskoe is worlds apart from the least village in the Black Forest. [. . .]

{ 215 }

Baden-Baden, July 16/28, 1868

TO NIKOLAI SERGEEVICH TURGENEV

[. . .] I spent two weeks in Spasskoe and, like Marius, can say that I have sat upon the ruins of Carthage. In the present year alone the "fetid elder" [1]

---

[1] Turgenev's uncle, Nikolai Nikolaevich Turgenev, had been managing his estates in Russia while the novelist was abroad.

—that plunderer of money, cattle, carriages, furniture, and other possessions—has fleeced me of 3,500 silver[2] rubles (I had to pay a 5,000-ruble debt of his). I will not mention that he left the estate in loathsome disorder and chaos, that he paid no one, tricked everyone, etc. I discovered that he was no longer at Katushishchi, and am very glad of that. During my entire stay at Spasskoe I was like a hare on the run; I could not stick my head into the garden without serfs, muzhiks, small merchants, retired soldiers, sluts, peasant women, the blind, the lame, neighboring landowners of both sexes, priests, and sextons—my own and other people's—rushing forward from behind trees, from behind bushes, and almost from out of the ground to assault me—all of them emaciated from hunger, with their mouths agape like jackdaws, throwing themselves at my feet, shouting hoarsely: "Dear master! Ivan Sergeevich! Save us! . . . Save us, we are dying!" I finally had to save myself by fleeing lest I be stripped of everything. Moreover, a terrible year is on the way: the spring crops have perished; the rye is enormous in the stalk, but the ears contain not a kernel. What a picture Russia presents now—this land everyone contends is so rich! The roofs are *all* uncovered, the fences are down, and not a single new building is to be seen except for taverns. The horses and the cows are dead; the people are thin—three coachmen could hardly lift my trunk! Dust is everywhere, like a bank of clouds; around St.

[2] The value of paper rubles in silver rubles varied considerably; back in 1839 the official rate had been set at seven to two, but the value of the paper ruble so deteriorated that paper money became unconvertible again about 1855. See Florinsky: *Russia: A History and an Interpretation* (New York: The Macmillan Co.; 1955).

Petersburg everything is burning up—the forests, the houses, the very *land*. . . . All you see is people, stretched out at full length, sleeping on their bellies. Feebleness, inertia, dismal filth, and poverty are everywhere. The picture is not a happy one, but it is *accurate*. [. . .]

. [216]

Baden-Baden, August 8, 1868

TO JULIAN SCHMIDT

[. . .] In addition, I also wrote articles of criticism, etc., as well as—*alas!*—verses and even long poems, which, however, are so miserably mediocre that they can only be compared to muddy and tepid water. This unfortunate period of my literary career lasted three years—1843 to 1846—and when my friends feel like getting me angry, they quote my verses. [. . .]

[217]

Karlsruhe, November 16/28, 1868

TO IVAN PETROVICH BORISOV

[. . .] I sent my latest story off to Pavel Annenkov and have already received encouraging comments from him. Let us see what the public will say. I do not know the purpose of the rumor about my attacking the Slavophiles in that story; nothing like that is in it. [The story] is simply an exposition of the tragic fate of a girl who flashed by me in my youth. By the by, about the Slavophiles—how faithfully you characterized the manner of Ivan Aksakov! I burst out laughing. The pen really squeaks. [. . .]

{ 218 }

Karlsruhe, December 1, 1868

TO LUDWIG PIETSCH

[. . .] Yes, my friend, I have become fifty years old—or, as you euphemistically express it, I have left behind the first half of my century. But I do not hope to see the end of the coming—the next—quarter [of a century]. Moreover, I know the éxact year of my death: 1881. My mother told it to me in a dream: the same integers as in the year of my birth—1818—only in different order. Yes, yes, I shall most certainly die in 1881, if not earlier (or later). [. . .]

{ 219 }

Karlsruhe, December 16 [O.S.], 1868

TO IAKOV PETROVICH POLONSKI

[. . .] Goncharov's peculiarities can be explained by his bad health and by his too exclusively literary life. When the people on earth imagined that our little globe was the center of the universe, they also ascribed an exaggerated importance to everything earthly. The idea that some fifty years hence not even a speck of dust will remain of your work has a chilling effect on your egotism, although, on the other hand, you ought not to give way to the idea completely and, perhaps, give up all work. But human happiness consists in acting out of momentary emotions and passions, at variance with the laws of logic. Your nose is built to wheeze—and you will wheeze, whether wheezing is useful or not. The result of all this philosophizing is that I am awaiting the appearance of [Goncharov's] *Precipice* with great impatience. [. . .]

I am now sitting over my literary *Reminiscences*, experiencing the distant past in my mind. . . . Sometimes I find it sad and sometimes pleasant . . . but even the pleasure is not without sadness. Whoever has turned 50 cannot abandon the minor key. [. . .]

[220]

Karlsruhe, January 12/24, 1869

TO PAVEL VASIL'EVICH ANNENKOV

Yesterday I received the first issue of the V*estnik Evropy* and finished [the first installment of] Goncharov's novel [*The Precipice*] within the day. . . . I am horrified even to state the degree of my disillusionment!! Not to mention the intolerable and impossible wordiness—it is beyond all measure—not to mention Mme Belovodov (who reminds me of a German pharmacist), not to mention her most repulsive conversations with Raiski (which smack of cud-chewing—and a cud-chewing produced by dry hay), how old-fashioned, conventional and *lieu commun* [commonplace] all of this is! What an absence of genuine and vital truth!

No! After L. N. Tolstoy on the one hand and [Fedor Mikhailovich] Reshetnikov (do not be astonished; I value him highly) on the other, such rancid and insubstantial literature is no longer possible! It must be filed in the archives. And what kind of a wish is it to spend time on such a hackneyed character as Raiski—to butter him up and re-butter him so verbosely and so lovingly, and put him into one's mouth and take him out again? And what kind of old maid's manners and a nervous, hysterical constitution is this? The very style, which once enraptured me, now suggests to me the face of a bureaucrat—well shaved, fine-look-

ing, and lifeless—with sideburns extending in a thread
from the ears to the corners of the lips. You are just
relaxing when you hit Tat'iana Markovna's house and
the district seat. . . . The book has some good things
—but second rate, at best. . . . Just think of any
description in *War and Peace.* No, I repeat, this is all
outdated. I do not know what public success is being
forecast for this novel, but I do know that most probably only banal people will become enthusiastic about
it—whether they are clever or stupid makes no difference. It is written by a bureaucrat for bureaucrats and
their wives. And what sort of women would like Mme
Belovodov! ! ! ! ! ! *Et maintenant, prenez ma tête.* [And
now, cut my head off.] [. . .]

[221]

Karlsruhe, February 9/21, 1869

TO PAVEL VASIL'EVICH ANNENKOV

[. . .] Well, my friend, I am reading the continuation of [Goncharov's] *Precipice,* and my hair is
falling out from boredom. I do not remember, in any
literature, such diabolically insufferable conversations.
Indeed, all the characters—Marfen'ka (I have just come
upon Vera, but even at this point she bears the im-
print of an eight-page conversation), Mark, and all the
others impress me as commonplace, with Goncharov
some sort of god, king, and poet of commonplace—
a deus loci communis. Only two of the women are
conceived with vitality and originality—Marina, and
the wife of the impossibly boring Leonti Kozlov. Ivan
Aleksandrovich [Goncharov] has grown very old, and
his philosophy is moldy. And what an unfortunate
figure Raiski is! Can there be anything uglier than his

silent rapture when Marfen'ka sits on his lap? Oh, how contrived the whole thing is! [. . .]

[222]

Karlsruhe, February 12/24, 1869
TO IVAN PETROVICH BORISOV

I am very happy to hear that the fifth volume of *War and Peace* will soon appear. Despite all his weaknesses and eccentricities, and even despite all his nonsense, Tolstoy is a veritable giant among the other literary brethren and impresses me as does an elephant in a zoo: clumsy, even ridiculous, but enormous—and how intelligent! May God grant that he write twenty more volumes. [. . .]

[223]

Karlsruhe, February 18/March 2, 1869
TO VASILI PETROVICH BOTKIN

[. . .] The V*estnik Evropy* contains the first two parts of Goncharov's novel [*The Precipice*]; it has some fine passages, but its length is more than intolerable—especially in the conversations; the work is essentially boring and almost obsolete. [. . .]

[224]

Karlsruhe, February 18/March 2, 1869
TO ALEKSANDR IVANOVICH HERZEN

[. . .] Having passed fifty, a man lives as if in a fortress which is besieged, and, sooner or later, will be taken by Death. He must defend himself, and not, in Totleben's style, without sorties. [. . .]

{ 225 }

Karlsruhe, February 20/March 4, 1869

TO IAKOV PETROVICH POLONSKI

[. . .] The second part of [Goncharov's] *The Precipice* is, of course, better than the first, but here too there are unbearable expanses! As soon as the work reaches conversations or contemplation, it makes one yawn. Goncharov has even managed to spoil his Vera; she too contemplates and wastes time. Here is someone whose self-assurance you ought to borrow at least a particle of! Unlike him, you, for one, will not put it in your cheek, spit it out again, and chew it some more —to the wonder of all Europe. [. . .]

{ 226 }

Karlsruhe, February 27/March 11, 1869

TO IAKOV PETROVICH POLONSKI

[. . .] I understand very well that my permanent stay abroad harms my literary work, and to such an extent as perhaps to betray it completely; but that cannot be changed. Inasmuch as, throughout my literary career, I have never started from *ideas* but always from *characters* (even Potugin is based on a certain character), and as the lack of *characters* becomes more and more evident, my Muse will have nothing left to draw her pictures from. Then I shall put my brush under lock and key and begin to see how others behave. [. . .]

[227]

Karlsruhe, March 4/16, 1869

TO VASILI PETROVICH BOTKIN

[. . .] We are still enjoying Mozart and Beethoven, plus Schubert—the divine Schubert who possessed me completely for a while. Have you heard his
[C-Major] Quintet for two violins, *two* violoncellos,
and a viola—Opus 163, *posthume?* Here all a man can
do, my friend, is to throw himself on his face and sink
into a bliss of reverence. Even Beethoven has no such
andante! [. . .]

[228]

Karlsruhe, March 8 [O.S.], 1869

TO KONSTANTIN KONSTANTINOVICH SLUCHEVSKI

I hasten to answer your letter. Frankly, any [auto-]
biographical publication has always seemed highly pretentious to me, but to turn it down and [at the same
time] ascribe importance to it in general would be even
more pretentious. You might have found the factual
data of my completely unremarkable life in the very
same issue of *Der Salon* from which you borrowed the
photograph I sent. I was born on October 28 [O.S.],
1818, in Orel, the son of Sergei Nikolaevich Turgenev
and Varvara Petrovna [née] Lutovinov. I received my
primary education in Moscow, and attended lectures
at Moscow University and later at [St.] Petersburg
University. I went abroad in 1838 and almost perished
during a fire aboard the steamship *Nikolai I.* I attended
lectures in Berlin, then returned, and was attached to

the chancellery of the Minister of the Interior for about
a year. I began to take up literature in 1842. Because
of an article I had published about Gogol (actually it
was for A *Sportsman's Sketches*), I was sent to live
in my village in 1852, and spent two years there. Ever
since, I have sometimes been living abroad and sometimes in Russia. You see that my biography recalls the
biography of Emile Augier, who answered a similar
inquiry as follows: "*Je suis né, j'ai été vacciné, puis
quand je suis devenu grand, j'ai écrit des comédies*"
["I was born, I was vaccinated, and then, when I had
grown up, I wrote comedies"]. And indeed, what kind
of a wish is it to publish my picture, etc., *now*, when
my credit is completely exhausted? Who could be interested? The rest is the business of the *Illiustratsiia*.

[229]

Karlsruhe, March 12/24, 1869

TO IVAN PETROVICH BORISOV

. . . I have not yet received the fifth volume of
War and Peace, but if I may judge from the reviews
received here, our eccentric genius has really taken the
bit between his teeth. Can he possibly, from his dislike
of philosophy and empty phrases, have got into his
head such philosophy and empty phrases? What every
muzhik knows (such as the use of bread, and even the
use of the human brain, and of reason) must really be
uprooted. . . . That is genuine nonsense. And such
nonsense really had to steal into the head of the *most
gifted writer* in contemporary European literature! But
I am touched in advance by all the charming things
that will certainly abound in the fifth volume.

{ 230 }

Baden-Baden, April 14/26, 1869

TO IVAN PETROVICH BORISOV

[. . .] What you say about [Goncharov's] *Precipice* is quite just. The fourth part, with its terrible and pathetic scenes, has finally appeared. . . . What merciless twaddle, what inexhaustible and flat arguments and reflections! . . . How can he constantly spoil himself so assiduously? And what kind of a figure is the tempter, Mark Volokhov? Why does that swineherd (I cannot imagine a better word) attract Vera? Where, finally, is the power, the beauty, and the intelligence? All one can see is the author squirming in the sweat of his brow. . . . But many people will like this work. [. . .]

I have been promised the fifth volume of *War and Peace*, but so far—nothing. This annoys me very much. Tolstoy infuriates and pleases—a real man, but crazy. [. . .]

{ 231 }

Baden-Baden, May 2/14, 1869

TO THE EDITOR OF THE *Sankt-Peterburgskie vedomosti*

Only today have I read the feuilleton in the *Golos* which mentions my "Reminiscences of Belinski." I have no intention of debasing myself by denying the shameful motives the writer ascribes to me, but I do not wonder that he does ascribe them to me: everyone judges others by what he himself is. In expatiating on my "stories," the writer of the feuilleton took the liberty of calling them lies. In giving back to him with

considerable loathing the expression that belongs to
that anonymous pen-pusher, I shall limit myself to
declaring that I do not renounce a single word of the
few lines about the "editor of the thick magazine." [3]
He is so insignificant in himself that I would not, of
course, have mentioned him even in passing had fate
not interwoven his life with the life of Belinski. But I
repeat: every word of those lines is in accord with the
strictest truth; everyone else knows it, and *Mr. Kraevski
himself knows it*.[4] I am almost ashamed to dwell upon
such trifles, but who on earth does not know that the
publisher of the "thick magazine" in whom Mr. Kraevski recognized himself is devoid of any aesthetic understanding, does not wield a pen, and is calculating? (I
did not say anything more about him.) The epithet
"calculating" should rather have flattered him as a man
(for the most part) of commerce. And that Belinski
was paid a completely insignificant *annual* salary by
Kraevski, that he [Belinski] would frequently point in
indignation and despair to the books being sent to him
for analysis—these are facts to whose accuracy anyone
who knew him can testify. But the writer of the feuilleton, not content with the above-mentioned libel, did
not scruple to publish the following:

"Mr. Turgenev must have known better than many
others from his own experience (italics in original) how
little this publisher calculated, and with what readiness
he loaned his contributors money, even without hope
of repayment."

Mr. Kraevski gave me, just as he did many other

[3] "The thick magazines" were—and are—generally month-
lies of roughly 100 to 250 pages which frequently serialize new
literature.

[4] Kraevski had been Belinski's employer.

beginning writers, small sums in advance, which we then repaid with literary work at suitable fees. Mr. Kraevski took his profit, and we did not complain. Similar arrangements are common in business; but merchants do not usually boast of their readiness to lend money. I settled all accounts with Mr. Kraevski long ago. As for the implication in the last phrase quoted, my entire past life gives me the right to treat those words with the utmost contempt. Everyone else knows that also, and *so does Mr. Kraevski.*

I would be very much obliged to you, my dear sir, if you would put this necessary explanation in the columns of your distinguished newspaper.

[232]

Baden-Baden, May 30, 1869

TO ALEKSEI MIKHAILOVICH ZHEMCHUZHNIKOV

[. . .] It would have been good if you yourself had collected and printed all your verses; I am sure that the general appearance of your talent would have been helped by being defined more clearly and completely in that manner. But do not accept Nekrasov's assistance; apparently you do not need his money, and he inevitably will either swindle you or do you mischief. He is a punchinello of his own kind who cannot go anywhere without leaving traces of his odor. [. . .]

[233]

Baden-Baden, May 19 [O.S.], 1869

TO IAKOV PETROVICH POLONSKI

[. . .] Even before I received your letter, I had

decided not to answer Kraevski. . . . Indeed, is attach-
ing importance to such dirty gossip worth while? To
tell the truth, I have become so indifferent to all literary affairs—what angered me about Kraevski was the
implication that I had almost stolen money—that if
I learned today that the young people who were . . .
after me until now had suddenly taken a notion to
gild me in a new way, I would not bend an ear or
lift a finger to achieve that. It is all vanity of vanities.
[. . .]

[234]

Baden-Baden, May 24/June 5, 1869

TO IVAN PETROVICH BORISOV

[. . .] I am now reading the fifth part of W*ar
and Peace* and I take turns getting angry and waxing
enthusiastic. The lack of a free approach, of genuine
artistic freedom, in so great a talent produces a painful
impression. [. . .]

[235]

Baden-Baden, June 8, 1869

TO LUDWIG PIETSCH

[. . .] Precisely because of Bazarov I have been
(and still am) pelted with so much mud and filth;
so much invective and abuse have been heaped on my
head (which was sentenced to the spirits of hell)—
Vidocq, Judas bought for gold, fool, ass, poison toad,
and spittoon were the least things said about me—I
would be glad to show that other nations do not look
at the matter that way at all. [. . .]

{ 236 }

Baden-Baden, June 18/30, 1869

TO IVAN PETROVICH BORISOV

[. . .] I have not yet been able to get the better
of the last part of [Goncharov's] *Precipice*, but I am
rereading *War and Peace* with the same contradictory
emotions. Whatever is good in that novel is wonderful,
while whatever is bad, weak, or pretentious is nevertheless not boring and is even interesting, in a certain
sense, as a monstrosity created by a man of genius.
[. . .]

{ 237 }

Baden-Baden, August 24/*September* 5, 1869

TO IVAN PETROVICH BORISOV

[. . .] A few days ago I went to Munich to see
the première of Wagner's opera *Das Rheingold*, and
something else, too. Munich is an interesting city. The
King of Bavaria, as you may know, is Wagner's bosom
friend, even his *strange* friend, and Wagner's music is
an affair of state in Bavaria. But what I attended was,
as a result of various most amusing and confused intrigues—from which Aristophanes could have derived
a very interesting moral, satirical, and political comedy
—only the dress rehearsal, not the opera [the première].
The music and the libretto are equally intolerable, but
you know there are Germans for whom Wagner is
almost Christ. The whole muddle amuses me greatly.
Someday I will tell about it, perhaps even in print.

I cannot work at all and have not even finished
my *Reminiscences*—the devil take them. My literary
screw has been smashed. [. . .]

[238]

Baden-Baden, October 25/November 6, 1869
TO ALEKSANDRA VASIL'EVNA PLETNEV

[. . .] Your spouse [Peter Pletnev] belonged to
the group of people who, both in life and after death,
have nothing to fear from the truth; and by telling the
truth about him [in my *Reminiscences*] as best I could,
I thought that I would show my respect for him.
[. . .]

Several times he himself used the words that apparently troubled you—"that everything came his way"
—in his talks with me. [. . .]

[239]

Baden-Baden, October 25/November 6, 1869
TO PAVEL VASIL'EVICH ANNENKOV

I knew that my *Reminiscences*,[5] however mild and
unpretentious, would cause me much unpleasantness,
and this partially excuses the unwillingness with which
I wrote them. You know what an uproar [my] article
on Belinski caused—Kraevski almost accusing me of
theft, etc. Now, because of the selection about Pletnev,
I have received a letter from his widow which I am
adding in the original with the request that it be returned to me. It already seems that the selection has—
how do you express it—*eu grisaille* [turned gray]. No!
I turn out to have libeled Pletnev by casting doubts on

___
[5] These memoirs are now available in English. See Ivan
Turgenev: *Turgenev's Literary Reminiscences*, translated and
with an Introduction by David Magarshack, and with a Prefatory
Essay by Edmund Wilson (New York: Farrar, Straus, and
Cudahy; 1958).

his erudition and intrepidity. I would not have paid
any attention except for my profound respect for Mme
Pletnev—one of the best women I have ever had occasion to meet. I am very sorry that my words have
grieved her; a feeling of piety toward a husband's memory is very honorable and, in this case, understandable.
But do my comments on Pletnev really go far beyond
what posterity will say about him—if it talks about him
at all? I hope that my letter [to her] will calm her
down somewhat. [. . .]

[240]

Baden-Baden, October 30 [O.S.], *1869*

TO AFANASI AFANAS'EVICH FET

[. . .] In my mind, I can see you first with a
gun in your hands and then simply chatting about
Shakespeare's being a fool and saying that, in Lev Tolstoy's words, only activity that is unconscious bears
fruit. How is it, do you think, that the Americans built
a railroad from New York to San Francisco—in their
sleep, and without consciousness? Or is that not *fruit?*
But as for philosophizing, we shall manage to indulge
in it at our next meeting.

[241]

Baden-Baden, November 13/25, 1869

TO IVAN PETROVICH BORISOV

[. . .] P.S. But what will you say about the
purely republican elections in the city of Paris? It
seems that the time for the downfall of the [Second
French] Empire is approaching. [. . .]

{ 242 }

Baden-Baden, December 16, 1869

TO JULIAN SCHMIDT

I have a request, my dear friend. The thing is that Pisemski, whom I told about the success of his novel,[6] would like to correspond with Mr. Keisler, the translator, and offer him his new novel, *Vzbalamuchennoe more* [*The Turbulent Sea*]. This is a vivid picture of the Russian way of life during the sixties which violently scourges our demagogues. It has some magnificent scenes, but the humor in it is even more ruthless than in *Tysiacha dush* [*A Thousand Souls*], although the general conception is weaker. If the German public liked *A Thousand Souls*, it will undoubtedly like *Sea* even more. Will you be kind enough to send me Dr. Kreisler's[7] address? [. . .]

{ 243 }

Baden-Baden, December 21 [*O.S.*]*, 1869*

TO AFANASI AFANAS'EVICH FET

To speak honestly, I, a sinner, little understood your last letter. I scented in it the same trend that fills half of Tolstoy's *War and Peace*, and I therefore shall not intrude. The *cruel* words "Europe, pistol, civilization" produce no effect upon you; on the other hand, other words—"*Rus*',[8] *gashnik*,[9] and nonsense"—do.

[6] *Tysiacha dush* [*A Thousand Souls*].
[7] The source spells the name Keisler (or Kreisler) both ways; the correct spelling has not been available to me.
[8] *Rus'* is the poetic name for Russia in Russian; it has no English equivalent, but roughly corresponds to "Albion" used in English for England.
[9] The source gives Fet's own definition of *gashnik* (which is not in Ushakov's standard Russian dictionary) as "a cotton braid or rope run through the upper limit of underwear in order to hold it up at the waist."

Everyone to his taste. I heartily rejoice in the success of your peasants' way of life which you talk about, but I do not believe at all in the mir or in the *fallow land*, which, in your opinion, is so necessary. I know only that all these praiseworthy special features of our life are in no way peculiar to us exclusively. They can all be found, down to the last iota, in the present or the past of that Europe which you reject so convulsively. The mir existed among the Arabs (hence they too died of hunger, but the Kabyle, who did not have it, did not). *Fallow land*, mutual guarantees—all this did exist or does exist in England and in Germany (for the most part, "did exist," because it has been abolished). There is nothing new under the sun, believe me, even in [your village of] Stepanovka; even the three stages of your philosophy are not new. As Vasili Botkin used to say, let Tolstoy discover the Mediterranean. [. . .]

[244]

Baden-Baden, December 24 [O.S.], *1869*
TO IAKOV PETROVICH POLONSKI

[. . .] P.S. It seems that everyone is dissatisfied with my article "On *Fathers and Children*." This shows me that one ought not to tell the truth all the time, for every word in the article is the truth itself—as I see it, of course.

[245]

Baden-Baden, December 24, 1869/January 4, 1870
TO IVAN PETROVICH BORISOV

[. . .] My little article about *Fathers and Children* turns out to have satisfied no one. [. . .] Even

Annenkov has rebuked me strongly. But, nevertheless, every word in it is the most sacred truth, at least in my opinion. Apparently the author does not always know what he creates; my emotions toward Bazarov— my personal emotions—were essentially confused. (God knows whether I loved him or hated him!) Nevertheless, the character was so delineated that he came to life immediately and began to act in his own way. What difference does it make in the long run what the author thinks of his own work? It is itself, and he is himself; but I repeat—my article is as sincere as a sermon.

[246]

Baden-Baden, January 10/22, 1870

TO PAVEL VASIL'EVICH ANNENKOV

[. . .] Death especially "stinks" to me because a few days ago I had an unexpected opportunity to smell my fill of it: to wit, I received an invitation from a friend in Paris [Maxime Ducamp] to be present not only at the execution of Tropmann, but [also] when the sentence of death was announced to him, at his *"toilette"* [getting dressed], etc. There were eight of us in all. I will never forget that terrible night, in the course of which *"I have supp'd full of horrors,"* [1] and acquired a definitive loathing for the death penalty in general and for the way it is carried out in France in particular. I have already begun a letter to you in which I narrate everything in detail and which, if you take a notion to do so, you may publish in the *Sankt-Peterburgskie vedomosti*. Let me say but one thing now:

[1] Quoted in English in the original. "I have supp'd full with horrors" comes from *Macbeth*, V,v,13.

such courage and contempt for death as Tropmann had, I could never have imagined. But the whole thing is horrible . . . , horrible. [. . .] [2]

[247]

Baden-Baden, January 25, 1870

TO MIKHAIL VASIL'EVICH ADEEV

[. . .] And now let me say a few words about myself. There is no doubt that a Russian writer who has settled in Baden by that very fact, condemns his writing to an early end. I have no illusions on that score, but since anything else is impossible, there is no point in even talking about it.

The "strange story" about which you talk is a trifle, but I am not capable of anything more now. Are you really so submerged in what is "contemporary" that you will not tolerate any *non-contemporary* characters? I have *"lagged behind"* with *my Sophia:* now, really! Why, perhaps I shall seize upon even more distant a past; *Sophia does not arouse anything but "contemptuous pity"*; but in my opinion that is a lot.

Must every character really and without fail be something like a copybook: "that is how one must (or must not) behave?" Such people have lived; hence, they have a right to be depicted in art. I admit no other immortality: and this immortality, the immortality of human life (in the eyes of art and history), is the basis for our entire work. You find that I am attracted to mysticism, and cite as examples the *Istoria*, "Phantoms," and "Ergunov" (although I myself cannot see

[2] "The Execution of Tropmann" is now available in English in David Magarshack's translation of *Turgenev's Literary Reminiscences* (New York: Farrar, Straus, and Cudahy; 1958).

anything mystical in Ergunov—I merely wanted to present the imperceptibility of the transition from reality to dream, which everyone has experienced for himself); but I can assure you that one thing especially interests me: the physiognomy of life and its truthful depiction. I am completely indifferent to mysticism in all its forms, and all I saw in the *plot* of "Phantoms" was an opportunity to present a series of pictures. You point to the inevitability of misunderstandings; but, my dear friend, you and I have passed through five decades and must know that to avoid such misfortunes is impossible—and what harm is done? [. . .]

{ 248 }

Weimar, March 15/27, 1870

TO IVAN PETROVICH BORISOV

[. . .] I am glad when I think that I shall see Fet again, and I shall try to argue with him from force of habit (which becomes increasingly difficult for me every year). I am becoming more and more imbued with the truth of Tiutchev's line: "A thought once uttered is a lie." [3]

[. . .] I read the sixth[4] volume of *War and Peace*; of course it contains first-class things, but, not to mention the childish philosophy, I was displeased to see the negation of *system* even in the characters Tolstoy has drawn. Why are all his good women inevitably not merely cows but even fools? And why does he try to convince the reader that if a woman is intelligent and cultured, she is inevitably a phrase-monger

[3] From Tiutchev's *Silentium*, one of the most famous poems in the Russian language.
[4] The sixth—and final—volume of *War and Peace* (first edition) had appeared in 1869.

and a liar? Why has he allowed the entire *Decembrist*[5] element to disappear, when it played such a huge role in the 1820's, and why are all his decent people also such blockheads with a touch of the *iurodivy?* [6] I am afraid lest Slavophilism, into whose hands he seems to have fallen, may spoil his beautiful and poetic talent by depriving him of his freedom of outlook, as it has already spoiled [Nadezhda Stepanovna] Kokhanovski and others. An artist who loses the ability to see both *black* and *white*—and both to the right and to the left —is on the brink of destruction. [. . .]

[249]

Weimar, April 1/13, 1870

TO IVAN PETROVICH BORISOV

Fet has really become rather strange; he writes me very long and, to tell the truth, unintelligible letters; the only thing apparent is that something is constantly irritating him. I submit that in no way has he been able

[5] The Decembrists staged their abortive uprising when Tsar Aleksandr I died in 1825, and it was unclear whether his brother Konstantin (who had been heir presumptive until his ultra-secret renunciation of his rights) or his brother Nikolai (who was the heir-presumptive but swore allegiance to Konstantin after Aleksandr's death) would succeed to the throne. Some troops of the St. Petersburg garrison revolted "for Konstantin and a constitution." Nikolai shot them down, and remarked: "This is a fine way to start a reign!" A revolt in the south was almost as much of a fiasco. (See Florinsky: *Russia: A History and an Interpretation.*)

Tolstoy had wanted to write a novel about the Decembrists, but realized he would have to go back further to understand them. He did go back further—all the way to 1805—and when he had finished his task, he called the result *War and Peace.*

[6] *Iurodivyi* has no exact English equivalent. Historically, according to Ushakov's dictionary (published in the U.S.S.R.), a *iurodivy* as a "Christian ascetic and madman (or pretended madman) who, in the opinion of believers, possessed the gift of prophecy."

to reconcile himself with the termination of his literary work. We shall have to try, and calm him down somewhat. [. . .]

[250]

Baden-Baden, June 17/29, 1870

TO ALEKSEI MIKHAILOVICH ZHEMCHUZHNIKOV

[. . .] Two weeks have already passed since I returned here. Although Baden is strangely deserted, and although we are anticipating invasion by the French any day, I am nevertheless remaining here. [. . .] What a marvelous anti-liberal instinct Katkov has! Now he has taken the French side! Prussia, God knows, is no liberal state, but if France wins—amen to any freedom in Europe. [. . .]

[251]

Baden-Baden, July 15/27, 1870

TO NIKOLAI SERGEEVICH TURGENEV

[. . .] At first this monstrous and repulsive [Franco-Prussian] war threw everything into terrible confusion, but now everything is gradually becoming orderly again, even though we expect an invasion by the French from across the Rhine any day. The Germans are all afire with patriotism, and the first result of Napoleon [III]'s escapade has been the unification of Germany. They all feel that this is not the time to quarrel among themselves, but stand together against the common enemy. Baden is completely deserted, but I am remaining here—and I shall remain here even if the French come; what on earth can they do to me? [. . .]

[252]

Letters on the Franco-Prussian War

[These letters were written for the *Sankt-Peter-burgskie vedomosti*, a newspaper published in St. Peters-burg. Turgenev disagreed with its editorial board about the significance of what was going on, and therefore stopped writing letters to that newspaper by the end of September.]

[252a]

Baden-Baden, July 27/August 8, 1870

Last Thursday I wrote you to the distant rumble of a cannonade; the next day, Friday, a telegram informed us that the Germans had taken Wissembourg by storm; while the Emperor of the French was showing his son, between breakfast and dinner, how *mitrailleuses* work and, with extraordinary effects, was taking the city of Saarbrücken (which had been defended by a single battalion); the Moltke Plan had been put into practice; the entire enormous army of the Crown Prince of Prussia was thrown into Alsace, and has cut the French army in two. On Saturday—i.e., the day before yesterday—my gardener came to tell me that an extraordinarily violent cannonade had been heard since morning; I went out on the porch and it was true: distant rumblings, rollings, and vibrations were reaching us distinctly, but they were resounding somewhat to the south of Thursday's; I calculated them at from thirty to forty per minute. I took a carriage and drove to Yburg—a castle on one of the highest peaks of the Black Forest near the Rhine—from which I could see the entire valley of Alsace as far as Strasbourg. The

weather was clear, and the line of the Vosges Mountains was clearly silhouetted against the horizon. The
cannonade had stopped for several minutes before my
arrival at Yburg, but enormous puffs of black, white,
dove-colored, and red smoke were rising beyond a long,
unbroken forest right against the mountains on the
other side of the Rhine; an entire city was burning
there. Beyond that, toward the Vosges, other cannon
shots were heard, but steadily weaker. . . . It was clear
that the French had been beaten and were retreating.
It was terrible and sad to see the monstrous traces of
war under the mild glow of the half-hidden sun upon
that peaceful and beautiful plain, and it was impossible
not to curse the war and the mad criminals responsible. I returned to Baden. The next day—i.e., yesterday
—early in the morning a telegram was posted everywhere in the city announcing the Crown Prince's new
and decisive victory over MacMahon, and toward evening we learned that the French had lost 4,000 prisoners,
30 guns, 6 *mitrailleuse*, and 2 flags, and that MacMahon
had been wounded! There is no limit to the astonishment of the Germans themselves; the roles have been
completely changed. *They* are attacking; *they* are beating the French on French soil—and not less [decisively]
than they beat the Austrians [in 1866]! The Moltke
Plan is being developed with rapidity and brilliance; the
right wing of the French army is annihilated; it is caught
between two fires, as at Königgrätz [Sadowa]. The King
of Prussia and the Crown Prince may meet today on a
battlefield that has decided the outcome of the war!
The Germans are so amazed that their patriotic joy
seems befuddled. *This* no one had expected! I was with
them with all my heart from the very beginning, you
know, because only in the irrevocable downfall of the

Napoleonic system do I see the salvation of civilization, and the possibility for the free development of free institutions in Europe; this was inconceivable as long as *that* monstrosity had not received the punishment it deserved. But I had anticipated a long and stubborn war—and suddenly this! All thoughts are now on Paris; what will she say? *Defeated*, Bonaparte *n'a plus raison d'être*, but now we can expect even so improbable an event as calm in Paris at the news of the French army's defeat. As you can easily imagine, I have been diligently reading the French and German newspapers all this time, and, with my hand on my heart, I must say that there is no comparison between them. I could not have even imagined such boasting, such calumnies, such extreme ignorance of the enemy, in short, such boorishness, as there has been in the French newspapers. Not to mention papers like *Figaro* or the most contemptible *Liberté* (which is completely worthy of its founder, E. de Girardin),[7] even such a sensible newspaper as, for example, the *Temps* reports, among other things, that Prussian sergeants follow the rank-and-file soldiers with steel rods in their hands to drive them into battle, etc. Ignorance has reached the point where the *Journal officiel*—the organ of the government (!) —states in all seriousness that *the Rhine flows* between France and the Palatinate. Only complete ignorance of the enemy can account for the confidence of the French in assuming that southern Germany would remain neutral—despite their clearly expressed wish to annex the Rhine province, with its historical cities of Cologne, Aachen, and Trier, that German borderland

[7] Emile de Girardin (1880–81), French publisher and politician who purchased *La Liberté* in 1868 and favored war in 1870.

which is almost the dearest to the German heart! The same *Journal officiel* asserted a few days ago that the French war aim was to return their freedom to the Germans!! And this is said at a time when all Germany from border to border has arisen against the age-old enemy! And it is really needless to comment on that assurance of the [presumed] inevitability of victory, or, for that matter, on the supremacy of the *mitrailleuse* and the chassepot. All the French newspapers are convinced that all the French have to do is to meet the Prussians and whoosh—it will all be over in a moment. But I cannot refrain from quoting to you one of the most charming boasts. In one paper (perhaps even the *Soir*), a correspondent describing the morale of the French soldiers exclaims: *"Ils sont si assurés de vaincre, qu'ils ont comme une peur modeste de leur triomphe inévitable."* (That is, they are so sure of winning that they have something like a modest fear of their inevitable triumph!) This sentence is something—although it cannot be compared to the classic Shakespearean words Prince Pierre Bonaparte[8] uttered about the Parisians when they followed the coffin of Noir, whom he had killed: *"C'est une curiosité malsaine, que je blâme"* (It is an unhealthy, inappropriate curiosity, and I condemn it). And what sayings, what mots are cited in the newspapers, which ascribe them to various high-placed personalities—the Emperor Napoleon among others! The *Gaulois*, for example, reports that when defenseless Saarbrücken was set afire on all four sides, the Emperor turned to his son with the question:

---

[8] Prince Pierre-Napoleon Bonaparte (1815–81), son of Lucien Bonaparte and thus nephew of Napoleon I and first cousin of Napoleon III. He pulled a revolver on Victor Noir, a newspaperman from *Le Peuple*, and killed him (January 10, 1870), after which he was tried for murder and acquitted.

"Es-tu fatigué, mon enfant?" ["Are you tired, my child?"] This means that they are finally losing all sense of shame!

There is also a good anecdote about the diplomatic attaché who declared, in the presence of the Empress Eugénie, that he did not desire victory over Prussia.

"What is that?"

"Yes, that's right—imagine how unpleasant it will be to live on Unter-Munter-Birschkrut Boulevard, or to tell the coachman to go to Nich Kaput-klops-mopsfurt Street! And, you know, this will be inevitable because we give our streets the names of our victories!"

Perhaps France counted on the neutrality of southern Germany on the basis of the same attaché's reports.

Without joking, I sincerely love and respect the French people; I admit their great and glorious role in the past; I have no doubt of their significance in the future. But it may be their turn to receive the lesson the Prussians received at Jena, the Austrians at Sadowa, and—why conceal the truth—we did at Sevastopol.[9] May God grant that they too will learn how to utilize [the lesson] and to extract the sweet fruit from the bitter root! It is time—it has long been time—for them to examine themselves within their own country, to see their ulcers and try to cure them; it is time to put a stop to the immoral system that has been ruling them for almost twenty years! Such retrospection is impossible without a violent jolt from the outside; it never takes place without profound sorrow and pain. But genuine patriotism has nothing in common with the arrogant and presumptuous pride which leads only to self-deception, ignorance, and irreparable mistakes.

[9] At Sevastopol the Russians were besieged and defeated by the British, the French, and their allies in 1855.

The French need a lesson . . . because they must still learn a great deal. The Russian soldiers who died by the thousand in the ruins of Sevastopol did not perish in vain; may the innumerable sacrifices of the present war not be in vain either; otherwise, they would seem senseless and monstrous.

As for our personal situation in Baden, the danger of invasion has now been removed; provisions have become even cheaper than they were, despite the assurance of the French newspapers that we are starving to death here.

[252b]

August 9, 1870

Blow after blow. I wrote you only yesterday about the Crown Prince's victory over MacMahon, and today came the news that the center of the main French army has also been defeated and is retreating toward Metz. A state of siege has been declared in Paris. The Chamber has been convoked for the 11th, and the French are fleeing everywhere, throwing their weapons away! Has not *their* Jena really arrived? [1] Let it be said, but not in anger, to Count Lev Tolstoy (who asserts that, in time of war, the adjutant babbles something to the general, the general mumbles something to the soldiers, and somehow and somewhere a battle is won or lost) that General Moltke's Plan is being carried out with genuinely mathematical precision, like the plan of an excellent chess player, such as, for example, Andersen (who is also a Prussian, and who, let me observe

---

[1] At Jena, Napoleon I smashed the Prussians in 1806; at Sadowa (also known as Königgrätz), the Prussians crushed the Austrians in 1866.

in passing, won a match here against the best chess players on the very day of the first Prussian victory at Wissembourg). And at that very time the Emperor Napoleon was amusing both himself and his sonny-boy *à la* Louis XIV with the performance of a military spectacle. But Napoleon is no Louis XIV; the latter endured failures in the course of many years, but his subjects' devotion to him did not waver; Napoleon will not survive a decisive defeat for two weeks. The French generals' lack of talent is demonstrated with ever-increasing frequency, and who are these Leboeufs, Frossards, Bazaines, and Faillys[2] surrounding the Emperor of the French? Court generals—*des généraux de cour*— also *à la* Louis XIV. The only sensible one of them, MacMahon,[3] seems to have been sacrificed. I am very

[2] Edmond Leboeuf (1809–88), Marshal of France and Minister of War. In July 1870 he told the French legislature that France "would not lack for a legging-button" should war come. He was interned after the surrender of Metz on October 27.

Charles-Auguste Frissard (1807–75), in charge of the French II Corps. Having attacked Saarbrücken on August 2, he was forced to withdraw at Spicheren on August 5, and was beaten at Forbach on August 6. Later he retired to Metz with Bazaine.

Achille Bazaine (1811–88), Marshal of France, in charge of the French III Corps in 1870 and named generalissimo on August 12. He surrendered Metz, after being besieged, on October 27.

Pierre-Louis-Charles de Failly (1810–92), in charge of French V Corps. On August 6 he remained motionless between Spicheren and Woerth battlefields, and on August 30 was surprised and almost surrounded by Bavarians at Beaumont. He was taken prisoner on September 3.

[3] Marie-Edmé-Patrice-Maurice MacMahon (1808–93), Duke of Magenta and Marshal of France, in charge of I Corps. His vanguard was destroyed at Wissembourg on August 4, and he was defeated at Reichshofen two days later. Ordered to relieve Bazaine at Metz, he was forced to surrender at Sedan on September 1. Later he was released to take charge of the troops that suppressed the Paris Commune in 1871. He served as President of France, 1873–9.

happy that during my trip through Berlin, on the very day that France declared war (June 15), I had occasion to dine at a *table d'hôte* directly opposite General Moltke.[4] His face is engraved in my memory. He was sitting in silence and looking around calmly. He seemed to be a professor, with his fair-haired wig and his smoothly shaven face (he does not have a mustache), but what tranquility, power, and intelligence are in his every feature, what a penetrating look in his blue, luminous eyes! Yes, intelligence and knowledge, united with a firm will—you rule this land! Napoleon's "star" is betraying him; he is not facing, as he was in Italy in 1859, an ungifted idiot such as Gyulai.[5]

What is going on in Paris? The newspapers have probably already told you of the alarm that has begun there. . . . But what will happen later on, when more and more of the truth will constantly be revealed to the French? The immoral government has finally brought foreigners onto the soil of the homeland. Having ruined the country, it has destroyed the army and has inflicted deep wounds upon the welfare, the freedom, and the dignity of France. It is now inflicting an almost fatal wound upon her self-respect! Can that government really yet be saved? Will it really not be swept away by the tempests?

And all those vile people—the Olliviers *"au coeur léger"* ["with their light heart"], the Girardins, the Cas-

---

[4] Helmuth Karl Bernhard, Count von Moltke (1800–91), was Chief of the Prussian General Staff and author of the campaign plan.
[5] Franz, Count Gyulai, Count of Maros-Németh and Rádaska (1798–1868), was the Austrian Governor General of the Kingdom of Lombardy and Venice in 1859. He was defeated by the French under MacMahon at Magenta that same year.

sagnacs,[6] the senators—what dust will they be turned to? But is lingering over them worth our while?

The Germans are not boasters and are not braggarts, but their heads have begun spinning from all these unheard-of events. A rumor is going around here today—Strasbourg has surrendered!! Of course, this is nonsense, but you know the time of miracles has arrived, so why not believe in this one, too? The day before yesterday the Baden [army] detachment captured all of a thousand Frenchmen without a shot. Demoralization has set in among them, and, after all, that is the same as the cholera.

[252c]

Baden-Baden, August 14, 1870

At the end of the past week, during the night, and without an especially strong wind, the oldest and hugest oak on the famous Lichtenthaler Allee collapsed. Its entire core turned out to be rotten, and only its bark had been holding it up. When I went to take a look at it in the morning, two German workmen were standing in front of it. "Look," said one of them laughingly to the other, "there it is, the French state!" (*"Da ist es, das französische Reich!"*) And really, judging from what has reached us from Paris and from France, one

[6] Olivier-Emile Ollivier (1825–1913) was Chief of the French Ministry formed on January 2, 1870. On July 15 he told the Chamber that he was accepting his "heavy responsibilities with a light heart."

Bernard-Adolphe Granier de Cassagnac (1806–80), a newspaper owner, was a defender of absolutism. He opposed Ollivier's reforms as too liberal. He was the father of Paul Granier de Cassagnac (1843–1902), a pro-Empire journalist captured by the Prussians in 1870.

might think that this colossus had been held up only
by its exterior and was ready to fall. The fruits of a
twenty-year reign have been disclosed at last. You know
that at the moment I am writing this, something like a
respite has ensued—i.e., no battle is going on; on the
other hand, the German army is moving forward
rapidly (according to the latest information, it has
occupied Nancy), and the French are retreating just
as rapidly. But a terrible battle, a decisive battle is
inevitable; both sides desire it, thirst for it, and tomorrow may be the fatal day. France especially—mad-
dened, in revolt, dishonored to the last filaments of
her national self-respect—is clamoring for skirmishes
with the Prussians; she demands *une revanche,* and it
is perhaps to this furious wish for "getting even" that
we ought to attribute the fact that the government
still holds sway and that the revolution which many
people have been expecting has not yet flared up in
Paris. "There is a time to be concerned with politics;
our country must be saved"—that is the common idea.
There is no doubt but that the French have become
drunk with a thirst for vengeance and for blood; every
one of them seems to have lost his head. I am not even
mentioning the scenes in the Chamber of Deputies or
on the streets of Paris; but today the news came that
all Germans are being expelled from France (not the
Austrians, of course)! Europe has not seen such a
barbarous violation of international law since the time
of the first Napoleon, who ordered the arrest of all
Englishmen on the Continent. But that measure affected only a few individuals; this time, ruin threatens
thousands of hard-working and honest families who had
settled in France, convinced that a civilized state was
taking them to its bosom. What if Germany takes a

notion to repay this in kind? The Frenchmen who have settled in Germany are no fewer than the Germans living in France, and perhaps they own more capital. Where will that lead us in the end? Even without that, the introduction of the bestial Turcos into a European war, with their cruel conduct toward prisoners, wounded, doctors and nurses, has justly aroused the indignation of the Germans. In addition, Mr. Paul de Cassagnac, the worthy offspring of his father, declares now that he does not wish to give money to the International Committee in Geneva because, he says, it will also take care of the Prussian wounded, and that is "a caricature of sentimentality" (*"une sentimentalité grotesque"*). Still, it is good that the Germans, who now have several thousand French wounded on their hands, do not maintain the principles of this favorite of the Tuileries court, this personal friend of the Emperor Napoleon, who calls him his son and says *"tu"* to him. You can judge what the French are rapidly coming to from the following. Yesterday *Liberté* reprinted with praise an article by a certain Marc Fournier in the *Paris-Journal*.[7] He demands the extermination of all Prussians, and exclaims *"Nous allons donc connaître enfin les voluptés du massacre! Que le sang des Prussiens coule en torrents, en cataractes, avec la divine furie du déluge! Que l'infâme qui ose seulement prononcer le mot de paix, soit aussitôt fusillé comme un chien et jeté à l'égout!"* ["We are at last going to know the delights of massacre! Let the blood of the Prussians flow in torrents, in waterfalls, with the divine fury of the flood! Let the wretch who merely dares to utter the word 'peace' be immediately shot like

[7] Marc Fournier (1818–?) was a French author born in Geneva. He specialized in the theater.

a dog and thrown into the sewers!"] And side by side
with these unheard-of monstrosities and ragings are
the most complete disorder, confusion, and lack of any
administrative talents (not to mention any others).
The Minister of War (Marshal Leboeuf), having asserted that everything was *ready*, and having given his
word of honor on the subject, has turned out to be
a mere child. Emile Ollivier has disappeared, swept
away like worthless refuse with his ministry and the
Chamber itself, which had cringed before him; and
who has replaced him? Count Palikao,[8] a man with so
sullied a reputation that a different Chamber, even
more devoted to the government than the present one,
refused him a donation and found that he had already
feathered his nest quite sufficiently in China! (As we
know, he was in command of the French expedition of
1860.) In view of the enormous resources of the French
nation, the patriotic enthusiasm that has taken possession of it, and the courage of the French army, no one
can doubt that the end of the war is far off. And no one
can predict with complete accuracy the outcome of
this colossal clash between the two races. For the
present, the odds are with the Germans; they have
shown such an abundance of variegated talents, such
power and exactitude of execution, their numerical
superiority is so great, their superiority in material resources is so obvious, that the question seems to have
been decided in advance. But *"le dieu de batailles"*
["the god of battles"], as the French say, is fickle, and

   [8] Charles - Guillaume - Marie - Appollinaire - Antoine Cousin-
Montauban (1796–1878) had been named Count of Palikao for
taking Peking and imposing peace on China in 1860. He formed
a cabinet to succeed the Ollivier ministry on August 9, 1870.
His ministry lasted twenty-four days. Refusing to become a
dictator, he disappeared from the political scene after the collapse at Sedan.

it certainly is not for nothing that they are the sons and grandsons of the victors of Jena, Austerlitz, and Wagram! We shall live, and see. But even now no one can fail to admit that, for example, King Wilhelm's proclamation upon entering France was clearly distinguished by its noble humaneness, its simplicity, and the dignity of its tone from all documents that have reached us from the opposing camp; the same can be said about the Prussian bulletins and the reports of the German correspondents. Sober and honest truth on the one side; falsehood—first furious and then sniveling—on the other. At any rate, history will not forget this.

Enough, however. As soon as something noteworthy takes place, I shall write you again. Everything is quiet here; the first sick and wounded have appeared in our hospital today.

[252d]

Baden-Baden, August 28, 1870

I will not talk to you this time about the battles near Metz or the movement of the Crown Prince on Paris, etc. The newspapers have been telling you enough about that without me. . . . I wish to draw your attention to a psychological fact that, at least within my memory, has never yet been presented in such dimensions—to wit, the thirst for self-delusion, for the conscious intoxication of falsehood, for the resolute aversion to truth—which has recently possessed Paris and France. To explain this by the vexation of a profoundly tormented self-respect alone is impossible. Such a "cowardice"—there is no other word—a cowardice to look the devil in the face, as the saying goes, at one and the same time shows the Achilles' heel of the nation's character and serves as one of the numerous symptoms of the moral level to which France has been reduced by the twenty-year rule of the Second Empire.

"For two weeks now you have been lying and deceiving the nation," honest Gambetta has exclaimed from the rostrum,[9] and his voice was immediately drowned by the howlings of the majority, and Granier de Cassagnac made the faint-hearted president adjourn the session. The French *do not wish* to learn the truth; incidentally, a man has just come along for them (Count Palikao) who outdoes all the Münchhausens and Khlestakovs in calm, concise, and imperturbable lying. Shakespeare has Prince Hal tell Falstaff that nothing can be more repulsive than an old fool, but an old liar is perhaps even worse; the old man—Palikao—cannot open his mouth without telling lies. Bazaine and the main French army have been shut up in Metz; he is threatened there by hunger, captivity, and the plague. . . .

"Pardon me, our army is in a superior position and Bazaine is on the point of uniting with MacMahon."

"But you have no news from him, do you?"

"Shhh! Quiet! We need absolute silence to execute a most astonishing military plan, and if I told you what I know, Paris would immediately have illuminations!"

"Well, tell me what it is you know!"

"I will say nothing—but Bismarck's entire *corps* of cuirassiers has been destroyed!"

[9] Léon Gambetta (1838–82) was chief of the opposition in the Chamber of Deputies in 1870. He announced the deposition of the Second Empire on September 4, 1870, and became part of the Government of National Defense. He said of Alsace-Lorraine: *"Pensons-y toujours; n'en parlons jamais."* ("Let us always think of it; let us never talk of it.") He became a leading figure in the first decade of the Third French Republic.

"But Bismarck has no cuirassiers at all, and there have not been any cuirassiers whatever in battle!"

"Oh! I see that you are a bad patriot," etc., etc.

And the French public pretends to believe all these fairytales. Is this really the way a great nation ought to behave in meeting the blows of fate? Without self-praise, we can state that the Russian public behaved differently during the Crimean campaign. Enthusiasm and readiness to sacrifice everything are fine qualities, of course, but knowing how to accept disaster and to acknowledge it may be an even greater quality, containing a better guarantee of success. Are these monstrous persecutions of individuals who are guilty of no crime whatever—but suspect anyhow—really worthy "of the great nation" (*"de la grande nation"*)? In one department they have even killed a Frenchman and set his body on fire merely because the crowd thought he was in favor of Prussia. "Ah! We cannot settle accounts with German soldiers, so let us beat German tailors, coachmen, and workingmen! Let us slander, lie —anything—in any way, as long as it comes out hot." But now is the time a man, despite himself, ought to ask with Figaro: *"Qui trompe-t-on ici?"* ["Who is being deceived here?"] A slave beats herself if she harvests badly. The French are shutting their eyes, pressing their hands against their ears, and crying like children, while the Prussians are already in Epernay[1] and Governor General Trochu[2]—the one sensible, honest, and

[1] Epernay is less than 100 miles from Paris.

[2] Louis-Jules Trochu (1815–96) was a general and political figure named Governor of Paris on August 17, 1870. He allowed the Empire to fall and became President of the Government of National Defense on September 4. He directed the military effort of besieged Paris, and resigned as Governor in January 1871 to facilitate the city's surrender.

sober person in the entire administration—is preparing
Paris to withstand a siege that will begin any day
now. . . .

I observed earlier, too, that the French are least
interested in the truth—*c'est le cadet de leurs soucis*
[that is the least of their worries]. In literature and in
art, for example, they very highly value wit, imagination, inventiveness, and taste—especially wit. But is
there truth in all that? Bah! As long as it is amusing.
Not one of their writers has decided to tell them the
complete and unlimited truth to their face—as, for example, Gogol has done to us, or Thackeray to the English—and tell it to them as Frenchmen and not as
people in general. Those rare works in which an author
tries to show his compatriots their basic shortcomings,
such as, for example, Edgar Quinets' *La Révolution* or,
in a more modest way, Flaubert's latest novel [*Une
Education sentimentale*], are ignored by the public.
This aversion to learning the truth about themselves at
home is combined with an even greater aversion and
indolence about learning what is taking place elsewhere,
among their neighbors. This does not interest a Frenchman; what could be interesting among foreigners? And
who does not know that the French are "the most
learned, the most advanced nation in the world, the
representatives of civilization who battle for ideas"?
They can get away with this in peacetime; but in the
terrible circumstances of the present this conceit, this
ignorance, this terror of the truth and aversion for it are
bringing horrible blows on Frenchmen themselves. . . .
But all the facts mentioned above show that they
have not sobered up yet. They have not shaken off
falsehood, and although they no longer sing the *Mar-
seillaise* (!) under the banners of the Emperor Napo-

leon (can greater blasphemy be imagined?), they still have a long way to go before they recover. . . . They are only just beginning to admit their illness, and what painful and bitter experiences they will have to go through!!

Incidentally, the *Sankt-Peterburgskie vedomosti* (in No. 214) quotes a letter from a correspondent of the *Birzhevye vedomosti* which states that people in Baden seem to shout: "Death to the French," as a result of which our young ladies have begun talking Russian. The journalistic gentleman is worthy of being a French chronicler; there is not a word of truth in his statement. The French families resident here enjoy the complete respect of the authorities and the population; their freedom has in no way been impaired, and in the large public hall where all the local ladies meet to prepare all kinds of trusses, bandages, sweaters, etc., for the sick and wounded, the French language is more in style than the German. Perhaps the journalistic gentleman was thinking of giving a skillful hint to the Russian ladies resident here, but alas! I can assure him that they are continuing to ignore the Russian language, and his patriotic outburst has been in vain.

A few days ago I went to Rastatt to visit the French wounded and prisoners. They are well cared for, but they are constantly complaining about their generals. Among them was an old Arab, a Turco—a real gorilla. Wrinkled, black, and thin, he was sitting on his bed and looking around vacantly and savagely, like a wild animal; his comrades said that he did not even understand French. It was necessary for the "country standing at the head of progress" to drag this child of the African plains off to Rastatt!

The shelling of Strasbourg is still going on con-

stantly; the measured, remote vibrations reach me even
with the windows shut. . . . News about the battle between the Crown Prince and MacMahon is expected at
any moment. If the French lose that one, too, the dic-
tatorship of Trochu is almost inevitable. Let me repeat:
we shall live, and see!

[252e]

Baden-Baden, September 6/18, 1870

You wish me to inform you about the impression
the momentous events at the start of this memorable
month have made on the German public—as far as I
have been able to observe those impressions. I shall not
talk about the outbursts of national pride, patriotic joy,
celebrations, etc. You already know all that from the
newspapers. I shall try briefly and with the necessary
impartiality to set forth for you the views of the Germans first on the change of government in France and
second on the question of "war and peace."

The revival of the republic in France, the appearance of a form of government which still fascinates so
many people, has not aroused even a shadow of the interest in Germany that once greeted the republic of
1848. The Germans realized quite quickly that after the
catastrophe at Sedan, the Empire had for the first time
become impossible, and that there was nothing to replace it with except a republic. They do not believe
(perhaps they are mistaken) that the republic has any
deep roots among the French, and do not count on its
long life; they are not in general examining it in absolute terms—*an und für sich* [in and for itself]—but
only from the standpoint of its influence on the conclusion of peace, of that prolonged and profitable peace

—*dauerhaft, nicht faul* [lasting, not shaky]—which now constitutes their *idée fixe*. From precisely this point of view, the appearance of a republic has even confused them; something impersonal, tottering, and unable to offer the necessary guarantees has replaced a definite governmental entity with which negotiations had been possible. This is just what makes them desire the energetic continuation of the war and an early capture of Paris—whose downfall, they think, will inevitably and quickly bring about just what France needs. In view of the remarkable and even unprecedented unanimity which has taken possession of them all, it would, plainly speaking, be childish to hope one could stop these swelling and oncoming waves, to expect the victor to stop or even turn back; only a Victor Hugo could have conceived of that idea, and I suppose that he has only seized upon it as a pretext for producing his usual logorrhea. King Wilhelm himself does not have the power to change matters; the waves are carrying him along too. But, having decided to settle things with France to the limit (*Abrechnung mit Frankreich*), the Germans are prepared to explain to you the reasons why they must do so.

Everything in the world has two sets of reasons, the open and the secret, the just and the unjust (the open, for the most part, are unjust), and two sets of justifications, one in good conscience and one not in good conscience. I have been living with the Germans for too long and have become too friendly with them to assume that in their talks with me they would resort to justifications that are not [presented] in good conscience; at any rate, they do not insist upon them. In demanding Alsace and German Lorraine from France (or Alsace in any case), they quickly drop the argu-

ment of race and origin of these provinces—because
that argument is massacred by another and most powerful one, to wit, the open and indubitable aversion of
these provinces themselves toward joining their former
homeland. But the Germans assert that they must have
these provinces for good as a protection against the
possibility of attack by and invasion from France, and
that they can see no other guarantee than the annexation of the left bank of the Rhine as far as the Vosges
Mountains. The razing of all the fortresses in Alsace
and Lorraine, the disarmament of a France humbled by
an army of two hundred thousand seems insufficient to
[the Germans]; the menace of eternal enmity, of an
eternal thirst for vengeance which they will arouse in
the hearts of their neighbors has no effect upon them.
"It is all the same," they say, "the French would never
forgive us their defeats. We really had better forestall
them and, as the cartoon in *Kladderadatsch*[3] shows,
pare the claws of an enemy whom we can never reconcile to us anyhow." It is true that the unjust and boldly
imprudent declaration of war by France in July would
seem to confirm the conclusions the Germans have
arrived at. Moreover, they do not conceal from themselves the great difficulties accompanying the *annexation* of two hostile provinces, but they hope that time,
patience, and understanding will help them there too,
as they helped in the Grand Duchy of Posen, in the
Rhine and Saxon areas, in Hanover itself, and even in
Frankfurt.[4]

[3] *Kladderadatsch* was a satirical and political weekly published in Berlin.
[4] Prussia reacquired Posen in 1815; she acquired Hanover,
Frankfurt am Main, the Duchy of Hesse-Cassel, and Nassau
after the war with Austria in 1866. After the same war, Saxony
was forced to join the North German Confederation.

Our habit is to cry out, frothing at the mouth, against this German seizure, but, as the newspaper *The Times* observes accurately, can anyone really doubt for a second that any other nation in the Germans' place, in their present position, would behave differently? Furthermore, we ought not to imagine that the idea of restoring Alsace appeared among them only as a result of their astonishingly unexpected victories; that idea came into the head of every German immediately after war had been declared; they conceived of it even when they were expecting a long, stubborn, defensive war on their own frontiers. I myself heard them talking that way in Berlin on July 15: "We have no regrets," they declared, "we shall give all our blood and all our gold, but Alsace will be ours."

"And if they defeat you?" I asked.

"If the French *beat* us," they answered, "let them make Rhine provinces out of our corpse."

The desperate game began; the stake was placed without any doubting by either side. Recall the declaration by Girardin, which was applauded by all France, that the Germans had to be thrown beyond the Rhine by means of rifle butts. . . . One player has lost the game; what is astonishing about the other player's picking up his stake?

Yes, you will say, that is logic—but where is justice?

I suppose that the Germans are behaving rashly and that their calculations are incorrect. In any case, they have already made a major mistake in that they have half destroyed Strasbourg and thus antagonized the entire population of Alsace. I suppose that a form of peace can be found which will secure the tranquillity of Germany for a long time without leading to the humiliation of France and without containing the embryos of new and even more horrible wars. But can we assume that after the terrible experience which she has undergone, France will again take a notion to try her strength? What Frenchman, in the depths of his heart, has not now renounced Belgium and the Rhine provinces forever? It would be worthy of the Germans —of the victorious Germans—also to renounce Alsace and Lorraine. Aside from material guarantees to which they have every right, they might be satisfied with the proud knowledge that, to use Garibaldi's expression, their hand has reduced the immoral monstrosity of Bonapartism to dust.

But at this moment only the extreme democratic party in Germany is renouncing Alsace and Lorraine. Read the speech of its main representative, Johann Jacoby, of Königsberg,[5] that unwavering and immense doctrinaire who for good reason has been compared to Cato the Younger. This party is weak in numbers; it is barely beginning to spread among the workmen, without whom no democracy is conceivable. However, that is not where all the aspirations of Germany are heading; their slogan is the unification of the German race and the consolidation of that unification. They are now consciously accomplishing what other nations achieved much earlier and almost unconsciously; who can blame them on that score? And is it not better to accept and record in the account books of history this fact, which is just as immutable and irrevocable as any physiological or geological phenomenon?

[5] Johann Jacoby (1805–77) was a member of the Prussian *Landtag* and an opponent of Bismarck, who condemned the annexation of Alsace-Lorraine and was interned in Boyen Fortress. Never re-elected to the *Landtag* after that incident he joined the Social Democratic Party in 1872.

But what will become of poor, confused, lacerated France? No country has ever been in a more desperate situation. There is no doubt that she will use all her strength for the fatal struggle; the letters I have received from Paris bear witness to the inflexible determination to defend it to the end, as at Strasbourg. The future of France now depends on the Parisians. "We shall have to re-educate ourselves," one of them writes us; "we are infected with Empire to the marrow of our bones; we have lagged behind; we have fallen; we have sunk in the mire of ignorance and conceit. . . . But that re-education is ahead; now we must save ourselves; we must really be baptized in the font of blood about which Napoleon merely chattered, and that is what we shall do." Let me say, without mincing words, that my sympathy for the Germans does not prevent me from wishing that they fail before Paris; this wish is no betrayal of that sympathy. The best thing that could happen to them would be their failure to take Paris. Unless they take Paris, they will not be tempted to make an effort to restore the imperial regime; several extra-zealous and patriotic newspapers are even now talking about that. [The Germans] will not spoil the best work of their hands; they will not inflict upon France the most bloody offense ever committed against a conquered nation. . . . It will be even worse than amputating provinces. "Even Waterloo can be forgiven," someone has justly observed, "but never Sedan!" "*The damned fool*"—*le maudit*—there is no other name for Napoleon [III] on the lips of French soldiers, and could it be otherwise? I am not mentioning the fact that a nation so profoundly and mercilessly defeated must, by the laws of psychology, choose a "scapegoat," but this time the "scapegoat" is no innocent creature; not even the *Moskovskie vedomosti* can doubt that.

But, I repeat, the role of the sword is not yet finished. . . . It alone will cut the Gordian knot.

And, nevertheless, let me say that although one must wish for the complete victory of the Germans, every victory must serve as a lesson to us; it is the triumph of greater knowledge, of greater art, of a most powerful civilization; we have been shown graphically and with striking clarity what achieves victory.

[252f]

Baden-Baden, September 18/30, 1870

Today I involuntarily recalled the opening verses of Goethe's poem *Hermann und Dorothea*. That is just the way it is now in this city; the population of Baden has taken to the highway to see "the sad procession of unfortunate people exiled from their homeland"—i.e., the seventeen thousand [French prisoners] of the Strasbourg garrison, who for the present have been assigned to Rastatt. Let me observe in passing that the "heroic" defense of Strasbourg scarcely justifies this epithet, which the French had given it beforehand. Not to mention Sevastopol at all, that defense cannot even brook comparison with Antwerp's in 1832, which also lasted for a month or so, but which General Chassé[6] surrendered only after Fort St. Laurens (which commanded the entire town) had been taken by storm. However, not a single friend of mankind will regret that

[6] David-Henri, Baron Chassé (1765–1840), was a Dutch general who late in 1832 held Antwerp fortress against Belgian rebels. Besieged by the British at sea and the French on land, he surrendered to Étienne-Maurice, Count Gérard (1773–1852), Marshall of France, after a twenty-two-day siege.

General Uhrich[7] avoided useless bloodshed by not waiting for the assault. They say he had no more powder.
The long column of prisoners, which had left Strasbourg on foot, approached Rastatt only at five o'clock
today, although they had been expected before twelve.
They exhibited the most variegated and picturesque
mixture of uniforms; here were infantrymen from
twenty different regiments, cuirassiers, artillerymen, gendarmes, zouaves, and Turcos—the remnants of Mac-
Mahon's army. The soldiers walked vigorously and even
merrily, and did not seem exhausted, even though many
of them were barefoot; almost every one of them held
a ramrod or a stick with vegetables or fruit—potatoes,
apples, carrots, or heads of cabbage—hanging on it.
The Turcos showed their teeth and looked around like
children; the officers walked in silence, in separate little
groups, eyes cast down and arms folded; it seemed that
they alone felt all the bitterness of their position. The
commandant of Rastatt had ridden out with all his
adjutants to meet the prisoners; he was riding at the
head of the column. A few French staff-officers were
also on horseback; they had all retained their swords.
The public, ten thousand strong, was standing on both
sides of the road and behaved quite decently—with
complete respect for the misfortune of the vanquished.
Not a shout, not a word insulting to the prisoners' self-
respect was audible. One old peasant woman burst out
laughing at the sight of a Turco who was a genuine
caricature, but she was immediately checked by a
workman in a blouse, who stated: *"Alles zu seiner*

[7] Jean-Jacques Alexis Uhrich (1802–86) was a French general who surrendered Strasbourg to the Prussians under General
August Werder (1808–87) on September 28, 1870. The following year the French Council of Inquiry on the Capitulations
found him guilty of not having defended the city to the last.

Zeit; heute lacht man nicht." ("Everything in its own
time; no laughing today.") This does not prevent all
the Germans from feeling great joy at the idea (as they
think) of the irrevocable return of the ancient German
city to the bosom of the united homeland; furthermore,
they well know that the fall of Strasbourg will hasten
the fall of Paris by giving them the opportunity to ship
all the siege artillery by the railroad which has been
completely open since the surrender of Toule.[8]

The blows do not cease falling upon unfortunate
France, one after another. A few days ago I had some
prolonged conversations with a Frenchman who had just
returned from Dijon, where he had gone with the idea
of trying to get into the future Constituent Assembly.
The elections to the Assembly were, as we know, postponed indefinitely because of the telegram[9] Favre sent
after talking with Bismarck, and which was then followed by Crémieux's[1] proclamation. This is what the
Frenchman who had returned from Dijon told me:
"We now have no assembly, no government, and no
army—and all we do have is the fury and determination to fight desperately to the end. The people of
moderation are silent—and they have to be silent; only
the devoted and insanely passionate extremists can act
now, and, he added, *"ce sont peut-être les plus fous
qui sont maintenant les plus sages; ils nous sauveront
peut-être* (perhaps the most insane are now the most

[8] Toule is on the Moselle, about twenty-two miles from
Nancy.
[9] Gabriel-Claude-Jules Favre (1809–80) was Vice-President
of the Government of National Defense after September 4, 1870,
and Minister of Foreign Affairs. He had been a member of the
opposition under the Empire.
[1] Isaac-Moïse (known as Adolphe) Crémieux (1796–1880)
had been elected a Deputy by the extreme left in 1869. He
joined the Government of National Defense as its Minister of
Justice on September 4, 1870.

sagacious; [maybe] they will save us). If Paris is in a
condition to hold out for three or four months; if the
Frenchmen demonstrate only some of the invincible
temperament that eventually brought the Spaniards
victory over Napoleon; if guerrillas are organized in all
the departments; if the downfall of Paris does not
throw us into confusion—the affair can still be won.
The Prussians must be forced to fight against a phantom, against a vacuum, against a complete absence of
any government. *Il faut faire le vide devant eux* [A
void must be created in front of them]. With whom
will they conclude peace when even now they do not
see a single responsible and authorized personage? Will
they not, in fact, resort to Napoleon himself? But,
meanwhile, their huge army will be melting like wax;
even they cannot remain so long outside Germany, far
away from their homes and families. . . . A nation in
arms is capable only of short campaigns, but our resources are inexhaustible."

These are some of the speeches with which my
acquaintance tried to drown some of his patriotic grief.
. . . One has to admit that they contain an important
part of the truth. And, in the meantime, the same
Frenchman has in no way concealed from himself any
of the gloomy aspects of the very situation that aroused
his hopes. He was especially shattered by the complete
breakdown of army discipline, at which Trochu had
already hinted in his famous pamphlet. . . . The Empire has turned the soldiers into Praetorians, and we
know from history what the discipline of Praetorians
was.

Everything depends, without any doubt, on how
Paris behaves: better than Strasbourg, we must hope.

[253]

Baden-Baden, July 28/August 9, 1870

TO HIS BROTHER, NIKOLAI SERGEEVICH TURGENEV

. . . You are worrying about me for nothing; you can see from the newspapers what an unexpected turn the war is taking; it is not the French who are beating the Germans, but the Germans [who are beating] the French, and the French army has not invaded Germany, but the German [army has invaded] France. Meanwhile, there is no danger here in Baden, for the German army has occupied all of Alsace on the other side of the Rhine. [. . .]

[254]

Baden-Baden, August 24, 1870

TO IVAN PETROVICH BORISOV

You might already have asked L. N. Tolstoy to give you the bottle you have won [in a bet on the Franco-Prussian War], for the latest blows the Prussians have dealt really seem to have decided the matter. One cannot fail to admire their skill in holding [Marshall] Bazaine's group back in Metz, then barring his way to Verdun, and finally beating him over the head and forcing him back to Metz again, where he now must either starve to death or surrender. The three battles (of August 14, 16, and 18) have cost them terrible sacrifices; on the other hand, the results are great. Nothing hinders the army of the Crown Prince from reaching Paris; [Marshal] MacMahon" will most probably abandon camp at Châlons. The final outcome of the war cannot be foreseen at present, but all the odds are with the Germans.

I can very well understand why Tolstoy supports the French side. He finds French phrase-mongering repulsive, but he hates sober-mindedness, system, and science (in a word, the Germans) even more. His entire latest novel [*War and Peace*] is constructed on enmity toward intellect, knowledge, and cognition—and suddenly the learned Germans beat the ignorant French!! (By the way, is the idiot who published some ridiculous plans and prophecies in the *Moskovskie vedomosti* really the same Prince Urusov with whom Tolstoy is so friendly?)[2] As for me, I rejoice "without any philosophizing" in the defeat of France, for with it Napoleon's Empire, whose existence was incompatible with the progress of freedom in Europe, has been defeated. [. . .]

I am also gladdened by what you write me about Tolstoy and about Fet; I regret only that the latter is still reluctant to part with the Muse.

[. . .] During the nights we can clearly hear the bombardment of Strasbourg, which is already half burned down. Even when I am in bed, with the windows closed, my ear picks up dull rumblings and shakings. Involuntarily I become absorbed in philosophical, historical, and social meditations of quite an unhappy nature. The iron age is not yet over, and we are all still barbarians! And we shall probably remain so until the end of our days. [. . .]

[2] This was Prince Sergei Semenovich Urusov, Tolstoy's old friend from the siege of Sevastopol. He had written a letter to the editor of the *Moskovskie vedomosti* proposing a plan for the French to beat the Prussians. Urusov's letter had been published on August 2 (O.S.), 1870.

{ 255 }

Baden-Baden, August 29, 1870

TO LUDWIG FRIEDLÄNDER

[. . .] I shall not repeat to you that I am whole-heartedly on the side of the Germans [in the Franco-Prussian War]. This positively is a war of civilization against the barbarians, but not in the sense the French gentlemen understand it. Bonapartism must receive the lesson it deserves regardless of the cost, if the social morality, the freedom, and the independence of Europe are to have any kind of a future at all.

How repulsive, false, and thoroughly rotten the "great [French] nation" has turned out to be! It must have its Jena, its Sevastopol, its Königgrätz.[3] But if it also fails to profit from these lessons, then its song will be over! [. . .]

{ 256 }

Baden-Baden, September 9, 1870

TO LUDWIG PIETSCH

[. . .] At the beginning of August, people here were very much on the *qui vive;* everybody had packed [his bags] to go to the hot springs as soon as the Turcos crossed the Rhine. [. . .]

{ 257 }

Baden-Baden, October 28, 1870

TO HIS DAUGHTER, PAULINE

Your letter is very tormented, and I understand;

[3] These are battles at which the Prussians, the Russians, and the Austrians respectively were defeated.

your position is very difficult, and I share all the terrors, especially when I see your husband obliged to go to war; moreover, I do not wish to discuss again your reproaches about my no longer thinking of you. I wish to prove by actions that I am thinking of you more than ever. I will begin with some advice.

Your father-in-law and mother-in-law have acted very badly in keeping half the Russian bonds back from you, but this is the time, if ever, to put a good face on a bad matter. You cannot force them to give up those bonds, and if you have a falling out with them, Gaston's heritage is gone. So, conceal your anger—all the more so because, when the war is over, there will be even less reason for them to keep the bonds, as I cannot suppose that M. Bruère wishes to rob his son.

Stay wherever your husband tells you to stay: at Vendôme or at Le Mans—and if he tells you to stay with his parents, do. Do you believe that you would be able to stay anywhere far from your husband? Why, you would die of anxiety! Even supposing that I could get to you and take you to Baden, look at the life you would have. So, I repeat, stay near your husband and go wherever he tells you to.

Now, let me repeat once more, and believe me, I implore you, despite the "flames" of Châteaudun, *wherever they are not being resisted by the main force, the Prussians are touching nothing and are not committing injuries* (witness Rheims, Nancy, Lunéville, and a host of other places). Also, I do not believe Rougemont is menaced to the slightest degree in the world—and it will not be the Prussians who devastate your house. You have enough real terrors not to create imaginary ones.

To be troubled in the trouble
Only makes the trouble double. [. . .] [4]

[258]

London, November 24/December 6, 1870

TO HIS BROTHER, NIKOLAI SERGEEVICH TURGENEV

[. . .] The French are going down violently, but they keep persisting and are not surrendering—which will only lead to greater destruction of the country and deprive them of any opportunity to *prendre leur revanche* in time.

But logic rules least in the affairs of the world, especially in a nation that, like the French, is guided by imagination. [. . .]

[259]

London, November 30 [O.S.], 1870

TO MIKHAIL EVGRAFOVICH SALTYKOV-SHCHEDRIN

Allow me to set aside the ceremonious "Dear Sir." A few days ago I received your *History of a Town,*[5] which you had given to Annenkov. My heartfelt thanks for your having remembered me and for the great pleasure your book has brought me; I read it immediately. Not to mention its other merits, the book is in its own way valuable historical material that must not be overlooked by any of our future depicters of mores. Beneath its unusually satiric and sometimes fantastic form, the sardonic humor recalls the best pages of [Jonathan] Swift. The *History of a Town* most truth-

---

[4] In English in the original.
[5] This book, to quote Turgenev's English review of it in *The Academy* for March 1, 1871, is "a sort of parody of Russian history."

fully depicts a basic side of the Russian physiognomy; "we have ears to hear with and eyes to see with," I would say with Benevolenski, the legislator.

Once again, my sincere thanks. [. . .]

{ 260 }

St. Petersburg, February 21/March 8, 1871 (sic)
TO PAULINE VIARDOT (NEE GARCIA)

[. . .] Yesterday I dined at old Countess Protasov's. [. . .] I found there several addicts of the new Russian musical school—not Cui, unfortunately, but the great Balakirev, whom they acknowledge as their leader. The great Balakirev played, rather badly, some selections from a fantasy for orchestra by Rimski-Korsakov (you remember, you were sent several pretty romances of his). The fantasy, on a subject from a rather bizarre Russian legend, struck me as really possessing imagination. Then the great Balakirev played, rather badly, some reminiscences of Liszt and of Berlioz, who, especially Berlioz, are the Absolute and the Ideal for these gentlemen. I believe that he [Balakirev] is an intelligent man, after all. *Kein Talent, doch ein Character* [No talent, but he has character].

{ 261 }

Moscow, March 13 [O.S.], 1871
TO SOFIA KONSTANTINOVNA BRIULLOV (NEE KAVELIN)

[. . .] Moscow is just the same—and, imagine, there are the very same people in the salons; not one young person has been added. It smells a little from lamp oil and Slavic blubber, but I am no lover of these aromas, and therefore feel that I will never build myself a nest in Moscow. Oh, if only Petersburg had Moscow's climate. [. . .]

[262]

London, April 2/14, 1871

TO SOFIA KONSTANTINOVNA BRIULLOV (NEE KAVELIN)

[. . .] In Berlin—rest. The Germans have developed to the point of indecency; they are supporting the sky with their helmets, but on this earth they want Bohemia. They despise others—most of all, us, out of friendship and kinship. Having rested, I continued on my way. There are huge numbers of black crosses with white borders everywhere. The wide cheeks of the *Landwehr* men is astonishing; [and so is] the hurried laugh of the French prisoners—the laugh of a beaten lackey, who remembers the smile of the master as he beat him. There is bitterness, pity, and a lot of mud on one's clothes. [. . .]

[263]

London, April 19/May 1, 1871

TO PAVEL VASIL'EVICH ANNENKOV

The following item appeared in yesterday's *Pall Mall Gazette*:

[. . .] A letter from Paris in the *Temps* announces the death of Madame Pauline Viardot, nee Garcia, sister of Malibran and creatress of the role Fides in Meyerbeer's *Prophète*. The celebrated artiste had just entered on her 54th year.[6]

You can imagine what an impression this announcement would have made upon me had I read it

---

[6] This paragraph is given in English in the original.

anywhere else but in Mme Viardot's salon and in her presence! But because such news is disseminated with lightning speed, and all the newspapers will reprint it immediately, may I ask you to forewarn them or refute the story, as you wish. Mme Viardot, thank God, is healthy, and she is not 54 but 49.

I seem to remember having asked you before to send me four copies of the latest notebook of [musical] romances, and have [copies of] *all* of Mme Viardot's romances delivered on her behalf to the musician and composer [Petr Il'ich] Tchaikovsky in Moscow; in any case, I repeat the request.

Regards to all [. . .]

{ 264 }

London, April 24 [*O.S.*], 1871

TO IAKOV PETROVICH POLONSKI

[. . .] This morning I received your letter with its enclosed article against Saltykov, and I am answering it immediately. The answer you gave to the critic of your *Snopy* [*Sheaves*] was completely logical and irrefutable, but nevertheless you would have done better not to publish it. To answer . . . means to justify oneself . . . which means something is not right—that is the syllogism which inevitably takes shape in the public mind in such cases. But if answering amused you, no great harm has been done. [. . .]

I have been told that Dostoevski has "unmasked" me. . . . What of it! Let him enjoy himself. He came to see me in Baden five years ago, not to pay back the money he had borrowed from me, but to curse me out because of *Smoke*, which, according to his ideas, ought to be burned by the executioner. I listened to his en-

tire philippic in silence—and what am I finding out
now? That I seem to have expressed to him every kind
of offensive opinion, which he hastened to communicate to Bartenev. (Bartenev has really written me about
this.) It would be out-and-out slander if Dostoevski
were not a madman, which I do not doubt in the
slightest. Perhaps it all came to him in a dream. But,
my God, what petty, dirty gossip! [. . .]

[265]

London, July 2/14, 1871

TO AFANASI AFANAS'EVICH FET

Your letter grieved me . . . because of what you
wrote about Lev Tolstoy's health. I am very afraid for
him; that two of his brothers have died of consumption
is not irrelevant, and I am glad he is going on *kumiss*,
in whose effectiveness and benefits I believe. Tolstoy is
the sole hope of our orphaned literature; he cannot
and must not disappear from the face of the earth so
early as his predecessors—Pushkin, Lermontov, and
Gogol. And suddenly he stumbles across Greek!

[266]

Baden-Baden, August 6/18, 1871

TO AFANASI AFANAS'EVICH FET

[. . .] I am very glad that Tolstoy is better,
and that he has mastered Greek so well; it does him
honor and will be of great use to him. But why is he
talking about the need to create some special kind of
Russian? To create a language (!!) is to create an ocean.
It spreads out in a circle of boundless and bottomless

waves; our business as writers is to direct part of those
waves to our channel, to our mill! And Tolstoy knows
this; therefore, his remarks disturb me only to the extent that they show he still feels like subtilizing everything.

A literary man is responsible only for what is published; when and where have I expressed myself in
print against classicism? Why am I guilty of what
various fools sponsor in my name? I grew up on the
classics, and I have lived and shall die in their camp,
but I do not believe in any *Alleinseligmacherei* [exclu-
sive beatifying power] even with respect to classicism,
and I therefore find that the new laws are absolutely
unjust and stifle one trend to the advantage of another.[7]
"Fair play," [8] say the English; I say, equality and freedom. Both classical and modern-language education
must be free and accessible, and enjoy *identical* rights.
Although Mr. Katkov says the opposite, I have hated
only one person in my life (not him, but one who,
thank God, has long been dead[9]), and I have despised
only three people: Girardin, Bulgarin, and the publisher
of the *Moskovskie vedomosti* [i.e., Katkov]. *Il s'en
f...t: et moi je me f...s de ce qu'il s'en f...t.*
[He does not give a damn: and, as for me, I do not
give a damn about what he does not give a damn
about.] [. . .]

[7] Count Dmitri Andreevich Tolstoy had been Minister of
Education since 1866. On June 30, 1871, Tsar Aleksandr II,
at Dmitri Tolstoy's request, decreed "Graeco-Roman bondage."
Both Greek and Latin were made compulsory in all secondary
schools with emphasis on parsing rather than on culture. (Florinsky.)

[8] English in the original.

[9] The Soviet-published source suggests that the man whom
Turgenev hated was undoubtedly Tsar Nikolai I (known to his
subjects as *Nikolai Palkin*—i.e., Nicholas the Stick).

[267]

Baden-Baden, August 24, 1871

TO LUDWIG PIETSCH

[. . .] There is really nothing to tell about the Edinburgh Festival[1] or my part in it; a completely unknown man—Torgunoff—spoke about a completely uninteresting subject, Russian literature. [. . .]

[268]

Baden-Baden, September 15, 1871

TO LUDWIG PIETSCH

[. . .] If Micawber were the type of a borrowing man, I would sooner have bitten my tongue off than have given you that nickname [in the letter of August 24, 1871]. In Micawber, Dickens wished to present a man who continually oscillates between the most profound despair and the greatest rejoicing—and in that sense you are Micawber. [. . .]

[269]

Baden-Baden, October 15/27, 1871

TO VLADIMIR VASIL'EVICH STASOV

[. . .] I have just read Ostrovski's comedy [*Ne vse kotu maslianitsa* (*Christmas Comes But Once a Year*)] in the *Otechestvennye zapiski* and it impressed me just as it did you. To clarify the reason for this and for similar phenomena in a few, or even in many, words is not easy. Here, in addition to insufficient education, monotony also produces its effect (for us), and

---

[1] In his letter of July 18, 1871, to Pietsch, Turgenev mentioned that he was going to Edinburgh to help celebrate the centennial of Sir Walter Scott's birth.

so does the isolation of literary life. Ostrovski, for example, never appears for even an instant outside his own environment. Workmanship matures in solitude, forms and devices are perfected, but the content withers and becomes tenuous. This happens—in magazines if not in books, and that is almost worse, even to those Russian writers who, as they say, follow "ideas" and "trends." [. . .]

{ 270 }

Paris, November 24 [O.S.], 1871

TO AFANASI AFANAS'EVICH FET

[. . .] Whatever he [Tolstoy] does will be good —if he himself does not mutilate his own work. Philosophy, which he hates, has taken vengeance on him in an original way; it has infected him himself, and our foe of argumentation has begun to argue desperately! Perhaps he has now shaken off all this, and only the pure and powerful artist remains. [. . .]

{ 271 }

Paris, January 16/28, 1872

TO HIS BROTHER, NIKOLAI SERGEEVICH TURGENEV

[. . .] From the *Moskovskie vedomosti*, which arrived here today, I see that my comedy, *A Month in the Country*, was given last Thursday, the 13th, in a benefit performance for Mme Vasil'ev (although I did my best to persuade Mme Vasil'ev not to give the comedy—because it is not for the stage and inevitably leads to boredom). I am certainly no playwright. My arguments, however, had no effect. Apparently there was nothing else on hand. I am not suggesting that you were in the theater on the 13th—but nothing is impossible. If you were there, take the trouble to write me your honest impressions and those of the public; if you were not there and the comedy is going to be given again, do not neglect to go, and let me know your impressions. Although I have cooled toward literature in general and even more toward the theater, I have not done so to the extent of losing interest in my own works completely. [. . .]

[272]

Paris, February 5/17, 1872

TO NIKOLAI SERGEEVICH TURGENEV

[. . .] My comedy, as I wrote earlier, had to suffer a fiasco.[2] That is why (since 1851) I have stopped writing for the stage; it is not my business. All I can do now is to reproach myself; why was I so weak as to agree to Mme Vasil'ev's request? [. . .]

[273]

Paris, March 1/13, 1872

TO VLADIMIR VASIL'EVICH STASOV

I have a request to make of you. In a few days you will receive a book by our good friend Ralston, *The Songs of the Russian People*.[3] It is compiled from the sources very conscientiously, and we Russians ought to encourage this work in every way. Nothing like it has yet appeared in a single [western] European language, and Ralston deserves a pat on the back from so competent a judge as yourself. He will thank you for

[2] *A Month in the Country.*
[3] English in the original.

it, and so will your humble servant. I suppose a short article in the *Vestnik Evropy* would be best. As for me, I shall write Stasiulevich. The book is luxurious, as all English editions are. [. . .]

[274]

Paris, March 15/27, 1872

TO VLADIMIR VASIL'EVICH STASOV

[. . .] You are wrong in imagining that I "have no special liking" for [Mikhail] Glinka; he was a very solid and original man. But the other gentlemen are something else again—especially Dargomyzhski and his *Stone Guest*. One of the greatest mysteries of my life is and will be how such intelligent people (as, for example, Cui and yourself) could, in these inert, colorless, impotent—impotent, excuse me, to the point of senile . . . recitatives, which are strewn in places with agonized howling "for the *sake* of" fantasy and color, how you, I repeat, could, in this insignificant squeaking, have discovered—what? not just music, but even a new, "epoch-making music" of genius! ! ? ! ! Is this really unconscious patriotism? I must say that in *that Stone Guest* I found nothing but sacrilegious trespassing on what is one of Pushkin's most beautiful works. Well, and now you can cut my head off, if you like!

Of all the "young" Russian musicians, only two have positive talent: Tchaikovsky and Rimski-Korsakov. All the others—not as people, of course, but as artists (as people they are charming)—will disappear without a trace. Rhadamiste XXIX is not so forgotten now as they will be in 15 or 20 years. That is my only consolation. [. . .]

{ 275 }

Paris, March 29/April 10, 1872

TO AFANASI AFANAS'EVICH FET

[. . .] And now, since you have treated the poet
Fet objectively in your *"exegi monumentum"* [4] [I have
demanded a monument], allow me to do the same. Fet
is a genuine poet, in the real sense of the word, but
he has one extremely serious shortcoming—while he
has a delicate and reliable sense for nature and the exterior forms of human life, he lacks a similar sense for
the inner man and the essence of his soul. In this
respect not only Schiller and Byron but even Iakov
Polonski rout him completely. To be touched or shaken
by any product of Fet's Muse is just as impossible as
to walk on the ceiling; hence, for all his gifts, he must
be relegated to the *dei minorum gentium* [gods of
minor peoples]. Even that is not to be laughed at; a
hundred years hence, about twenty of his beautiful
poems will still be remembered—what more can be
wished? But he should stop repeating himself the way
he has been doing these past ten years. An old night-
ingale is a *contradictio in adjecto*. [. . .]

{ 276 }

Paris, April 7 [O.S.], 1872

TO IAKOV PETROVICH POLONSKI

[. . .] I have also read a few words about Dargomyzhski's [opera] *The Stone Guest* [based on Pushkin's poem of the same name]. Believe me, it is the
most dismal stuff and nonsense, and in about ten years

---

[4] This line from Horace became very popular in Russia
after Pushkin had used it as the epigraph for a famous poem.

will bring a blush of shame to the cheeks of those who not only were not convinced of this at once, but even hailed this impotent [work]. . . .

[277]

Paris, March 23/April 4, 1872

TO NIKOLAI SERGEEVICH TURGENEV

[. . .] The picture of [Uncle] Nikolai Turgenev blind and in the hospital aroused my pity; despite everything, I loved him deeply, and I cannot refrain from giving the past its due. I certainly shall visit him, and you, brother, might do the same, remembering that we all are just people—pitiful and weak beings condemned to death. "He today, I tomorrow." How on earth can we fail to sympathize with our fellowman, and who among us is without sin? Who has the right to judge anyone else harshly? I do not doubt that your visit will be a joy to him in his present sorrowful situation. [. . .]

[278]

Moscow, June 14/26, 1872

TO HIS DAUGHTER, PAULINE

[. . .] As for my brother, who is certainly very rich, he would not lend me 50 francs—and you talk of 50 or 60,000!!! Get it into your head that he has always been very miserly and now is a Harpagon who could give some pointers to Molière's. [. . .]

[279]

Moscow, June 14/26, 1872

TO PAVEL VASIL'EVICH ANNENKOV

[. . .] My brother is grieved, but he is already beginning to calm down; he has developed into a first-class Harpagon, and no longer can see any pleasure in life except for trembling and sweating about money. [. . .] [5]

[280]

Paris, October 5/17, 1872

TO PAVEL VASIL'EVICH ANNENKOV

In the forties my friends used to tease me by digging up my poetic sins, which, unfortunately, had been printed. Now, in the seventies, you, you malicious *Bücherwurm* [bookworm], have dug up that nonsense with [Alphonse-Marie-Louis] Lamartine, which I long since thought engulfed by oblivion. But I myself was guilty in the first place; now I am like Christ before the Jews!

During the final years of his life, Lamartine (who had been ruined in every way) thought up the following device: he took about sixty or eighty pages from any author, French or foreign, prefaced them with insane eulogies in the guise of biographical and critical evaluations (so that, for example, he placed a certain Provençal poet, Mistral, above Homer, etc.), probably to disarm the authors and their publishers, and then sold the entire thing under the title *Conversations lit-*

---

[5] This is again about his financial difficulties with his uncle, who had been managing the estate at Spasskoe.

téraires [*Literary Conversations*]. I was caught along with others. I well remember how taken aback I was to find this nonsense on my desk. "Well," I thought, "here is material for the *Iskra*." [6] But Lamartinism fortunately did not reach Russia, and everything remained sewn up and covered until [you] my odd friend uncovered it and ripped out all the seams. However, I know this will go no further.

If at least I had seen and chatted with Lamartine frequently! I dined at his house exactly once. And what lies he told about his heroic conduct in 1848! I had been warned that he invented things *à la* Münchausen, but was amazed just the same! But what you say about the inability of the French to understand anything foreign and their ignorance about it is still completely true. . . .

P.S. So my old chief in the Ministry of the Interior, Vladimir Ivanovich Dal', has departed this life! He has left something [worth while] after him: his dictionary.[7] He was able to say: "*exegi monumentum.*"

[281]

Paris, October 17 [O.S.], *1872*

TO IAKOV PETROVICH POLONSKI

Your letter reached me in bed; I had another

[6] A contemporary satirical Russian periodical with cartoons. This *Iskra* must not be confused with Lenin's later publication of the same name.

[7] The dictionary of Dal' (or Dahl) is still one of the standard references for serious students of Russian—particularly nineteenth-century Russian. All four of its volumes, in a revised edition, were reprinted in 1954 (Paris, Librairie des cinq continents). There is also a recent Soviet reprint of a different edition.

attack of gout (the *eleventh* by count), and have again been transformed into a motionless statue with a swollen knee. [. . .]

I would like to tell you about extraordinary works of poetry in English or French . . . , but I cannot. The most recent English poets—all the Rosettis, etc.—are terribly precious. Glimmerings of undeniable talent flare up only in Algernon Swinburne; he is imitating Victor Hugo, but he has genuine passion and outbursts, whereas Hugo's are frequently artificial. Get his *Songs before Sunrise*;[8] he is sometimes obscure, but I think you will be pleased, anyhow. [. . .]

Why does Pisemski publish in the *Grazhdanin?* I shall not mention the [political] tendency of the magazine, but, after all, no one will read his comedy there. Do not other editors accept his works? I am glad his comedy has been successful, and I am awaiting its appearance impatiently. . . .

You keep asking why I pay no attention to the present (in my works). In the first place, I live abroad —so that to do so would be difficult—and second, I have conceived something of the sort, but it will not appear within the next year. Meanwhile, because good-hearted editors are still paying me, I shall get along on short stories and subject myself to the reviewers' contumely. [. . .]

{ 282 }

Paris, October 25/November 6, 1872

TO PAVEL VASEL'EVICH ANNENKOV

You are undoubtedly correct; *vous parlez d'or* [your

---

[8] English in the original.

words are golden], as the French say.[9] I only wish to tell you how the thing came into my head. The incident I narrated happened once to my neighbor Chertov (the real name of Chertopkhanov). It was told me by his own daughter, who may now become indignant at my lack of discretion. (Incidentally, she is not one who reads.) But that does not mitigate the force of your arguments.

Now, however, this is how things stand. Of the selections from *A Sportsman's Sketches*, 22 were published; 26 of them had been planned. Of the four that were not published, two had been started: *"Russki nemets i reformator"* ["The Russianized German and the Reformer"] and *"Zemleed"* ["The Land-Eater"]; two had merely been outlined: *"Primety"* ["Signs"] and *"Nezadacha"* ["Bad Luck"]. The first two were put aside because I knew that at the time the censor would not have passed them; the others because they were unimportant. [. . .]

After your arguments, I greatly hesitated [about whether to write more *Sketches*], although these arguments do not quite apply to the present case. I do not wish to write something new now, such as the continuation of "Chertopkhanov"; rather, I want to complete something old, which was begun and prepared twenty years ago. But [even] if I had better not touch the *Sportsman's Sketches* either way, I shall get along somehow. Write me immediately. That is what I shall do—either send off something else or give "The Land-Eater" a different look. (This is the story about some-

[9] Turgenev published "The End of Chertopkhanov" in 1872 and added it to his *Sportsman's Sketches*. Annenkov thereupon wrote him "imploring" him to leave well enough alone, which Turgenev later did.

thing that happened at home; the peasants killed their
landlord, who had been cutting down on their land
every year and whom they therefore called "the land-
eater," by forcing him to eat eight pounds of excellent
black earth. It is a jolly little plot.) [. . .]

[283]

Paris, November 8, 1872

TO GUSTAVE FLAUBERT

For some time we have been writing each other
very sad letters; they smack of ailments and death. That
is not our fault, but we must try to snap out of it. I
knew [Théophile] Gautier very slightly;[1] do you remember our dinner together at your place? Just the
same, I was very pained to learn of his demise, and
immediately thought of you; I know that you were
fond of him. Mme Sand wrote me about you in a
note I just received from her; she is uneasy about the
gloomy thoughts into which you have been plunged
and writes that I should try to suggest other and mer-
rier ones to you. I do not know what to tell you; I
merely know that a lengthy and heart-to-heart talk
would bring relief to both of us. Ah, but how in the
world can that talk be arranged? The damned gout
seems to have unsheathed its claws, and even for me to
think of a trip is pointless. I can walk now—lamely,
without shoes—but have not left my two rooms yet.
Consequently, I must await your arrival here.

Why are you so disquieted about the *plebs,* as you
say? It has power only over those who submit to its
yoke. This is when a person should say: *"Etiam si*

---

[1] Gautier had just died (October 23, 1872).

omnes, ego non." ["Even if everyone (else does so), I will not."] And then, is M. Alexandre Dumas *fils*— that meanness [*charognerie*], to use your expression, personified—a plebeian? And M. [Victorien] Sardou, M. [Jacques] Offenbach, M. [Auguste] Vacquerie, and all the others—are they really plebeians? And anyhow, they pretty much stink. The plebs also stinks—but in the sense of Cambronne's word.[2] The plebs is simply rotten. Finally, there is still at present someone in the world who is fond of you and who sympathizes with you. . . .

No, my friend, this is not what is oppressive at our age; what is oppressive is the general *taedium vitae* [tedium of life]. What is oppressive is the melancholy and the repulsion felt toward everything human. The important thing is not politics (which, in sum total, is nothing but a game); the important thing is the sadness of a person of fifty. And that is what delights me about Mme Sand: what lucidity, what simplicity, what an interest in everything, what kindness! And if, for that, a person must have a certain indulgence, a democratic attitude, and even evangelical features—what of it! Let us accept even these exaggerations.

You must come to Paris, bring your *Antoine* with you, then make plans for the future, and begin to live a full life. What if we are skeptics and criticasters, threadbare and tired—the lash of poesy urges us on; we must go on boldly to the end, especially when we can take courage from the sight of a friend urged forward by the same force.

[2] Cambronne was one of Napoleon's generals who allegedly answered the British demand for his surrender at Waterloo with one word—*"Merde!"*

I am not rereading this allegorical and metaphysical letter. I do not really know what I have written; I only know that I embrace you and say au revoir.

[284]

Paris, November 12, 1872

TO PAVEL VASIL'EVICH ANNENKOV

[. . .] And instead of a selection from A *Sportsman's Sketches*, I shall send Ragozin several lyric poems by a wonderful American poet—Walt Whitman (have you heard of him?)—in [my] translation, with a short preface. You cannot imagine anything more striking. [. . .]

[285]

Paris, December, 1872

ADDRESSEE UNKNOWN

In answer to your question, let me state that poetry is not necessary to anyone in any age; it is a luxury—but a luxury accessible to all, even the poorest; this is its meaning, its beauty, and its use.

[286]

Paris, November 26/December 8, 1872

TO PAVEL VASIL'EVICH ANNENKOV

[. . .] My translations from Whitman (not Whiteman) have also run aground [because of the gout]. [. . .]

{ 287 }

Paris, December 3 [O.S.], 1872

TO MAR'IA AGEEVNA MILIUTIN

Thank you sincerely for the kind emotion that inspired your letter. F. M. Dostoevski's conduct has not astonished me in the slightest; he hated me even when we were both young and at the beginning of our literary careers, although I have in no way deserved his hatred. But they say that groundless passions are the strongest and the most prolonged. . . . Dostoevski has permitted himself something worse than a parody; he has presented me, under the name of Karmazinov, as a secret sympathizer of the Nechaev party.³ The strange thing is that he chose to parody the one story I had placed in the magazine edited at one time by himself⁴—a story for which he showered me with letters of gratitude and praise.

I have kept those letters. It would be amusing to print them! But he knows that I will not do it. I only regret that he is using his undeniable talent to satisfy such vile emotions; evidently he does not care about debasing his talent as a pamphleteer. [. . .]

{ 288 }

Paris, December 21, 1872/January 2, 1873

TO SOFIA KONSTANTINOVNA BRIULLOV (NEE KAVELIN)

[. . .] P.S. Incidentally, do you know of a mono-

³ Sergei Nechaev (1847–83) was a student, teacher, and revolutionary disciple of Bakunin's who, in November 1869, had plotted and ordered Ivan Ivanov's murder. A *cause célèbre* of the time, this was used by Dostoevski in *The Devils* (also called *The Possessed*, in English), in which Dostoevski did parody Turgenev as "Karmazinov."

⁴ "Phantoms" first appeared in Dostoevski's magazine, *Epokha*, No. 1–2, 1864.

graph in English or German on the Emperor Pavel's
reign? If so, tell me the title quickly; Michelet is asking
about it.

[289]

Paris, February 21 [O.S.], *1873*

TO IAKOV PETROVICH POLONSKI

[. . .] Sometimes there are altogether flattering
opinions of me in the foreign press. One American
review, the *Atlantic Monthly*, has even called me a
genius!! [5] To state that this does not move me at all
would be untrue, but to assert that it gratifies me very
much would be just as false. All this is a "shadow fleeing from smoke." For several weeks of youth—most
stupid, broken, and mutilated, but youth—I would not
only give up my reputation, but also the glory of a
real genius, if I were one. And what would I do then,
you ask? I would at least run after partridges with a
gun for ten hours in a row, without a break. And that
would be enough—but now this is out of the question. [. . .]

[290]

Paris, March 22 [O.S.], *1873*

TO IAKOV PETROVICH POLONSKI

[. . .] Count Aleksei [Konstantinovich]Tolstoy's
"*Kanut*" is really a beautiful piece—perhaps the best
of all he has written. [. . .]

---

[5] The *Atlantic Monthly* in those years frequently praised
Turgenev. See Royal A. Gettman: *Turgenev in England and
America*, Illinois Studies in Language and Literature, Volume
XXVII, No. 2 (Urbana, Ill.: University of Illinois Press; 1941),
pp. 37–83.

Your story about Nekrasov did not astonish me at all. . . . His poem "Princess Volkonski" is, in my opinion, very repulsive and mawkishly liberal. . . . *Who Is Happy in Russia* is better, but there too all the hackneyed themes have been treated twenty times better by others.

Pisemski has sent me his comedy, *Podkopy* [*Mines*]. Between us, it is weak.

I have just bought an altogether beautiful naked woman (a painting). I am in general busy with this occupation—or lack of occupation (buying paintings) —because I have given up everything else, beginning with literature. [. . .]

[291]

Paris, April 9, 1873

TO MIKHAIL EVGRAFOVICH SALTYKOV-SHCHEDRIN

[. . .] I wish to thank you sincerely for having thought of me. To some extent, I have a right to be remembered by you; I am one of the oldest and most unwavering admirers of your talent. I have read your books with sincere delight, as I do everything that comes from your pen. You have staked out in our literature an entire region, in which you are the indisputable master and the first man. Once more, my heartfelt thanks. [. . .] [6]

---

[6] Saltykov-Shchedrin had sent two of his works to Turgenev in Paris: *Dnevnik provintsiala v Peterburge* (*The Diary of a Provincial in St. Petersburg*), and *Gospoda tashkentsy* (*The Tashkent People*).

[292]

Château de Nohant,[7] *September 13* [O.S.], *1873*

TO AFANASI AFANAS'EVICH FET

You speak in vain so harshly about Vergil. The constructions, characters, and so on of his *Aeneid* are of no importance—in his individual expressions, in his epithets, and in his vividness, he is not only a real poet but also a bold innovator and a romantic. Let me remind you of *per amica silentia lunae* [through the friendly silence of the moon] (if only Tiutchev could do that), or *futura iam pallida morte* [pale with imminent death] (about Dido when, mad, she ascends her pyre in order to kill herself), etc. I read Ovid with young Viardot *etwas Latein treiben* [to practice some Latin]. Ovid is not so bad, either, as you say.

[. . .] I am glad that Lev Tolstoy does not hate me and even happier that he is about to finish a major novel. I hope to God that it contains no philosophy.

[293]

Paris, November 23/December 5, 1873

TO MIKHAIL MATVEEVICH STASIULEVICH

The bearer of this letter, Mr. Mikhailov, will give you the manuscript of the translation his father, V. M. Mikhailov, made of [Heinrich] Heine's famous *Deutschland*. I recommend the translation as a completely conscientious and successful work, which would be an ornament to the pages of the *Vestnik Evropy*. Twice I went over the entire poem with the translator verse by verse, collating it with the original, and the results seem completely satisfactory. In any case, the new

---

[7] The residence of George Sand.

translation far excels the one by [V. N.] Vodovozov which was printed several years ago; I can vouch for that. There is one problem: what will be said by the censorship (which is almost harsher today than it was in the blessed times of Nikolai)?[8] The translator would not like to be subjected to distortions that are too violent, and would rather withdraw his manuscript in such a case. [. . .]

[294]

Paris, January 13 [O.S.], 1874

TO IAKOV PETROVICH POLONSKI

Wishing to put my bit into the *Skladchina,* and not having anything ready, I began digging among my old papers and came up with a supplementary selection from *A Sportsman's Sketches,* which I am asking you to forward to the proper address. 22 of them were printed in all, but about 30 had been planned. Some of these remained unfinished because I feared that the censor would not pass them; others, because I thought them insufficiently interesting or suitable. A rough draft entitled "A Living Relic" belongs to the latter group. Of course, I would have preferred sending you something more important, but you are welcome to what I have. Furthermore, the indication of our people's "long suffering" may not be completely out of place in a publication such as the *Skladchina.*

Incidentally, let me tell you a story that also has a bearing on the time of famine in Russia. In 1841, as we know, Tula Province and the provinces adjacent to it almost died out because of the famine. Several years later, while I was traveling in the same Tula Province

---

[8] Nikolai I reigned from 1825 to 1855.

with a friend, we stopped at a village inn and sat down to tea. My friend began to tell a story about some incident—I do not remember which one—from his life, and mentioned a man dying of hunger who was as "thin as a skeleton."

"Permit me to say, sir," intruded the old innkeeper who was present at our conversation, "people don't get thin from hunger: they get bloated."

"What's that?"

"Yes, sir, that's just the way it is; a man gets bloated. He swells up just like a bottle. (There are apples like that.) Why, we were all walking around bloated in 1841."

"Ah," I replied, "in 1841! Was that a terrible time?"

"Yes, sir, it was terrible."

"Well, and what happened?" I asked. "Were there disorders and robberies then?"

"What disorders, sir?" the old man replied in astonishment. "If God punishes you like that, will you sin even more?"

It seems to me that to help such a people when misfortune strikes is a sacred duty for each of us.

{ 295 }

Paris, March 4/16, 1874

TO AFANASI AFANAS'EVICH FET

[. . .] I am very grateful both to you and to L. N. Tolstoy. The season is now drawing to a close, but I shall try just the same to place his *"Three Deaths"* in the *Revue des deux mondes* or the *Temps*, and toward Autumn I certainly shall have the *Cossacks* published [in French]. The more I reread the *Cossacks*,

the more convinced I become that it is the chef
d'oeuvre of Tolstoy and of all Russian narrative literature. [. . .]

[296]

Paris, March 15/27, 1874

TO MIKHAIL MATVEEVICH STASIULEVICH

[. . .] Pushkin is my idol, my teacher, a model
I can never hope to equal, and I can say to each of his
works, as did Statius about Vergil: "*Vestigia semper
adora.*" ["Always respect traces of the past."] [. . .]

[297]

Paris, April 2, 1874

TO W. R. S. RALSTON

[. . .] I wish to ask you to do me a favor (as I
frequently have before). My friend Gustave Flaubert
has published a remarkable book *La Tentation de Saint
Antoine,* and he would be very happy to submit it to
competent English critics. Be so obliging as to give me
the names, let us say, of four of these (from the *Athe-
naeum,* the *Contemporary Review,* etc.) to whom the
book must be sent immediately.[9] I would be very grateful to you for a prompt reply.

The *Tentation* is one of the most extraordinary
works I know. [. . .]

[298]

Paris, April 2, 1874

TO LUDWIG PIETSCH

[. . .] You will shortly receive a book by my

[9] The names of the English periodicals are given in English.

friend Gustave Flaubert—*La Tentation de Saint An-toine*—or perhaps you already have. Read it, and if you like it (and I do not doubt that you will), write something about it with your fine and witty pen. Write a very impressive article. I shall be very grateful to you indeed. Let me know in which newspaper your article will appear. [. . .]

[299]

Paris, March 21/April 2, 1874

TO HIS BROTHER, NIKOLAI SERGEEVICH TURGENEV

The news about a thousand francs being sent is completely accurate, and is explained in this way: taking advantage of the lack of a literary [copyright] agreement between Russia and America, my publishers there have printed translations of my works without paying me so much as a kopeck; finally, their conscience spoke out and they sent me, together with an alto-gether flattering letter, those thousand francs by way of remuneration, which was all the kinder because no law forced them to do so. I admit that I found this very pleasant. And that is all. [. . .]

[300]

Spasskoe, June 19 [O.S.], 1874

TO SEMEN AFANAS'EVICH VENEROV

I received your letter today, and am answering your frank questions frankly.

My father passed away not in 1836 but on Oc-tober 30 [O.S.], 1834. I was all of 16 years old. My hatred of serfdom was alive even then; by the way, that is the reason why I, who grew up among beatings and tortures, have never dirtied my hands with a single blow—but A *Sportsman's Sketches* were a long way off. I was only a boy—almost a child. Moreover, my father was a poor man; he left 130 serfs in all, but they were not settled and produced no income; and we were three brothers. My father's property was merged with that of my mother—a headstrong and power-loving woman who alone gave us (and sometimes took away from us) the means to live on. It never entered either her head or ours that the insignificant estate (I am talking about my father's) was not hers. I spent three years abroad without receiving so much as a kopeck from her, but I never thought of asking for my inheritance; incidentally, that inheritance —including both what my mother inherited, as the widow, and our portion, as brothers [sons]—was not much above zero.

Just as soon as my mother passed away in 1850, I immediately set the manor serfs free; I changed over to quitrent the peasants who so desired; I assisted the general emancipation in every way; I gave them one fifth off the redemption price, and took nothing for the land on the main farmstead (which was worth a large sum). Perhaps someone else in my place would have done more—and more quickly—but I have promised to tell the truth, and I am telling it, as it is. It is nothing to boast of, but I don't think it would bring me dishonor, either.

As for your other wish, to grant it would be much more difficult. I feel a positive, almost a physical, repugnance toward my poetry, and not only do I not have a single copy of my poems, but I also would pay a good deal to know that none of them are in existence. "Andrei" was printed in the *Otechestvennye zapiski*;

but I do not remember the year—either 1845 or 1846.
Parasha appeared in a separate edition in 1843. You
might stumble across it in Cherkesov's book store on
the Nevski Prospekt [in St. Petersburg], where they
preserve all kinds of trash. [. . .]

[301]

Karlsbad, August 7, 1874

TO HENRY JAMES[1]

I ought to have written you long ago—but I have
some excuses of my silence. The letter you wrote to
me never reached me. I was in Russia at the time—I
know that it was sent to me from Paris, but it did not
come to my hands. I received the April number of the
North American Review with your article on my writings only in July; and the very day of its arrival I had
a violent attack of gout, which has not disappeared
even now—so that I had the greatest difficulty of reaching this place, where I hoped to get rid of my ailings.
But I am not willing to put further off the expression
of my thanks.

I have read your article very attentively. It is rather
difficult for an author to judge fairly a critical analysis
of his own works—I must confess that I, for instance,
find always the praise too great and the blame too
weak. I do not attribute this impression to diffidence
or modesty: it is perhaps one of the many disguises
which self-love enjoys in. All that I can say—is, that
your article strikes me as being inspired by a fine sense
of what is just and true; there is manliness in it and
psychological sagacity and a clear litterary [*sic*] taste.

[1] For a number of letters in English and French from
Turgenev to James, see the source. This letter was written in
English.

Carlsbad.
(Bohemia.)
König von England.
August 7th 1874.

My dear Sir,

I ought to have written you long ago—but
I have some excuses of my silence. The
letter you wrote to me never reached me.
I was in Russia at the time—I know
that it was sent to me from Paris—
but it did not come to my hands.
I received the April N? of the North-Ameri-
can Review with your article on my writings
only in July; and the very day of its arrival
I had a violent attack of gout, which
has not disappeared even now—so
that I had the greatest difficulty of reaching
this place, where I hope to get rid of
my ailings. But I am not willing to
say further of the progress of my
things.

I have read your article very attentively.
It is rather difficult for an author to
judge fairly a critical analysis of his own
works. — I must confess that I, for instance,
find always the praise too great and
the blame too weak. I do not attribute
this impression to diffidence or modesty:
it is perhaps one of the many disguises
which self-love enjoys in. All that I
can say — is, that your article strikes me
as being inspired by a fine sense of
what is just and true; there is manliness in it and psychological sagacity
and a clear litterary taste. — I have
only to observe that the seriousness
you reproach me — is perhaps — is certainly —
an involuntary one. — My "excess of
irony", as you call it — does not give
me any pleasure — not even the bitter one,
of which some people speak.

      I have a great sympathy for all

that is American and a great desire to
see your country. But I ought to have
indulged it earlier in life. I am falling
in the "sere, the yellow leaf" — and that's
not the best time for travelling. Still
I do not altogether abandon the idea.
It would please me very much indeed
to make your acquaintance as well
as that of some of your compatriots.
In the mean time, believe me, my
dear sir

                    Yours most sincerely,
                        Ivan Turgeniew.

P. S. My permanent adress is:
     Paris, Rue de Douai, 50.

Mr Henry James, Jr.
                                    c. t. r.

P. S. Truth compels me to say (v. page
249) — that I have large hands and
feet, an ugly nose — and nothing of an
"aristocratic" temperament: and I do
not regret it.

I have only to observe, that the pessimism you reproach me—is perhaps—is certainly—an involuntary one.—My "excess of irony," as you call it—does not give me any pleasure—not even the bitter one, of which some people speak.

I have a great sympathy for all that is American —and a great desire to see your country. But I ought to have indulged it earlier in life—I am falling in the "sere, the yellow leaf"—and that's not the best time for travelling. Still I do not altogether abandon the idea. It would please me very much indeed to make your acquaintance as well as that of some of your compatriots. [. . .]

P.S. Truth compels me to say (v. page 249)—that I have large hands and feet, an ugly nose—and nothing of an "aristocratic" temperament—and I do not regret it.

[302]

Bougival, August 18 [O.S.], 1874

TO ANNA PAVLOVNA FILOSOFOV[2]

[. . .] And you, you say that in Bazarov [in *Fathers and Children*] I wanted to present a caricature of young people. You repeat that . . . —excuse the unceremonious expression—senseless reproach! Bazarov is my favorite brain-child; I quarreled with Katkov because of him. I expended all the colors at my disposal on him. Bazarov, that wise man, that hero—a caricature?!? But apparently it cannot be helped. Just as Louis Blanc, despite all his protestations, has hitherto been

---

[2] The complete name of the addressee comes from Turgenev's *Sobranie sochineni v dvenadtsati tomakh*, Moscow, GIKhL, 1953–8, XII, 465 1.

accused of leading the national workshops (*ateliers na-tionaux*),[3] so I am saddled with a wish to libel young people through caricature! [. . .]

Now let us turn to your "old woman," i.e., to the critics—or to the public.

Like any other old woman, she stubbornly main-tains preconceived or current notions, regardless of how groundless they are. For example, she steadily as-serts that all my works since *A Sportsman's Sketches* have been bad as a result of my absence from Russia, which country, it seems, I cannot therefore even know. But that reproach can only apply to what I have writ-ten since 1863. Before that (i.e., before I was 45), I lived in Russia almost without interruption (except for 1848–50, during which time I was writing the same *Sportsman's Sketches*); *Rudin*, *A House of Gentlefolk*, *On the Eve*, and *Fathers and Children* were written in Russia. But that means nothing to the old woman; *son siège est fait* [her ways are set].

A second failing of the old woman's is that she constantly follows fashions. The fashion in literature now is for politics; everything that is not politics is non-sensical or even absurd to her.

However clumsy I am in the defense of my works, you nevertheless will understand that I cannot agree that even "Knock, Knock, Knock" is absurd. What is it, then . . . , you ask? This is what it is: a general study of the Russian suicide, who rarely shows any-thing poetic or pathetic but, on the contrary, almost always performs the act as a result of egotism and nar-row-mindedness, with an admixture of mysticism and

[3] In 1848, Louis Blanc forced the government to implement, with the *ateliers nationaux*, the principle of guaranteed employ-ment for workingmen.

fatalism. You will tell me that my study has not succeeded. . . . Perhaps, but I merely wanted to point out the justification and the appropriateness of treating purely psychic (not political, and not social) questions.

The old woman also reproaches me for lacking convictions. My entire thirty-year career in literature will serve to answer that. Not one line I have written has caused me to blush, and I do not repudiate a single one. Let that be said about those who say otherwise! And, moreover, let the old woman chatter to herself! I have never paid any attention to her before, and I am certainly not going to begin now!

I do not know whether I shall write my novel; I do know it will have many shortcomings. . . . But excuse me, my dear Anna Pavlovna, why do not the young people undertake these tasks? We, the old ones, would willingly yield "honor and place" to them, be the first to rejoice in the influx of new power. [. . .]

[303]

Bougival, September 11 [O.S.], 1874
TO ANNA PAVLOVNA FILOSOFOV[4]

[. . .] You began with Bazarov [in *Fathers and Children*], and I shall begin with him. You look for him in real life, but you will not find him; in a minute I shall tell you why. The times have changed; Bazarovs are not needed now. Society in the times ahead of us will not need any special talents, or even a special kind of mind—or anything strong, outstanding, or too in-

[4] The complete name of the addressee comes from Turgenev's *Sobranie sochineni v dvenadtsati tomakh*, Moscow, GIKhL, 1953–8, XII, 465 *f*.

dividualistic; it will need industriousness and endurance. People will have to know how to sacrifice themselves without any glitter or fuss; they will have to know how to humble themselves and how to take on petty and obscure and even mean work without abhorrence. I choose the word "mean" in the sense of the plain, the artless, the *terre à terre* [commonplace]. For example, what can be meaner than teaching a muzhik to read, helping him, starting hospitals, etc. Why should talents and even erudition be needed for that? All that is needed is a heart able to sacrifice its egotism; we cannot even talk about a mission here (not to mention the star of Mr. X.!) . . . * A feeling of duty, a glorious feeling of patriotism in the real sense of the word—that is all that is needed.

But Bazarov nevertheless is still a type, a harbinger, endowed with some fascination, and not devoid of a certain halo. All this is not out of place here; and it is ridiculous to talk about *heroes* or *artists* of toil. Brilliant natures will probably not turn up in literature; those who rush into politics are merely ruining themselves for nothing. That is how things are, but many people—especially impressionable and enthusiastic women such as yourself—cannot at once become reconciled to this fact, to this ordinary milieu, to this modest resolution. No matter what you say, you still would like to become enraptured and be carried away; you yourself write that you wish to show reverence, but one does not revere *merely useful* people . . . and they will be the best people. There will probably be many of them, but there will be very few beautiful and captivat-

---

* The source just mentioned identifies Mr. X. as Vladimir Gavrilovich Dekhterev (1854–1903), a medical student and revolutionary, whose verses Turgenev disliked.

ing ones. And your search for a "present-day" Bazarov implies—perhaps unconsciously—a thirst for beauty (of course, of an original kind). All these dreams must be given up. [. . .]

[304]

Paris, October 7, 1874

TO LUDWIG PIETSCH

[. . .] I am sending you in today's mail the *Tentation de Saint Antoine.* Do you know whether Julian Schmidt received his copy? I read Lindau's excellent article and, upon his instructions, sent it to Gustave Flaubert. [. . .]

[305]

Paris, October 14 [O.S.], 1874

TO IAKOV PETROVICH POLONSKI

[. . .] "Andrei Kolosov" appeared in the *Otechestvennye zapiski* during 1844 and, of course, passed away without even a trace. A young person who had paid attention to the tale at that time would have been a special phenomenon. Young people do not read such works, which are unable to attract (and, to speak fairly, do not merit) attention. [. . .]

I read Aksakov's book about F. I. Tiutchev.[5] The first half is very good and astute; the second, with its Slavophile policy, is bad and confused. But it could not have been different. [. . .]

[5] Ivan Sergeevich Aksakov: *Biografiia Fedora Ivanovicha Tiutcheva* (*Biography of Fedor Ivanovich Tiutchev*).

{ 306 }

Paris, November 26, 1874

TO JULIAN SCHMIDT

[. . .] As for the *Tentation* [*de Saint Antoine*], you are unfortunately correct, and I must admit that this wonderful book is really an unreadable and barbarous work. [. . .]

{ 307 }

Paris, January 2/14, 1875

TO ALEKSANDR VASIL'EVICH TOPOROV

[. . .] Be kind enough to subscribe to the *Russki vestnik*, especially because rumor has it that Lev Tolstoy's novel will appear in it. [. . .]

{ 308 }

Paris, February 13, 1875

TO JULIAN SCHMIDT

[. . .] I am very glad that you liked the photographs. I myself would have sent you pictures of Flaubert and Zola, but this is no easy matter. Flaubert has not had his picture taken for fifteen years, and Zola never at all. He [Zola] is what the French call *un sanglier* [literally, a wild boar; figuratively, a determined person not easy to distract]; he stays at home with his wife all the time, does not wear gloves, has no frock-coat, and does not wish to hear about any of the trifling vanities of life, including his being photographed. [. . .]

Do you know Flaubert's *Education sentimentale*

(a terribly stupid title)? I scarcely think so. It is perhaps his most significant work, although it is hardly pleasant. It has been a failure in France, as it was too bitter a truth for the French. It appeared shortly before the [Franco-Prussian] war and turned out to be prophetic. Would you like me to send you this book?

{ 309 }

Paris, February 5/17, 1875

TO ALEKSANDR VASIL'EVICH TOPOROV

The forties are the most difficult years in life, and you are in the most difficult period of those years. Bear it for a while, and the idea of old age, even a lonely one, will no longer terrify you so. And life in general is not a happy business—that question was decided long ago.

I ought to tell you as Chichikov tells Tentetnikov [in Gogol's *Dead Souls*]: "Everything indicates that you must get married." To provide oneself with children is the main thing. The rest is nonsense. [. . .]

{ 310 }

Paris, 1875 [?]

TO PAVEL VASIL'EVICH ANNENKOV

[. . .] That Tolstoy's novel is unsatisfactory is distressing. I do not know how you will like *Anna Karenina*, but I found it—i.e., the beginning—mannered, shallow, *léché* [labored] (as the painters say), and uninteresting. Perhaps the rest will be better. Let us wait. [. . .]

{ 311 }

Paris, February 13/25, 1875

TO ALEKSANDRA VASIL'EVNA PLETNEV

[. . .] My health is all right, but my laziness is boundless. [. . .]

I read the beginning of Lev Tolstoy's novel [*Anna Karenina*] in the *Russki vestnik*. To you I can say that I am dissatisfied with it. Despite all its seeming simplicity, it is precious, shallow, with a preconceived idea, and boring, to boot. Perhaps he will spread his wings later on. The reader has the right to demand the excellent from him. I would like to know your opinion; do not hesitate to tell it to me, even if it directly contradicts my own. [. . .]

{ 312 }

Paris, February 14 [O.S.], 1875

TO ALEKSEI SERGEEVICH SUVORIN

[. . .] The times in which we are living are nastier than those of our youth. Then we were standing before a boarded-up door; now the door seems to have been opened a crack—but it is even more difficult to get past it. [. . .]

Toporov has probably already delivered to you a copy of the latest edition of my works. Accept it from a man who is in the same camp as you, who is interested in you and values your interest. Take the trouble to reread "Punin and Baburin." I revised and corrected the story and I am still dissatisfied with it, but it strikes me as having something to it. But could not this also be an old man's self-flattery about his latest brain-child? [. . .]

{ 313 }

Paris, February 22 [O.S.], *1875*

TO MAR'IA AGEEVNA MILIUTIN

You have really set me a task! I do not think that any writer has ever taken on such a task. To define my outlook on life . . . and in the compressed form of a letter, to boot!?

To treat the question either negatively or humorously would be easy and even natural. . . . It would be no less natural and accurate to say: "God knows!" I do not know my own personality at all. But because I do not wish to grieve your son (although, frankly, I cannot fail to wonder at the strange assignments given to the pupils in our educational institutions!!),[6] I shall say in brief that I am mainly a realist and interested most in the living truth of the human physiognomy; I am indifferent to everything supernatural; I do not believe in any absolutes or [philosophical] systems, and—as far as I can judge—I am vulnerable to poetry. Everything human is dear to me; Slavophilism is alien—as is any other *orthodoxy*. I seem to have said enough, and all this is really only words! I have nothing more to report to you about myself. [. . .]

{ 314 }

Paris, March 14 [O.S.], *1875*

TO ALEKSEI SERGEEVICH SUVORIN

Tuesday, April 1/13

[. . .] I am impatiently awaiting the first part of

[6] According to her daughter, Mrs. Miliutin had asked this question of Turgenev jestingly after Mrs. Miliutin's little boy had been given a school assignment to prepare for examinations on "Turgenev's Outlook on Life as Shown in His Works."

your essays. Your picture of L. N. Tolstoy will most likely come out well. He has an extraordinary talent, but in *Anna Karenina* he, as they say here, *a fait fausse route* [has taken the wrong road]; [this work shows] the influence of Moscow, the Slavophile gentry, Orthodox old maids, his own isolation, and the lack of genuine, artistic freedom. The second part is merely boring and *shallow*—and that is a misfortune!

As for biographical details about me, the data in Polevoi[7] are correct, and gathering others is not worth while (but remember that he gives my father the wrong first name; [my father] was called Sergei Nikolaevich, my mother Varvara Petrovna Lutovinov; I was born on October 28 [O.S.], 1818). There is really a lot that is autobiographical in "Punin and Baburin." [. . .]

{ 315 }

Paris, March 20/April 1, 1875

TO ALEKSANDR VASIL'EVICH TOPOROV

[. . .] Rather a bigger disappointment to us [than Anton Rubinshtein's opera *The Demon*] (because the expectations were greater) is Lev Tolstoy's novel [*Anna Karenina*]. For his talent to stray into the swamp of high society and tramp and push around in one spot there, and treat all that nonsense without humor but, on the contrary, with pathos and earnestness—what kind of stuff is that!! Moscow has ruined him; he is not the first and will not be the last. But I am more sorry for him than for the others. [. . .]

If I manage to shake off my laziness and finish my

[7] Perhaps Petr Nikolaevich Polevoi (1839–1902), author of *Istoria russkoi literatury* (*A History of Russian Literature*), St. Petersburg, 1872 (second edition, 1874).

long tale [*Virgin Soil*], we shall see each other at the
end of the year. [. . .]

[316]

Bougival, April 9, 1875

TO PETR LAVROVICH LAVROV

[. . .] The author [Sergei Mikhailovich Step-
niak-Kravchinski] is a man with talent; he knows the
language,[8] and his entire work is warmed by the fire
of youth and conviction. But his tone is not consistent.
He is not clearly aware of whom he is writing for—for
exactly what stratum of the reading public. The result
is confusion and unevenness in the exposition. Now he
writes for the people, and now for an audience that is,
if not more educated, more literary. Nor has the author
avoided what I would be ready to call the melodious
and rhetorical—or Moscow—manner, for example, at
the very beginning. It seems to me that the fewer such
ornaments, the better. But, I repeat, your acquaintance
has talent and fire; let him continue to labor in this
field. [. . .]

[317]

Paris, April 13, 1875

TO LUDWIG PIETSCH

[. . .] In my letter, I asked you to find out why
Julian Schmidt has not answered my question as to
whether he knows Flaubert's *Education sentimentale*
[and not reflected on my offer to] send him the book if
he so wishes. [. . .]

---

[8] Lavrov had sent Turgenev a story by Stepniak, who was
a Populist (*narodnik*) and terrorist. Years later Stepniak wrote
The Career of a Nihilist in English.

[318 }

Paris, April 3/15, 1875

TO VLADIMIR VASIL'EVICH STASOV

I received your letter, and am losing no time in carrying out your instructions about Zola, which were really, I know, rather short. His address is Paris, 21 rue St.-Georges, Batignolles. However, I do not vouch for success. Working like a horse from morning to night, he barely makes both ends meet, and he will not begin to spend his time on a correspondence with no financial value. If you are really getting ready to come to Paris, that will furnish you with the most convenient opportunity to have some talks with him. [. . .]

[319 }

Paris, May 13 [O.S.], 1875

TO IAKOV PETROVICH POLONSKI

[. . .] My health is pretty good; my idleness, colossal. Kharlamov, whose portraits have scored a major success at the exhibition here, is finishing my portrait; it is coming out excellently, but what I have to pay him for two two-hour sittings a day is not excellent!! [. . .]

That Nekrasov has the blues, I confess, leaves me completely indifferent: the old ——, the satiated kite, has ruffled his feathers. Well, to hell with him.

Grigorovich will no longer find me here; I will not cry about that, either. [. . .]

I do not like *Anna Karenina*, although it does contain some genuinely magnificent pages (such as the horse race, the mowing, and the hunt). But it is all

sour; it reeks of Moscow, incense, old maids, dirty
Slavicism, and the gentry.

{ 320 }

Karlsbad, May 24/June 6, 1875

TO ALEKSANDR VASIL'EVICH TOPOROV

[. . .] I have never written a line [of creative lit-
erature] that was not in Russian. And how can anyone
write except in his own language? [. . .]

{ 321 }

Karlsbad, June 9, 1875

TO LUDWIG PIETSCH

[. . .]The death of Bizet, the young French
composer, is a great loss. If his *Carmen* is given anywhere in Germany, do not miss it. It is the most
original thing to appear in France since Gounod's
Faust. [. . .]

{ 322 }

Karlsbad, June 6/18, 1875

TO ALEKSANDR VASIL'EVICH TOPOROV

[. . .] As for [Aleksandr Nikolaevich] Pypin's
article on Belinski and his argument with me in the
last number of the *Vestnik Evropy,* upon reading it
through carefully, I have become convinced that he is
right and views the activities of our great critic more
accurately than I did. [. . .] [9]

[9] Turgenev added a postscript to the 1880 edition of his
reminiscences of Belinski, acknowledging this.

[323]

Bougival, September 5, 1875

TO VLADIMIR VASIL'EVICH STASOV

[. . .] I am reading *Rappel,* and have also read Victor Hugo's new articles. I regret that I do not possess sufficient power of expression to state the degree to which I despise them—as I do *all* his *prose.* [. . .]

[324]

Bougival, October 28 [O.S.], *1875*

TO MIKHAIL EVGRAFOVICH SALTYKOV-SHCHEDRIN

[. . .] Let me turn to your last story in the *Otechestvennye zapiski.* I received the October issue yesterday and, of course, immediately read [your] *"Semeiny sud"* ["A Family Court"], which I liked very much indeed. The characters are all drawn powerfully and faithfully. I shall not mention the mother, who is typical and is not appearing in your work for the first time; evidently, she has been captured alive—from real life. But the character of the lost and drunken "booby" is especially well done. It is so good that I involuntarily wonder why Saltykov does not write, instead of sketches, an important novel with groupings of characters and events, with a guiding idea and large-scale exposition? The answer may be that novels and stories are, to some extent, written by others—but what Saltykov does, no one else can. Whatever may happen, I very much liked *"Semeiny sud,"* and I am impatiently awaiting the continuation of Judas's exploits. [. . .] [1]

[1] Saltykov later did expand his *"Semeiny sud"* to a full-length novel: *Gospoda Golovlevy* [*The Golovlyov Family*].

And that Mother Russia escorts you everywhere should not cause you to complain; she will have to submit to your operations for a long time, and that is why, even if she shouts, she thrusts herself upon you. [. . .]

[325]

Paris, November 12 [O.S.], 1875

TO MIKHAIL EVGRAFOVICH SALTYKOV-SHCHEDRIN

[. . .] In the first place, do you not wish (on behalf of the *Otechestvennye zapiski*) to start an arrangement with Edmond de Goncourt similar to that which the *Vestnik Evropy* has with Emile Zola? I am not talking about feuilletons, but about a novel. Goncourt is about to finish a novel that might appear first in Russian translation, as *La Faute de l'abbé Mouret* did. The author could send his manuscript. If you like the idea, let me know—and the price could be just the same as for Zola (from 1,500 to 2,000 francs). Second, as for Zola, you told me that you would pay considerably more for his novel than Stasiulevich [of the *Vestnik Evropy*]. I gave Zola a hint about that, of course in vague terms and without mentioning anyone. His face lit up. If you still have such intentions—and what is the offer?—drop me a line on the subject. [. . .]

[326]

Paris, November 25 [O.S.], 1875

TO MIKHAIL EVGRAFOVICH SALTYKOV-SHCHEDRIN

They say that Peter the Great, when he met an intelligent man, would kiss him on the head; I am neither Peter nor great, but having read your letter of

November 30 [presumably N.S.], I would willingly kiss you, my dear Mikhail Evgrafovich, because what you say about the Goncourts' and Zola's novels is accurate and true. Deep down, I had vague inklings of all this myself, but only now have I said "Ah!" and seen it clearly. And not because they (especially Zola) have no talent, but because they are not going along the right road—and they invent very powerfully. Their writing smacks of literature; that is what is bad. But everything shows that all this is just what our Russian public wishes at this moment, and although we ought not to indulge that taste blindly, neither ought we to forget that novels and stories are not written for our confreres, and that what the public finds as fresh as early snow may well set our teeth on edge. And so let us wait to see what the editorial board of the *Otechestvennye zapiski* will say. The contents of Goncourt's novel are rather bold; it is, in his words, a serious and harsh study of a public woman.

In any case, it is not Dostoevski's *Raw Youth*. After I had received the latest (November) issue of the *Otechestvennye zapiski*, I took a look at that chaos. God, what a taste of sourness and what a hospital stench it has—and also mumblings and ignorant psychological tinkering which no one needs!! He is the one to whom what you said in your letter about the latest generation applies completely. [. . .]

There is no doubt of any kind that our compatriots both hate and avoid you. If they see every writer as a criticaster, you are even more so. [. . .]

[327]

Paris, December 26 [O.S.], 1875

TO MIKHAIL EVGRAFOVICH SALTYKOV-SHCHEDRIN

[. . .] As for the article about Aleksei Konstantinovich Tolstoy, you are both right and not right. Of
course, it is a panegyric in the sense of the old saying:
De mortuis nil nisi bene. But there are *circonstances
atténuantes.*

First of all, I was requested to do the article,
and could not refuse because I was *personally* indebted
to A. K. Tolstoy; second, I still think that A. K. Tolstoy
was nevertheless a poet—even if second-rate (third-rate,
if you like); third, he was a man who, if not terribly
brainy, was good, kind, and humane. Finally, I must observe that Stasiulevich cut out several sentences containing my reservations. To protest against this was not
worth while.

To praise such persons as A. K. Tolstoy—after
their death—is permissible; during their lifetimes, praise
would be something else again. You will [certainly] feel
the nuance here and not ascribe it to any ulterior considerations. [. . .]

[328]

Paris, January 3 [O.S.], 1876

TO MIKHAIL EVGRAFOVICH SALTYKOV-SHCHEDRIN

[. . .] I was enraptured by your draft of the
humorous story about the correspondence between
Miss N—— P——ch and Paul de Kock; you must write
it up *without fail,* for it will be a gem of the purest
water. I also read *"Po rodstvennomu"* ["By Kinship"]
and liked it very much; the old woman who weeps

when the sun rises is what the French call *une trouvaille* [a real find]; the entire characterization is superb. To know how to arouse the reader's sympathy for her without softening a single one of her features can be done only by a great talent.

And now a few words about *Fathers and Children* because you spoke of it. Do you really suppose that everything you reproach me with has not entered my head? That is why I should not have wished to disappear from the face of the earth without having finished my major novel, which, as far as I can see, would have clarified many misunderstandings and placed me somehow and somewhere I ought to be. I do not wonder that many people still find Bazarov a riddle; I myself cannot picture him exactly as I wrote him. He has had —please do not laugh—something fateful, something stronger than the author and independent of him. I know one thing: I had no preconceived idea, and no [political] tendency at the time; I wrote naïvely, as if wondering myself at what was emerging from me. You refer to the teacher; but it was really after *Fathers and Children* more than at any other time that I moved away from the circle I had never really been admitted to, and for which I would consider it stupid and shameful to write or toil. Tell me honestly whether anyone could really be offended at being compared to Bazarov. You yourself observe that he is the most sympathetic of all my characters. "A certain delicate aroma" is ascribed to him by the readers, but I am ready to admit (and I have already done so in print in my *Reminiscences*) that I had no right to give our reactionary scoundrels a chance to catch hold of a sobriquet, of a name; the writer in me had to make that sacrifice to the citizen, and hence I acknowledge that both the

alienation of the young people from me and every kind
of obloquy are justified. The question that arose was a
little more important than artistic truth, and I had to
know it beforehand. [. . .]

{ 329 }

Paris, January 19 [O.S.], 1876

TO MIKHAIL EVGRAFOVICH SALTYKOV-SHCHEDRIN

[. . .] The weather there [in St. Petersburg]
now is really very nasty; the suppressions and the sus-
pensions of publications are coming down hard and
heavy. . . . Come to Paris before going to St. Petersburg.

As for me and the disadvantages of living abroad,
far from my native soil—far from the clashes and con-
troversy—you are a thousand times right, but it cannot
be changed. . . . In my literary work, I am forced
like a bear in the winter to suck my own paw, and
nothing comes of that. [. . .]

All these days I have been living with my impressions of the part of Herzen's manuscript for *Byloe i
Dumy*[2] in which he narrates the story of his wife, her
death, etc. It was all written with tears and blood; it
flames and burns. I am sorry that it cannot be published. He was the only Russian who could write like
that. [. . .]

{ 330 }

Paris, January 27, 1876

TO JULIAN SCHMIDT

[. . .] I am using the departure of a kind ac-

[2] Mirsky refers to the Herzen book as *My Past and
Thoughts.*

quaintance to send you Flaubert's *Education sentimentale*. In all probability, you will receive it simultaneously with this letter. It is not very compelling reading, but the book is extremely important, and its complete fiasco in France is characteristic. The French do not like to swallow such bitter pills. [. . .]

[331]

Paris, March 2/14, 1876

TO ALEKSANDR FEDOROVICH ONEGIN (NÉ OTTO)

Upon receiving your letter, I rummaged through my entire correspondence, and at last found the subjoined letter of Mr. Dostoevski's. The result is that I had loaned him not 100 thalers as I thought, but 50. I shall be obliged to you if you would remit to him this letter together with the receipt, in lieu of the receipt I had sent him through you as the intermediary.

I shall not conceal from you that you have hurt me more deeply than anyone else has ever done.[3] You have not hesitated to accuse me of having consciously given offense as a rich man can to a poor one. You talk of your despotism, but I, I might have expected you to show me your friendship. Indeed, believing me capable not of such "baseness," as you say, but of cowardly behavior, you should not have hesitated to decline taking on the errand in the first place. Or you might have supposed that my memory had betrayed me, that I was mistaken about the sum (as was the case), and then, how

[3] At Turgenev's request, A. F. Onegin had called on Dostoevski to get the money Turgenev had lent him in Germany during 1865. Turgenev had earlier received 50 thalers from Dostoevski, and had asked Onegin to get what he believed to be the balance of the loan—another 50. As Dostoevski could prove that only 50 thalers had been loaned to him originally, Onegin felt like a fool and wrote a hot letter to Turgenev.

could you have failed to warn me, to tell me to look through my papers again? Instead, after a hesitation that I find offensive, you did not hesitate [sic] to cast the insult in my face. (All I can do is to hope you did not realize the magnitude of its force.) After having given long consideration to your attribution of so many vile and despicable emotions to me, I beg you—and this will not surprise you at all—after you have fulfilled my last request (that is to say, the exchange of receipts), to forget my existence. [. . .]

[332]

Paris, March 10/22, 1876

TO IULIA PETROVNA VREVSKI

[. . .] Read Zola's *Son Excellence Rougon* [*His Excellency Rougon*]—a wonderful book; one character in it, Clorinde, is drawn with a masterful hand.

I have not yet read the continuation of *Anna Karenina*,[4] but I see with regret where the entire novel is heading. However great the talent of Lev Tolstoy may be, he will not tear himself away from the Moscow swamp he has crawled into. Orthodoxy, nobles, Slavophilism, gossip, the Arbat, Katkov, Antonina Bludov,[5] ignorance, conceit, customs of the gentry, officers, enmity to everything foreign, sour cabbage soup, and the absence of soap—in a word, chaos. And a gifted man must perish in that chaos!! That is the way things always are in Russia. [. . .]

[4] In January 1876 Tolstoy published Chapters XI through XXVIII of Part Three, and in February, Chapters I through XIV of Part Four. Both selections appeared in the *Russki vestnik.*
[5] Antonina Dmitrievna Bludov ran a salon in Moscow famous for its reactionary attitudes; she herself was a Maid of Honor.

{ 333 }

Paris, March 25, 1876

TO JULIAN SCHMIDT

[. . .] The chief mistake of this remarkable
novel [Zola's *Les Rougon-Macquart*] is the petty provincial milieu that surrounds Rougon. It is all too petty for
such a man, but Zola, unfortunately, does not know
high society well enough and is too timid to study it as
it deserves. The Emperor and the Empress are remark-
ably similar [to the originals]. Today I am sending you
[Zola's] *La Faute de l'abbé Mouret*. The beginning and
the end of this book are perhaps the best things Zola
has ever written. The middle, in which he tries to
depict the solitude of Paradou and adapts an ultra-
poetic tone (rather astonishing for a realist), is the
Achilles' heel of the novel. [. . .]

{ 334 }

Paris, March 16/28, 1876

TO PAVEL VASIL'EVICH ANNENKOV

[. . .] Even the famous and celebrated *Anna
Karenina* satisfies me little, although one does run
across charming things in it which are worthy of a
great master. But the whole work exudes a musty
odor. [. . .]

{ 335 }

Paris, March 22/April 3, 1876

TO ALEKSANDR VASIL'EVICH TOPOROV

[. . .] I have been given *Anna Karenina* to read
in the *Russki vestnik*; I cannot say that I am satisfied

with it, although Tolstoy's strong talent does sometimes become apparent in all its brilliance. [. . .]

[336]

Paris, March 22 [O.S.], 1876

TO ALEKSEI SERGEEVICH SUVORIN

[. . .] My friend, Emile Zola, has written the
sixth novel of his *Rougon-Macquart* series entitled *The
Slaughterhouse (L'Assommoir)*. He wished to give it
to the *Vestnik Evropy* on the earlier terms, but because
his latest work (*Son Excellence Rougon*) has scored
such a success, he has received an altogether advan-
tageous offer from the magazine *Bien public*. *The
Slaughterhouse* will be serialized in the feuilleton section of that magazine, beginning April 15 (N.S.). All
this has made its appearance in the May issue of the
Vestnik Evropy (i.e., on May 13) impossible because
other translators will have almost an entire month's
head-start—and, of course, they will not pass up the
opportunity. I have been wondering whether you would
like to use this for your *Novoe vremia*. Zola could arrange for you to receive the beginning—and also the
continuation—of his novel a full week ahead of all the
others, so that it would be new to the public. But to do
this, you must:

1) if you agree, telegraph me immediately;

2) let me also know in the telegram what price
you could set. *Vestnik Evropy* paid 1400 francs *pour
la primeur* [for his first book]. I suppose that he would
let you have the novel for perhaps 1000 (250 silver
rubles). In any case, as soon as we receive your telegram here, the beginning of the novel will be set up
immediately and mailed to you; today is the 3rd [N.S.];

the telegram could arrive the 6th; the novel would go
to you on the 10th—and *Bien public* will not appear
before the 15th. You would have a lead your competi-
tors could never overtake. And judging from all I know
about the novel, it is excellent. It is taken from the life
of the Parisian workmen whom Zola knows better than
anyone else. . . .

[337]

Paris, April 9 [*O.S.*], *1876*

TO ALEKSEI SERGEEVICH SUVORIN

Excuse my not answering you at once, but many
things were piling up. Moreover, the damage is not
great because the question of Zola's novel has been set
aside for the reasons that you have stated. He also is
unable to supply you with a few galley proofs for feuilletons because he has decided to replace them this time
with his usual monthly letter to the *Vestnik Evropy*.
I told him of your suggestion (about contributing to
the *Novoe vremia* twice a month), but he now has so
much work on his hands (by the way, he has become
the drama critic for the *Bien public*) that he is compelled to turn down this offer, too, although he thanks
you for your confidence and will keep that in mind.

As for Leopold Sacher-Masoch, I know that he
would be very glad to get in touch with you. His permanent residence is Graz (Austria); his publisher is
Haller in Berne (Switzerland). I do not know him personally, and I admit that I am no great lover of his
books. They smack too much of "literature" and "spice"
—two good things that become intolerable with too
much repetition. I could never understand the viewpoint that compares him to me. [. . .]

[338]

Spasskoe, June 9 [O.S.], 1876

TO ALEKSEI SERGEEVICH SUVORIN

Upon going through St. Petersburg, I read in one of your feuilletons: "George Sand is dead—and I do not feel like talking about it." You probably meant by that that a man must say either a lot or nothing about her. I do not doubt that *Novoe vremia* has subsequently filled this gap and, like the other magazines, has at least given a biographical sketch of the great author. Nevertheless, permit me to say a word about her in your magazine, although I too do not have the time or the opportunity to say "much," and although, as you shall see, this "word" is not even mine. I was lucky enough to have the pleasure of knowing George Sand personally, and please do not take that expression for the usual phrase; whoever was able to see that rare creature close up had to consider himself lucky.

A few days ago I received a letter from a Frenchwoman who also knew her intimately; this is what her letter says:

"The last words of our dear friend were: 'Leave . . . greenery!' (*Laissez . . . verdure . . .*)—i.e., place no stone on my grave; let the grass grow on it! And her wish will be respected; only wild flowers will grow on her grave. I find these last words very touching, very significant, and so much in accord with her life, which had been given for so long to everything good and unaffected. . . . Her love of nature, of the truth, her humbleness before it, her inexhaustible kindness— quiet, always uniform and always inherent! . . . [. . .] No matter how rare genius is, *such* kindness is even rarer. [. . .] When they buried her, one of the peasants from the environs of Nohant[6] went up to the grave, placed a wreath on it, and said: 'From the peasants of Nohant—not from the poor; thanks to her, there have been no poor here.' And mind you, George Sand was not rich, and working to the very end of her life, she only managed to make ends meet."

I have almost nothing to add to these lines; I can only guarantee their complete truthfulness. When I first met George Sand about eight years ago, the enthusiastic wonder she once inspired in me had long since disappeared, and I no longer worshipped her. But no one could enter the circle of her personal life and fail to become a worshipper in a different, and perhaps better, sense. Everyone felt immediately that he was in the presence of an infinitely generous and benevolent nature, in which everything egotistic had long since been burned away completely by the inextinguishable flame of poetic enthusiasm, and faith in the ideal [in the presence of a person] who could be reached by everything human, who found it valuable, and who radiated help and sympathy. . . . And, above all, this was an unconsciously worn halo, something lofty, free, and heroic. . . . Believe me, George Sand was one of our saints; you, of course, will grasp what I mean by that word.

Excuse the disjointedness and the jerkiness of this letter. [. . .]

{ 339 }

Spasskoe, June 16 [O.S.], 1876

TO VLADIMIR LIUDVIGOVICH KIGN

. . . If the study of the human appearance of

6 George Sand's chateau. (Turgenev's note.)

someone else's life interests you *more* than the exposition of your thoughts and emotions—if, for example, you find it more *pleasant* faithfully and precisely to transmit the external appearance not merely of a person but of an ordinary thing than to state beautifully and heatedly what you feel upon seeing that thing or that person—then you are an objective writer and can undertake a story or a novel. As far as toil is concerned, without it, without persistent work, any artist invariably remains a dilettante; he cannot wait for the so-called beneficent moments of inspiration; if it comes, so much the better. But you must work just the same!

And you must not merely work on your piece to have it express precisely what you wish it to express, both in degree and kind; you must read it again, study it incessantly, try to grasp everything around you, try not only to catch life in all its manifestations, but also to understand it, to understand the laws that make it move and that do not always break through to the surface; you must strive for patterns through the play of chance and, with all this, must remain faithful to the truth, you must not be satisfied with superficial study, and must shun false effects. An objective writer takes a large burden upon himself; his muscles must be strong. That is the way I used to work—but not always even then; now I have grown lazy and old. [. . .]

[340]

Spasskoe, June 20/July 2, 1876

TO HIS BROTHER, NIKOLAI SERGEEVICH TURGENEV

[. . .] Let me turn to you with the following request: if I die before you, and you inherit [my estate at] Spasskoe, may I count on the brotherly friendship you have always shown me? Let me fervently hope that you will give to Mme P[auline] Viardot the 100,000 [rubles] you wanted to leave to me in your will, or, if she is no more, to her two daughters, Claudie and Marianne. The sale of Spasskoe alone should, from all accounts, bring in 150,000 rubles, which will recompense you with interest, and if you can possibly give an additional 10,000 or 15,000 to my daughter, Pauline Bruère, I shall thank you from beyond the grave. (And, you know, you would then also acquire other estates— Tanki and Kaznoe.) Please set me at ease, my dear brother, and tell me that in case you inherit my estate after my death, you will fulfill my request. [. . .]

{ 341 }

Bougival, August 7, 1876

TO MIKHAIL MATVEEVICH STASIULEVICH

[. . .] I am secretive about the title [of V*irgin Soil*] only because I am afraid lest someone else hit upon the same thing. But if you would like to announce it in the V*estnik Evropy* and call the novel by its title, I would still retain my priority. However, it is too late now for the August issue.

As for its contents, I can assure you of one thing: the [metal] *plow* in my epigraph does not mean revolution, but enlightenment,[7] and the very idea of the novel has the best of intentions; only a *very* stupid censor could think I am winking at the young people— and our censorship now is not stupid. [. . .]

---

[7] The epigraph reads: "Virgin soil ought to be turned over not with a *sokha* [a wooden plow] which glides along the surface but with a *plug* [a metal plow] which penetrates deeply."

[342]

Bougival, September 17 [O.S.], *1876*

TO MIKHAIL EVGRAFOVICH SALTYKOV-SHCHEDRIN

I received your letter and also the copy of [your] *Blagonamerennye rechi* [*Well-intentioned Speeches*], for which I sincerely thank you; the copy came to me with the inscription to N. A. Nekrasov (and he probably has the one with mine). You made a mistake in not sending *Blagonamerennye rechi* to Zola; he would have been very flattered; he asks about you every time I see him, just as Flaubert does.

Incidentally, about Zola, I have seen L——chov, and I know that he has been hard hit by losses. My "invincible" zeal for him has nothing to do with it. The fact is that Stasiulevich, on his last trip to Paris, became acquainted with Zola and loaded him with money from head to foot—but on condition that Zola would entirely belong to him. As a result, V*estnik Evropy* seems to Zola like the fabulous *poule aux oeufs d'or* [goose with the golden eggs], which must be guarded like the apple of one's eye. [. . .]

[343]

Bougival, October 23, 1876

TO EMMA LAZARUS[8]

My dear Miss Lazarus,

I have just received in the same day—your letter and your drama—and I beg you to receive my very best

---

[8] This letter was written by Turgenev in English. It has been reproduced here with his original punctuation and in its entirety.

thanks. I am just now very occupied: I finish a novel of a considerable length, which will appear in the January number of a Russian Review.[9] But as soon as I will have some leisure—I will give me the pleasure of reading "the Spagnoletto." [1] I do not doubt that I will find it worthy of the Author of "Alide"—and I will be so free as to express you my opinion of it.

In the beginning of November I go back to Paris. . . . (50, Rue de Douai) and I will remain there all the winter, with the exception of a few week's [sic] sojourn in Petersburg.

Believe me, my dear Miss Lazarus

Yours very truly
Iv. Tourguéneff

[344]

Bougival, November 9/21, 1876

TO MIKHAIL MATVEEVICH STASIULEVICH

[. . .] The day before yesterday Zola came to me completely upset. He brought his manuscript and asked me to compare it with the [Russian] translation that had appeared in the November issue of the *Vestnik Evropy*.[2] You not only had deleted some quotations, but had even eliminated a considerable part of his text. He could have become reconciled to the first fact (because he admitted that he had included too many quotations), but he was extremely pained by the second. His words and also his articles written for the *Bien public* (as a drama critic) show that no one could con-

[9] *Virgin Soil* first appeared in the January and February 1877 issues of the *Vestnik Evropy*.
[1] A work by Emma Lazarus.
[2] For which Zola was a correspondent in France.

sider his attitude to *Rome vaincue* negative; on the contrary, he liked it in general and, in any case, did not introduce his quotations merely to puff up his text. Henceforth, of course, this will not be repeated; your letter to him has also somewhat hurt him, but you will remain friends as before. [. . .]

[345]

Paris, November 23, 1876

TO PAVEL VASIL'EVICH ANNENKOV

[. . .] All your observations have been taken into account: the ending has been completely redone, and several other changes have been made.[3] But I would like to know in more detail the meaning of your words "the pamphlet element." In addition to the apparent (and unconcealed) hints at Stasov, Prince Viazemski, and the singer Slavianski, do you consider, for example, that the dinner at the merchant Galushkin's also belongs in a pamphlet, or is it only a kind of caricature *à la* Dickens? I must know this: please write me, because as soon as I receive the proofs here, this will have to be considered. [. . .]

[346]

Paris, November 25/December 6, 1876

TO MIKHAIL MATVEEVICH STASIULEVICH

[. . .] What you have said about Solomin [a character in *Virgin Soil*] has made me very happy. I seem to have hit the bull's eye. Some time I shall show you Solomin's file (before I begin to write the work

---

[3] *Virgin Soil.*

itself, I always compose files for all the characters),[4] and the main epithet characterizing Solomin was the word, written in large letters at the top, *sober*. And now you have guessed it! [. . .]

[347]

Paris, November 27, December 8, 1876

TO HIS BROTHER, NIKOLAI SERGEEVICH TURGENEV

[. . .] A play, "*The Danishevs* (*Les Danicheff*), has scored just as great a success at the Odéon; its author is a certain Mr. Korvin-Kriukovski. But it was revised by Alexandre Dumas *fils*; in it, by the way, there is a big-hearted coachman, Ossin, who expresses himself in the following phrases: "*La pudeur de la vierge est comme une fleur délicate et pure, mais celle de la femme a je ne sais quoi d'auguste et de sacré!*" ["Modesty in a virgin is like a delicate and pure flower, but in a wife it is something indescribably lofty and sacred!"] And here he added: "*Apportez un samoouar!*" ["Bring a samowar!"] And the public said: "*Quelle couleur locale! Quelle étude profonde des moeurs russes!*" ["What local color! What a profound study of Russian mores!"]

The two Russian princes for whom the plays were ordered for two theaters have turned out to be only one—and he is a Pole, Liubomirski, who is trying to carry on his trade under the wing of Sardou. Inciden-

[4] Henry James states: "The first thing [Turgenev did in writing a story] was to make clear to himself what he did know to begin with; and to this end, he wrote out a sort of biography of each of his characters, and everything that they had done and that had happened to them up to the opening of the story. He had their *dossier*, as the French say. . . ." See Henry James: *Partial Portraits* (London: The Macmillan Co.; 1888), p. 315.

tally, one must admit that Russia has recently come into style, and many quasi-Russian tales and novels with the *couleur locale* indicated above are being placed everywhere. [. . .]

[348]

Paris, December 28, 1876

TO LUDWIG PIETSCH

[. . .] Germans always have two shortcomings when they narrate: mediocre motivation, and the damned idealization of the truth. Conceive of the truth simply and poetically; the Ideal will come along with it, too. No, the Germans may conquer the whole world, but they have forgotten how to narrate—they have never really known how. If a German author narrates something touching,[5] he cannot help pointing tenderly to one of his own tear-filled eyes and giving me, the reader, a modest wink with the other lest I allow the object of his emotion to go unobserved! [. . .]

[349]

Paris, December 17/29, 1876

TO KONSTANTIN DMITRIEVICH KAVELIN

[. . .] My novel [*Virgin Soil*] has special significance for me; the subject now is not the decline or the preservation of talent, and not the degree of success with the public. (I treat the latter, if not indifferently, then calmly, as befits a tired man whose gray hair is turning white.) The subject is whether I accomplished the task that I had believed true, but whose execution

[5] The reference was specifically to a novella by Theodor Storm.

(and, you know, the entire essence is in the execution!) aroused my justified doubts and apprehensions. These apprehensions were all the more natural because my task was so painfully difficult! And then you, a person who is just as sensitive as he is truthful, a genuine friend and at the same time a genuine judge, come and tell me: "The work is good; everything is completely accurate and all right." And you even add your thanks, and in phrases that could not fail to touch me. . . . How could I possibly fail to rejoice? Thanks to you, I pat myself on the back and now, whatever the "literary" fate of *Virgin Soil* may be, I already know—I most probably know—that I did not spend my time in vain, but rendered a service, and have finished my service to my generation and perhaps even to my nation.

And if the young critics beat me with sticks, it will mean nothing; it is good exercise for them; and then everything will calm down, and perhaps they themselves will guess that they have been hitting one of their own.

I agree with your critical observations. And do not think that I am saying this from a heart made tender by your praises. Fomushka and Fimushka is an inserted bit; it can be cut out without detriment to the whole. . . . That alone condemns it irrevocably. I simply did not withstand the wish to sketch in an old Russian scene by way of *un repoussoir* [*a foil*]— or an oasis, if you like. As for my picture of the peasants, there was some premeditation on my part. Because my novel could not include them also (for two reasons: first, it would have become too broad and I would have lost the threads, and second, I do not know them well and intimately enough now to grasp the still unclear and indefinite thing that moves them inside), all I could do was to present the harsh and cruel side with which they touch the Nezhdanovs, the Markelovs, etc. Perhaps I should have limned the picture of Paul—Solomin's factotum and a future populist revolutionary—more sharply, but he is too large-scale a character. He will become with time (but not from my pen, of course; I am too old for that and I have been living outside Russia for too long) the central figure of a new novel. For the present, I have merely indicated his contours.

That I have succeeded with Solomin is what gladdens me most. He was the most difficult one. [. . .]

[350]

Paris, December 22, 1876/January 3, 1877

TO MIKHAIL MATVEEVICH STASIULEVICH

[. . .] I do not consider it superfluous to remind you, in a few words, of the considerations that guided me in writing *Virgin Soil* and that, you will recall, I set forth to you orally at our meeting last fall in Bougival. Hitherto, the younger generation has been presented in our literature either as a crew of crooks and scoundrels (which, first of all, is unjust, and secondly, can only offend our young readers as lies and libels) or as much as possible idealized (which again is unjust and harmful, to boot). I decided to choose the middle way and to get closer to the truth—to take young people who, for the most part, are good and honest and show that despite their honesty their very cause is so false and impractical that it cannot fail to lead them to complete fiasco. How well I succeeded is not for me to judge, but that was my idea, and you can see that it is essentially well-intentioned and *acceptable to the censor*. In any case, young people cannot say that it was an enemy who has undertaken to depict them; on the contrary, they must sense the sympathy that is alive in me—if not for their aims, then for their personalities. And only in such a way can a novel written for them and about them be of any use to them.

I expect reproaches to be showered upon me from both camps, but, after all, the very same thing happened with *Fathers and Children*. Nevertheless, of all my past literary activity, I have reason to be satisfied with just that work, and I would sooner agree to wipe out *A Sportsman's Sketches* than that. I hope that the same fate lies ahead of *Virgin Soil*, and that it will not be an object [of] or a pretext for any misunderstandings. [. . .]

[351]

Paris, January 22, 1877

TO W. R. S. RALSTON

Dear Friend,

I received your two letters and the clipping from *The Times* with your article about Mr. [Donald Mackenzie] Wallace's book, *Russia*, about which he must be very flattered.[6] I completely agree with you that *Dream*[7] will not do for the English translation [of *Phantoms*]. Undoubtedly, you are the best judge of the matter. I shall merely tell you that in writing that little story, I felt no malaise, the French desire for

---

[6] Wallace's *Russia* (particularly in its twentieth-century editions) still forms one of the best one-volume introductions to the life and culture of late tsarist Russia.

[7] English in original.

rapprochement (*French desire for touching*)[7]—something, perhaps, a bit shocking (*a rather scandalous matter*).[7] I tried to resolve a physiological problem with which I was somewhat familiar from my own experience. [. . .]

Try to become friendly with Henry James; he is a very pleasant man who has a lot of talent and a certain bent for sadness which, no doubt, will not frighten you. [. . .]

[352]

Paris, January 23, 1877

TO ELIZAVETA V —— L'VOV

[. . .] Try to tell a simple and vital incident involving two or three persons, without adding arguments or considerations of your own. Take a subject from your environment or the memories of your youth, but do not let your *I* be in the foreground, and we shall see what this leads to. [. . .] For example, apparently you regret that you have frequently run into ideas that seem to be yours. A true creative writer, who thinks in images, would never have felt any such thing. And if you turn out to possess even a particle of the creative gift, the rest will come to you—for you certainly have no lack of intelligence. [. . .] Prove that you know how to narrate. Remember:

Scribitur ad narrandum, non ad probandum.
[We write to narrate, not prove.]

Perhaps you do not yet suspect how difficult it is; you will scarcely believe, for example, that to tell about a drunken muzhik's beating his wife is incomparably

---

[7] English in original.

harder than to compose a whole tract about the "woman question." These are two completely separate spheres; the entire question is which of them is more natural for you. One more short remark: write simply; although, I remember, your descriptions of nature are beautiful, they are artificial and precious; do not forget, the most fragrant flower never smells of perfume. [. . .]

[353]

Paris, February 4, 1877

TO LUDWIG PIETSCH

[. . . Zola's *L'Assommoir*] is a completely confused book. The word *merde* occurs a dozen times *"en toutes lettres"* ["in all five letters"], but a great talent is there. This will probably be too much for the Germans. I too have read the work with a mixture of aversion and admiration; finally, disgust won the upper hand. But the novel is *"un signe du temps"* ["a sign of the times"], as the French say. [. . .]

[354]

Paris, February 13, 1877

TO JULIAN SCHMIDT

Here at last is a photograph of Zola for you—it resembles him, but the shading and expression are too light. He has jet black hair, but here he seems almost blond. His entire person reminds me of an intelligent, somewhat clumsy, and sluggish Parisian *ouvrier* [worker]. His book (which you have received, I hope?) is creating an unusual furor here. Thirteen editions in three weeks! I am curious as to what you think of this.

[355]

Paris, February 18, 1877

TO W. R. S. RALSTON

[. . .] Do you know the address of [Henry] James? If you do, be kind enough to send it to me. [. . .]

[356]

Paris, February 12/24, 1877

TO PAVEL VASIL'EVICH ANNENKOV

[. . .] I have been busy with the proofs of the German and French translations of *Virgin Soil* (there are also English, Italian, and even Swedish proofs; but those, fortunately, are not sent to me), and this can serve me as an excuse for not talking to you about my novel. I have had my fill of it even without that. Let me tell you only that Stasiulevich has communicated with me about the second part. It was almost annihilated. The Censorship Committee was divided into two factions: one suggested burning the second part; the other wanted to return it to me for corrections. But do you know who saved it? Timashev!! He declared that if he had known the entire work beforehand, he would have banned it, but to ban the second part after the first had appeared would mean to create an uproar, to provoke the public, etc. How do you like that? That is something I did not expect at all. [. . .]

[357]

Paris, February 18 [O.S.], 1877

TO IAKOV PETROVICH POLONSKI

[. . .]There was a time when I asked you not

to speak any more about Cherniaev; I ask you the very same thing now with regard to *Virgin Soil*. Whatever its final fate may be, it is my last original literary work; that is my irrevocable decision; my name will not appear any more. I might wish that my final word had met with a more indulgent reception, but that it is my final word you can doubt as little as . . . well, as you doubt my friendship for you. And there is nothing further to discuss.

So as not to give up my pen, I shall probably undertake translations. I am thinking of *Don Quixote* and Montaigne. Incidentally, I have translated one of Gustave Flaubert's *Legends*; it is not long, but it has unusual beauty.[8] It will appear in the April issue of the *Vestnik Evropy* (perhaps even *two* of them will appear), and I recommend it to you. I have tried to convey as best I could the colors and the tone of the original. [. . .]

Two thick volumes of Victor Hugo's *Légendes des siècles* have appeared here. A lot of ballast and bombast, without even a single restrained poem—but there are wonderful verses by the dozen. The local critics have all bowed down to the ground, and everywhere there are eulogies and incense-burnings. And I really cannot help wondering when I think that it was written by an old man of 75. But hardly anywhere save in France will the book produce so great an effect. [. . .]

[358]

Paris, February 27/March 11, 1877

TO MIKHAIL MATVEEVICH STASIULEVICH

[. . .] I am enclosing a short preface to the

[8] *St. Julien l'Hospitalier.*

Flaubert *Legends*. Regardless of my exertions, *Héro-diade* will not make the April issue; it must be inserted in the May number. I hope these pieces will be liked; I tried with all my strength, and suppose I have not disgraced myself as a stylist. Tell me how much you will pay per signature, and consult with your mag-nanimity, for I will not take a kopeck; the money will all go to Flaubert, who needs it. The book itself will appear *comme une primeur* [for the first time] in Russia; even when the second *legend* appears, the book will not have come out here yet. You can send me the proofs of [St.] *Julien l'Hospitalier* in just the way you did with *Virgin Soil*. [. . .] [9]

[359]

Baden-Baden, March 5/17, 1877

TO ALEKSEI MIKHAILOVICH ZHEMCHUZHNIKOV

[. . .] To say that your remarks about the ac-tivities of Marianna and Nezhdanov [in *Virgin Soil*] are accurate is not enough. As the Germans say, you *haben den Nagel auf den Kopf getroffen* [have hit the nail on the head]. I said all this—approximately—to myself. (One exception: Nezhdanov would think nothing of visiting five taverns; in the vicinity of my estate, where there are no large villages, there are eleven taverns within a seven-verst radius, and a man can very easily make the rounds of them in one day.)

But the fact is that because of my absenteeism I

[9] *The Legend of St. Julian the Hospitaler* appeared in Rus-sian in April, and *Hérodiade* followed in May; both of them thus were printed in Russian translation before they appeared in French. Turgenev himself called his translation "love's labour," and expressed the hope that it would not be "love's labour lost." (He used both these phrases in English.)

would not know how to perform the task as it ought to be done: faithfully and vividly. That and many other reasons that would take too long to tell have forced me to become silent. I myself am dissatisfied with my work and, in the depths of my soul, agree with the majority of the critics (and never have they been so unanimous). [. . .]

[360]

Paris, March 7/19, 1877

TO HIS BROTHER, NIKOLAI SERGEEVICH TURGENEV

[. . .] The clipping you sent from the article that criticizes my novel has not taught me anything new. There is no doubt that, as you say, *Virgin Soil* has been a failure, and I am beginning to think that its fate was deserved. One cannot really suppose that all the magazines have entered a conspiracy against me. Rather, I ought to admit that I have been mistaken: I undertook a work beyond my powers and fell beneath its weight. To write about Russia without living there is really impossible. It would have been better if I had become silent a few years ago, but, in any case, this latest lesson will not be lost on me. My literary career is closing forever, and my name will no longer appear over any original work. That is not quite easy; life ahead seems rather empty—but the devil (or, if you like, the truth) must, as they say, be looked in the eye. Diderot has said somewhere: *"Avant sa mort l'homme suit plusieurs fois son propre convoi."* ["A man follows his own funeral procession several times before he dies."] And now I have had to walk behind my own literary coffin. I shall find some occupation or other, and old age will set in for good. . . . And the daily

worries about preserving life, etc., will engulf everything
else. . . .

[361]

Paris, April 19, 1877

TO W. R. S. RALSTON

[. . .] The trial of the revolutionaries [in Russia]
is certainly a very sad thing, but you would be deceived
were you to think that all these girls resemble Miss
Mashurin more than they do Marianna [in *Virgin
Soil*].[1] Some of the girls are pretty and interesting and
(as the barbarous custom of physical examination of
prisoners still exists under our legal system) they all
have been found to be virgins. That is something to
think about seriously. [. . .]

Russian statesmen ought to think about all that
and come to the conclusion that constitutional reforms
would be the only means of stopping the wave of revolutionary propaganda in Russia. But all such considerations will now be destroyed by the war [between Russia
and Turkey in 1877]. I am convinced that we are at
the threshold of very grave events. [. . .][2]

[362]

Bougival, August 1, 1877

TO EMMA LAZARUS

Let me begin by asking permission to write

[1] The reference is to the "Trial of the Fifty," which had
just taken place (in February and March 1877). (See Florinsky,
p. 1,078.)
[2] Terrorism in Russia increased during the next few years
and was climaxed by the assassination of Aleksandr II about four
years later.

in French: that language is as familiar to you as your own, and I have greater facility in handling French than English. [. . .] I could not have been more touched by the flattering things you tell me, and I am very happy that you liked my latest work. Of all my novels, it[3] caused me the most trouble and had—I must say—the least success in my native country. The critics have been very harsh—and so has the public, especially at first; things became somewhat better afterward—or rather, other and graver preoccupations have directed public attention elsewhere. Whatever your opinion may be, I value it highly. [. . .]

{ 363 }

Paris, October 26/November 7, 1877

TO HIS BROTHER, NIKOLAI SERGEEVICH TURGENEV

[. . .] Iablochkov,[4] our fellow Russian, has really invented something new in illumination, but his method is rather expensive for the present. If he manages to make it cheaper, a complete revolution in the manufacture of gas is imminent, while he will make millions. He has been here in Paris because only here has he found capitalists who agreed to take the risk and loaned him the necessary money for his experiments, research, etc. [. . .]

---

[3] *Virgin Soil.*
[4] According to the second edition of the *Bol'shaia Sovetskaia Entsiklopediia* (the *Large Soviet Encyclopedia*), Iablochkov had received Patent No. 112024 for his electric light from the French patent office on March 23, 1876.

[364]

Paris, December 4, 1877

TO PAVEL VASIL'EVICH ANNENKOV

[. . .] And affairs here are "even astonishing." [Marshall] MacMahon also deserves serious thought. France, like a locomotive that has got loose, is racing at full speed into the abyss, while the fireman looks . . . around with dignity.[5] I suppose that the Chamber will submit *volens-nolens* [willy-nilly] to such a personage, and, having shouted *j'ai fait tout mon possible* [I have done all I could], will find the loophole you talk about and into which *one* . . . will start crawling. Or, even more likely, the Chamber will be obstinate, and the Marshall will turn to the Senate—which, regardless of what is said there, will *inevitably* agree to dissolve for the second time. Again [Adolphe-Théodore] Borgniart and Co. will come onstage. They will autocratically take last year's budget, which is not at all so difficult or so unprecedented (*vive Bismarck*, up to 1866)—and the writing will begin! France is finally being turned into another Persia, which even now she rather resembles. I would like to be a false prophet.

Wednesday morning

The Chamber is being really obstinate—but that does not change the essence of the matter. What lying impudence the party running the Elysée is [resorting to]?!! The traditions of the Jesuits and the traditions of the Empire have blended into one fine whole. [. . .]

[5] "Early in the autumn of 1944 François Mauriac told me that living in France between 1934 and 1940 was 'like being in an automobile that wouldn't respond to the steering wheel, the brakes—anything.' . . ." A. J. Liebling: "A Reporter at Large: M. Mauriac's Automobile," *The New Yorker*, June 21, 1958, p. 39.

[365]

Paris, January 3/15, 1878

TO HIS BROTHER, NIKOLAI SERGEEVICH TURGENEV

[. . .] The past week has really been a week of funerals for me; first I learned about the death of Uncle [Nikolai Nikolaevich Turgenev],⁶ then about Grinval'd's, and last about Nekrasov's. These were people of different kinds, but all 3 were connected with my past. *Et l'on fait involontairement un retour sur soi-même* [And involuntarily one retraces one's past].

After fifty, the life of every man becomes something like Plevna:⁷ death besieges him and he must fight to defend himself, for the present, against its almost daily assaults.

But let us hope that our capitulation is not yet too near. [. . .]

[366]

Paris, January 9/21, 1878

TO PAVEL VASIL'EVICH ANNENKOV

[. . .] Yes, Nekrasov is dead, and a large part of our past and of our youth has died with him. Do you remember what he was like when you and I saw him in June? . . . Now he has become a legend for young people. . . . But sense will emerge from these very young people only after they have freed themselves from that legend, i.e., when a new, powerful, and vital talent appears. [. . .]

⁶ This report was false; Nikolai Nikolaevich Turgenev did not die until 1881.

⁷ Plevna is a town in Bulgaria which the Russians assaulted unsuccessfully three times during the Russo-Turkish War of 1877–9. On December 10, 1877, the town was forced to surrender to the Russians for lack of supplies.

{ 367 }

Paris, January 12/24, 1878

<small>TO HIS BROTHER, NIKOLAI SERGEEVICH TURGENEV</small>

[. . .] As far as the letters of Pushkin, etc., are concerned, I am astonished that so confirmed a magazine reader as you should not be convinced of the need for the following rule: "Of any news item about a person, we ought to throw out one half as complete nonsense and disbelieve the idle chatter of the other half."

What would be the point of my editing Pushkin's letters in French? What Frenchman needs them? Where would I get the money to buy them from Countess Merenburg? The story is simply this: the editorial board of the *Vestnik Evropy* bought from Pushkin's daughter her father's letters to her mother and is printing them in the magazine; Pushkin's daughter asked me to be the editor (which I consider a great honor)—i.e., to write a preface and delete from the letters whatever is not fit to print. I have finished all this, and if you get the *Vestnik Evropy* (which you will not do without some reason), you will find half of these very interesting letters in the very first number.

Pushkin left two sons and two daughters. . . . It is most astonishing that his younger daughter, who at his death was a six-month-old baby (the same Countess Merenburg), resembles him as much as one drop of water resembles another! And he suspected his wife! The older daughter was married to the General Gartung who shot himself in the government offices in Moscow. [. . .]

{ 368 }

Spasskoe, August 10/22, 1878

TO ALEKSANDR VASIL'EVICH TOPOROV

[. . .] I stayed in Moscow longer than I thought I would. I spent two days at Lev Tolstoy's estate near Tula. [. . .] [8]

{ 369 }

Paris, September 30/October 12, 1878

TO MISS LIUBOV' IAKOVLEVNA STECH'KIN[9]

[. . .] In a work such as yours, everything that does not advance the action of the drama seems superfluous and even tiresome to the reader. He has time to pause; whereas he ought to be inevitably drawn forward. [. . .]

{ 370 }

Bougival, October 1 [O.S.], 1878

TO COUNT LEV NIKOLAEVICH TOLSTOY

[. . .] You have probably received a letter from my friend, W. R. S. Ralston (an English literary man and a lover of our literature), in which he asks you for a few autobiographical remarks. I hope you will not turn him down; he is a very good and serious man— neither a reporter nor a feuilletonist. You probably know by now that an English translation of your *Cossacks* has appeared both in London and in America,

[8] After the seventeen-year break that followed their duel *manqué*.
[9] Miss Stech'kin (Liubov' Iakovlevna) should not be confused with her mother (Liubov' Nikolaevna), who was also a correspondent of Turgenev's.

and, from the rumors that have reached me, is enjoying a major success. Ralston has undertaken to write a long article about *War and Peace*. As for me, I have sent him a short list of the facts I know about your literary and general life, and I do not suppose that you will complain to me about that. *The Cossacks* is also being printed in a French translation in the *Journal de St.- Pétersbourg*. That annoys me a little because I had planned to translate it myself this fall with Mme Viardot. Anyhow, if the translation is good, there will be no cause for annoyance. I do not know whether you have taken any steps to publish it in book form in Paris. (I do not even know whether the translation has been done with your consent.) But, in any case, I offer my services as your middleman. . . . I would be very pleased to introduce to the French public the best novelette written in our language. [. . .]

[371]

Bougival, October 13, 1878

TO JULIAN SCHMIDT

[. . .] He [Richepin] is an astonishing poet— and what a poet! [1] Some of the pieces you will scarcely understand because they are written in Parisian argot, which even many Frenchmen do not understand. But pieces such as *"Le Banc aux enfants,"* for example, are classically beautiful. I recommend *"Fleurs de boisson"* to you as especially bold and powerful. There is in every line such a gushing and sanguine temperament that in our pale, contemplative, and impotent times it

---

[1] Turgenev was sending Schmidt a copy of Richepin's *La Chanson des gueux* with this letter.

produces a definitely wholesome effect. Unfortunately,
Richepin is a confirmed drunkard. [. . .]

{ 372 }

Paris, November 15 [O.S.], *1878*

TO COUNT LEV NIKOLAEVICH TOLSTOY

[. . .] I am glad that you are physically healthy,
and hope that the mental "indisposition" you write
about has passed. I too have known it; sometimes it
came as an inner restlessness before I started on some
piece of work; I suppose this sort of restlessness has
also struck you. Although you ask me not to speak
about your writings, I cannot refrain from remarking
that to laugh "even a little" at you has never entered
my head. I have liked some of your works very much;
some others I have disliked very much; still others
(such as *The Cossacks*, for example) have given me
great pleasure and filled me with wonder.

What would be the point of laughing? I assumed
that you had long ago got rid of such "recurrent" emotions. Why do only writers know what they are, and
not painters, musicians, or other artists? Probably because a literary work reveals more of that part of the
soul whose exposure is not quite pleasant. But as we
are no longer in the early years of our creative work,
the time has come to get used to that.

[. . .] The English translation of *The Cossacks*
is faithful but dry and "matter of fact" [2]—like Mr.
Schuyler himself, who visited me here a few days ago
on his way to Birmingham, where he has been appointed consul. I have not seen the French translation;

[2] English in the original.

I am afraid that it has really been unsuccessful, for I know the style of our Russian ladies who do translations. On the one hand, I am afraid—but on the other, I am almost happy. To translate your novelette and publish it here will thus still be possible.

You have been exterminating hares at home, while I also have been hunting this fall. I went to a friend's place in England—an estate situated between Cambridge and Oxford—and I banged away at a rather large number of pheasants, partridges, etc. But hunting without dogs is rather monotonous. In such a case one must shoot superbly, but I have always been a mediocre shot . . . and am no longer used to even that. Incidentally, I visited both universities—Cambridge and Oxford. These English educational institutions are marvelous and very intricate things! And how fiercely they hate us!

Tchaikovsky's *Eugene Onegin* has arrived here in a piano arrangement. Mme Viardot has been examining it in the evenings. The music is undoubtedly wonderful; the lyrical and melodious spots are especially good. But what a libretto! Imagine: Pushkin's verses about the characters are put into their own mouths. For example, he wrote about Lenski:

He sang the faded flower of life
Before he had quite reached eighteen. [. . .]

But the libretto has: "*I sing* the faded flower of life," etc. And it is constantly like that!

Tchaikovsky's reputation has grown here since the concerts of Russian music at the Trocadéro; in Germany he has long enjoyed, if not honor, at least attention. At Cambridge an English professor of music told me very seriously that Tchaikovsky was the most re-

markable figure of our times in music. My jaw
dropped. [. . .]

[373]

Bougival, December 30 [O.S.], 1878
TO AFANASI AFANAS'EVICH FET

I was very happy to meet Tolstoy again, and I
spent three very pleasant days at his place. His entire
family is very congenial, and his wife is charming. He
himself has calmed down very much, and has grown
up. His name is becoming famous in Europe; we Russians have long known that he is without peer.

[374]

Paris, January 9, 1879
TO PAVEL VASIL'EVICH ANNENKOV

[. . .] The "Domestic Survey" in the December
number [of the *Vestnik Evropy*] is excellent. I have
not spoken about it with Petr Lavrov (whom, by the
way, I saw a few days ago), but I know what he will
say. He is a pigeon trying hard to pass himself off as
a hawk. You must hear him cooing about the need
for Pugachevs and Razins. [. . .] [3] The words are terrible, but the glance is gentle, the smile is very kind,
and even the enormous and unkempt beard has an
affable and idyllic appearance. [. . .]

[3] Emilian Pugachev in the eighteenth century followed the
example of Stepan Razin in the seventeenth century by leading
disaffected Cossacks in an unsuccessful revolt against Moscow.

[375]

Paris, February 13 [O.S.], 1879

TO GUSTAVE FLAUBERT

My dear friend,

From the telegram I sent you this morning, you knew about the collapse of our plans.[4] Here are the details. When I returned to Paris, we decided upon the following: I should try to have a talk with [Léon] Gambetta, then with [Jules] Ferry, and, if need be, with [Paul] Baudry. On Thursday evening I received Zola's first letter (enclosed herewith), and as a result—delay. I asked for an interview with Mme Edmond Adam—no answer. On Monday morning [came] the letter from Zola together with a note from Mme [Georges] Charpentier (which I am also sending you). You can imagine my astonishment. I took a cab and went right to the President's palace to see Gambetta (the Charpentiers had promised to obtain a final answer on Saturday). I was not received, but did manage to see his personal secretary, M. Arnaud (the son of Mme Arnaud de l'Ariège). I explained the whole matter to him. He listened to me affably (although he squirmed in his seat), wrote something on a scrap of paper, and promised definitely to send an answer the very next morning. Of course, there was no answer. I went to his mother, whom I had just met. A stone face. I returned home, wrote a letter to Gambetta, and, on the very same evening, took it to Mme Arnaud, asking her to pass it on to Gambetta through her son. I added

[4] Turgenev and some of Flaubert's other friends had been trying to secure a post for the French novelist in the Mazarini Library in Paris.

that I would come to her place again the following day for an answer.

On the next day—that is, yesterday, Wednesday— I went to Mme Arnaud's: no answer! At the very same time [*sic*] I received a letter from Mme Arnaud in which she seemingly said that she had gone to Cannes (I am enclosing her letter). I put on my frock-coat and white tie—and there I was in her salon, where almost all the political celebrities of France gather, and from which they rule over and take care of France. She received me very well, and I stated my business to her. . . . "Well, you know, Gambetta is here just now; he is having a smoke after dinner; we shall know everything in a moment." She returned a couple of minutes later. "It is impossible, Monsieur; Gambetta already has candidates."

Then the dictator himself came in. He appeared to be at ease. I have never seen trained dogs dance before their master the way the ministers and senators did before him. He began talking with one of them. Mme Arnaud took me, by the arm, up to him, but the great man declined the honor of meeting me and said in a voice loud enough for me to hear: "I do not wish to: the impossibility has already been stated." I disappeared inconspicuously. I returned home, overwhelmed (as they say) by thoughts I surely need not communicate to you. That is how much one can rely on sweet words and promises.

The posts Mme Charpentier talked about will go to Messrs. Baudry and [Jules-Auguste] Soury.

Well, then, old man, all this must be put out of your head and you must again devote yourself to work, literary work—the only kind worthy of a man like yourself. I am leaving on *Saturday* (at seven in the morning). Please manage to write me. Let me know about yourself. Can you walk on crutches yet?

I shall write from Moscow. [. . .]

{ 376 }

Paris, May 17/29, 1879

TO ALEKSANDR VASIL'EVICH TOPOROV

[. . .] I also have an excellent translation of a biographical and critical foreword to *Don Quixote* by Louis Viardot; the work is a classic.

{ 377 }

Bougival, June 2/14, 1879

TO MISS LIUBOV' IAKOVLEVNA STECH'KIN

[. . .] I am really going to England because I have received the completely unexpected news that Oxford University is awarding me, for my "literary services," a *doctorate of natural science!* [5] It is a great honor—I am almost the first Russian to receive it—but how, why! I still cannot understand it!! I can imagine how incensed certain gentlemen in the dear homeland will be at me! [. . .]

{ 378 }

Bougival, June 12/24, 1879

TO BORIS ALEKSANDROVICH CHICHELEV

As I promised, I am writing you a few words about the ceremony that took place at Oxford. To tell the truth, even these few words are superfluous, for who

[5] The degree was really a D.C.L. (Doctorate of Civil Law).

could really be interested in them? My having been
made a doctor of Oxford University will give our magazines cause to mock me once again, and that is all;
I shall therefore be brief.

Oxford is an extraordinarily interesting city. The
weather was magnificent. At noon we, the newly created
doctors (in our red gowns and four-cornered caps),
moved out from the Vice-Chancellor's quarters to a
special building at which the *commémorations* [cere-
monies] take place. We walked two abreast; the crowd
gaped at us. The building was filled with students
and ladies; we were presented one at a time to the
Vice Chancellor, enthroned in a velvet chair, by the
Public Orator, who also wore a red gown and who
accompanied each presentation with a short speech in
Latin full of flattery. The Vice Chancellor answered
in Latin, too; he shook hands with every newly desig-
nated doctor, and the latter then went to take his seat
while the public applauded.

When my turn came, I felt highly nervous, but
everything went off all right. I was forewarned that the
students would use their right to whistle and hiss that
day (it is something like university saturnalia, which
usage permits), and that because they still cannot stand
Russians in England, an uproar was to be expected.
But there was no uproar despite the expectations, and
(according to *The Times*) I was applauded even more
than the others. None of us gave a speech or received
a diploma. The professors there presented me with my
cap and gown as a sign of special esteem, and I can
now, if I have to act out a charade, flaunt my doctoral
attire. Then there were dinners, suppers, dances, etc.—
but all of that without speeches (thank God). I am
enclosing for you the program of the entire ceremony.

. . . I am only the second Russian to merit such an honor. . . .[6]

If you find that you can squeeze some juice out of this little lemon, well and good. Only one condition: do not talk on my behalf.

[379]

Bougival, June 20/July 2, 1879

TO ALEKSANDR VASIL'EVICH TOPOROV

[. . .] I reached Oxford all right, and was very favorably received; the students applauded me during the reception, and the professors presented me with a red gown and a four-cornered cap, which I sported all day, and which I can now use if I take a notion to act out charades. [. . .]

[380]

Bougival, August 7, 1879

TO GUSTAVE FLAUBERT

[. . .] As for the state of my soul, you can get an exact idea of it by raising the cover of a privy and looking inside; only do not let it be an English water closet; they are generally clean. [. . .][7]

---

[6] R. P. Clifford, the Head Clerk at the University Registry of Oxford University, informs me in a letter dated January 13, 1959, that the Oxford "list of honorands" does not go back before 1870. "However, I was informed at Pushkin House in Leningrad that the first Russian so honored was Tsar Aleksandr I in 1814."

[7] This passage has been deleted in the Victorian English translation of the original French source.

[381]

Bougival, September 16 [O.S.], 1879

TO IAKOV PETROVICH POLONSKI

[. . .] Although the Paskeviches have written
you that a translation of Tolstoy's novel [8] is available
in Paris, I can assure you that it is not at a single book-
store and that no one knows *anything* about it.

Please have six copies sent to me; I shall distribute
them in the right quarters, and [also] shall give the
book some publicity in the magazines—without which
no book (especially no foreign one) can be sold here.
I am very much afraid of the translation the Russian
lady has done. The French publishers almost have fits
when they are presented with a mixture of French and
(high society) *Nizhegorod*.[9] But do not forget to pass
my offer on to the Paskeviches. We shall try to help as
much as we can.

[. . .] Lev Tolstoy, as a major and vital talent,
has leaped out of the swamp he had got himself into—
and that will be to the advantage of literature—but
Fet-Shenshin is so mired in philosophasting that he is
only blowing bubbles, and these bubbles are not
fragrant. [. . .]

[382]

Bougival, October 3 [O.S.], 1879

TO IAKOV PETROVICH POLONSKI

[. . .] As soon as I receive the copies of W*ar
and Peace* [in French] I shall immediately distribute

[8] W*ar and Peace*.
[9] *"Nizhegorod"* Russian, a phrase first used by A. S. Griboe-
dov in his *Gore ot uma* [W*oe from Wit*], is as provincially Russian as Russian can get.

them to the people who ought to get them. I [also] will concern myself with publicity—although, of course, the name of the woman who did the translation will not be mentioned; but everything will be arranged decently —you can tell her so.[1] It will be quite pleasant to meet her this winter. [. . .]

[383]

[*Bougival* (?)], *October* 17, 1879

TO M. HÉBRARD, EDITOR OF *Le Temps*

Here is a selection from some autobiographical memoirs that seem to me worthy of being communicated to the readers of your newspaper. The author is one of those young Russians, too numerous at present, whose opinions have been adjudged dangerous and punishable by the government of my country. Without in any way approving of his opinions, I believe that the naïve and sincere story of what he had to suffer could, while arousing interest in the man himself, serve to show how little justified preventive imprisonment in a cell is from the viewpoint of sound legislation. I hope that you will be struck as I was by the accents of truth which permeate these pages, and also by the lack of useless, if not misplaced, reproaches and recriminations. You will see that the nihilists, who have been talked about for some time, are neither so black nor so callous as people are eager to depict them.

[1] The translator was Princess Paskevich.

[384]

Bougival, October 27/November 8, 1879

TO PAVEL VASIL'EVICH ANNENKOV

[. . .] I liked Daudet's novel *Les rois en exil* [*Kings in Exile*] less than you did. Probably because of the very subject, only pictures—covered with an almost transparent haze—emerge instead of characters. And, you know, only characters are interesting. . . . But his talent is nevertheless altogether major, and the success of the book is enormous—not like Zola's *Nana*, which has been or is a glorious failure, despite the obscenity of its plot and its multitude of unprintable expressions. I am reading this work in the *Voltaire* and feel extraordinarily bored. That is something which, most probably, my friend Zola did not anticipate. [. . .]

[385]

Paris, December 28 [O.S.], 1879

TO COUNT LEV NIKOLAEVICH TOLSTOY

Before your letter arrived, Tchaikovsky came to see me and I informed him of your intention; I then gave him 260 francs (100 rubles). He is really a very good man; unfortunately, I saw him but little because he spent almost all his time in a village that is not close to Paris. . . .

I was very touched by the interest you expressed about my article in the *Moskovskie vedomosti* and I, for my part, am almost ready to rejoice in its appearance because it has prompted you to tell me such kind and friendly things. When I left the *Russki vestnik*, Katkov forewarned me that I did not know what it meant to have him as an enemy; now he is trying to show me. Let him! My soul is not in his power.

Princess Paskevich, who translated your *War and Peace* [into French], has finally delivered 500 copies here, of which I have received 10. I distributed them to the local influential critics (among others, to [Hippolyte] Taine and [Edmond] About). We must hope that they will grasp all the power and beauty of your epic. The translation is somewhat weak, but was done with zeal and love. The past few days I have reread with new delight your real, great work [in the original] five or six times. Its entire cut is far from what the French like and what they look for in books; but, in the long run, the truth will claim its own. I hope, if not for a brilliant victory, for a solid (but slow) conquest.

You do not tell me anything about your new work, and meanwhile rumor has it that you are toiling assiduously. I can see you at your desk in the isolated hut that you pointed out to me. However, I shall soon have firsthand information about all that.

I am glad about your domestic well-being. May I ask you to give everyone my ardent greetings and regards. Russia is now really living through painful and gloomy times, and right now to live as an alien is a shame. This emotion keeps growing stronger within me, and for the first time I am going to our country without thinking at all about when I shall return here —and not even wishing to return soon. [. . .]

[386]

Paris, January 2, 1880

TO THE EDITOR OF THE V*estnik Evropy*
[M. M. STASIULEVICH]

As my old friend, you well know the distaste I
have for concerning the public with questions touching
me personally; but reading the correspondence of the
"Resident of a Different Town" [2] in the *Moskovskie
vedomosti* a few days ago compels me to take up my
pen.

That correspondence appeared because *Le Temps*
had printed a letter of mine which prefaced the story
of a [Russian] exile who had been kept in solitary confinement for four years—a story of exceptional psychological and perhaps forensic interest.[3]

If the "Resident of a Different Town" had limited
himself merely to the insults at his command, I would
not have paid any attention to them, knowing what
"cloud" this "thunder" comes from;[4] but he takes it
upon himself to make my convictions and manner of
thinking suspect—and I have no right to answer that
with mere contempt.

While ascribing all kinds of ignoble motives and
almost criminal intentions to me, the "Resident of a
Different Town" accuses me of servility, of flattery, and
of "turning handsprings" for a certain part of our youth.
Flattery of that sort means that a man has deserted his
own convictions and is counterfeiting those of others.

[2] "Resident of a Different Town" was the pen name used
in this instance by Boleslav Mikhailovich Markevich (1822–84),
a reactionary writer.
[3] See Turgenev's letter to M. Hébrard, Editor of *Le Temps*,
dated October 17, 1879, above.
[4] Read *"tuchi"* for *"kuchi"* in the source.

But, without boasting or mincing words, and merely stating a fact—I have the right to assert that the convictions I have expressed both in print and in speech have not changed by an iota during the past forty years; nor have I ever concealed [these convictions] from anyone. In the eyes of our young people—as they are the subject—in their eyes, regardless of what party they may belong to, I always was and still am a "gradualist," a liberal of the old stamp in the English, dynastic sense, a man who anticipates reforms *only from above,* an opponent, on principle, of revolution (not to mention the recent monstrosities).[5] The young people have been correct in their evaluation, and I would consider it unworthy of both them and me to present myself to them in a different light. The ovations (which "Resident of a Different Town" mentions) have been pleasant and dear to me precisely because *I did not go to the younger generation,* whose dislike I have borne completely philosophically for fifteen years (since the appearance of *Fathers and Children*), but because they came to me; these ovations were dear to me as proof of the sympathy shown toward the convictions I have always been loyal to, and which I have expressed loudly in my speeches to the people who chose to honor me.

What would be the point of lying to them and flattering them, when they themselves offered me their hands, and believed me?

And what do you think, from whose lips do these libels and accusations come?! From the lips of a man who has earned a reputation as a virtuoso in matters of servility and "turning handsprings" from his earliest childhood on—at first voluntarily but now involuntarily

[5] This was the period when terrorists were repeatedly trying to kill Aleksandr II (as well as some other high Russian officials).

as well! True, he has nothing to lose or be afraid of; his name has become a byword, and he is not a man an answer can be expected from. But caution does not hurt even in his position; in any case, to remind me of "having disgraced gray hair" is not for him; there is no need to direct the eyes of the reading public to his own head. The public knows him even without that . . . and, I dare add, knows me too.

[387]

[*place not given*] *January 20, 1880*
TO EDMOND ABOUT, EDITOR OF *Le XIX-e Siècle*

You have been willing to publish in *Le XIX-e Siècle* a letter in which I announced the exhibition of Vereshchagin's pictures. The success [of this exhibition], which I ventured to predict and which has surpassed my expectations, encourages me to turn to you again. This time the subject is once again the work of a painter—but a painter with a pen in his hand.

I wish to talk about a historical novel by my compatriot, Count Lev Tolstoy [entitled], *War and Peace,* a [French] translation of which has just been published by Hachette. Lev Tolstoy is the best-known author we have in Russia, and *War and Peace* is—I do not hesitate to say it—one of the most remarkable books of our time. The breath of an epic runs through this vast work, in which the public and private life of the Russians during the first years of our century is traced by the hand of a master. An entire epoch, rich in great deeds and great figures (the story begins a bit before the Battle of Austerlitz and goes up through that *de la Moscowa* [Borodino]), an entire world, a multitude of the most lifelike characters in all ranks of society, un-

rolls before the reader. The manner in which Count
Tolstoy treats his subject is as original as it is new; it is
neither that of Walter Scott nor, I need hardly add,
that of Alexandre Dumas. Count Tolstoy is a Russian
writer to the marrow of his bones; and those French
readers who will not be repelled by some prolixity and
some peculiarities of evaluation will be able to say that
War and Peace has given them a more intimate and a
more truthful insight into the Russian character and
its temperament, in short into Russian life, than hundreds of ethnographical and historical works. There are
entire chapters [whose subject matter] will never re-
quire another treatment; historical figures [such as]
Kutuzov, Rastopchin, and others, whose traits have
been fixed forever, will last.

You see, my dear sir, that I am not niggardly in my
statements; and yet, they render my opinion only im-
perfectly. Perhaps the utter originality of Count Lev
Tolstoy, by its very power, will impede a sympathetic
and rapid understanding by foreign readers, but I repeat—and I would be happy if my words were taken
as the gospel truth: this is a great work by a great writer
—and this the real Russia. [. . .]

[388]

Paris, January 12 [O.S.], *1880*
TO COUNT LEV NIKOLAEVICH TOLSTOY

I am copying for you with diplomatic precision a
selection from M. Flaubert's letter to me—I sent him
the translation of *War and Peace* (which, unfortunately, is rather pallid):

Thanks for having had me read the novel by
Tolstoy. It is first-rate. What a painter and what

a psychologist! The first two volumes are *sub-lime*, but the third topples terribly. He repeats himself! And he philosophizes!! We finally see the gentleman, the author, and the Russian, while before, we had seen only Nature and Humanity. It seems to me that he sometimes has things worthy of Shakespeare. I uttered cries of admiration as I read it . . . and it is long.

Yes, it is powerful! Very powerful! [6]

I suppose that *en somme* [all in all] you will be pleased.

I have distributed W*ar and Peace* to all the main critics here. No separate review has yet appeared . . . , but 300 copies have already been sold. (500 were sent in all.) [. . .]

P. S. I am enclosing a newspaper clipping from *Le XIX-ème Siècle*.

[389]

Moscow, April 24/May 6, 1880

TO PAVEL VASIL'EVICH ANNENKOV

I suppose that this letter will catch you just as you are leaving Baden-Baden, and I am therefore limiting myself to a few words. Come here and come quickly, for the Pushkin Festival (which will last for

[6] It is interesting to note the part of Flaubert's letter which Turgenev does not quote: "Tell me something about the author. Is this his first book? In any case, he has a *brain*." The Flaubert selection, of course, is translated from the French given by Turgenev. It checks completely with the edition of Flaubert's works published in Paris by Louis Canard in 1954 (*Oeuvres complètes de Gustave Flaubert*, ed. by Mme René Dumesnil *et alii*, Supplément [*juillet* 1877–*mai* 1880], p. 299).

three days, May 25, 26, and 27 [all O.S.])[7] is inconceivable without you, and everyone is waiting for you
with the greatest impatience.[8] At the dinner on the
26th, you will inevitably have to give a short speech on
any of Pushkin's works you choose, and [thus] be added
to the list which contains the names of Goncharov,
Dostoevski, Ostrovski, Pisemski, Petekhin, Polonski,
Maikov, Ivan Aksakov, Tikhonravov, your friend Bartenev, your humble servant, and others. Every unpleasant element will be removed.

I myself arrived here last Friday. (N.B. on the
very next day, a telegram came about [Dmitri] Tolstoy's
downfall [9] and never before had I seen such an outburst
of general happiness.) I am remaining here until Monday, and then I am going to the village—Spasskoe—
but shall be here again at my friend Maslov's house on
May 24. I plan to visit Lev Tolstoy on the way and shall
try to persuade him to come also, but I shall scarcely
succeed. So, I shall see you soon! Greetings to all yours,
and best regards.

[390]

Moscow, April 24 [O.S.], 1880

TO MAR'IA GAVRILOVNA SAVIN

[. . .] Yesterday, late in the evening, I suddenly
received both your letters and was very happy (but

---

[7] The editor in the Soviet source states here that the festival
began on June 6 rather than on May 26; I wonder if he is not
confusing the two calendars, inasmuch as Pushkin's birthday is
May 26 (O.S.).

[8] Annenkov was an editor of Pushkin's works.

[9] Count Dmitri Tolstoy had been Minister of National Education since 1866. He had championed the teaching of the syntax of classical languages as a way to keep young intellectuals
away from politics.

naturally not about the fact that you are not completely well). I felt how sincerely I loved you. I felt (and not for the first time since my departure from St. Petersburg) that you have become something in my life from which I shall never part. [. . .]

[391]

Spasskoe, May 8, 1880

TO MIKHAIL MATVEEVICH STASIULEVICH

[. . .] Upon my arrival here, I was greeted by the following bit of news: rumors have been circulating among all the local peasants and their women that as a result of the explosion in the Palace,[1] the sovereign has ordered me immured, with a twelve-pound cast-iron cap on my head, within a stone column. These are the flowers that grow from the seeds so carefully planted by the Katkovs and their ilk. [. . .]

[392]

Spasskoe, May 17 [O.S.], 1880

TO MAR'IA GAVRILOVNA SAVIN

It is now 12:30. I returned here an hour and a half ago, and now I am writing to you. The night I spent at Orel was both good (because you alone were constantly in my mind) and bad (because I could not shut my eyes). I hope that you, in your comfortable

---

[1] This was the period when the terrorists of the *Narodnaia Volia* (the People's Will) were making every effort to assassinate Aleksandr II. On February 5 [O.S.], 1880, Stepan Khalturin's attempt to blow him up in a banquet hall at the Winter Palace in St. Petersburg failed because of an unexpected change in the Tsar's plans. What was at least the seventh attempt to assassinate him within less than two years finally succeeded on March 1 [O.S.], 1881. (See Florinsky.)

railroad car, slept better than I did; my thoughts are
with you on the way to Kiev. Today, the day set aside
for your stay at Spasskoe, is like paradise—as if by
decree. Not a single cloud in the sky; no wind; warm
. . . If you were here, we would now be sitting on the
terrace—you [your fellow actress], Raisa Alekseevna
Potekhin, and I—admiring the view. I would be talking
about various irrelevant subjects, but in my mind I
would constantly be kissing your feet in a burst of gratitude. That, at least, was my dream . . . but dreams
have remained only dreams. They ought to be banished,
but to do so is not easy. I suppose that once you have
arrived, you will be kind enough to write me a few
words. I have not managed to talk to you about the
"nasty thing which must have an influence upon your
future. . . ." I can guess, but I would like to know
something more definite.

At the station yesterday evening, when you were
at the open window, I silently stood in front of you,
and then uttered the word: *"Otchaiannaia"* ["The
Desperate One"]. . . . You took it personally, but I
had something completely different in mind. . . . I
had a really desperate idea. . . . To seize you and
carry you off to the station. . . . The third bell would
have sounded, and right after it a cry from Raisa Alekseevna—and maybe from you—but it would have been
too late. . . . And you would have had to stay twenty-
four hours—where and how? . . . That is what I was
thinking when I uttered that word. But unfortunately
reason triumphed, and then the bell rang, and *ciaò* [so
long], as the Italians say. But imagine what would have
been in the papers!! I can see the story now, headed:
SCANDAL AT OREL STATION. "Yesterday an extraordinary
event occurred here. The writer T. (an old man, to

boot!), while accompanying the famous actress Miss S. (who was leaving to fill a brilliant engagement in Odessa), suddenly, at the exact moment of departure, as if possessed by a devil, snatched Miss S. through the train window, despite her desperate resistance . . ." etc., etc. What fussing and thundering throughout Russia! And at the time the thing was hanging by a hair. . . . I ought to add that so does almost everything else in life. [. . .]

{ 393 }

Spasskoe, May 19 [O.S.], 1880

TO MAR'IA GAVRILOVNA SAVIN

[. . .] All you are doing by calling me your "sin" is to reproach me for nothing. Alas! I shall never be [your "sin"]. And if we see each other in two or three years, I shall have become an extremely old man, while you will probably be entering the ultimate path of your life—and nothing will remain of the past. This is half a sorrow for you; [. . .] your whole life lies ahead; mine lies behind, and the hour spent in the railroad coach, when I felt almost like a twenty-year-old, was the final flaring of the lamp. It is even difficult for me to explain to myself the emotion which you kindled in me. Whether I am in love with you, I do not know; love used to be different for me. This is an indeterminate aspiration toward a blending, toward the complete surrender of myself, in which everything earthly disappears in some delicate fire. . . . I am probably talking nonsense, but I would be indescribably happy if . . . if . . . But now, when I know that this is not to happen, I am not unhappy; I do not even feel any special melancholy, but I am profoundly sorry that this enchanting instant is thus lost forever, without having touched me with its wings. [. . .] I am sorry for myself and—I dare to add—for you, because I am sure that you too would never have forgotten the happiness you would have given me. [. . .]

[394]

Spasskoe, June 13 [O.S.], 1880

TO MIKHAIL MATVEEVICH STASIULEVICH

I do not know which one of you on the *Vestnik Evropy* will write about the Pushkin celebrations, but such knowledge would not stop my observing the following to him: Ivan Aksakov and all the newspapers have said that I personally submitted completely to Dostoevski's speech, and entirely approve of it. But that is not so, and I have not yet cried out: "Thou hast conquered, O Galilean!" That clever, brilliant, and craftily deft speech, with all its peculiarities, is based totally on deceit. . . . And what is the purpose of that *universal man* whom the public so furiously applauded? [. . .] To be an original Russian is better than to be that characterless universal man. The whole thing is the same old pride—disguised as humility. . . . But it is easy to understand why the public has swooned at that flattery; the prettiness and tact of the speech were really remarkable. It seems to me that something of this sort ought to be stated. The Slavophiles have not swallowed us yet. . . .

[395]

Spasskoe, June 14 [O.S.], 1880

TO VSEVOLOD MIKHAILOVICH GARSHIN

I am writing you although I do not have the pleasure of knowing you personally. I have learned that you are not well at present, and would like to express my interest and sympathy to you.[2] I was hoping to meet you through Gleb Ivanovich Uspenski in St. Petersburg, but you had already left. I have been paying attention to your indubitable and original talent since your first appearance in literature, and have been following your activities. Your latest work, V*oina i liudi* [*War and People*] (unfortunately unfinished), has, in my opinion, finally earned you first place among all beginning writers. Count Lev Nikolaevich Tolstoy, to whom I gave *War and People* to read, shares this opinion. I would be very sorry if your illness impeded your talent's further development and hope that it will not be delayed, and that once you have recovered you will immediately take up your pen with doubled powers. Every aging writer who honestly loves his work is glad when he finds heirs—of whom you are one. [. . .]

[396]

Bougival, November 1 [O.S.], *1880*

TO VIKTOR PAVLOVICH GAEVSKI

From my prolonged silence, you have concluded that I did not succeed in doing what I had promised you; I have not found an explanation for the inscription on Pushkin's ring,[3] which was given to me by the Oxford professor, and I have not received Pushkin's letters to Aleksandr Ivanovich Turgenev from the Tur-

[2] Garshin was already on the brink of madness, a condition that lasted until his suicide in 1888. *War and People* was the title for a planned series of stories which Garshin never finished. The story Turgenev mentions was translated by Captain Rowland Smith under the title "Officer and Soldier-Servant."

[3] The ring was at the Pushkin exhibition in St. Petersburg that year.

genevs. I am beginning to think that the letters have simply been mislaid. Instead, the Turgenevs handed me (and that only yesterday) a note from Pushkin sent to A. I. Turgenev on the eve of [Pushkin's fatal] duel, and a notebook with a fair copy, in Pushkin's own hand, of the *first chapter of* [*Eugene*] *Onegin*, with certain corrections† I am sending both these documents to you through Mme L. I. Stasiulevich, who is leaving Paris tomorrow for St. Petersburg: please send me a receipt as soon as you get them. The Turgenevs gave me these two things with fear and trepidation. The receipt will calm them down. [. . .]

Although I see from the newspapers that the Pushkin exhibit has already opened, perhaps the afore-mentioned two documents will manage to get there yet. [. . .]

[397]

Paris, December 26, 1880

TO MOISEI L'VOVICH VELLER

In answer to your letter, which has aroused my sincere interest in your fate, I advise you as follows. Write a letter to Count Mikhail Tarielovich Loris-Melikov in which you set forth your past with complete frankness, and inform him of your wish to return to Russia, adding a promise henceforth not to be concerned with politics but to dedicate yourself to science exclusively. Send the letter to me and I shall send it off together with a note of my own. Of course, I cannot guarantee anything (I do not know Count Loris-Melikov personally), but perhaps things will work out; in

† "This manuscript, after having been at the Public Library in St. Petersburg, is now in Pushkin House, Leningrad."

any case, trying will not hurt. Send this letter without losing any time; this is an opportune moment. [. . .]

{ 398 }

[*Paris* (?)], *January 10/22, 1881*

TO GLEB IVANOVICH USPENSKI

[. . .] I read your last sketches in the *Otechestvennye zapiski* with particular satisfaction; they are beautiful, and "the boy who does not wish to learn" [in "Mishka"] is a little *chef d'oeuvre* in its own way. The work contains not only knowledge of village life (which you have always had), but a penetration into its very depths, an artistic grasp of its characteristic traits and individuals. In these sketches, you have almost entirely shaken off the shortcomings which, you will remember, I pointed out to you when I saw you in Moscow—the analytical, and (in view of your talent) the superfluous arguments and notions. When knowledge is adduced,[4] the woods (without which it would not exist) disappear, you know. [. . .]

{ 399 }

Paris, March 18, 1881

TO PAVEL VASIL'EVICH ANNENKOV

[. . .] Yes, our homeland is an unfortunate country. I could not suppress a smile at your appeal to the Russian god for aid, and I was reminded of Béranger's verses:

Si je conçois comment l'on s'y comporte,
Je veux, mes enfants, que le diable m'emporte.

[4] **Vyvedeno**, the Russian word translated here as "adduced," may also mean "exterminated."

[If I understand how they behave in this matter/
May the devil take me, fellows.]

The Russian god has thus far helped only by doing
nothing; somehow, everything has become disentangled
by itself. And now, it seems, a knot has been tightened
which cannot be compared to the Gordian. . . . And
here is something else: if they take a notion to make
an attempt [on the life] of the new tsar,[5] then really, as
people say, shut your eyes and run to the end of the
world before the muzhik noose tightens around your
civilized throat. Involuntarily, I repeat after Stasiulevich: we are living through fine times! He has written
me a letter that reminded me vividly of the bell on a
troika in motion, when its clapper no longer strikes but
only swishes against the sides with ah—ah—ah—, ai—
ai—ai, and you cannot make out anything.

The nihilist gentlemen magnanimously assure us
that they will give both the new tsar and Russia several weeks of respite. To make up for it later! Because
now these rattle-brained fools are a power, we must
take their foolish words into consideration, but how
will they be applied to reality? [. . .]

[400]

Bougival, November 10, 1881

TO LUDWIG PIETSCH

[. . .] I sent Tolstoy's novel [*War and Peace*] to
Julian Schmidt a month ago [in French], but do not
know whether he has received it or read it. Did he, perhaps, dislike it? In any case, ask him about it and, if

---

[5] Tsar Aleksandr II had been assassinated on March 1
[O.S.], 1881, and was succeeded by his son, Aleksandr III.

possible, read it yourself. My judgment about it remains firm: it is the most sublime modern Epos. [. . .]

{ 401 }

Paris, November 24 [*O.S.*], 1881

TO ZHOZEFINA ANTONOVNA POLONSKI

[. . .] I have not received a letter from Grigorovich, but, knowing his friendly attitude toward me, I am grateful to him for having defended me against the attacks of that black cock Stasov. The fate of my Italian novella is unexpected! In Russia, they not only are not swearing at it, but are even praising it, while in France, I am assured most seriously that I have never written anything better; two translations have already appeared in Germany, etc. I can really say with Sollogub: "I thank you. I did not expect it!"

The second sketch for my *Vospominanii svoikh i chuzhikh* [*Reminiscences of My Own and of Others*] (entitled "A Desperate Character") has been copied and will be sent to St. Petersburg tomorrow for the January issue of the *Vestnik Evropy*. Who knows, perhaps the fate of that sketch will be the opposite of *The Song of Triumphant Love's*. [. . .]

{ 402 }

Paris, December 3/15, 1881

TO MAR'IA GAVRILOVNA SAVIN

[. . .] I am angry with my fellow countrymen, who are making such fools of themselves over the intolerable Sarah Bernhardt. All she has is a charming voice; everything else is false, cold, affectation and repulsive Parisian chic. She is a charlatan and a publicity-hound to the extent that she telegraphed (she herself, mind you!) all the newspapers about the firemen's rescuing *her* things from the unfortunate theater in Vienna. . . .[6] How do you like that? A thousand people perish. . . . Let them! But Sarah's things have been saved, and therefore there is no cause for grief. Upon such occasions, my ancestors' old serf-blood grows wild in me; I would truly flog that poser myself. . . . The trouble is that she is so thin there is *no place* to whip! [. . .]

[403]

Paris, January 1, 1882

TO PAVEL VASIL'EVICH ANNENKOV

[. . .] From Stasiulevich, I have already received (I continue on [January] 5th), various compliments about "A Desperate Character." Even the severe Kavelin is content. Let us see what the public will say. By the way, imagine: a Russian lady has most seriously assured me that in Russia they have guessed the *real* significance of "The Song of Triumphant Love": Valeriia is Russia; Fabius is the government; Mucius, who fertilizes Russia even though he perishes, is nihilism, and the mute Malayan is the Russian muzhik (also mute), who calls nihilism back to life!! What an unexpected allegory?! Like M. Jourdain [in Molière's *Bourgeois Gentilhomme*] *qui parlait en prose sans le savoir* [who spoke prose without being aware of it], I created all this profundity without suspecting it myself! [. . .]

---

[6] The Ringtheater in Vienna burned down on December 8, 1881; Mme Bernhardt had first appeared in Russia the previous month.

{ 404 }

Paris, January 9/21, 1882

TO VLADIMIR VASIL'EVICH STASOV

[. . .] I expressed my opinion about Mr. . . .'s
article on Sarah Bernhardt in a personal letter to Mr.
. . . and, of course, I could not have expected it to
become public. But I am not in the habit of denying
my opinions even when they become public, against
my will, after I expressed them in a friendly, private
conversation. Yes, I find Mr. . . .'s appraisal of Sarah
Bernhardt completely true and accurate. She is an intelligent and dexterous woman, who knows her *métier*
inside out. She is gifted with a charming voice and
good schooling, but she has no suitable personality and
no artistic temperament (which she tries to replace
with Parisian sensuality). She is completely rotten
from chic (*pourrie de chic*), advertising, and posing.
She is monotonous, cold, and dry—in a word, she is
without a spark of what, in the highest sense, is called
talent. Her walk is like a chicken's; her dumb show does
not exist; the motions of her hands are purposely and
awkwardly piquant: it all stinks of the boulevard, *Figaro*, and patchouli. . . .

{ 405 }

Paris, February 25, 1882

TO PAVEL VASIL'EVICH ANNENKOV

[. . .] I read my "Desperate Character" (not
"Furious Character") in our circle—with success; the
Grand Duke [Konstantin Nikolaevich] deigned to
laugh; incidentally, he and I are on friendly terms; he
even brought me to his *quasi*-wife's—Miss Kuznetsov,

with whom he lives here *maritalement* [as man and wife]. There are three children, and she is an ordinary, plain-looking, modest, and very quiet housemaid.[7] The critics in Russia have reacted unfavorably to the "Desperate Character" while the "illegals"[8] here have taken offense. It is, on a small scale, the same story as with Bazarov [in *Fathers and Children*]. The French *lettrés* [men of letters] liked the work. Taine even embarrassed me with his compliments. [. . .]

[406]

Bougival, May 26 [*O.S.*], *1882*

TO MIKHAIL EVGRAFOVICH SALTYKOV-SHCHEDRIN

I intended several times to write you, but you probably know that I have been sick for three months and more, two months in bed. They took me here in the hope that a change of air would help me after the doctors' efforts had proved futile. I have been hooked by some sort of very vile disease whose very name I did not even know—*angine de poitrine goutteuse* [angina pectoris induced by the gout] *cardialgie névralgique* [neuralgic cardialgia], etc.—and which consists in a person's not being able to walk or stand lest cruel pains attack his breast and left shoulder; recently *névralgie intercostale* [intercostal neuralgia], in the right shoulder and in the side, has been added, which does not permit me to recline. The only thing left is for me to sit and take morphine through hypodermics. The situation, as you see, is not a happy one. Add to this cruel attacks of the gout in the legs, a tormenting biliary

[7] Miss Kuznetsov had been a ballerina.
[8] The "illegals" were Russians resident abroad who were active politically against the Russian Empire.

colic, and—the main thing—ignorance as to when and how this will end, and the result is a jolly little landscape. Meantime, I sit here like the Prisoner of Chillon, but I do not even have the consolation of knowing that a Byron will celebrate me, and that a Zhukovski will translate it [into Russian]. (The latter is scant consolation.) . . .

[407]

Bougival, May 26/June 7, 1882

TO MAR'IA GAVRILOVNA SAVIN

Yesterday I was partly carried and partly driven here, and my first duty, of course, is to write you at the address you left. Do not conclude from my transfer, however, that my health has become significantly better; the doctors are counting on the influence of a change of atmosphere—and that is all. I am becoming convinced that I cannot get completely healthy, and that I shall never be able to stand, to walk, and the rest, as ordinary living people do. The illness is one of those which assail many artists, writers, and the like at about sixty years of age, and which does not leave them again until the end of their days—a sort of faithful spouse. I must become reconciled to it, even if doing so is certainly difficult. If only the illness had waited for a short year, I could have gone down to Spasskoe, etc., etc. I had so many plans—in literature, in business—all kinds of plans! But all that is water under the bridge and I am in all respects an obliterated man. My sole consolation is the idea that those whom I sincerely love are *well*, and you occupy one of the first places among those people. You, of course, have no doubt about that. [. . .]

[408]

Bougival, May 27 [O.S.], 1882

TO ZHOZEFINA ANTONOVNA POLONSKI

[. . .] I must become reconciled to this [illness]. I am a man who is *canceled*, although I can creak for a long time to come.

And all around, everything is green and in bloom, the birds are singing, etc. But all that is beautiful and sweet only while a person is healthy, but now he can't help remembering "indifferent" nature. [. . .]

P.S. Iakov Petrovich [Polonski] [9] once advised me to conquer my illness through will power. Tell him that I shall try to follow his advice if he manages through will power *alone*, without frowning, without waving his arm, and without shaking himself but *through will power alone*, to chase a fly off his nose—especially if his nose is sweaty and offers the fly abundant food.

[409]

Bougival, August 25, 1882

TO PAVEL VASIL'EVICH ANNENKOV

The Polonski [family] are still staying at my place in the village [of Spasskoe]. So is Vsevolod Garshin, the young writer one can have the greatest hopes for of all the present writers. Perhaps you know that he had gone out of his mind; now, however, he has become better and, I hear, has set to work. [. . .]

[9] The addressee's husband.

[410]

Bougival, September 4, 1882

TO THE PEASANTS OF SPASSKOE VILLAGE

I have received your letter, and I thank you for your kind memories of me and for your good wishes. I myself am very sorry that illness has prevented me from visiting Spasskoe during the present year. My health is improving, and I hope to spend next summer in Spasskoe.

Rumors have been reaching me that you recently have been drinking much less alcohol; I am very glad about that and hope that you will abstain from it in the future; drunkenness is the first cause of a peasant's ruin.

But I regret that—also according to rumors—your children rarely visit the school. Remember that in our times a man who cannot read or write is just like a blind man, or a man without arms. Following the example of earlier years, I am giving you a few acres[1] of land in a spot which [the manager] Nikolai Aleksandrovich [Shchepkin] will show you. I am sure that you will do no damage to my house or garden, or my property in general, and am counting on you in this respect.

With this, I greet you all, peasants of Spasskoe, and wish you every happiness.

Your former landowner,

[411]

Bougival, September 3/15, 1882

TO VSEVOLOD MIKHAILOVICH GARSHIN

[. . .] Of all our young writers, you are the one

[1] The Russian says one *desiatina* (2.7 acres).

who arouses the greatest hopes. You have all the signs of a genuine and large-scale talent: artistic temperament, a subtle and accurate understanding of the *characteristic* features in life (both human and public), a sense of truth and measure, simplicity and beauty of form, and—as a result of all this—originality. I do not even see what advice I could give you; I can only express the wish that life will not impede you but, on the contrary, will give your creations breadth and variety—and the tranquillity without which no creative work is thinkable. [. . .]

[412]

Bougival, September 23, 1882

TO W. R. S. RALSTON

[. . .] Henry James paid me a visit. He is still just as pleasant, and has become much stouter; he is almost as stout as Albert Turgenev, with whom he came to see me. [. . .]

[413]

Bougival, September 24 [O.S.], 1882

TO MIKHAIL EVGRAFOVICH SALTYKOV-SHCHEDRIN

I received your letter and the September issue of the *Otechestvennaia zapiski* right after it. I immediately read your "*Sovremennaia idill'ia*" [Contemporary Idyll"] and found that your innate *vis comica* [comic force] has never been displayed with greater brilliance. Yes, you must work like a fiend for a long time to come. Perhaps the censor will eat you up. But you are on a large scale; perhaps he will chew you, but not gulp you down. I also read Mikhailovski's article on Dostoevski.

He has accurately noted the basic feature of Dostoevski's work. He might have recalled that French literature has also had a similar phenomenon—to wit, the
celebrated Marquis de Sade. The latter even wrote a
book, *Tourments et supplices* [*Tortures and Torments*],
in which he insists, with special delight, upon the
voluptuous debauchery of inflicting refined torture and
suffering. Dostoevski also, in one of his novels, carefully
paints the pleasure of such an enthusiast. . . . And
just think—for our De Sade the entire Russian prelacy
performed memorial services, and even read sermons
about this man's universal love! Truly, we live in
strange times.

That you are indisposed is not good (who can
know this and value it better than I?), but that you
complain about the hatred of certain persons who even
turn pale at your very name is pointless. Whoever
arouses hatred also arouses love. Had you simply been
M. E. Saltykov, a hereditary nobleman, nothing like
this would have happened. But you are Saltykov-Shchedrin, a writer destined to leave a profound mark on our
literature, and that is why you are loved by some and
hated by others. And this is the "result of your life"
which you are talking about, and you can be satisfied
with it. As for the loneliness and isolation, who, oh
who, is not essentially alone after fifty, and not a "fragment" of the older generation? Nothing can be done
about it; death is gradually preparing us not to be so
sad at parting from life.

You are unjust about our mutual friend, P. V. A.[2]
I know what a high opinion he has of you. He has
never treated anyone haughtily or ironically; would he
really begin with you? Perhaps you have not observed

[2] Perhaps Annenkov.

that he is an extremely bashful—and even timid—person. You have failed to sense that beneath his pretended breeziness.

I shall remain here for about six weeks more. Then, I plan to go back to Paris. . . . But when I shall hit Russia only the gods know (if they are concerned with such trifles). [. . .]

[414]

Bougival, October 22, 1882

TO PETR ISAEVICH VEINBERG

In answer to your letter, I must inform you that, with all my desire to advance your useful enterprise, I am in no condition to promise you any translations.[3] I owe my publishers original works, which I have promised them; how on earth can I think of translating? Moreover, I would rather translate some pages from Montaigne or Rabelais—but in any case not Balzac, of whom I could never read more than ten pages at a time, so repulsive and alien do I find him. But, I repeat, I cannot pledge myself in any way. [. . .]

[415]

Bougival, October 19/31, 1882

TO COUNT LEV NIKOLAEVICH TOLSTOY

[. . .] Of course I shall, as you want me to, read your article ["A Confession"]. I know that it was written by a very intelligent, very talented, and very *sincere* man; I may disagree with him, but first of all I shall try to understand him, to put myself completely in his place. . . . This will be more instructive and

---

[3] Veinberg, a well-known translator of Shakespeare, had started a magazine that specialized in translations of literature.

more interesting than to measure him by my own
yardstick, or to find out why he disagrees with me. But
for me to get really *angry* is completely inconceivable.
Only young people, who imagine that only what comes
in through their window is light, get angry. . . .
And I shall be 64 in a few days. A long life teaches one
not to doubt everything . . . (because to doubt everything means to believe in oneself), but to doubt oneself, i.e., to believe in, and even need, something else.
That is the spirit in which I shall read you. [. . .]

{ 416 }

Bougival, October 31 [O.S.](?), 1882
TO DMITRI VASIL'EVICH GRIGOROVICH

[. . .] A few days ago I received from a very
sweet Moscow lady the sermon by Lev Tolstoy which
the censor had banned. I read it through with great
interest; it a work remarkable for its sincerity, truthfulness, and strength of conviction. But the entire
thing is constructed on false premises, and leads in the
long run to the most gloomy denial of human and all
other life. . . . This in its own way is also nihilism. I
wonder what causes Tolstoy, who incidentally also
denies art, to surround himself with artists—and what
can they gain from his conversations? Nevertheless,
Tolstoy is almost the most remarkable person in present-
day Russia. [. . .]

{ 417 }

Paris, November 12/24, 1882
TO MIKHAIL MATVEEVICH STASIULEVICH

[. . .] A young novelist whom you know, Guy

de Maupassant, undoubtedly the most talented of all
contemporary French writers, has written a novel that
will be serialized in the feuilleton section of *Gil Blas*
beginning with the February 15 [1883] issue. I know
the contents of this novel; they are in no way scabrous
(as some of his other things are). He read me some
major selections a few days ago, and I became absolutely
ecstatic. Nothing like it has appeared since [Flaubert's]
Madame Bovary. He is not like Zola and the others. I
know that I have the reputation of being too indulgent
a judge and critic, but either I have no understanding
at all or the novel by Maupassant is an extraordinarily
outstanding phenomenon—a *most capital work!* He
would not be averse to selling it in manuscript, with
the proviso that the translation must not appear before
February 3/15 of next year—i.e. the first part; the
second part could appear a month later, i.e. in the
March issue of the *Vestnik Evropy* (assuming that the
first part has appeared in February). The *Vestnik
Evropy* does not seem to have done anything like this,
but, let me repeat, this is an unusual work and will
create a powerful impression. Maupassant would let
you have it for 600 silver rubles. I would find a good
translator here, and I myself would keep an eye on the
translation. Think it over, and also give me as quick
an answer as you can.

That is what I had to tell you.

The title of the novel is *Une Vie* [*A Life*]. It is
the entire life of an honest and good woman, a complete and intimate drama depicted by a first-class
artist. Its length does not exceed that of *Madame
Bovary*. [. . .]

{ 418 }

Paris, November 26 [O.S.], 1882

TO ALEKSANDR VASIL'EVICH TOPOROV

Today I sent you the corrected fifth volume of my works (*Smoke* and *Virgin Soil*). The sixth and seventh (the stories) have been received, and will be sent back next week. Incidentally, I have forgotten one important thing: on the title page for *Fathers and Children* the following must be put, in parentheses, *without fail:*

"Dedicated to the memory of Vissarion Grigor'evich Belinski."

Do not forget. [. . .]

{ 419 }

Paris, December 2, 1882

TO SIDNEY JERROLD

In accordance with your wish, I am answering your kind letter in Russian. I sincerely rejoice that a man of your abilities loves our language and our literature, and I hope that your labors will not be lost on the English public, but will arouse their interest. As for the biographical data, you will find everything you need in the sources you have indicated. As for the rest, my life does not offer anything particularly outstanding. I can merely say that the two stories you have selected ["The Torrents of Spring" and "Punin and Baburin"] contain much from my own life. In fact, I constantly depend on actual experiences in all my work, and, as far as I can, I try to make only chance phenomena into characters.

[420]

Paris, December 6, 1882

TO IVAN NIKOLAEVICH KRAMSKOI

[. . .] There is no doubt that the French public has become interested in Russian art *precisely since Russian art achieved self-dependence,* displayed originality, and became Russian and national. (The very same thing also happened to our literature in France.) Hence, we have no reason for doubt and hesitation about this question. But this itself imposes on us the obligation to choose strictly and impartially. The works of our school which express *ax-grinding* and *underlining* (the usual sign of everything that is still young and *immature*) must be removed as an unfree representation of national life, as a burdensome afterthought. This tinkering and this flaunting of originality are frequently and largely accompanied by a weakness in technique, and are forced to serve as substitutes; this strikes the eyes immediately and causes a special coolness among Europeans, whose long experience has developed taste and a feeling for [recognizing] hypocrisy. Repin's [painting] *Burlaki* [*Barge-Haulers*] and Vereshchagin's works can serve as examples which have scored major successes here, while other seemingly national pictures which I will not mention have had a total fiasco. *Ax-grinding* in art, in poetry, etc. gives itself away by its very name. It is not achievement. [. . .]

[421]

[*Paris, published December* 10 [O.S.], 1882]
[TO THE STUDENTS IN THE WOMEN'S MEDICAL COURSES]
Dear Ladies,

Allow me first of all to thank you for your letter, and also for the sympathy you have expressed in such flattering terms for my work, and especially for the opportunity you have given me to participate in such a humane and patriotic cause, which I think will consolidate the future of women's medical courses. In proof that this is really a patriotic and a Russian cause, I repeat here the beautiful words of your letter:

"We wish one thing: that the paths to knowledge not be closed to us. Will the Russian public really deny us our just aspiration, and force us with wretched hearts to acquire the necessary knowledge abroad?"

As far as I know, the Russian public will not only fail to answer you with a denial but has already answered—heatedly and energetically answered—your very just aspirations. The public has shown that, despite all the false and unscrupulous comments, it remembers your services in war and peace and is equally convinced of the purity of your intentions (to which the unanimous opinion of your teachers has testified) and of the great benefits you are called upon to bring to our country. One can definitely state that in the present situation our country needs women doctors even more than it needs doctors in general; the number of doctors is disproportionately small in proportion to the present need.[4] The historical destinies of Russia place on the

---

[4] The women's medical school in St. Petersburg was closed in 1882 as part of Aleksandr III's policy toward higher education (see Florinsky, p. 1,113).

Russian woman special and lofty obligations. In their
fulfillment she has already displayed so much self-
sacrifice, so much honest and steadfast toil, that it
would be unwise, indeed sinful—I shall not say to place
obstacles on the road destined for her—not to employ
every conceivable measure in helping her to accom-
plish her mission. Believe me, everything honest in
Russia, everything that loves our country, everything
desiring her welfare and a regular and peaceful development—both in the human sense and with respect to law
and government—is on your side.

And therefore success must not be doubted. Allow
me also to join in, and to contribute my mite.

[422]

Paris, January 6, 1883

TO EUGEN ZABEL

[. . .] As for my biography, the main dates are
well known and none of the rest, in view of its intimate
nature, is of any interest to the public. Those details
are not necessary for an evaluation of my literary work
—and, after all, this is the main purpose of your
study. [. . .]

[423]

Paris, December 28, 1882/January 9, 1883

TO ALEKSANDR VASIL'EVICH TOPOROV

[. . .] On Sunday I shall have to undergo a
rather painful operation. They will remove from my
stomach a "neuroma," which began to develop twenty-
four years ago in consequence of a minor surgical operation. All that time it had remained motionless and no

bigger than a small pea, but three months ago it began to grow and swell, and it is bigger now than a walnut. To my annoyance, they cannot give me chloroform because of my heart disease, and I shall be in real torment for four hours. I shall then have to stay in bed for about three weeks. [. . .]

[424]

Paris, December 29, 1882/January 10, 1883

TO PAVEL VASIL'EVICH ANNENKOV

[. . .] Inasmuch as a man must, as far as he can, always anticipate everything, especially everything that is not good, you will find in this letter a note by virtue of which you will have the right, in case of my death, to buy up my correspondence and to take whatever you find interesting. I have informed my friends, the Viardots, about this. [. . .]

[425]

Bougival, June 27 or 28, 1883

TO COUNT LEV NIKOLAEVICH TOLSTOY

I have not written you for a long time because, to speak plainly, I was and am on my deathbed. I cannot recover, and to think I could is pointless. I am really writing you, therefore, to tell you how happy I have been to be your contemporary, and to express to you my final, sincere request. My friend, return to literature! You know, this gift of yours comes from the same place as everything else. Oh, how happy I would be to think that my request has had an effect upon you! As for me, I am a man who is finished; the doctors do not even know what to call my ailment—*névralgie stoma-*

cale goutteuse [neuralgia of the stomach induced by the gout]. No walking, no eating, no sleeping—and why go on! Even to repeat it all is futile! My friend, great writer of the Russian land, hearken to my request! Let me know if you receive this sheet, and let me embrace you, your wife, and all yours closely, closely once more. . . . I cannot go on. . . . Tired!

APPENDIXES

A Letter from Pauline Viardot to Ludwig Pietsch, Bougival, September 8, 1883. Turgenjew an Pietsch: *Briefe* . . . , p. 159 (In French.)

B Turgenev's Reminiscences of His Childhood. Z: "*Ivan Sergeevich Turgenev na vechernei besede v SPb., 4-go marta 1880 g.*," *Russkaia starina*, October 1883, pp. 202–4.

C Turgenev Recounts a Writing Lesson. N. Ia. Stech'kina: *Iz vospominanii ob I. S. Turgeneve* (St. Petersburg; 1903), pp. 8–9, as quoted in N. L. Brodski, ed.: *I. S. Turgenev, materialy i issledovaniia* (Orel: Izdatel'stvo Orlovskogo Oblastnogo Soveta deputatov trudiashchikhsia; 1940), p. 155.

D The Incident with Tolstoy at Stepanovka. Evgeni Garshin: "*Vospominaniia ob I. S. Turgeneve,*" *Istoricheski vestnik*, November 1883, pp. 389–90.

E The incident with Dostoevski at Baden-Baden. Ibid., p. 387.

F Spasskoe on August 13 [O.S.], 1881. Ibid., pp. 378–9.

G Count L. N. Tolstoy on Ivan Turgenev. "*Novoe o proshlom: L. N. Tolstoi ob I. S. Turgeneve (Pis'mo k A. N. Pypinu),*" *Sovremennik*, 1913, No. 3, p. 313.

Bougival, September 8, 1883

FROM PAULINE VIARDOT TO LUDWIG PIETSCH

[On Turgenev's death the previous August 22.]
He did not suffer; his life stopped slowly, after two hic-
cups; we were all there. [. . .] The religious ceremony took place in the Russian church. There were
many curious people and a few friends, society being
away from Paris. They will take the body to Russia in
a few days. He expressed the desire to be buried in
Russia, close to his friend Belinski. [. . .]

St. Petersburg, March 4 [O.S.], *1880*
[*Turgenev's Reminiscences of his Childhood*]

My mother was a woman who belonged completely to the pattern of the eighteenth century and
the first decades of the nineteenth. She just barely
admitted that Pushkin was a remarkable writer, but
she absolutely would not admit the existence of any
Russian literature after Pushkin. Hence, although she
died in 1850—i.e., when I had been contributing to
magazines for about seven years—she never acknowledged the writer in me, and certainly never read a single
piece of mine, not even A *Sportsman's Sketches*.

I was a mischievous child and frequently aroused
my mother's wrath by putting her in awkward situa-
tions.

I can see one occasion even now; as a boy of six

or seven, I was presented to a tremendously worthy old man. I was told that he was the writer Ivan Ivanovich Dmitriev, and that I would recite one of his fables to him. But imagine the horror of my mother and of everyone else around when I looked the venerable old man right in the eye and blurted out: "Your fables are good, but Ivan Andreevich Krylov's are much better."

My mother became so angry that she flogged me, and that fixed in my mind the image of my first meeting and acquaintance with a Russian writer.

Another time they brought me to an equally worthy old lady; this was the Most Serene Princess Catherine Golenishchev-Kutuzov-Smolenski, nee Bibikov,[5] who died, as far as I can remember, in 1824. I was six years old, no more, when they brought me up to this antiquated old lady (whose headdress and entire appearance reminded me of an icon of some saint which, blackened by time, had a very poor outer appearance); instead of treating her with the same reverence that both my mother and the old ladies around had shown her, I burst out in her face: "You look just like a monkey." I received a severe scolding from my mother for this new sally.

Quite a fair number of tutors passed through my father's house, but the teacher who first interested me in the works of Russian literature was a manor serf. He would frequently take me into the garden, and there he read to me—what do you think?—Kheraskov's *Rossiad*. Each verse of the poem he would read at first, as it were, in a rough draft and quickly, and then he would read the same verse in finished copy, in a loud voice, and with a special delight. . . . I loved to listen to the *Rossiad*, and it was a great pleasure for

[5] The widow of the hero of 1812.

me when our home-grown elocutionist called me to the garden for the hundredth time to listen to him read selections from Kheraskov's ponderous work.

A German, who spoke Russian very badly, introduced us to German literature.

I vividly remember that this eccentric came to us one day with a cage in which there was the most ordinary, average, and even untrained raven. The entire serf-retinue ran in to look at the curious German who was making a to-do about his raven; they were puzzled as to why the German was dragging the bird around as there were enough of its kind in the courtyard.

An old serf glanced at his fussing and phlegmatically remarked: "Oh. you *fuflyga*," applying the epithet, of course, to the German. The German took offense, began to think [about it], and at breakfast or dinner the next day, he unexpectedly turned to my father and, explaining himself in extremely poor Russian, announced that he had a subject to ask my father a question about.

"Will you allow me to learn from you the meaning of the word *fuflyga*? That is what your man called me yesterday."

My father, having looked at the serf who had just left the room, at my brother, and at me, guessed what was happening, smiled, and said: "It means a lively and polite gentleman."

It was obvious that the German did not entirely trust the explanation. "And if they said to you," he continued, addressing my father, "oh, what a *fuflyga* you are!—wouldn't you take offense?"

"On the contrary, I would take it as a compliment."

This German was very sensitive. He would begin

reading us something from Schiller and would always burst into tears at the very first lines. He did not stay with us long. We soon learned that he had been nothing more than a saddler, that he had had no pedagogical training before coming to us, and he was let go.[6]

Turgenev Recounts a Writing Lesson[7]

This is what happened to me once. A budding playwright brought me his drama in order to get my reaction. It was terrible. I said to him: "Let me give you a thorough examination."

"How?"

"This way. I'll give you a subject for a powerfully dramatic scene, and you will sit down at my desk and sketch it out. Then I shall show you what your shortcomings are."

He agreed, but not at once.

"This is the subject," I said. "A tyrant has killed his legitimate sovereign in a country, and has occupied the throne. The murdered man's son has hidden in a neighboring country. His adherents join him there, one after another. Just as he is speaking with one of them, a new refugee arrives. Asked by the prince's interlocutor about what is happening in the homeland and how his family is getting along, the newcomer reports that the cruelty of the tyrant is increasing not by the day but by the hour, and that the inquirer's wife and children

---

[6] This excerpt is given by the man who had it published as coming from a speech delivered by Turgenev in St. Petersburg on March 4 [O.S.], 1880 and transcribed the same evening.

[7] This is given in the source as being told by Turgenev himself.

have been wickedly put to death. How does the aggrieved husband and father react to this news?"

I sat the dramatist at my desk and went into another room. An hour later the scene was ready. The aggrieved husband and father shouted terrible soliloquies. I then took my Shakespeare from the shelf, opened it to the last scene in Act IV of *Macbeth* and in the Russian translation, read to the playwright how and what Macduff says upon learning about his misfortune from Ross in Malcolm's presence. Macduff only repeats: "My children too?" (i.e. killed), "My wife kill'd too?" while Ross answers: "I have said [so]." The playwright understood, again took up the scene which he had written, and went away, never to return.

APPENDIX D

The incident with Tolstoy at Stepanovka[8]

[. . .] Before the departure, at breakfast, someone asked Turgenev where his daughter was living.

He answered that his daughter was abroad, as before, that hitherto she had been receiving an exclusively French education, but that he did not like that, and was putting her into the hands of a good English governess.

Count Tolstoy had turned his usual searching glance upon Turgenev throughout this conversation and then asked him: "And will the governess, during strolls and drives, drop in with your daughter on the poor and leave them money and medicine?"

[8] This incident that almost led to a duel between Turgenev and Lev Tolstoy occurred at Stepanovka (Fet's estate) in 1861. It is quoted here as it appears in the reminiscences of Evgeni Garshin (the brother of the author of "Four Days"), who states that it was told him by Turgenev himself.

Turgenev retorted that in any case he did not see any harm in that. On the one hand, the poor are helped even if only a little, and on the other, the child develops a sense of the necessity to help those who suffer.

"There is still another meaning: if your daughter does not get a genuine education, at least the poor will be receiving something. Isn't she, after all, your illegitimate daughter?"

"She is. But what on earth follows from that?"

"That you are conducting an *experimentum in anima vili* [experiment on a base soul]."

At these words, everything went dark before Turgenev, and he managed only to shout: "Tolstoy, shut up or I'll stick a fork in you." [9]

"I only saw," said Turgenev, "a smile of satisfaction twinkling in his eyes at the idea that he had succeeded in his goal." [. . .]

The incident with Dostoevski at Baden-Baden[1]

[. . .] "This book [*Smoke*] ought to be burned by the public executioner," said Dostoevski, taking the book in his hands. Turgenev (unfortunately the entire scene took place with only the two of them present) modestly inquired about the reasons, and in answer was given a complete accusatory speech on the subject: you hate Russia, you do not believe in her future, etc. —in short, Dostoevski identified Potugin [in *Smoke*] with Turgenev. Turgenev said that he preferred to hear all this out in silence, and to wait for Dostoevski to

[9] This is a play on words: *vilka* in Russian is "fork," while *vilis* in Latin is "base."

[1] Told by Evgeni Garshin.

finish and leave. And that is what actually happened.

But several weeks later Turgenev received a communication from Mr. Bartenev, the publisher of [the magazine] *Russki arkhiv*, informing him that Dostoevski had sent Bartenev a letter in which the above-mentioned soliloquy was reproduced, not as an accusation against Turgenev but as Turgenev's own sermon on the theme "I hate Russia, etc." At the same time, Dostoevski had requested that his letter not be published before a given period had passed (ten or fifteen years, if memory serves me right).

Turgenev answered Bartenev's question about what to do in the given instance by stating that he [Turgenev] felt completely indifferent about the matter. I am narrating this incident just as Turgenev recounted it to me. . . .

APPENDIX F

Spasskoe on August 13 [*O.S.*], *1881*

[. . .] I then drove up the broad street of the village of Spasskoe-Lutovinovo, which is lined on both sides with white willows. As in any other Great-Russian village, the houses were gray and unattractive. At the entrance, I caught sight of a small chapel, which was still unfinished at the time. At the end of the street, there was an extensive grove of green trees which completely concealed the manor house; until I had driven up to it, only the church steeple was to be seen. The wooden house was built in the Russian style, with a balcony on two sides and a small attic. Adjoining the house was a long, arch-shaped, stone outbuilding—the remains of a three-story gallery, with its own outbuildings and wings—that had been built during the first half of the [nineteenth] century and which had burned down later. One of the wings, the so-called musicians' wing, has been turned into the present house, which is buried in the verdure of a garden covering over fifty acres of ground and sloping down to a pond as long and as wide as a lake.

A church was built right in the garden, and close by is a small wooden building that houses the school. [. . .][2]

APPENDIX G

January 10 [O.S.], 1884

Count L. N. Tolstoy on Ivan Turgenev

[. . .] I am not writing anything about Turgenev because I have too much to say about him and all in the same connection. I always liked him, but only after his death did I value him as he deserved. I am sure that you see Turgenev's importance in the same way as I do, and thus I am very happy about your study.[3] I cannot, however, refrain from saying what I have thought of him. The main thing about him is his *truthfulness*. In my opinion, every work of literature (including belles-lettres) has three factors: 1) who and what sort of a person is speaking; 2) how does he speak, well or poorly, and 3) does he say what he is thinking, and all of what he is thinking and feeling. The various combinations of these three factors determine for me the entire product of human thought.

Turgenev was a fine person (not very profound, very weak—but a good, kind person), who always said

[2] Description by Evgeni Garshin.
[3] This is part of a letter to Professor Aleksandr Pypin, who wished to write a study of the late 1840's and the 1850's in Russia, and had written to Tolstoy.

well *exactly* what he thought and felt. Rarely do these three factors coincide so felicitously. More cannot be demanded of a person, and therefore Turgenev's impact upon our literature has been very good and fruitful. He lived, he sought, and he expressed in his works, what he found—everything he found. He did not use his talent (his skill at depicting so well) to hide his heart, as has been done and is being done, but to bring all of it out into the open. He had nothing to fear.

In my opinion, his life and works show three phases. 1) Faith in beauty (woman's love, art); This is expressed in very many of his writings. 2) Doubt about this and about everything else; This is expressed both touchingly and charmingly in "Enough." 3) An unformulated—as if on purpose, from fear of grasping it (he himself has said somewhere that only the unconscious acted powerfully and genuinely within him)—an unformulated love which drove him toward the good, both in his life and his writings, and a self-denial, expressed by all his self-denying characters and most clearly and charmingly in *Hamlet and Don Quixote,* where the paradoxicalness and the special quality of the form freed him from his bashfulness at being a preacher of the good. I would like to say much more about him. I very much regret that I have been hampered from speaking about him. [. . .]

SOURCES OF
LETTERS

1   To N. N. Turgenev, Moscow, March 31–April 2 [O.S.], 1831. I. S. Turgenev: *Sobranie sochineni*, Moscow, Pravda, Biblioteka Ogonek, 1949, XI, 45–6 (hereinafter referred to as Ogonek, 1949), and I. S. Turgenev: *Sobranie sochineni v dvenadtsati tomakh*, Moscow, GIKhL, 1958, XII, 9–11 (hereinafter referred to as GIKhL, 1958).

2   To A. V. Nikitenko, St. Petersburg, March 26/April 7, 1837. GIKhL, XII, 11–13.

3   To S. M. Figlev, place not given, June 12, 1837. V. V. Danilov, ed.: *"Pis'ma I. S. Turgeneva k S. M. Figlevu,"* *Literaturny arkhiv*, 1951, III, 172.

4   To A. P. Efremov, Frankfurt am Main, May 17, 1840. Sergei Orlovski, ed.: *"Iz proshlogo: tri pis'ma I. S. Turgeneva k A. P. Efremovu,"* *Novy mir*, May 1926, pp. 135–6.

5   To T. N. Granovski, Berlin, July 4 [O.S.], 1840. *Pervoe sobranie pisem I. S. Turgeneva, 1840–83 gg.* (St. Petersburg: Obshchestvo dlia posobiia nuzhdaiushchimsia literatoram i uchenym; 1884), pp. 1–4. (hereinafter referred to as *Pervoe*, 1884).

6   To A. P. Efremov, Marienbad, September 18, 1840. Orlovski, op. cit., p. 138.

7   To A. V. Nikitenko, place not given, end of 1846 or start of 1847. M. P. Alekseev, ed.: *"Pis'ma I. S. Turgeneva k A. V. Nikitenko,"* *Literaturny arkhiv*, 1953, IV, 185.

8   To the *Sovremennik*, Berlin, March 1, 1847. I. S. Turgenev: *"Pis'ma iz Berlina," Sobranie sochineni v dvenadtsati tomakh,"* Moscow, 1953–8, XI, 286–90 (hereinafter referred to as GIKhL, 1956).

9   To Pauline Viardot (nee Garcia), Paris, October 19, 1847. Ivan Tourguéneff: *Lettres à Mme Viardot* (publiées et annotées par E. Halpérine-Kaminsky, Paris: Charpentier; 1907), p. 8.

10   To V. G. Belinski, Paris, November 14/26, 1847. GIKhL, 1958, XII, 43–5.

11   To Pauline Viardot (nee Garcia), Paris, December 8, 1847. *Lettres à Mme Viardot*, p. 16.

12   To the same, Paris, December 19, 1847. Ibid., pp. 24–5.

13   To the same, Paris, December 25, 1847. Ibid., pp. 29–30.

14   To the same, Paris, January 5/17, 1848. Ibid., p. 40.

15   To the same, Paris, April 30, 1848. Ibid., pp. 45–6.

16   To the same, Paris, May 15, 1848. Ibid., pp. 52–9.

17   To the same, Paris [?], January 10, 1849. Ibid., p. 67.

18   To the same, Courtavenel, June 19, 1849. Ibid., p. 82.

19   To the same, Paris, June, 1849. Ibid., p. 69.

20   To the same, place not given [perhaps July 1849]. Ibid., p. 93.

21   To the same, Courtavenel, July 4, 1849; added July 6, 1849. Ibid., pp. 86–8.

22   To the same, Courtavenel, July 28, 1849. Ibid., pp. 113–14.

23   To the same, Courtavenel, August 16, 1849. Ibid., p. 127.

24   To the same, Courtavenel, May 16, 1850. Ibid., pp. 129–30.

25   To A. I. Herzen, Paris, June 10/22, 1850. *Pis'ma Dm. Kavelina k Al. Iv. Gertsenu, s ob"iasnitel'nymi primechaniiami M. Dragomanova* (Geneva: Switzerland: Ukrainskaia tipografiia; 1892), p. 89.

26   To Pauline Viardot (nee Garcia), Moscow, January 1/13, 1851. *Lettres à Mme Viardot*, pp. 145–6.

27   To E. M. Feoktistov, St. Petersburg, March 4/16, 1851. GIKhL, 1958, XII, 100–1.

28 To K. N. Leont'ev, St. Petersburg, December 3/15, 1851. *"Pis'ma I. S. Turgeneva k K. N. Leont'evu (1851–1876 gg.)," Russkaia mysl'*, 1886, No. XII, p. 66.

29 To I. S. Aksakov, St. Petersburg, December 4/16, 1851. B. N. Kapeliush, ed.: *"Pis'ma I. S. Turgeneva k I. S. Aksakovu," Literaturny arkhiv*, 1953, IV, 189.

30 To S. T. Aksakov, February 2 [O.S.], 1852. *"Iz perepiski I. S. Turgeneva s sem'eiu Aksakovykh," Vestnik Evropy*, January 1894, p. 332.

31 To Pauline Viardot (nee Garcia), St. Petersburg, February 21, 1852. *Lettres à Mme Viardot*, p. 155.

32 To I. S. Aksakov, St. Petersburg, March 3/15, 1852. GIKhL, 1958, XII, 107–8.

33 To Louis and Pauline Viardot (nee Garcia), St. Petersburg, May 1/13, 1852. E. Halpérine-Kaminsky, ed.: *"Lettres inédites d'Ivan Tourguéneff à Mme Viardot," Revue politique et littéraire*, Paris, 1906, 5–éme série, V, 773–4.

34 To Pauline Viardot (nee Garcia), Spasskoe, October 13 [O.S.], 1852. *Lettres à Mme Viardot*, pp. 160–1.

35 To N. A. Nekrasov, Spasskoe, October 28 [O.S.], 1852. GIKhL, 1958, XII, 124.

36 To K. N. Leont'ev, Spasskoe, December 12 [O.S.], 1852. *"Pis'ma I. S. Turgeneva k K. N. Leont'evu (1851–76)," Russkaia mysl'*, December 1886, p. 70.

37 To N. A. Nekrasov, Spasskoe, December 16 [O.S.], 1852. *"Pis'ma I. S. Turgeneva k N. A. Nekrasovu," Russkaia mysl'*, January 1902, second pagination, p. 118.

38 To I. S. Aksakov, Spasskoe, December 28 [O.S.], 1852. GIKhL, 1958, XII, 131–3.

39 To P. V. Annenkov, Spasskoe, January 10 [O.S.], 1853. Ibid., p. 136.

40 To K. S. Aksakov, Spasskoe, January 16 [O.S.], 1853. Ibid., pp. 140–2.

41 To S. T. Aksakov, Spasskoe, January 22 [O.S.], 1853. Ibid., pp. 142–4.

42 To the same, Spasskoe, February 5/17 [O.S.], 1853. *"Iz perepiski I. S. Turgeneva s sem'eiu Aksakovykh,"* pp. 342–3.

43 To E. M. Feoktistov, Spasskoe, March 6 [O.S.], 1853. M. V. Izmailov, ed.: *"Pis'ma Turgeneva k E. M. Feoktistovu,"* in anthology *Turgenev i krug Sovremennika, neizdannye materíaly, 1847–61* (Moscow and Leningrad; Academia; 1930), pp. 158–9.

44 To P. V. Annenkov, Spasskoe, March 14 [O.S.], 1853. GIKhL, 1958, XII, 154.

45 To S. T. Aksakov, K. S. Aksakov, and I. S. Aksakov, Spasskoe, April 2 [O.S.], 1853. Ibid., pp. 156–7.

46 To I. F. Minitski, Spasskoe, May 12 [O.S.], 1853. Ibid., pp. 158–9.

47 To Pauline Viardot (nee Garcia), Spasskoe, May 12/24, 1853. *Lettres à Mme Viardot*, p. 174.

48 To S. T. Aksakov, Spasskoe, June 5 [O.S.], 1853. *"Iz perepiski I. S. Turgeneva s sem'eiu Aksakovykh,"* *Vestnik Evropy*, February 1894, p. 475.

49 To the same, Spasskoe, June 29 [O.S.], 1853. Ibid., pp. 475–6.

50 To the same, August 30 [O.S.], 1853. Ibid., pp. 476–7.

51 To Mrs. Sofia Andreevna Miller, Spasskoe, October 12 [O.S.], 1853. GIKhL, 1958, XII, 163.

52 To S. T. Aksakov, Spasskoe, November 20 [O.S.], 1853. *"Iz perepiski I. S. Turgeneva s sem'eiu Aksakovykh,"* *Vestnik Evropy*, February 1894, p. 480.

53 To the same, St. Petersburg, February 10 [O.S.], 1854. GIKhL, 1958, XII, 167.

54 To K. N. Leont'ev, St. Petersburg, April 3 [O.S.], 1854. *"Pis'ma I. S. Turgeneva k K. N. Leont'evu (1851–76 gg.),"* pp. 74–5.

55 To S. T. Aksakov, Peterhof, May 31 [O.S.], 1854. GIKhL, 1958, XII, 168–9.

56 To the same, Peterhof, August 7 [O.S.], 1854. *"Iz perepiski I. S. Turgeneva s sem'eiu Aksakovykh,"* *Vestnik Evropy*, February 1894, p. 486.

57 To the editor of *Le Journal de St. Pétersbourg*, St. Petersburg, August 7/19, 1854. GIKhL, 1956, XI, 306–8. (French text.)

58 To S. T. Aksakov, Spasskoe, October 8 [O.S.], 1854. *"Iz perepiski I. S. Turgeneva s sem'eiu Aksakovykh,"* *Vestnik Evropy*, February 1894, p. 487.

59 To E. I. Kolbasin, Spasskoe, October 29 [O.S.], 1854. *Pervoe*, 1884, p. 9.

60 To I. F. Minitski, Spasskoe, November 1 [O.S.], 1854. I. A. Linnichenko, compiler: *"Pis'ma I. S. Turgeneva k doktoru I. F. Minitskomu,"* Vestnik Evropy, 1909, CCLVIII 635.

61 To Countess M. N. Tolstoy (nee Tolstoy) and Count V. P. Tolstoy, St. Petersburg, December 4 [O.S.], 1854. GIKhL, 1958, XII, 176.

62 To P. V. Annenkov, Spasskoe, June 15 [O.S.], 1855. I. S. Zil'bershtein and P. E. Shchegolev, eds.: *"Iz proshlogo: Pis'ma I. S. Turgeneva k P. V. Annenkovu,"* Novy mir, Book 9, 1927, pp. 161–2.

63 To V. P. Botkin, Spasskoe, June 17 [O.S.], 1855. GIKhL, 1958, XII, 179.

64 To the same, Spasskoe, July 9 [O.S.], 1855. V. P. Botkin i I. S. Turgenev: *Neizdannaia perepiska, 1851–69 gg., po materialam pushkinskogo doma i tolstovskogo muzeia* (prigotovil k pechati N. L. Brodski, Moscow and Leningrad: Academia; 1930), p. 57.

65 To N. A. Nekrasov, Spasskoe, July 10 [O.S.], (?) 1855. Ogonek, 1949, XI, 128–9.

66 To I. I. Panaev, Spasskoe, July 10 [O.S.], 1855. S. A. Koplan-Shakhmatova and P. I. Zisserman: *"Perepiska I. S. Turgeneva s I. I. Panaevym,"* in anthology *Turgenev i krug Sovremennika* . . . , pp. 38–9.

67 To V. P. Botkin and N. A. Nekrasov, Spasskoe, July 25 [O.S.], 1855. GIKhL, 1958, XII, 186.

68 To P. V. Annenkov, Spasskoe, July 25 [O.S.], 1855. M. P. Alekseev, ed.: *"Neizdannye pis'ma I. S. Turgeneva, tri pis'ma M. L. Velleru,"* Byloe, 1925, No. 1 (29), pp. 83–4.

69 To Count L. N. Tolstoy, Pokrovskoe, October 3 [O.S.], 1855. GIKhL, 1958, XII, 193–4.

70 To V. P. Botkin, St. Petersburg, December 3 [O.S.], 1855. Ibid., p. 195.

71 To P. V. Annenkov, St. Petersburg, December 9 [O.S.], 1855. Ibid., p. 197.

72 To N. A. Nekrasov, St. Petersburg [end of 1855, start of 1856]. N. I. Motovilova: *"Iz pisem Turgeneva k*

Nekrasovu," in anthology *Turgenev i krug Sovremennika* . . . , p. 119.

73 To Countess E. E. Lambert, Spasskoe, June 10 [O.S.], 1856. G. P. Georgievski, ed.: *Pis'ma I. S. Turgeneva k grafine E. E. Lambert* (Moscow; 1915), p. 8.

74 To A. I. Herzen, Courtavenel, September 22, 1856. *Pis'ma Dm. Kavelina k Al. Iv. Gertsenu* . . . , p. 90.

75 To V. P. Botkin, Courtavenel, September 18/30, 1856. Botkin i Turgenev: *Neizdannaia perepiska* . . . , p. 89.

76 To his daughter, Pauline, London, September 4, 1856. E. Séménoff: *La Vie douloureuse d'Ivan Tourguéneff avec des lettres inédites de Tourguéneff à sa fille* (Paris: Mercure de France; 1933), p. 37.

77 To A. V. Druzhinin, Paris, November 11, 1856. GIKhL, 1958, XII, 222–3.

78 To Count L. N. Tolstoy, Paris, November 16/28, 1856. Ibid., pp. 233–4.

79 To V. P. Botkin, Paris, November 25/December 7, 1856. Ibid., pp. 237–8.

80 To A. V. Druzhinin, Paris, December 5/17, 1856. Ibid., pp. 243–5.

81 To Count L. N. Tolstoy, Paris, December 8/20, 1856. Ibid., pp. 246–7.

82 To the same, Paris, December 16/28, 1856. Ibid., pp. 251–2.

83 To I. I. Panaev, Paris, December 16/28, 1856. S. A. Koplan-Shakhmatova and P. I. Zisserman in anthology *Turgenev i krug Sovremennika* . . . , pp. 66–8.

84 To Countess M. N. Tolstoy (nee Tolstoy), Paris, January 6, 1857. GIKhL, 1958, XII, 254–5.

85 To S. T. Aksakov, Paris, January 8, 1857. Ibid., pp. 259–60.

86 To Count L. N. Tolstoy, Paris, January 3/15, 1857. Ibid., pp. 261–3.

87 To I. I. Panaev, Paris, January 12/24, 1857. S. A. Koplan-Shakhmatova and P. I. Zisserman in anthology *Turgenev i krug Sovremennika* . . . , pp. 72–3.

88 To A. V. Druzhinin, Paris, January 13 [O.S.], 1857. *Pervoe*, 1884, pp. 43–4.

89 To V. P. Botkin, Paris, February 17/March 1, 1857. GIKhL, 1958, XII, 270–1.

90 To A. I. Herzen, Paris, March 5, 1857. *Pis'ma Dm. Kavelina k Al. Iv. Gertsenu* . . . , p. 108.

91 To V. N. Kashperov, Paris, March 7, 1857. GIKhL, 1958, XII, 272.

92 To I. I. Panaev, Paris, March 6/18, 1857. S. A. Koplan-Shakhmatova and P. I. Zisserman in anthology *Turgenev i krug Sovremennika* . . . , p. 82.

93 To P. V. Annenkov, Paris, April 3/15, 1857. GIKhL, 1958, XII, 273–5.

94 To A. I. Herzen, Sinzig bei Remagen am Rhein, July 17, 1857. *Pis'ma Dm. Kavelina* . . . , p. 109.

95 To V. P. Botkin, Boulogne, August 4, 1857. Botkin and Turgenev: *Neizdannaia perepiska* . . . , p. 156.

96 To N. A. Nekrasov, Rome, November 22/December 4, 1857. "*Pis'ma I. S. Turgeneva k N. A. Nekrasovu* . . . ," pp. 123–4.

97 To Count L. N. Tolstoy, Rome, November 25/December 7, 1857. GIKhL, 1958, XII, 287–8.

98 To I. I. Panaev, Rome, January 1/13, 1858. S. A. Koplan-Shakhmatova and P. I. Zisserman in anthology *Turgenev i krug Sovremennika* . . . , pp. 98–9.

99 To Count L. N. Tolstoy, Rome, January 17/29, 1858. GIKhL, 1958, XII, 295–6.

100 To the same, Vienna, April 8, 1858. Ibid., pp. 299–300.

101 To Pauline Viardot (nee Garcia), Spasskoe, June 25/July 7, 1858. Ivan Tourguéneff: *Lettres à Mme Viardot*, p. 181.

102 To A. A. Fet, St. Petersburg, December 27 [O.S.], 1858. Evgeni Bogoslovski, ed.: *Turgenev o L've Tolstom: 75 otzyvov* (Tiflis, Tipografiia kantsl. Glavnonach. grazhd. chast'iu na Kavkaze; 1894), p. 53.

103 To Count L. N. Tolstoy, St. Petersburg, February 11 [O.S.], 1859. A. E. Gruzinski and M. A. Tsiavlovski, eds.: *Tolstoi i Turgenev: perepiska* (Moscow: M. and S. Sabashnikov; 1928), p. 53.

104 To Countess E. E. Lambert, Spasskoe, March 27

[O.S.], 1859. Georgievski, ed.: *Pis'ma Turgeneva k gr. Lambert*, p. 25.

105 To I. A. Goncharov, Spasskoe, April 7, 1859, GikhL, 1958, XII, 304–5.

106 To V. P. Botkin, Spasskoe, April 12 [O.S.], 1859. Botkin and Turgenev: *Neizdannaia perepiska* . . . , p. 156.

107 To P. V. Annenkov, Vichy [received June 10/22, 1859]. P. V. Annenkov: *"Shest' let perepiski s I. S. Turgenevym, 1856–62," Vestnik Evropy*, March 1885, pp. 27–8.

108 To his dughter, Pauline, Vichy, June 26, 1859. E. Séménoff: *La Vie douloureuse* . . . , pp. 94–5.

109 To A. A. Fet, Courtavenel, July 16 [O.S.], 1859. Bogoslovski: *Turgenev o L've Tolstom*, p. 23.

110 To Countess E. E. Lambert [France, summer of 1859]. Georgievski, ed.: *Pis'ma Turgeneva k gr. Lambert*, p. 37.

111 To P. V. Annenkov, Courtavenel, August 1/13, 1859. GIKhL, 1958, XII, 307.

112 To A. A. Fet, Spasskoe, October 9 [O. S.], 1859. Bogoslovski, ed.: *Turgenev o L've Tolstom*, p. 23.

113 To Countess E. E. Lambert, Spasskoe, October 14 [O. S.], 1859. Georgievski, ed.: *Pis'ma Turgeneva k gr. Lambert*, p. 50.

114 To the same [perhaps Spasskoe or Moscow, November or December 1859]. Ibid., p. 3.

115 To K. N. Leont'ev, St. Petersburg, February 16 [O.S.], 1860. *"Pis'ma Turgeneva k Leont'evu (1851–76 gg.),"* pp. 82–3.

116 To A. A. Fet, St. Petersburg, February 22 [O. S.], 1860. Bogoslovski, ed.: *Turgenev o L've Tolstom*, p. 23.

117 To E. M. Feoktistov, Courtavenel, July 19/31, 1860. N. V. Izmailov, ed.: *"Pis'ma Turgeneva k Feoktisovu,"* p. 160.

118 To A. A. Fet, Paris, September 8 [O.S.], 1860. Bogoslovski, ed.: *Turgenev o L've Tolstom*, p. 25.

119 To K. N. Leont'ev, Courtavenel, October 3, 1860. First paragraph: Ogonek, 1949, XI, 198–9; second para-

graph: *"Pis'ma Turgeneva k Leont'evu* (1851-76 gg.),"
p. 84.

120 To P. V. Annenkov, Paris, October 12, 1860.
GIKhL, 1958, XII, 318–19.

121 To I. I. Panaev, Paris, October 1/13, 1860. Annenkov: *"Shest' let perepiski s I. S. Turgenevym, 1856–62,"*
pp. 36–7.

122 To A. I. Herzen, Paris, November 4, 1860. *Pis'ma Dm. Kavelina* . . . , p. 130.

123 To the same, Paris, January 9, 1861. Ibid., p. 134.

124 To Countess E. E. Lambert, Paris, January 8/20, 1861. Georgievski, ed.: *Pis'ma Turgeneva k gr. Lambert*, p. 110.

125 To Princess O. D. Khilkovoi, Paris, January 19/31, 1861. B. N. Kapeliush, ed.: *"Pis'ma I. S. Turgeneva k O. D. Khilkovoi,"* *Literaturny arkhiv*, 1951, III, 215–16.

126 To P. V. Annenkov, Paris, February 15/27, 1861. Annenkov: *"Shest' let perepiski s I. S. Turgenevym, 1856–62,"* p. 479.

127 To Countess E. E. Lambert, Paris, February 16/28, 1861. Georgievski, ed.: *Pis'ma Turgeneva k gr. Lambert*, p. 113.

128 To A. I. Herzen, Paris, March 9, 1861. *Pis'ma Dm. Kavelina* . . . , p. 139.

129 To Count L. N. Tolstoi, Paris, March 10/22, 1861. Gruzinski and Tsiavlovski, eds.: *Tolstoi i Turgenev: perepiska*, p. 56.

130 To V. I. Kartashevski (nee Makarov), Paris, March 14/26, 1861. S. Pereselenikov, ed.: *"Iz perepiski Turgeneva s V. Ia. Kartashevskoi,"* *Golos minuvshego*, No. 1–4 (one issue), January–April 1919, p. 215.

131 To I. P. Polonski, Spasskoe, May 21 [O. S.], 1861. *Pervoe*, pp. 89–90.

132 To Count L. N. Tolstoi, Spasskoe, May 27 [O. S.], 1861. Gruzinski and Tsiavlovski, eds.: *Tolstoi i Turgenev: perepiska*, pp. 65–6.

133 To P. V. Annenkov, Spasskoe, June 7/19, 1861. Annenkov: *"Shest' let perepiski s I. S. Turgenevym,"* pp. 487–8.

134 To Countess E. E. Lambert, Spasskoe, June 7/19, 1861. Georgievski, ed.: *Pis'ma Turgeneva k gr. Lambert*, pp. 124–5.

135 To D. I. Kolbasin, Spasskoe, June 14 [O. S.], 1861. *Pervoe*, pp. 91–2.

136 To his daughter, Pauline, Spasskoe, July 8/20, 1861. E. Séménoff: *La Vie douloureuse . . .* , p. 131.

137 To P. V. Annenkov, Spasskoe, July 10 [O. S.], 1861. Annenkov: *"Shest' let perepiski s I. S. Turgenevym,"* p. 493.

138 To Countess E. E. Lambert, Spasskoe, July 19 [O.S.], 1861. Georgievski, ed.: *Pis'ma Turgeneva k gr. Lambert*, p. 132.

139 To L. N. Tolstoy, Paris, second half of September 1861. Gruzinski and Tsiavlovski, eds.: *Tolstoi i Turgenev: perepiska*, p. 69.

140 To P. V. Annenkov, St. Petersburg, October 26/November 7, 1861. Annenkov: *"Shest' let perepiski s I. S. Turgenevym, 1856–62 gg.,"* p. 492.

141 To M. N. Katkov, Paris, October 30/November 11, 1861. GIKhL, 1958, XII, 324–5.

142 To A. A. Fet, Paris, November 8 [O.S.], 1861. Bogoslovski, ed.: *Turgenev o L've Tolstom*, pp. 33–4.

143 To P. V. Annenkov, Paris, December 11/23, 1861. GIKhL, 1958, XII, 328.

144 To Friedrich von Bodenstedt, Paris, December 29, 1861. *"Ivan Sergeevich Turgenev v ego pis'makh k Fr. Bodenshtedtu, 1861–65 gg.,"* Russkaia starina, 1887, LIV, 448 (In French.)

145 To F. M. Dostoevski, Paris, December 26, 1861/January 7, 1862. GIKhL, 1958, XII, 329–30.

146 To A. A. Fet, Paris, January 7 [O.S.], 1862. Bogoslovski, ed.: *Turgenev o L've Tolstom*, pp. 34–5.

147 To the same. GIKhL, 1958, XII, 331–2.

148 To A. I. Herzen, Paris, February 11, 1862. *Pis'ma Dm. Kavelina . . .* , p. 145.

149 To V. P. Botkin, Paris, March 10, 1862. Botkin and Turgenev: *Neizdannaia perepiska . . .* , p. 165.

150 To A. A. Fet, Paris, March 5/17, 1862. Ogonek, 1949, XI, 209.

151 To F. M. Dostoevski, Paris, March 18/30, 1862. GIKhl, 1958, XII, 334–5.

152 To A. A. Fet, Paris, April 6/18, 1862. Ibid., pp. 337–8.

153 To V. P. Botkin, Paris, April 12/24, 1862. Botkin and Turgenev: *Neizdannaia perepiska* . . . , p. 174.

154 To K. K. Sluchevski, Paris, April 14/26, 1862. GIKhL, 1958, XII, 339–41.

155 To A. I. Herzen, Paris, April 28, 1862. *Pis'ma Dm. Kavelina* . . . , pp. 146–7.

156 To "Marko Vovchok" (M. A. Markovich), Baden-Baden, September 28, 1862. Ogonek, 1949, XI, 219.

157 To A. I. Herzen, Baden-Baden, October 8, 1862. *Pis'ma Dm. Kavelina* . . . , p. 153.

158 To the same, Baden-Baden, October 8, 1862 (second letter to Herzen so dated). Ibid., pp. 160–2.

159 To the same, Paris, November 8, 1862. Ibid., pp. 170–2.

160 To the Editor of the *Severnaia pchela*, Paris, December 10, 1862. GIKhL, 1956, XI, 332–3.

161 To I. P. Borisov, Paris, December 3/15, 1862. "*Pis'ma I. S. Turgeneva k I. P. Borisovu, 1858–71 gg.,*" *Russki arkhiv*, 1910, No. 4, pp. 587–8.

162 To P. V. Annenkov, Paris, January 19/31, 1863. P. V. Annenkov: "*Iz perepiski s I. S. Turgenevym v 60-kh godakh,*" *Vestnik Evropy*, January 1887, p. 11.

163 To A. I. Herzen, Paris, February 12, 1863. *Pis'ma Dm. Kavelina* . . . , p. 178.

164 To A. A. Fet, Paris, April 7/19, 1863. GIKhL, 1958, XII, 351.

165 To Countess E. E. Lambert, Baden-Baden, April 27/May 9, 1863. Georgievsik, ed.: *Pis'ma Turgeneva k gr. Lambert*, pp. 161–2.

166 To P. V. Annenkov, Baden-Baden, September 15/27, 1863. Annenkov: "*Iz perepiski s I. S. Turgenevym v 60-kh godakh,*" p. 13.

167 To V. P. Botkin, Baden-Baden, November 26/December 8, 1863. Botkin and Turgenev: *Neizdannaia perepiska* . . . , p. 194.

168 To P. V. Annenkov, Baden-Baden, December 9/21,

1863. Annenkov: "*Iz perepiski s I. S. Turgenevym v 60-kh godakh*," p. 18.

169 To A. A. Fet, St. Petersburg, January 25, 1864. GIKhL, 1958, XII, 354.

170 To his daughter, Pauline, Baden-Baden, March 15, 1864. E. Séménoff: *La Vie douloureuse* . . . , p. 146.

171 To A. I. Herzen, Paris, March 21/April 2, 1864. *Pis'ma Dm. Kavelina* . . . , p. 181.

172 To P. A. Pletnev, Baden-Baden, June 1/13, 1864. M. P. Alekseev, ed.: "*Pis'ma I. S. Turgeneva P. A. Pletnevu*," *Literaturny arkhiv*, 1951, III, 195.

173 To I. P. Borisov, Baden-Baden, June 5/17, 1864. "*Pis'ma Tusgeneva k Borisovu, 1858–71 gg.*," p. 589.

174 To Friedrich von Bodenstedt, Baden-Baden, July 12, 1864. "*Turgenev v ego pis'makh k Bodenshtedtu, 1861–65*," pp. 462–3. (In German.)

175 To Countess E. E. Lambert, Baden-Baden, September 3 [O. S. (?)], 1864. Georgievski, ed.: *Pis'ma Turgeneva k gr. Lambert*, p. 170.

176 To Miss Innis, Baden-Baden, January 10, 1865. E. Séménoff: *La Vie douloureuse* . . . , p. 153.

177 To I. P. Borisov, Paris, January 28/February 9, 1865. GIKhL, 1958, XII, 355–6.

178 To Pauline Viardot (nee Garcia), Paris, February 16, 1865. *Lettres à Mme Viardot*, pp. 199–200.

179 To F. M. Dostoevski, Baden-Baden, February 21 [O.S.], 1865. *Pervoe*, 1884, pp. 122–3.

180 To I. P. Borisov, Baden-Baden, March 16/28, 1865. GIKhL, 1958, XII, 357–8.

181 To the same, Baden-Baden, August 5/17, 1865. "*Pis'ma Turgenev k Borisovu, 1858–71 gg.*," p. 593.

182 To P. V. Annenkov, Baden-Baden, December 19, 1865/January 1, 1866, Annenkov: "*Iz perepiski s I. S. Turgenevym v 60-kh godakh*," p. 469.

183 To the same. Baden-Baden, January 17/29, 1866. Ibid., p. 470.

184 To the same. Baden-Baden. February 9/21, 1866. Ibid., pp. 471–2.

185 To the same. Baden-Baden. February 17/March 1, 1866. Ibid., p. 473.

186 To the same. Baden-Baden, March 25/April 6, 1866. Ibid., p. 474.

187 To Ludwig Pietsch, Baden-Baden, April 21, 1866. Iwan Turgenjew an Ludwig Pietsch: *Briefe aus den Jahren 1864–83* (herausgegeben von Alfred Doren, mit Zeichnungen von Ludwig Pietsch, Berlin: Propyläen-Verlag; n.d.), p. 30.

188 To A. A. Fet, Baden-Baden, March 25/April 6, 1866. GIKhL, 1958, XII, 360.

189 To the same, Baden-Baden, June 27 [O.S.], 1866. Bogoslovski, ed.: *Turgenev o L've Tolstom*, p. 39.

190 To I. P. Borisov, Baden-Baden, September 30/October 12, 1866. *"Pis'ma Turgeneva k Borisovu, 1858–71,"* p. 595.

191 To the same, Karlsruhe, January 12/24, 1867. Ibid., p. 603.

192 To Pauline Viardot (nee Garcia), Moscow, March 25/April 6, 1867. *Lettres à Mme Viardot, pp.* 223–4.

193 To the same, Moscow, March 28/April 9, 1867. Ibid., p. 225.

194 To the same, Moscow, April 10, 1867. *Ibid.,* p. 228.

195 To P. V. Annenkov, Baden-Baden, April 10/22, 1867. *"Pis'ma I. S. Turgeneva k P. V. Annenkovu,"* predislovie L. N. Maikova, *Russkoe obozrenie*, January 1894, pp. 13–14.

196 To A. I. Herzen, Baden-Baden, May 22, 1867. Ogonek, 1949, XI, 233.

197 To the same, Baden-Baden, May 23/June 4, 1867. *Pis'ma Dm. Kavelina . . .* , p. 195.

198 To P. V. Annenkov, Baden-Baden, May 23/June 4, 1867. *"Pis'ma I. S. Turgeneva k P. V. Annenkovu,"* pp. 19–20.

199 To D. I. Pisarev, Baden-Baden, May 23/June 4, 1867. GIKhL, 1958, XII, 376–7.

200 To P. V. Annenkov, Baden-Baden, June 16/28, 1867. *"Pis'ma I. S. Turgeneva k P. V. Annenkovu,"* p. 21.

201 To I. P. Borisov, Baden-Baden, June 16/28, 1867. *"Pis'ma Turgeneva k Borisovu,"* p. 598.

202 To V. P. Botkin, Baden-Baden, September 24/Oc-

tober 6, 1867. Botkin and Turgenev: *Neizdannaia pere-piska* . . . , pp. 271–2.

203   To P. V. Annenkov, Baden-Baden, October 7/19, 1867. *"Pis'ma I. S. Turgeneva k P. V. Annenkovu,"* pp. 24–5.

204   To A. I. Herzen, Baden-Baden, December 12, 1867. Z.: *"Iz perepiski I. S. Turgeneva s A. M. Gertsenom v 1867 godu,"* *Russkoe obozrenie,* January 1895, XXXI, 114.

205   To the same, Baden-Baden, December 13/25, 1867. Ibid., p 119.

206   To I. P. Polonski, Baden-Baden, January 13 [O.S], 1868. *Pervoe,* 1884, pp. 130–1.

207   To P. V. Annenkov, Baden-Baden, February 14/26, 1868. GIKhL, 1958, XII, 385–6.

208   To I. P. Borisov, Baden-Baden, February 27/March 10, 1868. Ibid., pp. 387–8.

209   To I. P. Polonski, Baden-Baden, March 6 [O.S.], 1868. *Pervoe,* 1884, pp. 135–6.

210   To his daughter, Pauline, Baden-Baden, March 13, 1868. E. Séménoff: *La Vie douloureuse* . . . , p. 187.

211   To A. A. Fet, Baden-Baden, February 12/April 12 [*sic*], 1868. Bogoslovski, ed.: *Turgenev o L've Tolstom,* p. 41.

212   To I. P. Borisov, Baden-Baden, April 8/20, 1868. *"Pis'ma Turgeneva k Borisovu,"* p. 601.

213   To P. V. Annenkov, Baden-Baden, April 13/25, 1868. GIKhL, 1958, XII, 391.

214   To Pauline Viardot (nee Garcia), Spasskoe, June 13/25, 1868. *Lettres à Mme Viardot,* pp. 236–7.

215   To N. S. Turgenev, Baden-Baden, July 16/28, 1868. GIKhL, 1958, XII, 392–3.

216   To Julian Schmidt, Baden-Baden, August 8, 1868. E. Halpérine-Kaminsky, ed.: *"Pis'ma I. S. Turgeneva k ego nemetskim druz'iam,"* *Vestnik Evropy,* February 1909, p. 259   The original of this letter being unavailable, it has been translated from the Russian.

217   To I. P. Borisov, Karlsruhe, November 16/28, 1868. *"Pis'ma Turgeneva k Borisovu, 1858–1871 gg.,"* p. 602.

218   To Ludwig Pietsch, Karlsruhe, December 1, 1868.

Iwan Turgenjew an Ludwig Pietsch: *Briefe* . . . , p. 61.
219 To I. P. Polonski, Karlsruhe, December 16 [O.S.], 1868. *Pervoe*, 1884, pp. 145–6.
220 To P. V. Annenkov, Karlsruhe, January 12/24, 1869. *GIKhL*, 1958, XII, 397–8.
221 To the same, Karlsruhe, February 9/21, 1869. Ibid., pp. 403–4.
222 To I. P. Borisov, Karlsruhe, February 12/24, 1869. "*Pis'ma Turgenev k Borisovu, 1858–1871 gg.*," p. 604.
223 To V. P. Botkin, Karlsruhe, February 18/March 2, 1869. Botkin and Turgenev: *Neizdannaia perepiska* . . . , p. 276.
224 To A. I. Herzen, Karlsruhe, February 18/March 2, 1869. *Pis'ma Dm. Kavelina* . . . , p. 195.
225 To I. P. Polonski, Karlsruhe, February 20/March 4, 1869. GIKhL, 1958, XII, 405.
226 To the same. Karlsruhe, February 27/March 11, 1869. Ibid., pp. 408.
227 To V. P. Botkin, Karlsruhe, March 4/16, 1869. Botkin and Turgenev: *Neizdannaia perepiska* . . . , p. 281.
228 To K. K. Sluchevski, Karlsruhe, March 8 [O.S.], 1869. *Pervoe*, 1884, pp. 155–6.
229 To I. P. Borisov, Karlsruhe, March 12/24, 1869. Ogonek, 1949, XI, 253–4.
230 To the same, Baden-Baden, April 14/26, 1869. GIKhL, 1958, XII, 411-12.
231 To the Editor of the Sankt-Peterburgskie vedomosti, Baden-Baden, May 2/14, 1869. GIKhL, 1956, XI, 355–6.
232 To A. M. Zhemchuzhnikov, Baden-Baden, May 30, 1869. "*Materialy po istorii russkoi literatury i kul'tury: Pis'ma I. S. Turgeneva k A. M. Zhemchuzhnikovu,*" *Russkaia mysl'*, January 1914, p. 132.
233 To I. P. Polonski, Baden-Baden, May 19 [O.S.], 1869. *Pervoe*, 1884, p. 160.
234 To I. P. Borisov, Baden-Baden, May 24/June 5, 1869. "*Pis'ma Turgeneva k Borisovu,*" p. 607.
235 To Ludwig Pietsch, Baden-Baden, June 8, 1869. Turgenjew an Pietsch: *Briefe* . . . , p. 75.

236 To I. P. Borisov, Baden-Baden, June 18/30, 1869. *"Pis'ma Turgeneva k Borisovu,"* p. 609.

237 To the same. Baden-Baden, August 24/September 5, 1869. Ibid., p. 610.

238 To A. V. Pletnev, Baden-Baden, October 25/November 6, 1869. M. P. Alekseev, ed.: *"Pis'ma I. S. Turgeneva k A. V. Pletnevoi," Literaturny arkhiv,* 1951, III, 201.

239 To P. V. Annenkov, Baden-Baden, October 25/November 6, 1869. Maikov, ed.: *"Pis'ma I. S. Turgeneva k P. V. Annenkovu,"* p. 29.

240 To A. A. Fet, Baden-Baden, October 30 [O.S.], 1869. Bogoslovski, ed.: *Turgenev o L've Tolstom,* pp. 45–6.

241 To I. P. Borisov, Baden-Baden, November 13/25, 1869. *"Pis'ma Turgeneva k Borisovu,"* p. 612.

242 To Julian Schmidt, Baden-Baden, December 16, 1869. E. Halpérine-Kaminsky, ed.: *"Pis'ma Turgeneva k ego nemetskim druz'iam,"* pp. 260–1. The original of this letter being unavailable, it has been translated from the Russian in the source.

243 To A. A. Fet, Baden-Baden, December 21 [O.S.], 1869. Bogoslovski, ed.: *Turgenev o L've Tolstom,* pp. 46–7.

244 To I. P. Polonski, Baden-Baden, December 24 [O.S.], 1869. *Pervoe,* 1884, p. 168.

245 To I. P. Borisov, Baden-Baden, December 24, 1869/January 4, 1870. *"Pis'ma Turgeneva k Borisovu,"* p. 613.

246 To P. V. Annenkov, Baden-Baden, January 10/22, 1870. GIKhL, 1958, XII, 425–6.

247 To M. V. Avdeev, Baden-Baden, January 25, 1870. Ibid., pp. 427–8.

248 To I. P. Borisov, Weimar, March 15/27, 1870. Ibid., pp. 429–30.

249 To the same. Weimar, April 1/13, 1870. *"Pis'ma Turgeneva k Borisovu,"* p. 616.

250 To A. M. Zhemchuzhnikov, Baden-Baden, June 17/29, 1870. *"Materialy . . . : Pis'ma Turgeneva k Zhemchuzhnikovu,"* p. 136.

251 To N. S. Turgenev, Baden-Baden, July 15/27, 1870.

"Ivan Sergeevich Turgenev v pis'makh k ego bratu Nikolaiu Sergeevichu, 1863–78," Russkaia starina, August 1885, p. 332.

252   To the *Sankt-Peterburgskie vedomosti*, Baden-Baden, a) July 27/August 8, 1870; b) August 9, 1870; c) August 14, 1870; d) August 28, 1870; e) September 6/18, 1870; f) September 18/30, 1870. GIKhL, 1956, XI, 357–76.

253   To N. S. Turgenev, Baden-Baden, July 28/August 9, 1870. *"Turgenev v pis'makh k ego bratu,"* p. 333.

254   To I. P. Borisov, Baden-Baden, August 24, 1870. GIKhL, 1958, XII, 430–2.

255   To Ludwig Friedländer, Baden-Baden, August 29, 1870. E. Halpérine-Kaminsky, ed.: *"Pis'ma Turgeneva k ego nemetskim druz'iam,"* p. 655. The original of this letter being unavailable, it has been translated from the Russian in the source.

256   To Ludwig Pietsch, Baden-Baden, September 9, 1870. Turgenjew an Pietsch: *Briefe . . . ,* p. 87.

257   To his daughter, Pauline, Baden-Baden, October 28, 1870. E. Séménoff: *La Vie douloureuse . . . ,* pp. 211–12.

258   To N. S. Turgenev, London, November 24/December 6, 1870. *"Turgenev v pis'makh k ego bratu,"* p. 334.

259   To M. E. Saltykov-Shchedrin, London, November 30 [O.S.], 1870. *Pervoe,* 1884, pp. 184–5.

260   To Pauline Viardot (nee Garcia), St. Petersburg, February 21/March 8, 1871 (sic). Tourguéneff: *Lettres à Mme Viardot,* p. 255.

261   To S. K. Briullov (nee Kavelin), Moscow, March 13 [O.S.], 1871. D. A. Korsakov, ed.: *"Iz pisem I. S. Turgeneva S. K. Briullovoi, rozhdennoi Kavelinoi (1870–1871),"* Russkaia mysl', June 1897, p. 20.

262   To the same, London, April 2/14, 1871. Ibid., p. 22.

263   To P. V. Annenkov, London, April 19/May 1, 1871. *"Perepiska I. S. Turgeneva s P. V. Annenkovym s 1871 po 1883 god.,"* predislovie L. N. Maikova, Russkoe obozrenie, March 1898, p. 13.

264   To I. P. Polonski, London, April 24 [O.S.], 1871. *Pervoe,* 1884, pp. 193–4.

265 To A. A. Fet, London, July 2/14, 1871. Ogonek, 1949, XI, 269.

266 To A. A. Fet, Baden-Baden, August 6/18, 1871. GIKhL, 1958, XII, 436–7.

267 To Ludwig Pietsch, Baden-Baden, August 24, 1871. Turgenjew an Pietsch: *Briefe* . . . , p. 94.

268 To the same, Baden-Baden, September 15, 1871. Ibid., p. 97.

269 To V. V. Stasov, Baden-Baden, October 15/27, 1871. V. V. Stasov: *"Dvadtsat' pisem Turgeneva i moe znakomstvo s nim,"* *Severny vestnik*, October 1888, pp. 163–4.

270 To A. A. Fet, Paris, November 24 [O.S.], 1871. Bogoslovski, ed.: *Turgenev o L've Tolstom*, p. 54.

271 To N. S. Turgenev, Paris, January 16/28, 1872. *"Turgenev v pis'makh k ego bratu,"* *Russkaia starina*, September 1885, p. 496.

272 To the same, Paris, February 5/17, 1872. Ibid., p. 497.

273 To V. V. Stasov, Paris, March 1/13, 1872. V. V. Stasov: *"Dvadtsat' pisem Turgeneva* . . . , p. 165.

274 To the same, Paris, March 15/27, 1872. Ibid., pp. 166–7.

275 To A. A. Fet, Paris, March 29/April 10, 1872. GIKhL, 1958, XII, 439.

276 To I. P. Polonski, Paris, April 7 [O.S.], 1872. *Pervoe*, 1884, p. 204.

277 To N. S. Turgenev, March 23/April 4, 1872. *"Turgenev v pis'makh k ego bratu, 1863–78,"* *Russkaia starina*, September 1885, pp. 497–8.

278 To his daughter, Pauline, Moscow, June 14/26, 1872. E. Séménoff: *La Vie douloureuse* . . . , p. 223.

279 To P. V. Annenkov, Moscow, June 14/26, 1872. Maikov, ed.: *"Perepiska Turgeneva s Annenkovym s 1871 po 1883 god.,"* p. 372.

280 To the same, Paris, October 5/17, 1872. Ogonek, 1949, XI, 275.

281 To I. P. Polonski, Paris, October 17 [O.S.], 1872. *Pervoe*, 1884, pp. 206–7.

282 To P. V. Annenkov, Paris, October 25/November 6, 1872. GIKhL, 1958, XII, 443–4.

283 To Gustave Flaubert, Paris, November 8, 1872. M. Gorlin, ed.; André Mazon, author of introduction: "*Neizdannye pis'ma I. S. Turgeneva k Diu-Kanu, Floberu i E. de Gonkuru,*" translated from French to Russian by E. Gunst. *Literaturnoe nasledstvo*, 1937, XXXI–XXXII, 680–2. The original of this letter being unavailable, it has been translated from the Russian in the source.

284 To P. V. Annenkov, Paris, November 12, 1872. Maikov, ed.: "*Perepiska Turgeneva s Annenkovym s 1871 po 1883 god.,*" p. 24.

285 Addressee unknown, Paris, December, 1872. Quoted in M. K. Kleman: "*Iz perepiski Turgeneva s nachinaiush-chimi avtorami,*" in anthology, N. L. Brodski, ed.: *I. S. Turgenev, materialy i issledovaniia* (Orel: Izdatel'stvo Orlovskogo Oblastnogo Soveta deputatov trudiashchikhsia; 1940), p. 149.

286 To P. V. Annenkov, Paris, November 26/December 8, 1872. Maikov, ed.: "*Perepiska Turgeneva s Annenkovym s 1871 po 1883 god.,*" p. 26.

287 To M. A. Miliutin, Paris, December 3 [O.S.], 1872. *Pervoe*, 1884, p. 208.

288 To S. K. Briullov (nee Kavelin), Paris, December 21, 1872/January 2, 1873. Korsakov, ed.: "*Iz pisem Turgeneva k Briullovoi,*" p. 28.

289 To I. P. Polonski, Paris, February 21 [O.S.], 1873. *Pervoe*, 1884, pp. 213–14.

290 To the same, Paris, March 22 [O.S.], 1873. Ibid., p. 215.

291 To M. E. Saltykov-Shchedrin, Paris, April 9, 1873. GIKhL, 1958, XII, 448.

292 To A. A. Fet, Château de Nohant, September 13 [O.S.], 1873. Bogoslovski, ed.: *Turgenev o L've Tolstom*, p. 53.

293 To M. M. Stasiulevich, Paris, November 23/December 5, 1873. Ogonek, 1949, XI, 282.

294 To I. P. Polonski, Paris, January 13 [O.S.], 1874. *Pervoe*, 1884, pp. 225–6.

295   To A. A. Fet, Paris, March 4/16, 1874. GIKhL, 1958, XII, 456.

296   To M. M. Stasiulevich, Paris, March 15/27, 1874. Ogonek, 1949, XI, 284.

297   To W. R. S. Ralston, Paris, April 2, 1874. J. W. Bienstock, ed. and tr.: "Lettres inédites de Tourguénev," *Revue mondiale*, Paris, January 1925, CLXIII, 3. The Russian original of this letter being unavailable, it has been translated from the French in the source.

298   To Ludwig Pietsch, Paris, April 2, 1874. Turgenjew an Pietsch: *Briefe* . . . , p. 117.

299   To N. S. Turgenev, Paris, March 21/April 2, 1874. "Turgenev v pis'makh k ego bratu, 1863–78," *Russkaia starina*, October 1885, p. 127.

300   To S. A. Vengerov, Spasskoe, June 19, [O.S.], 1874. *Pervoe*, 1884, pp. 233–4.

301   To Henry James, Karlsbad, August 7, 1874. Jean Seznec: "Lettres de Tourguéneff à Henry James," *Comparative Literature*, Vol. I, No. 3 (Summer 1940), pp. 197–8.

302   To A. P. Filosofov, Bougival, August 18 [O.S.], 1874. *Pervoe*, 1884, pp. 238–9.

303   To the same, Bougival, September 11 [O.S.], 1874. *Ibid.*, pp. 241–2.

304   To Ludwig Pietsch, Paris, October 7, 1874. Turgenjew an Pietsch: *Briefe* . . . , p. 123.

305   To I. P. Polonski, Paris, October 14 [O.S.], 1874. *Pervoe*, 1884, pp. 245–6.

306   To Julian Schmidt, Paris, November 26, 1874. E. Halpérine-Kaminsky, ed.: "Pis'ma Turgeneva k ego nemetskim druz'iam," p. 270. The original of this letter being unavailable, it has been translated from the Russian in the source.

307   To A. V. Toporov, Paris, January 2/14, 1875. L. N. Nazarova, ed.: "Pis'ma I. S. Turgeneva k A. V. Toporovu," *Literaturny arkhiv*, 1953, IV, 217.

308   To Julian Schmidt, Paris, February 13, 1875. E. Halpérine-Kaminsky, ed.: "Pis'ma Turgeneva k ego nemetskim druz'iam," pp. 270–1. The original of this letter being unavailable, it has been translated from the Russian in

the source.

309   To A. V. Toporov, Paris, February 5/17, 1875. L. S. Utevski: *"Niezdannye pis'ma I. S. Turgeneva k A. V. Toporovu,"* Novy mir, February 1930, p. 212.

310   To P. V. Annenkov, Paris, 1875 [?]. N. Bel'chikov, ed.: *"Pis'ma I. S. Turgeneva k P. V. Annenkovu,"* Krasny arkhiv, 1929, XXXII, 206.

311   To A. V. Pletnev, Paris, February 13/25, 1875. Alekseev, ed.: *"Pis'ma Turgeneva k Pletnevoi,"* pp. 204–5.

312   To A. S. Suvorin, Paris, February 14 [O.S.], 1875. *Pervoe*, 1884, p. 251.

313   To M. A. Miliutin, Paris, February 22 [O.S.], 1875. Ibid., p. 252.

314   To A. S. Suvorin, Paris, Marsh 14 [O.S.], 1875. Ibid., p. 257.

315   To A. V. Toporov, Paris, March 20/April 1, 1875. Nazarova, ed.: *"Pis'ma Turgeneva k Toporovu,"* p. 217.

316   To P. L. Lavrov, Bougival, April 9, 1875. GIKhL, 1958, XII, 479.

317   To Ludwig Pietsch, Paris, April 13, 1875. Turgenjew an Pietsch: *Briefe . . . ,* p. 128.

318   To V. V. Stasov, Paris, April 3/15, 1875. V. V. Stasov: *"Dvadtsat' pisem Turgeneva . . . ,"* p. 173.

319   To I. P. Polonski, Paris, May 13 [O.S.], 1875. *Pervoe*, 1884, pp. 259–60.

320   To A. V. Toporov, Karlsbad, May 24/June 6, 1875. *Literaturny arkhiv*, 1953, IV, 224.

321   To Ludwig Pietsch, Karlsbad, June 9, 1875. Turgenjew an Pietsch: *Briefe . . . ,* p. 130.

322   To A. V. Toporov, Karlsbad, June 6/18, 1875. Nazarova, ed.: *"Pis'ma Turgeneva k Toporovu,"* p. 226.

323   To V. V. Stasov, Bougival, September 5, 1875. V. V. Stasov: *"Dvadtsat' pisem Turgeneva . . . ,"* p. 176.

324   To M. E. Saltykov-Shchedrin, Bougival, October 28 [O.S.], 1875. *Pervoe*, 1884, pp. 267–8.

325   To the same, Paris, November 12 [O.S.], 1875. Ibid., p. 269.

326   To the same, Paris, November 25 [O.S.], 1875. Ibid., pp. 271–2.

327   To the same, Paris, December 26 [O.S.], 1875. Ibid., pp. 276–7.

328   To the same, Paris, January 3 [O.S.], 1876. Ibid., pp. 277–8.

329   To the same, Paris, January 19 [O.S.], 1876. Ibid., p. 281.

330   To Julian Schmidt, Paris, January 27, 1876. E. Halpérine-Kaminsky, ed.: *"Pis'ma Turgeneva k ego nemetskim druz'iam,"* p. 272. The original of this letter being unavailable, it has been translated from the Russian source.

331   To A. F. Onegin (nee Otto), Paris, March 2/14, 1876. J. W. Bienstock, ed. and tr.: *"Lettres inédites de Tourguénev,"* pp. 238–9. The original of this letter being unavailable, it has been translated from the French source.

332   To I. P. Vrevski, Paris, March 10/22, 1876. GIKhL, 1958, XII, 488–9.

333   To Julian Schmidt, Paris, March 25, 1876. E. Halpérine-Kaminsky, ed.: *"Pis'ma Turgeneva k ego nemetskim druz'iam,"* p. 273. The original of this letter being unavailable, it has been translated from the Russian source.

334   To P. V. Annenkov, Paris, March 16/28, 1876. *"Pis'ma I. S. Turgeneva k P. V. Annenkovu,"* Pechat' i revoliutsiia, April–June (one issue), 1922, p. 100.

335   To A. V. Toporov, Paris, March 22/April 3, 1876. Nazarova, ed.: *"Pis'ma Turgeneva k Toporovu,"* p. 238.

336   To A. S. Suvorin, Paris, March 22 [O.S.], 1876. *Pervoe,* 1884, pp. 288–9.

337   To the same, Paris, April 9 [O.S.], 1876. Ibid., pp. 289–90.

338   To the same, Spasskoe, June 9 [O.S.], 1876. Ibid., pp. 292–4.

339   To V. L. Kign, Spasskoe, June 16 [O.S.], 1876. Ibid., pp. 295–6.

340   To N. S. Turgenev, Spasskoe, June 20/July 2, 1876. *"Ivan Sergeevich Turgenev v pis'makh k ego bratu Nikolaiu Sergeevichu,"* Russkaia starina, October 1885, pp. 138–9.

341   To M. M. Stasiulevich, Bougival, August 7, 1876. GIKhL, 1958, XII, 494.

342   To M. E. Saltykov-Shchedrin, Bougival, September 17 [O.S.], 1876. *Pervoe*, 1884, p. 300.

343   To Emma Lazarus, Bougival, October 23, 1876. Ralph L. Rusk, ed.: *Letters to Emma Lazarus in the Columbia University Library* (New York: Columbia University Press; 1939), p. 18.

344   To M. M. Stasiulevich, Bougival, November 9/21, 1876.   M. M. Stasiulevich, ed.: *"Iz pisem I. S. Turgeneva k M. M. Stasiulevichu (po povodu pechataniia Novi v 1876 godu),"* in anthology *Sbornik obshchestva liubitelei rossiskoi slovesnosti na 1891 g.* (Moscow; 1891), p. 72.

345   To P. V. Annenkov, Paris, November 23, 1876, M. D. Beliaev, ed.: *"Nov'. K perepiske P. V. Annenkova s I. S. Turgenevym. Materialy Pushkinskogo Doma,"* *Literaturnaia mysl'*, Petrograd, Book 1, 1922, p. 199.

346   To M. M. Stasiulevich, Paris, November 25/December 6, 1876. GIKhL, 1958, XII, 495.

347   To N. S. Turgenev, Paris, November 27/December 8, 1876. *"Turgenev v pis'makh k ego bratu,"* *Russkaia starina*, October 1885, pp. 140–1.

348   To Ludwig Pietsch, Paris, December 28, 1876. Turgenjew an Pietsch: *Briefe . . . ,* p. 137.

349   To K. D. Kavelin, Paris, December 17/29, 1876. GIKhL, 1958, XII, 497–8.

350   To M. M. Stasiulevich, Paris, December 22, 1876/January 3, 1877. GIKhL, 1958, XII, 502.

351   To W. R. S. Ralston, Paris, January 22, 1877. J. W. Bienstock, ed. and tr.: *"Lettres inédites de Tourguénev,"* p. 5. The Russian original of this letter being unavailable, it has been translated from the French source.

352   To E. V. L'vov, Paris, January 23, 1877. Kleman: *"Iz perepiski Turgeneva s nachinaiushchimi avtorami,"* p. 152.

353   To Ludwig Pietsch, Paris, February 4, 1877. Turgenjew an Pietsch: *Briefe . . . ,* p. 138.

354   To Julian Schmidt, Paris, February 13, 1877. E. Halpérine-Kaminksy, ed.: *"Pis'ma Turgeneva k ego nemetskim druz'iam,"* p. 274. The original of this letter being unavailable, it has been translated from the Russian source.

355   To W. R. S. Ralston, Paris, February 18, 1877. J. W. Bienstock, ed, and tr.: *"Lettres inédites de Tourguénev,"* p. 7. The Russian original of this letter being unavailable, it has been translated from the French source.

356   To P. V. Annenkov, Paris, February 12/24, 1877. Beliaev, ed.: *"Nov'. K perepiske Annenkova s Turgenevym,"* p. 206.

357   To I. P. Polonski, Paris, February 18 [O.S.], 1877. *Pervoe, 1884, pp. 312–13.*

358   To M. M. Stasiulevich, Paris, February 27/March 11, 1877. GIKhL, 1958, XII, 509; for the material in the note, see GIKhL, 1956, X, 642–3.

359   To A. M. Zhemchuzhnikov, Baden-Baden, March 5/17, 1877. *"Materialy . . . : Pis'ma Turgeneva k Zhemchuzhnikovu,"* p. 138.

360   To N. S. Turgenev, Paris, March 7/19, 1877. Ogonek, 1949, XI, 321–2.

361   To W. R. S. Ralston, Paris, April 19, 1877. J. W. Bienstock, ed. and tr.: *"Lettres inédites de Tourguénev,"* p. 7. The Russian original of this letter being unavailable, it has been translated from the French source.

362   To Emma Lazarus, Bougival, August 1, 1877. Rusk, ed.: *Lettres to Emma Lazarus*, pp. 18–19. (In French.)

363   To N. S. Turgenev, Paris, October 26/November 7, 1877. *"Turgenev v pis'makh k ego bratu, 1863–78,"* Russkaia starina, December 1885, p. 623.

364   To P. V. Annenkov, Paris, December 4, 1877. *"Pis'ma Turgeneva k Annenkovu,"* p. 94.

365   To N. S. Turgenev, Paris, January 3/15, 1878. *"Turgenev v pis'makh k ego bratu, 1863–78,"* Russkaia starina, December 1885, p. 627.

366   To P. V. Annenkov, Paris, January 9/21, 1878. *"Pis'ma Turgeneva k Annenkovu,"* p. 99.

367   To N. S. Turgenev, Paris, January 12/24, 1878. *"Turgenev v pis'makh k ego bratu, 1863–1878,"* Russkaia starina, December 1885, p. 628.

368   To A. V. Toporov, Spasskoe, August 10/22, 1878. Nazarova, ed.: *"Pis'ma Turgeneva k Toporovu,"* p. 269.

369   To L. I. Stech'kin, Paris, September 30/October 12, 1878. M. G. Pogruzhenko, ed.: *Pis'ma I. S. Turgeneva*

k L. N. i L. Ia. Stech'kinym (Odessa: Count M. M. Tolstoy; 1903), pp. 10–11.

370 To Count L. N. Tolstoy, Bougival, October 1 [O.S.], 1878. *Pervoe*, 1884, pp. 335–6.

371 To Julian Schmidt, Bougival, October 13, 1878. E. Halpérine-Kaminsky, ed.: "*Pis'ma Turgeneva k ego nemetskim druz'iam*," pp. 275–6. The original of this letter being unavailable, it has been translated from the Russian source.

372 To Count L. N. Tolstoy, Paris, November 15 [O.S.], 1878. *Pervoe*, 1884, pp. 338–40.

373 To A. A. Fet, Bougival, December 30 [O.S.], 1878. Bogoslovski, ed.: *Turgenev o L've Tolstom*, pp. 67–8.

374 To P. V. Annenkov, Paris, January 9, 1879. "*Pis'ma Turgeneva k Annenkovu*," p. 96.

375 To Gustave Flaubert, Paris, February 13 [O.S.], 1879. GIKhL, 1958, XII, 536–8. The French text of this letter being unavailable, it has been translated from the Russian source.

376 To A. V. Toporov, Paris, May 17/29, 1879. Nazarova, ed.: "*Pis'ma Turgeneva k Toporovu*," p. 283.

377 To L. I. Stech'kin, Bougival, June 2/14, 1879. Pogruzhenko, ed.: *Pis'ma Turgeneva Stech' kinym*.

378 To B. A. Chichelev, Bougival, June 12/24, 1879. *Ogonek*, 1949, XI, 344.

379 To A. V. Toporov, Bougival, June 20/July 2, 1879. Nazarova, ed.: "*Pis'ma Turgeneva k Toporovu*," p. 288.

380 To Gustave Flaubert, Bougival, August 7, 1879. E. Halpérine-Kaminsky, ed.: *Ivan Tourguéneff d'après sa correspondance avec des amis français* (Paris: Charpentier; 1901), p. 124.

381 To I. P. Polonski, Bougival, September 16 [O.S.], 1879. *Pervoe*, 1884, p. 347.

382 To the same, Bougival, October 3 [O.S.], 1879. Ibid., p. 348.

383 To Hébrard, editor of *Le Temps*, Bougival (?), October 17, 1879. GIKhL, 1956, XI, 393. (In French.)

384 To P. V. Annenkov, Bougival, October 27/November 8, 1879. Ibid., 1958, XII, p. 539.

385   To Count L. N. Tolstoy, Paris, December 28 [O.S.], 1879. *Pervoe*, 1884, pp. 351–3.

386   To M. M. Stasiulevich, Editor of the *Vestnik Evropy*, Paris, January 2, 1880. GIKhL, 1956, XI, 395–6.

387   To Edmond About, editor of *Le XIX-e Siècle*, place not given, January 20, 1880. Ibid., 1956, XI, pp. 209–10. (In French.)

388   To Count L. N. Tolstoy, Paris, January 12 [O.S.], 1880. *Pervoe*, 1884, p. 354.

389   To P. V. Annenkov, Moscow, April 24/May 6, 1880. Bel'chikov, ed.: "*Pis'ma Turgeneva k Annenkovu*," pp. 192–3.

390   To M. G. Savin, Moscow, April 24 [O.S.], 1880. A. F. Koni and A. E. Molchanov, eds.: *Turgenev i Savina, pis'ma I. S. Turgeneva k M. G. Savinoi, Vospominaniia M. G. Savinoi ob I. S. Turgeneve* (Petrograd: Izdanie Gosudarstvennykh teatrov; 1918), p. 9.

391   To M. M. Stasiulevich, Spasskoe, May 8, 1880, GIKhL, 1958, XII, 545.

392   To M. G. Savin, Spasskoe, May 17 [O.S.], 1880. Koni and Molchanov, eds.: *Turgenev i Savina . . .* , pp. 13–14.

393   To the same, Spasskoe, May 19 [O.S.], 1880. Ibid., p. 15.

394   To M. M. Stasiulevich, Spasskoe, June 13 [O.S.], 1880. Ogonek, 1949, XI, 353–4.

395   To V. M. Garshin, Spasskoe, June 14 [O.S.], 1880. GIKhL, 1958, XII, 546.

396   To V. P. Gaevski, Bougival, November 1 [O.S.], 1880. *Pervoe*, 1884, pp 363–4.

397   To M. L. Veller, Paris, December 26, 1880. Alekseev, ed.: "*Neizdannye pis'ma I. S. Turgeneva, tri pis'ma M. L. Velleru*," p. 79.

398   To G. I. Uspenski, Paris (?), January 10/22, 1881. N. V. Alekseev, ed.: *Pis'ma I. S. Turgeneva k G. I. Uspenskomu*," *Literaturny arkhiv*, 1951, III, 227.

399   To P. V. Annenkov, Paris, March 18, 1881. Bel'chikov, ed.: "*Pis'ma Turgeneva k Annenkovu*," pp. 196–7.

400   To Ludwig Pietsch, Bougival, November 10, 1881. Turgenjew an Pietsch: *Briefe . . .* , p. 151.

401   To Z. A. Polonski, Paris, November 24 [O.S.], 1881. *Pervoe*, 1884, p. 391.

402   To M. G. Savin, Paris, December 3/15, 1881. Koni and Molchanov, eds.: *Turgenev i Savina* . . . , p. 35.

403   To P. V. Annenkov, Paris, January 1, 1882. GIKhL, 1958, XII, 553.

404   To V. V. Stasov, Paris, January 9/21, 1882. Stasov: *"Dvadtsat' pisem Turgeneva* . . . , p. 178.

405   To P. V. Annenkov, Paris, February 25, 1882. Bel'chikov, ed.: *"Pis'ma Turgeneva k Annenkovu,"* p. 200.

406   To M. E. Saltykov-Shchedrin, Bougival, May 26 [O.S.], 1882. *Pervoe*, 1884, 431–3.

407   To M. G. Savin, Bougival, May 26/June 7, 1882. Koni and Molchanov, eds.: *Turgenev i Savina* . . . , pp. 46–7.

408   To Z. A. Polonski, Bougival, May 27 [O.S.], 1882. *Pervoe*, 1884, p. 434.

409   To P. V. Annenkov, Bougival, August 25, 1882. Bel'chikov, ed.: *"Pis'ma Turgeneva k Annenkovu,"* p. 202.

410   To the Peasants of Spasskoe Village, Bougival, September 4, 1882. GIKhL, 1958, XII, 555–6.

411   To V. M. Garshin, Bougival, September 3/15, 1882. Ibid., p. 556.

412   To W. R. S. Ralston, Bougival, September 23, 1882. J. W. Bienstock, ed. and tr.: *"Lettres inédites de Tourguénev,"* p. 7. The Russian original of this letter being unavailable, it has been translated from the French source.

413   To M. E. Saltykov-Shchedrin, Bougival, September 24 [O.S.], 1882. *Pervoe*, 1884, pp. 497–8.

414   To P. I. Veinberg, Bougival, October 22, 1882. GIKhL, 1958, XII, 562.

415   To Count L. N. Tolstoy, Bougival, October 19/31, 1882. Ibid., pp. 564–5.

416   To D. V. Grigorovich, Bougival, October 31 [O.S.], 1882. *Pervoe*, 1884, p. 510.

417   To M. M. Stasiulevich, Paris, November 12/24, 1882. GIKhL, 1958, XII, 566–7.

418   To A. V. Toporov, Paris, November 26 [O.S.], 1882. *Pervoe*, 1884, p. 519.

419   To Sidney Jerrold, Paris, December 2, 1882. GIKhL, 1958, XII, 567–8.

420   To I. N. Kramskoi, Paris, December 6, 1882. Ibid., pp. 571–2.

421   (To the Students in the Women's Medical Courses, Paris, published December 10 [O.S.], 1882.) GIKhL, 1956, XI, 471–2.

422   To Eugen Zabel, Paris, January 6, 1883. E. Halpérine-Kaminsky, ed.: "*Pis'ma Turgeneva k ego nemetskim druz'iam,*" p. 659. The original of this letter being unavailable, it is translated from the Russian source.

423   To A. V. Toporov, Paris, December 28, 1882/January 9, 1883. Utevski, ed.: "*Neizdannye pis'ma Turgeneva k Toporovu,*" p. 217.

424   To P. V. Annenkov, Paris, December 29, 1882/January 10, 1883. "*Pis'ma Turgeneva k Annenkovu,*" p. 96.

425   To Count L. N. Tolstoy, Bougival, June 27 or 28, 1883. *Pervoe,* 1884, pp. 550–1.

BIBLIOGRAPHY

This bibliography includes *only* articles from which letters have been used in the preparation of this volume. For a more complete bibliography of Turgenev's letters, see Mikhail Karlovich Kleman: *Letopis' zhizni i tvorchestva I. S. Turgeneva* (Redaktsiia N. K. Plekhanova, Moscow and Leningrad: Academia; 1934), pp. 330–9.

Alekseev, M. P., ed.: *"Neizdannye pis'ma I. S. Turgeneva. Tri pis'ma M. L. Velleru." Byloe*, No. 1 (29), 1925, pp. 78–84.
———, ed.: *"Pis'ma I. S. Turgeneva k A. V. Nikitenko." Literaturny arkhiv*, 1953, IV, 172–87.
———, ed.: *"Pis'ma I. S. Turgeneva k A. V. Pletnevoi." Literaturny arkhiv*, 1951, III, 195–213.
———, ed.: *"Pis'ma I. S. Turgeneva k P. A. Pletnevu." Literaturny arkhiv*, 1951, III, 183–95.
Alekseeva, N. V., ed.: *"Pis'ma I. S. Turgeneva k G. I. Uspenskomu." Literaturny arkhiv*, 1951, III, 221–9.
Annenkov, P. V.: *"Iz perepiski s I. S. Turgenevym v 60-kh godakh." Vestnik Evropy*:
January 1887, pp. 5–29;
February 1887, pp. 561–78.
———: *"Shest' let perepiski s I. S. Turgenevym, 1856–62 gg." Vestnik Evropy*:
March 1885, pp. 5–41;
April 1885, pp. 465–505.

Bel'chikov, N., ed.: *"Pis'ma I. S. Turgeneva k P. V. An-nenkovu."* *Krasny arkhiv*, 1929, XXXII, 181–208.
Beliaev, M. D., ed.: *"Nov'. K perepiske P. V. Annenkova s I. S. Turgenevym. Materialy Pushkinskogo Doma."* *Literaturnaia mysl'*, Petrograd,Book 1, 1922, pp.188–207.
Bienstock, J. W., ed. and tr.: *"Lettres inédites de Tour-guénev."* *Revue mondiale*, Paris:
January 1925, pp. 3–10, and 115–21.
February 1925, pp. 233–9.
Bogoslovski, Evgeni, ed.: *Turgenev o L've Tolstom: 75 otzyvov* (Tiflis: Tipografiia kantsl. Glavnonach. grazhd. chast'iu na Kavkaze; 1894), 79 pp.
Brodski, N. L., ed.: *V. P. Botkin i I. S. Turgenev, Neizdannaia perepiska, 1851–69 gg., po materialam Pushkinskogo Doma i Tolstovskogo Muzeia.* (Moscow and Leningrad: Academia; 1930), 349 pp.
Danilov, V. V., ed.: *"Pis'ma I. S. Turgeneva k S. M. Figlevu."* *Literaturny arkhiv*, 1951, III, 170–9.
Georgievski, G. P., ed.: *Pis'ma I. S. Turgeneva k grafine E. E. Lambert.* (Moscow; 1915), 244 pp.
Gorlin, M., ed., and Mazon, André, author of Introduction: *"Neizdannye pis'ma I. S. Turgeneva k Diu-Kanu, Floberu i E. de Gonkuru."* Translated from French to Russian by E. Gunst. *Literaturnoe nasledstvo*, 1937, XXXI–XXXII (one volume), 663–706.
Gruzinski, A. E., and Tsiavlovski, M. A., eds.: *Tolstoi i Turgenev: perepiska* (Moscow: M. and S. Sabashnikov; 1928), 118 pp.
Halpérine-Kaminsky, E., ed.: Ivan Tourguéneff, *Lettres à Mme Viardot* (Paris: Charpentier; 1907), 263 pp.
—— ed.: *"Lettres inédites d'Ivan Tourguéneff à Mme Viardot."* *Revue politique et littéraire*, Paris, 1906, 5-ème série, V, 773–4.
——ed.: Ivan Tourguéneff *d'après sa correspondance avec ses amis français* (Paris: Charpentier; 1901), 359 pp.
——, ed.: *"Pis'ma I. S. Turgeneva k ego nemetskim druz'-iam."* *Vestnik Evropy*, February 1909, pp. 251–76. (In Russian.)
"Ivan Sergeevich Turgenev v ego pis'makh k Fr. Boden-

shtedtu, 1861–1865 gg." *Russkaia starina*, 1887, LIV,
443–96. (In French and German.)

"*Ivan Sergeevich Turgenev v pis'makh k ego bratu Nikolaiu
Sergeevichu, 1863–1878 gg.*" *Russkaia starina:*
    August 1885, pp. 313–36;
    September 1885, pp. 495–510;
    October 1885, pp. 126–42;
    December 1885, pp. 613–32;
    February 1886, pp. 597–608.

"*Iz perepiski I. S. Turgeneva s sem'eiu Aksakovykh.*"
Vestnik Evropy:
    January 1894, pp. 329–44;
    February 1894, pp. 469–99.

Izmailov, N. V., ed.: "*Pis'ma Turgeneva k E. M. Feoktistovu,*" in anthology "*Turgenev i krug Sovremennika, q. v.*

Kapeliush, B. N., ed.: "*Pis'ma I. S. Turgeneva k O. D.
Khilkovoi.*" *Literaturny arkhiv*, 1951, III, 214–17.

Kavelin, Dmitri: *Pis'ma Dm. Kavelina k Al. Iv. Gertsenu.
S ob"iasnitel'nymi primechaniiami M. Dragomanova*
(Geneva, Switzerland: Ukrainskaia tipografiia; 1892),
227 pp.

Kleman, M. K.: "*Iz perepiski Turgeneva s nachinaiush-
chimi avtorami,*" in anthology, N. L. Brodski, ed.: *I. S.
Turgenev, materialy i issledovaniia* (Orel: Izdatel'stvo
Orlovskogo Oblastnogo Soveta deputatov trudiashchikhsia; 1940).

Koni, A. F., and Molchanov, A. E., eds.: *Turgenev i Savina. Pis'ma I. S. Turgeneva k M. G. Savinoi. Vospominaniia M. G. Savinoi ob I. S. Turgeneve* (Petrograd:
Izdanie Gosudarstvennykh teatrov; 1918), 114 pp.

Koplan-Shakhmatova, S. A., and Zisserman, P. I., eds.:
"*Perepiska I. S. Turgeneva s I. I. Panaevym,*" in anthology *Turgenev i krug Sovremennika, q. v.*

Korsakov, D. A., ed.: "*Iz pisem I. S. Turgeneva k S. K.
Briullovoi, rozhdennoi Kavelinoi (1871–77 gg.).*"
Russkaia mysl', June 1897, pp. 18–29.

Linnichenko, I. A., ed.: "*Pis'ma I. S. Turgeneva k doktoru
I.F. Minitskomu.*" *Vestnik Evropy*, 1909, CCLVIII, pp.
626–38.

Maikov, L. N., ed.: "Pis'ma I. S. Turgeneva k P. V. An-
nenkovu." Russkoe obozrenie:
  January 1894, pp. 5–28;
  February 1894, pp. 485–99;
  March 1894, pp. 19–31;
  April 1894, pp. 511–19.
——, ed.: "Perepiska I. S. Turgeneva s P. V. Annenkovym
s 1871 po 1883 gg." Russkoe obozrenie:
  March 1898, pp. 5–19;
  April 1898, pp. 365–79;
  May 1898, pp. 5–28.
"Materialy po isotorii russkoi literatury i kul'tury: Pis'ma
I. S. Turgeneva k A. M. Zhemchuzhnikovu." Russkaia
mysl'. January 1914, pp. 126–39.
Motovilova, N. I., ed.: "Iz pisem Turgeneva k Nekrasovu,"
in anthology Turgenev i krug Sovremennika, q.v.
Nazarova, L. N., ed.: "Pis'ma I. S. Turgeneva k A. V.
Toporovu." Literaturny arkhiv, 1953, IV, 196–341.
Orlovski, Sergei, ed.: "Iz proshlogo: tri pis'ma I. S. Tur-
geneva k A. P. Efremovu." Novy mir, May 1926, pp.
134–43.
Pereselenikov, S., ed.: "Iz perepiski Turgeneva s V. Ia.
Kartashevskoi." Golos minuvshego, No. 1–4 (one issue),
January–April 1919, pp. 207–27.
Pervoe sobranie pisem I. S. Turgeneva, 1840–83 gg
(St. Petersburg: Obshchestvo dlia posobiia nuzhdaiush-
chimsia literatoram i uchenym; 1884), 564 pp.
Pietsch, Ludwig, ed.: Iwan Turgenjew an Ludwig Pietsch:
Briefe aus den Jahren 1864–83 (herausgegeben von
Alfred Doren, mit Zeichnungen von Ludwig Pietsch,
Berlin: Propyläen-Verlag; n.d.), 176 pp.
"Pis'ma I. S. Turgeneva k I.P. Borisovu, 1858–71 gg."
Russki arkhiv, 1910, No. 4, pp. 585–622.
"Pis'ma I. S. Turgeneva k K. N. Leont'evu (1851–76
gg.)." Russkaia mysl', 1886, No. XII, pp. 62-87.
"Pis'ma I. S. Turgeneva k N. A. Nekrasovu," Russkaia
mysl', January 1902, second pagination, pp. 116–26.
"Pis'ma I. S. Turgeneva k P. V. Annenkovu." Pechat' i
revoliutsiia, April–June (one issue) 1922, pp. 89–102.
Pogruzhenko, M. G., ed.: Pis'ma I. S. Turgeneva k L. N.

i L. Ia. Stech'kinym (Odessa: Count M. M. Tolstoy; 1903), 61 pp.

Rusk, Ralph L., ed.: *Letters to Emma Lazarus in the Columbia University Library* (New York: Columbia University Press; 1939), 84 pp. (In French and English.)

Séménoff, E.: *La Vie douloureuse d'Ivan Tourguéneff avec des lettres inédites de Tourguéneff à sa fille* (Paris: Mercure de France; 1933), 253 pp.

Seznec, Jean: "Lettres de Tourguéneff à Henry James." *Comparative Literature*, Vol. I, No. 3 (Summer 1949), pp. 193–209.

Stasiulevich, M. M., ed.: "*Iz pisem I. S. Turgeneva k M. M. Stasiulevichu (po povodu pechataniia Novi v 1876 godu)*," in anthology *Sbornik obschestva liubitelei rossiskoi slovesnosti na 1891 g.* (Moscow; 1891), pp. 69–76.

Stasov, V. V.: "*Dvadtsat' pisem Turgeneva i moe znakomstvo s nim.*" *Severny vestnik*, October 1888, pp. 145–94.

Turgenev, I. S.: *Sobranie sochineni* (Moscow: Pravda, Biblioteka Ogonek; 1949), Vol. XI, 434 pp.

——: *Sobranie sochineni v dvenadtsati tomakh.* Moscow, GIKhL; 1953–8. Vol. XI, 1956, 571 pp., and Vol. XII, 1958, 695 pp.

Turgenev i krug Sovremennika: neizdannye materialy,1847–61 gg (Moscow and Leningrad: Academia; 1930), 490 pp.

Utevski, L. S., ed.: "*Neizdannye pis'ma I. S. Turgeneva k A. V. Toporovu.*" *Novy mir*, February 1930, pp. 210–18.

Z.: "*Iz perepiski I. S. Turgeneva s A. M. Gertsenom v 1867 godu.*" *Russkoe obozrenie*, January 1895, XXXI, 114.

Zil'bershtein, I. S., and Shchegolev, P. E., eds.: "*Iz proshlogo: Pis'ma I. S. Turgeneva k P. V. Annenkovu.*" *Novy mir*, Book 9, 1927, pp. 155–68.

INDEX

Weber, Karl Maria von, 18
Werder, Karl, 11, 15
What to Do, 149
Whitman, Walt, xii, 252
Who Is Happy in Russia?, 255
Wilhelm I, King of Prussia, 203–4, 221
Will, Dr. Samuel F., Jr., xxv
Wilson, Edmund, 194 *n*
Winner, Dr. Thomas G., xxv
women medical students, *letter to*, 355
"Wood Cutting," 68, 70, 72
Wordsworth, William, xvi

Yarmolinsky, Avrahm, xvii
Years of Childhood, xv, 38 *n*, 88 *n*
Yermolai, *see* Afanasi

"Yermolai and the Miller's Wife," 121 *n*
Youth, 74, 79, 83, 86

Zabel, Eugen, 356
Zagoskin, Mikhail Nikolaevich, 49–51, 130
Zakhar, 100
Zapiski ruzheinogo okhotnika, 51
"Zatish'e," 65
Zhemchuzhnikov, Aleksei Mikhailovich, *letters to*, 191, 202, 306
Zhitova, Varvara, 36 *n*
Zhukovski, Vasili Andreevich, 345
Zola, Emile, x, 271, 277, 280–1, 286, 288–9, 294–5, 303, 318, 325, 352

EDGAR H. LEHRMAN was born in 1926 in New York City. He holds a Ph.D. from Columbia University, where he also was connected with the Russian Institute. He taught at Duke University, Dartmouth, and Pennsylvania State University, and since 1959 has been Associate Professor of Russian at Emory University, Atlanta, Georgia. He has translated Vladimir Seduro's *History of the Byelorussian Theatre and Drama* (1955) and Nikolai A. Gorchakov's *The Theatre in Soviet Russia* (1957).

1960

A NOTE ON THE TYPE

This book is set in *Electra,* a Linotype face designed by W. A. Dwiggins (1880-1956), who was responsible for so much that is good in contemporary book design. Electra cannot be classified as either modern or oldstyle. It is not based on any historical model, nor does it echo a particular period or style.

Composed, printed, and bound by The Colonial Press Inc., Clinton, Mass. Paper manufactured by S. D. Warren Co., Boston. Typography and binding design by Vincent Torre.